Brazilian Derivatives and Securities

Brazilian Derivatives and Securities

Pricing and Risk Management of FX and Interest-Rate Portfolios for Local and Global Markets

Marcos C. S. Carreira
Quantitative Finance Practitioner, Brazil

Richard J. Brostowicz
Executive Director and Head of Brazil Quants, Banco Morgan Stanley, Brazil

palgrave
macmillan

First published 2016 by
PALGRAVE MACMILLAN

Palgrave Macmillan in the UK is an imprint of Macmillan Publishers Limited, registered in England, company number 785998, of Houndmills, Basingstoke, Hampshire RG21 6XS.

Palgrave Macmillan in the US is a division of St Martins Press LLC, 175 Fifth Avenue, New York, NY 10010.

Palgrave Macmillan is the global academic imprint of the above companies and has companies and representatives throughout the world.

Palgrave® and Macmillan® are registered trademarks in the United States, the United Kingdom, Europe and other countries

ISBN: 978–1–137–47726–2

This book is printed on paper suitable for recycling and made from fully managed and sustained forest sources. Logging, pulping and manufacturing processes are expected to conform to the environmental regulations of the country of origin.

A catalogue record for this book is available from the British Library.

Library of Congress Cataloging-in-Publication Data
Brostowicz, Richard J., author.
Brazilian derivatives and securities : pricing and risk management of FX and interest-rate portfolios for local and global markets / Richard J. Brostowicz, Marcos Carreira.
pages cm
ISBN 978-1-137-47726-2 (hardback)
1. Foreign exchange market–Brazil. 2. Derivative securities–Brazil.
3. Investments–Brazil. 4. Finance–Brazil. I. Carreira, Marcos, author. II. Title.

HG3933.B76 2015
332.64'570981–dc23 2015033263

Contents

List of Figures

List of Tables

Foreword

My first encounter with Brazilian derivatives and securities arose when I was a doctoral student in finance at UCLA 32 years ago. I was fortunate enough to share an office with a gentleman named Eduardo Facó Lemgruber, whose dissertation covered the valuation of executive stock options (ESOs). In the mid 1980s, a strong theory had developed for pricing exchange-traded options. However, the applicability of this theory for off exchange ESOs was far from immediate. In his UCLA dissertation, my enterprising office-mate showed how to adapt the standard theory to cover ESOs. Dr. Lemgruber is now a much sought after management consultant, after spending 31 years as a distinguished academic. We meet from time to time at international conferences, and reminisce about the glory days, a past time especially appealing to people of our vintage.

Fast forward 32 years and the Brazilian derivatives market has become the largest in Latin America. BM&FBovespa is the only Latin American exchange to crack the top ten largest derivatives exchanges in the world. The prominence of the Brazilian derivatives and securities market tracks larger trends. The Federative Republic of Brazil is the largest country in both South America and in the Latin American region. Brazil is the world's fifth largest country, both by geographical area and by population. It is the largest Portuguese-speaking country in the world, with roughly 20 times the population of Portugal. The 2014 FIFA World Cup was held in Brazil and the next summer Olympics are scheduled for Rio in 2016.

Given these trends, it is only fitting that we have now been blessed with the first book to take a serious look at the Brazilian derivatives and securities market. Brazilian financial markets have been criticized in the past for a lack of transparency, so it is exciting to see the curtain pulled back by our two esteemed co-authors. It is quite rare to find a pair of practitioners with the requisite energy needed to share their deep understanding of financial markets in book form, while somehow managing to keep the lights on in their day jobs. It is equally rare to find a pair of financial institutions willing to stand up to the culture of closedness that permeates typical institutional mindsets.

This book adapts the theory of mathematical finance to the realities of the Brazilian financial marketplace. Since its development at MIT in the early 1970s, mathematical finance has led to a deepened understanding of derivatives markets, which in turn has had a profound impact on financial markets as a whole. The pioneers in the field of mathematical finance were compelled to posit several simplifying assumptions, in order to expose the basic intuition underlying derivatives pricing. While not necessarily relevant to Brazilian financial markets, these assumptions included price transparency and the continuity of asset prices over time. Price or rate jumps of Poisson type were later added to extend the theory, but price or rate jumps occurring at known times are not considered part of the mainstream. These latter type of jumps have come to be known as events, which are all too important in Brazilian securities markets. Included in events are discrete changes in interest rates or jumps in FX rates that arise due to skipped interest and principal payments on sovereign borrowing. While the Brazilian government's credit has substantially improved over time, there remains a vibrant market in hedges against a possible default. About ten years ago, I co-authored a paper with Liuren Wu that compared the implicit pricing of sovereign default event risk in both credit default swap (CDS) and foreign exchange (FX) markets. Our research led to a Bloomberg function called CDFX that compares the implied risk-neutral probabilities from the two markets.

The interest in applying mathematical finance to Brazilian financial markets is stronger than ever. My former Bloomberg colleague Bruno Dupire studied in Brazil for three years and has for the last nine years co-organized a highly regarded annual conference called Research in Options (RIO!) at IMPA with Jorge Zubelli. It is just a matter of time before specialized journals emerge to cover this growing field. The contents of this book reflect almost half a century of combined experience of the two co-authors. I truly hope that the current generation of traders and risk managers will take the lessons of the ensuing pages to heart. Our shared financial future depends on it.

Peter Carr, PhD,
Managing Director at Morgan Stanley, Global Head of Market Modeling, and Executive Director of NYU Courant's Masters in Mathematical Finance.

Preface

Brazil is not a simple country; one could say that for any other country, but Brazilians seem to utter this evocation with a quite peculiar sort of resignation, as if giving up hope that the country will ever change to become more standardized. Anyone who sees the electrical plugs mandated by law will understand that.

And yet it is a fascinating country, where you could find double-digit interest rates and an investment grade (maybe not for long). The history and products of this financial market are quite unique, and we are glad to help the reader understand this corner of the world a bit better.

This book will refer to other books that already explain concepts like managing option risks and stochastic calculus instead of repeating them, but once we delve into the details of the products we will provide the mathematical background and the heuristics for these, in a level somewhat beyond an undergraduate course. In fact, we used the draft of this book as the reference for a Masters' course.

Chapter 1 introduces the history of the markets over the past 20–30 years, and some definitions and concepts will be detailed later. In Chapter 2 we define the main fixings, for which the markets and curves described in Chapters 3 through 6, 9 and 15 will provide a framework for trading and hedging.

Chapters 7 and 13 cover IR and FX options, respectively. Much more could have been written on FX options, but again we defer to other excellent books on this subject.

The link between local fixings and offshore markets is discussed in Chapters 8 and 10; Chapter 11 covers the opposite case (onshore markets and offshore fixings).

We briefly cover cash products in Chapter 14, mainly worried about market dynamics rather than trying to exhaust all possible cash instruments available.

The microstructure of the Brazilian markets has been sadly underrepresented in the literature, and Chapter 16 is a brief introduction to our work in this subject.

The (hopefully satisfied but still curious) reader should finish the book at Chapter 17 with the reminder that some of the rules, products and markets described in the book are subject to sudden and puzzling changes, and we swear that these are not our fault. In fact, they will provide us with an opportunity to publish further editions of the book, and we will be glad to receive any feedback that might improve those future versions. The publisher's website will help with that.

Acknowledgments

Richard thanks Dorival Leão for interesting discussions regarding financial topics and for asking him to be a lecturer on the new MECAI Master's course in Brazil. He also thanks Stefan Andreev, an outstanding quant who has been very patient with him since his first days at Morgan Stanley and a very good friend. A special thank you also goes to the triplet, Dolina, Nina and Ruby, who rock his life like a free jazz trio. Dolina keeps the rhythm like a steady bass player, Nina is the sax player, with Coltrane-like improvisation, and Ruby is the hard-hitting drum player. Last but not least, a big thank you goes to his tight, warm and small family nucleus: Mama, Baba, Bisna and Brígida [R.I.P.]. You are all great!

Marcos thanks Emanuel Derman for, among other things, showing that most of quantitative finance is just a way to find the price of fruit salad, and for the encouragement and help with the decision to write this book. He also thanks Robert Almgren for the advice on learning Python, for pointing out Mathias Rosenbaum's work on market microstructure and more useful advice. Special thanks to Kathya, Gabriel and Gustavo, for understanding the time spent away from family while at the same time making sure I kept the focus on writing the book, which could not have been written without Kathya's energy and support.

Disclaimer

The views represented are the authors' own and do not necessarily represent the views of Morgan Stanley or its affiliates, and are not a product of Morgan Stanley Research.

The information herein has been prepared solely for informational purposes and is not an offer to buy or sell or a solicitation of an offer to buy or sell any security or instrument or to participate in any trading strategy. Any such offer would be made only after a prospective participant had completed its own independent investigation of the securities, instruments or transactions and received all information it required to make its own investment decision, including, where applicable, a review of any offering, circular or memorandum describing such security or instrument, which would contain material information not contained herein and to which prospective participants are referred. No representation or warranty can be given with respect to the accuracy or completeness of the information herein, or that any future offer of securities, instruments or transactions will conform to the terms hereof. Morgan Stanley and its affiliates disclaim any and all liability relating to this information. Morgan Stanley, its affiliates and others associated with it may have positions in, and may effect transactions in, securities and instruments of issuers mentioned herein and may also perform or seek to perform investment banking services for the issuers of such securities and instruments.

The information herein may contain general, summary discussions of certain tax, regulatory, accounting and/or legal issues relevant to the proposed transaction. Any such discussion is necessarily generic and may not be applicable to, or complete for, any particular recipient's specific facts and circumstances. Morgan Stanley is not offering and does not purport to offer tax, regulatory, accounting or legal advice and this information should not be relied upon as such. Prior to entering into any proposed transaction, recipients should determine, in consultation with their own legal, tax, regulatory and accounting advisors, the economic risks and merits, as well as the legal, tax, regulatory and accounting characteristics and consequences, of the transaction.

Notwithstanding any other express or implied agreement, arrangement, or understanding to the contrary, Morgan Stanley and each recipient hereof are deemed to agree that both Morgan Stanley and such recipient (and their respective employees, representatives, and other agents) may disclose to any and all persons, without limitation of any kind, the U.S. federal income tax treatment of the securities, instruments or transactions described herein and any fact relating to the structure of the securities, instruments or transactions that may be relevant to understanding such tax treatment, and all materials of any kind (including opinions or other tax analyses) that are provided to such a person relating to such tax treatment and tax structure, except to the extent confidentiality is reasonably necessary to comply with securities laws (including, where applicable, confidentiality regarding the identity of an issuer of securities or its affiliates, agents and advisors).

The projections or other estimates in these materials (if any), including estimates of returns or performance, are forward-looking statements based upon certain assumptions and are preliminary in nature. Any assumptions used in any such projection or estimate that were provided by a recipient are noted herein. Actual results are difficult to predict and may depend upon events outside the issuer's or Morgan Stanley's control. Actual events may differ from those assumed and changes to any assumptions may have a material impact on any projections or estimates. Other events not taken into account may occur and may significantly affect the analysis. Certain assumptions may have been made for modeling purposes only to simplify the presentation and/or calculation of any projections or estimates, and Morgan Stanley does not represent that any such assumptions will reflect actual future events. Accordingly, there can be no assurance that estimated returns or projections will be realized or that actual returns or performance results will not be materially different than those estimated herein. Any such estimated returns and projections should be viewed as hypothetical. Recipients should conduct their own analysis, using such assumptions as they deem appropriate, and should fully consider other available information in making a decision regarding these securities, instruments or transactions. Past performance is not necessarily indicative of future results. Price and availability are subject to change without notice.

The offer or sale of securities, instruments or transactions may be restricted by law. Additionally, transfers of any such securities, instruments or transactions may be limited by law or the terms thereof. Unless specifically noted herein, neither Morgan Stanley nor any issuer of securities or instruments has taken or will take any action in any jurisdiction that would permit a public offering of securities or instruments, or possession or distribution of any offering material in relation thereto, in any country or jurisdiction where action for such purpose is required. Recipients are required to inform themselves of and comply with any legal or contractual restrictions on their purchase, holding, sale, exercise of rights or performance of obligations under any transaction. Morgan Stanley does not undertake or have any responsibility to notify you of any changes to the attached information.

With respect to any recipient in the U.K., the information herein has been issued by Morgan Stanley & Co. International Limited, regulated by the U.K.

Financial Services Authority. This communication is directed in the U.K. to those persons who are market counterparties or intermediate customers (as defined in the UK Financial Services Authority's rules).

Additional information is available upon request.

1
Financial Archeology

This chapter aims to give the reader a historical background on Foreign Exchange and Interest Rate derivatives in Brazil, through tables, charts and anecdotes.

By studying the past, one can understand why some things are the way they are. If you see a turtle on top of a post, you wonder: "Who put it there?". Well, in this book there are some turtles not only sitting on top of posts, but they're juggling chainsaws as well.

Here we'll show how the most important contracts work, with a formal approach (Richard knows a martingale from a nightingale) and some tinkering with numbers and charts (challenge the first two things Marcos says about something and he might get it right on the third try).

The reader (you, also known throughout the book as "the one") will learn that, when looking at Brazilian data, it helps to look at events like someone studying dinosaurs: Here a meteor extinguished several species, there the Real Plan extinguished the huge overnight rates. It is quite helpful to break down Brazil's financial history into periods, and in the differences among strata, distinguish volatility from structural changes.

We'll also introduce some of the tools used throughout the book, and we encourage the reader to come along this exploration, test our results, and in the process gather knowledge and increase skills in preparation to the next economic plan, change of currency or whatever comes out of Brasilia next.

1.1 Interest rates and inflation

1.1.1 Record levels (the old days of overnight rates of 2% per day and the Real Plan); desperate times call for desperate measures

When studying Brazil's financial history, it's easy to be amazed by the number (and nature) of events: Here the currency lost 3 zeros, the bank accounts were frozen (the words "bank holidays" carrying an ominous feeling), here comes a new finance minister, there goes another, and so on. Let's go over the list of the

Table 1 Presidents of Brazil's Central Bank since 1965

Name	Interim	Start	Years
Denio Chagas		12-Apr-65	1.94
Ruy Leme		31-Mar-67	0.87
Ary Burguer	I	08-Feb-68	0.03
Ernane Galvêas		21-Feb-68	6.06
Paulo Lira		15-Mar-74	5.00
Carlos Brandão		15-Mar-79	0.42
Ernane Galvêas		17-Aug-79	0.42
Carlos Langoni		18-Jan-80	3.63
Affonso Pastore		05-Sep-83	1.52
Antonio Lemgruber		15-Mar-85	0.45
Fernão Bracher		28-Aug-85	1.46
Francisco Gros		11-Feb-87	0.21
Lycio de Faria	I	30-Apr-87	0.01
Fernando Milliet		05-May-87	0.85
Elmo Camões		09-Mar-88	1.29
Wadico Bucchi	I	23-Jun-89	0.34
Wadico Bucchi		25-Oct-89	0.38
Ibrahim Eris		15-Mar-90	1.17
Francisco Gros		17-May-91	1.50
Gustavo Loyola		13-Nov-92	0.37
Paulo Cesar Ferreira		26-Mar-93	0.46
Pedro Malan		09-Sep-93	1.31
Gustavo Franco	I	31-Dec-94	0.03
Persio Arida		11-Jan-95	0.42
Gustavo Loyola		13-Jun-95	2.19
Gustavo Franco		20-Aug-97	1.54
Arminio Fraga		04-Mar-99	3.83
Henrique Meirelles		01-Jan-03	8.00
Alexandre Tombini		01-Jan-11	3.40

presidents of Brazil's Central Bank (BCB) (Table 1) and Finance Ministers since 12-Apr-1965 (Table 2) as of mid-2014.

The period from Mar-1985 to Jan-1995 saw more than 10 different people commanding the BCB and also more than 10 people with the title of Finance Minister; from 13-Jun-1995 to Jun-2014 we've had only 5 BCB Presidents and 3 Finance Ministers.

One can see the instability of the period by looking at the currency itself. Named Real (although mostly used in the plural "Réis") since Portugal discovered Brazil in 1500, and used until 1942, Brazil's currencies experienced name changes and was divided by 1000 several times, and the last cut (division by 2750 in 01-Jul-1994) brought its name back to Real (Table 3 shows the names and the factors that divided the currency). Twice there was only a name change (Factor=1).

Table 2 Brazil's Finance Ministers since 1965

Name	Interim	Start	Years
Otávio Bulhões		15-Apr-1964	2.92
Delfim Netto		17-Mar-1967	7.00
Mário Simonsen		16-Mar-1974	5.00
Karlos Rischbieter		16-Mar-1979	0.84
Ernane Galvêas		18-Jan-1980	5.15
Franciscos Dornelles		15-Mar-1985	0.45
Dilson Funaro		26-Aug-1985	1.67
Luiz Carlos Bresser		29-Apr-1987	0.65
Maílson da Nóbrega	I	21-Dec-1987	0.04
Maílson da Nóbrega		06-Jan-1988	2.19
Zélia Cardoso		15-Mar-1990	1.15
Marcílio Marques		10-May-1991	1.40
Gustavo Krause		02-Oct-1992	0.21
Paulo Haddad		16-Dec-1992	0.21
Eliseu Resende		01-Mar-1993	0.22
Fernando Henrique		19-May-1993	0.86
Rubens Ricupero		30-Mar-1994	0.44
Ciro Gomes		06-Sep-1994	0.32
Pedro Malan		01-Jan-1995	8.00
Antonio Palocci		01-Jan-2003	3.23
Guido Mantega		27-Mar-2006	8.17

Table 3 Brazil's currencies since 1942

Year	Name	Symbol	Factor
1822	Real (plural Réis)	Rs	1
1942	Cruzeiro	Cr$	1000
1967	Cruzeiro Novo	NCr$	1000
1970	Cruzeiro	Cr$	1
1986	Cruzado	Cz$	1000
1989	Cruzado Novo	NCz$	1000
1990	Cruzeiro	Cr$	1
1993	Cruzeiro Real	CR$	1000
1994	Real (plural Reais)	R$	2750

Indeed, the 1985–1995 period experienced 5 name changes and 4 cuts (so 1 Real at 1994 was equal to 2,750,000,000,000 Cruzeiros from 1985). One could say that there's no sense in a currency that has no cents (the "Centavos" were abolished in 1964 and again in 1984, but life without commas lasted only three and two years, respectively).

Brazil's hyperinflation will be discussed later; for now let's remember that those currency conversions will probably be useful later.

We will continue our journey through Brazil's past at the BCB's website (http://www.bcb.gov.br/?ENGLISH). Here we can find some interesting time series, while learning some of the formats used throughout the book. The environment configuration: Idiom = English; Date format: European – dd/MM/yyyy (we'll also use dd-Mmm-yyyy); Number format: American – 123,456,789.00 (although one will likely find the format 123.456.789,00 when importing data from most Brazilian sources).

Fortunately, our curiosity is shared by many others, and the "Ranking" option on the Time Series Management module reveals the most looked up series, which include:

- CDI (the overnight interbank rate for unsecured lending and borrowing) expressed as % per day.
- CDI as % per year.
- Selic (the overnight rate for secured lending and borrowing) as % per year.
- Selic target (the rate determined by the Monetary Policy Committee – COPOM) as % per year.

We'll use all the data since 1986, and download a CSV file in english (instead of using the website tools), and a quick look reveals that we'll have to deal with incomplete data.

Now it's a good time to introduce our approach to data:

- Spreadsheets are useful for looking at some of the data, quick calculations and charts, but we'll avoid them.
- Ideally results should include the data and the code also, in order to ensure reproducibility.

A good alternative is to use Python (https://www.python.org/), an open-source software that, with the addition of packages like numpy and pandas, provides an environment for scientific, numeric and time-series analysis. If you have to read one book in order to follow our use cases [12] would be perfect.

For those used to Matlab and/or Mathematica, the IPython notebook is a similar experience. Your code (or text) goes into cells, you can get your results just below your commands. Here [13] is the weapon of choice.

After some cleaning (notebook available at the book's website), we can plot the data to see the history of Brazil's interest rates.

The Selic target rate is available since 1999 (the same year in which Brazil adopted the Inflation Targeting Regime), as shown in Figure 1.

We'll go back to the period between 1996 and 1999 later to discuss the TBC and the TBAN, but it is worth looking at the Selic rate itself (and its explosive past) in Figure 2.

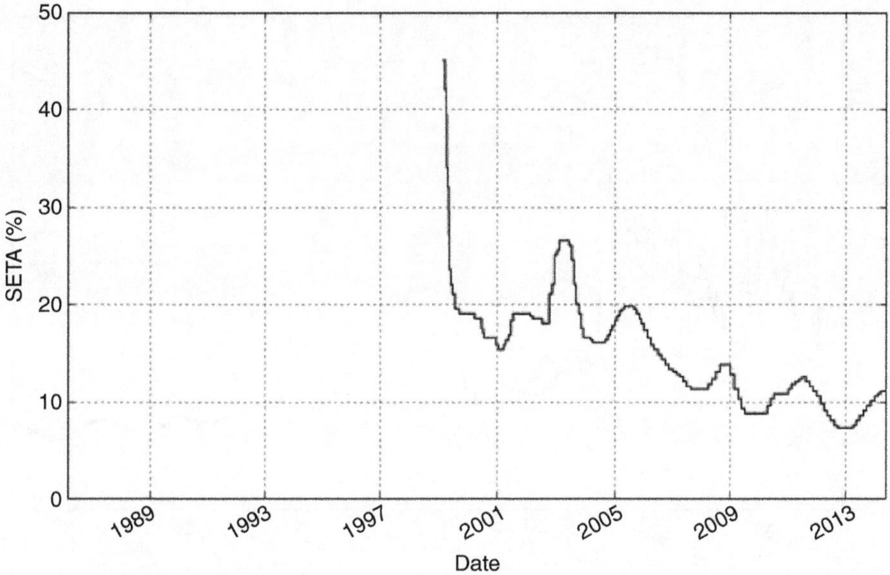

Figure 1 Selic target

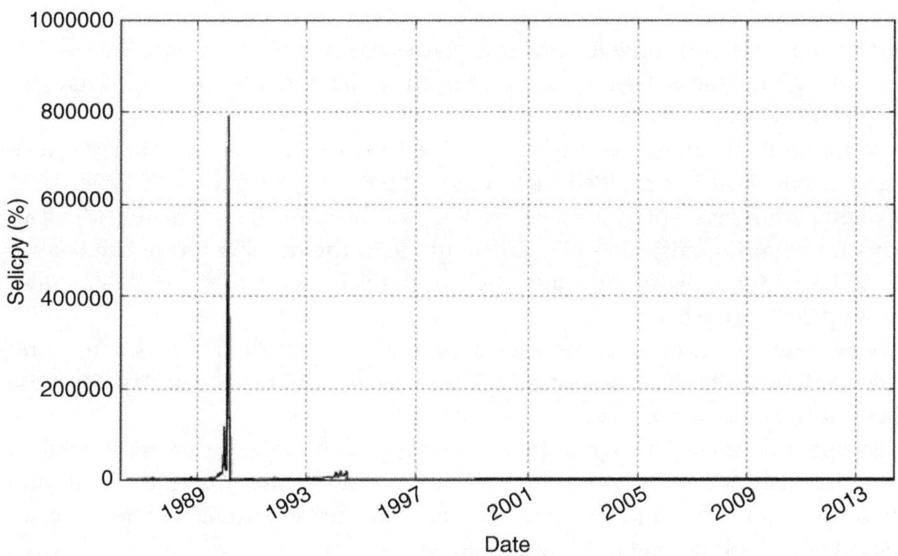

Figure 2 Selic since 1986

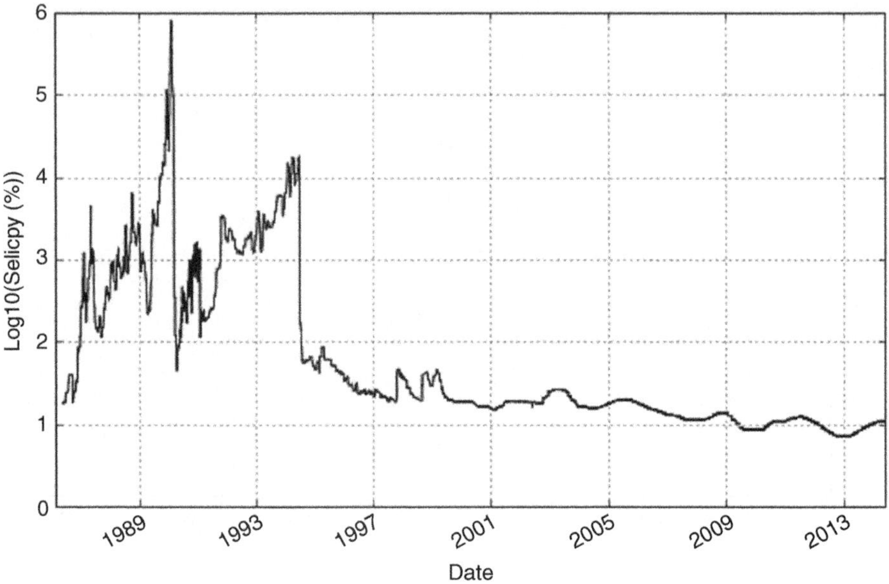

Figure 3 Selic (log scale)

We need to put on some logarithmic glasses to see it better (Figure 3).

To bring this home, Figure 4 shows the daily CDI rate (2% per day? That will keep real investment away).

Zooming in (Figures 5 and 6, still in Log10 scale), we can see that the Real Plan ("Plano Real") succeeded in bringing down interest rates to a lower level (2 digits) quite permanently. As Figure 7 shows, even further increases (Mexican crisis in 1995, EM crisis in 1997, Russia in 1998, the devaluation of the Real in 1999) lasted for a few months and the overnight rates approached lower values (around 20% per year).

Now, one can explain those increases in the overnight rates as a reaction against the possibility of investors taking money out of the country: increase the return, and investors will bear the risk.

Because the level of foreign currency reserves was quite low, this risk was taken quite seriously. Also worth noticing is that the currency was managed from mid-1995 until Jan-1999, and therefore it could not easily devalue as a reaction to shocks: interest rates had to increase a lot.

But after the 1999 devaluation another framework was put in place to determine the overnight Interest Rates, and we will describe these events in Subsection 1.1.2.

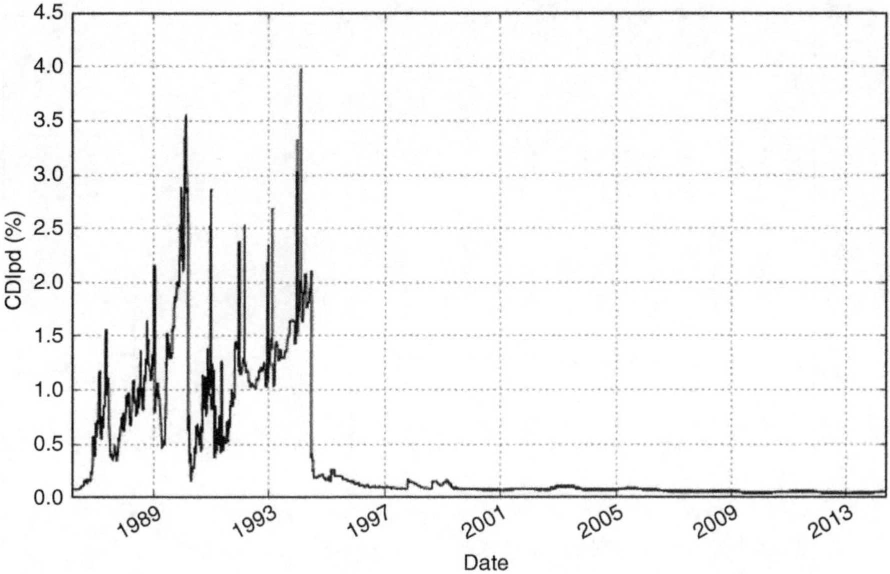

Figure 4 CDI (daily rate)

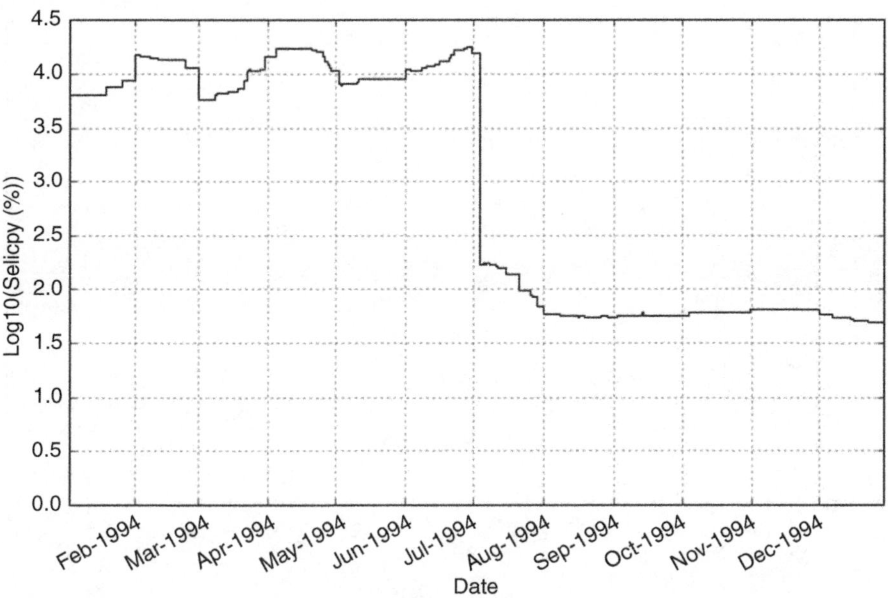

Figure 5 Change in overnight rates with the Real Plan (Jul-1994)

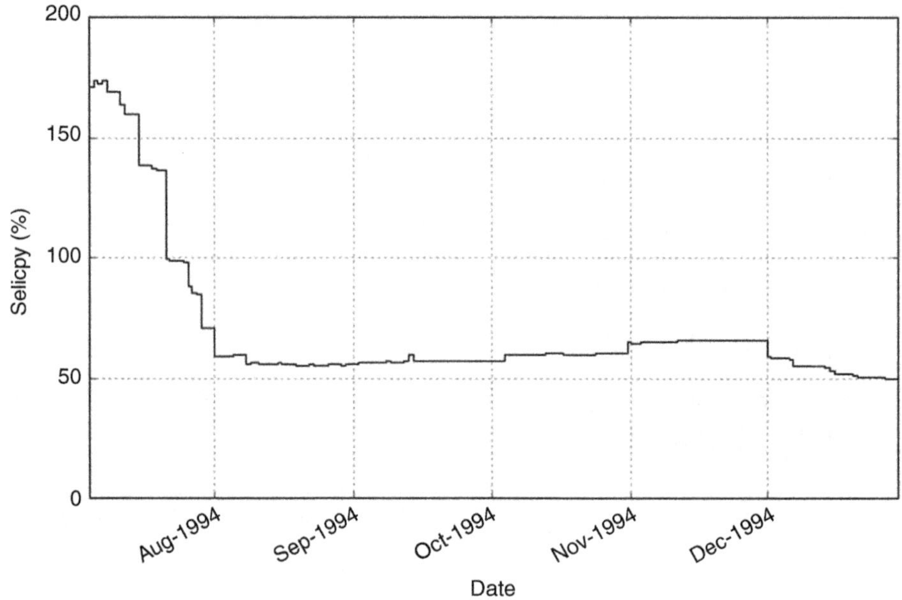

Figure 6 Overnight rates after the Real Plan (1994)

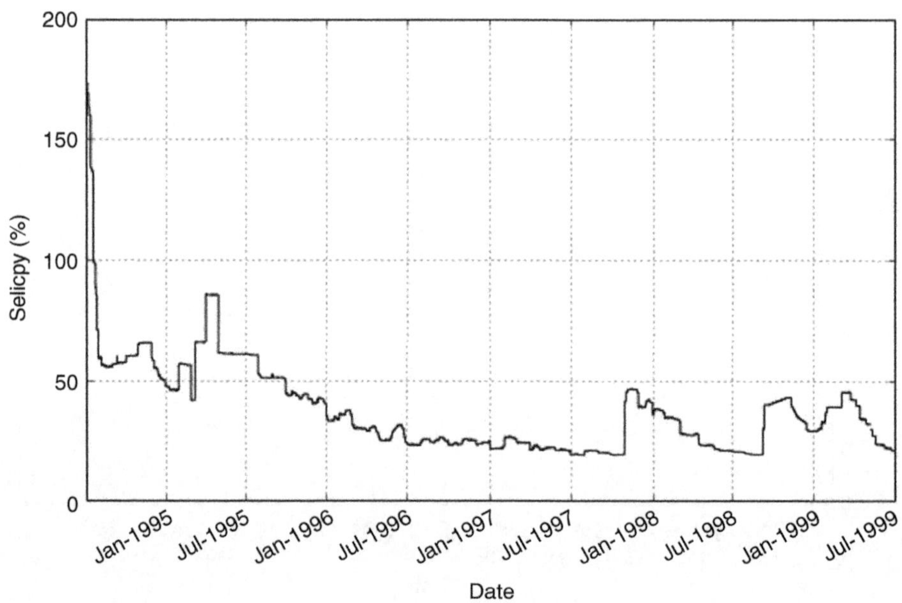

Figure 7 Overnight rates from Jul-1994 to Jul-1999

1.1.2 COPOM (The Brazilian FOMC): behavior, language, influence, targets and bands

From the BCB's website (http://www.bcb.gov.br/?OBJECTIVES):

"The Central Bank of Brazil's (BCB) Monetary Policy Committee (COPOM) was created on June 20th 1996, and was assigned the responsibility of setting the stance of monetary policy and the short-term interest rate. The aim in creating the COPOM was to enhance monetary policy transparency and confer adequate regularity to the monetary policy decision-making process."

There's a history of interest rates decisions available at http://www.bcb.gov.br/?INTEREST.

We can divide the decisions in four groups.

The first group can be seen as Pre-Inflation Targeting (Table 7), and lasts from 20-Jun-1996 to 04-Mar-1999. It was marked by 3 crises: Emerging Markets in Oct/Nov-1997, Russia/LTCM in Aug/Sep-1998, Brazil's Devaluation in Jan-1999.

Originally the meeting was held on the second half of the month, and the decisions changed the rates that would be practiced for the following month; but, in response to the market events, sometimes the script was changed. The decision of the 17th meeting was not implemented (an extraordinary meeting held on 30-Oct-1997 increased rates for the following month). And another extraordinary meeting on 10-Sep-1998 increased rates midway through the scheduled duration of the previous decision.

Another interesting aspect of this table is how rates are defined up to 31-Dec-1997: as effective rates for the period. How can we find the values on the table?

Going back to our Selic Time Series, we'll filter all the rates for the month of Jul-1996 and calculate the overnight discount factors (Figure 8). Therefore the accrual of the Selic for the period is equal to the inverse of the product of the discount factors, matching the result of 1.93% .

Also worth noticing is how rates were expressed. Let's jump to the website of CETIP (www.cetip.com.br) to get the CDI time series since 1986. Downloading the data returns a spreadsheet that opens with a series of observations. About the rates:

- Up to 30-Jun-1989, for the days that precede weekends and holidays rates are divided by the number of calendar days between business days.
- Up to 31-May-1990, rates are published as linear, actual days/360.
- Between 01-Jun-1990 and 31-Dec-1997, daily rates were published as linear per month (multiplied by 30) => discount factor.
- Starting from 01-Jan-1998, rates are published as exponential, business days/252.

Figures 9 and 10 show a comparison of the different standards. The first column comes from the CETIP database, and the last column matches the

Table 4 Interest rate decisions before the inflation targeting regime

Meeting	Type	Date	Start	End	TBC	TBAN	Selic (period)	Selic (average)
1	–	26-Jun-1996	01-Jul-1996	31-Jul-1996	1.90		1.93	23.28
2	–	30-Jul-1996	01-Aug-1996	31-Aug-1996	1.90		1.97	25.01
3	–	21-Aug-1996	01-Sep-1996	30-Sep-1996	1.88		1.90	25.40
4	–	23-Sep-1996	01-Oct-1996	31-Oct-1996	1.82	1.93	1.86	23.48
5	–	23-Oct-1996	01-Nov-1996	30-Nov-1996	1.78	1.90	1.80	25.27
6	–	27-Nov-1996	01-Dec-1996	31-Dec-1996	1.74	1.90	1.80	23.94
7	–	18-Dec-1996	01-Jan-1997	31-Jan-1997	1.70	1.88	1.73	21.73
8	–	22-Jan-1997	01-Feb-1997	28-Feb-1997	1.66	1.84	1.67	26.14
9	–	19-Feb-1997	01-Mar-1997	31-Mar-1997	1.62	1.80	1.64	24.11
10	–	19-Mar-1997	01-Apr-1997	30-Apr-1997	1.58	1.78	1.66	21.84
11	–	16-Apr-1997	01-May-1997	31-May-1997	1.58	1.78	1.58	21.91
12	–	21-May-1997	01-Jun-1997	30-Jun-1997	1.58	1.78	1.61	21.08
13	–	18-Jun-1997	01-Jul-1997	31-Jul-1997	1.58	1.78	1.60	19.04
14	–	23-Jul-1997	01-Aug-1997	31-Aug-1997	1.58	1.78	1.59	20.78

Table 4 Continued

Meeting	Type	Date	Start	End	TBC	TBAN	Selic (period)	Selic (average)
15	–	20-Aug-1997	01-Sep-1997	30-Sep-1997	1.58	1.78	1.59	19.81
16	–	17-Sep-1997	01-Oct-1997	30-Oct-1997	1.58	1.78	1.53	19.05
17	–	22-Oct-1997	01-Nov-1997	30-Nov-1997	1.58	1.78		
18	E	30-Oct-1997	31-Oct-1997	30-Nov-1997	3.05	3.23	3.18	45.67
19	–	19-Nov-1997	01-Dec-1997	31-Dec-1997	2.90	3.15	2.97	39.87
20	–	17-Dec-1997	02-Jan-1998	28-Jan-1998	38.00	43.00	2.43	37.47
21	–	28-Jan-1998	29-Jan-1998	04-Mar-1998	34.50	42.00	2.72	34.20
22	–	04-Mar-1998	05-Mar-1998	15-Apr-1998	28.00	38.00	2.74	27.51
23	–	15-Apr-1998	16-Apr-1998	20-May-1998	23.25	35.25	1.92	23.16
24	–	20-May-1998	21-May-1998	24-Jun-1998	21.75	29.75	1.85	21.23
25	–	24-Jun-1998	25-Jun-1998	29-Jul-1998	21.00	28.00	1.86	20.45
26	–	29-Jul-1998	30-Jul-1998	02-Sep-1998	19.75	25.75	1.76	19.25
27	–	02-Sep-1998	03-Sep-1998	10-Sep-1998	19.00	29.75	0.45	25.49
28	E	10-Sep-1998	11-Sep-1998	07-Oct-1998	19.00	49.75	2.58	40.18
29	–	07-Oct-1998	08-Oct-1998	11-Nov-1998	19.00	49.75	3.26	42.12
30	–	11-Nov-1998	12-Nov-1998	16-Dec-1998	19.00	42.25	3.02	34.93
31	–	16-Dec-1998	17-Dec-1998	18-Jan-1999	29.00	36.00	2.16	29.21
32	–	18-Jan-1999	19-Jan-1999	04-Mar-1999	25.00	41.00	3.98	37.34

Date	Selic (252)	Discount Factor (Daily)
1-Jul-96	24.08	0.99914419
2-Jul-96	23.46	0.999164052
3-Jul-96	23.66	0.999157634
4-Jul-96	23.25	0.999170802
5-Jul-96	23.25	0.999170802
8-Jul-96	23.25	0.999170802
9-Jul-96	23.15	0.99917402
10-Jul-96	23.04	0.999177563
11-Jul-96	23.25	0.999170802
12-Jul-96	23.56	0.999160842
15-Jul-96	23.46	0.999164052
16-Jul-96	23.15	0.99917402
17-Jul-96	23.15	0.99917402
18-Jul-96	23.15	0.99917402
19-Jul-96	23.25	0.999170802
22-Jul-96	23.15	0.99917402
23-Jul-96	23.15	0.99917402
24-Jul-96	23.25	0.999170802
25-Jul-96	23.15	0.99917402
26-Jul-96	23.04	0.999177563
29-Jul-96	23.04	0.999177563
30-Jul-96	23.15	0.99917402
31-Jul-96	23.35	0.999167586
		=(1+B25/100)^(-1/252)
	Product	0.981081336
	Inverse	1.019283481
	Effective Rate	1.9283481

Figure 8 Effective Selic rate

series downloaded from the BCB, which is already standardized. It is always worth remembering that in Brazil, after receiving a time series, one must ask: “Standardized or raw?”.

The second group of decisions (Tables 5 and 6) is composed of the meetings held with Arminio Fraga as BCB's helm, from 04-Mar-1999 to the end of Fernando Henrique Cardoso's second mandate as Brazil's President.

Gone are the TBC and the TBAN (used as reference rates by the Central Bank before inflation targeting), and the downward trajectory of the rates after the

Standards for overnight rates

1. Up to 30-Jun-1989 100*((1+D6/36000)^252-1)

Date	CDI (%)	Calendar days	CDI * CalDays (%)	CDI (252, %)
16-Apr-1986	23.35	1	23.35	17.75
17-Apr-1986	23.39	1	23.39	17.78
18-Apr-1986	5.76	4	23.04	17.50
22-Apr-1986	23.27	1	23.27	17.68
23-Apr-1986	23.34	1	23.34	17.74
24-Apr-1986	23.29	1	23.29	17.70
25-Apr-1986	7.73	3	23.19	17.62
28-Apr-1986	23.33	1	23.33	17.73
29-Apr-1986	23.40	1	23.40	17.79
30-Apr-1986	11.62	2	23.24	17.66
2-May-1986	7.78	3	23.34	17.74
5-May-1986	23.50	1	23.50	17.87
6-May-1986				

Figure 9 CDI standards in 1986

Standards for overnight rates

2. From 01-Jul-1989 to 31-May-1990 and
3. From 01-Jun-1990 to 31-Dec-1997

100*((1+D29/100)^252-1)

Date	CDI (%)	Daycount	CDI / Daycount (%)	CDI (252, %)
25-May-1990	99.84	360	0.28	100.96
28-May-1990	100.32	360	0.28	101.63
29-May-1990	102.60	360	0.29	104.86
30-May-1990	103.08	360	0.29	105.55
31-May-1990	111.48	360	0.31	117.96
1-Jun-1990	10.96	30	0.37	150.67
4-Jun-1990	10.68	30	0.36	144.86
5-Jun-1990	10.51	30	0.35	141.40
6-Jun-1990				

Figure 10 CDI standards in 1990

devaluation is hastened by the (quite frequent) use of a Downward Bias, which allows the COPOM to act before the next meeting. Not all of those Bias were acted upon, though. Sometimes the next move was Upwards (even with a Downward Bias at the previous meeting).

As the BCB puts it: "Brazil implemented a formal inflation-targeting framework for monetary policy in June of 1999. Under the inflation-targeting regime,

Table 5 Interest rate decisions under Arminio Fraga (1999–2000)

Meeting	Type	Date	Bias used	Bias intended	Start	End	Selic Target	Selic (period)	Selic (average)
33	–	04-Mar-1999		Down	05-Mar-1999	24-Mar-1999	45.00	2.08	44.95
	B	25-Mar-1999	Down		25-Mar-1999	05-Apr-1999	42.00	0.84	41.96
	B	06-Apr-1999	Down		06-Apr-1999	14-Apr-1999	39.50	0.93	39.42
34	–	14-Apr-1999		Down	15-Apr-1999	28-Apr-1999	34.00	1.05	33.92
	B	29-Apr-1999	Down		29-Apr-1999	07-May-1999	32.00	0.77	31.91
	B	10-May-1999	Down		10-May-1999	12-May-1999	29.50	0.31	29.53
	B	13-May-1999	Down		13-May-1999	19-May-1999	27.00	0.47	26.96
35	–	19-May-1999		Down	20-May-1999	08-Jun-1999	23.50	1.09	23.36
	B	09-Jun-1999	Down		09-Jun-1999	23-Jun-1999	22.00	0.87	21.92
36	–	23-Jun-1999		Down	24-Jun-1999	28-Jul-1999	21.00	1.90	20.88
37	–	28-Jul-1999			29-Jul-1999	01-Sep-1999	19.50	1.78	19.51
38	–	01-Sep-1999			02-Sep-1999	22-Sep-1999	19.50	1.00	19.52
39	–	22-Sep-1999			23-Sep-1999	06-Oct-1999	19.00	0.69	19.01
40	–	06-Oct-1999		Down	07-Oct-1999	10-Nov-1999	19.00	1.59	18.87
41	–	10-Nov-1999			11-Nov-1999	15-Dec-1999	19.00	1.67	18.99
42	–	15-Dec-1999			16-Dec-1999	19-Jan-2000	19.00	1.74	19.00
43	–	19-Jan-2000			20-Jan-2000	16-Feb-2000	19.00	1.45	18.87
44	–	16-Feb-2000			17-Feb-2000	22-Mar-2000	19.00	1.59	18.88
45	–	22-Mar-2000		Down	23-Mar-2000	28-Mar-2000	19.00	0.28	18.94
	B	29-Mar-2000	Down		29-Mar-2000	19-Apr-2000	18.50	1.09	18.60
46	–	19-Apr-2000			20-Apr-2000	24-May-2000	18.50	1.57	18.55
47	–	24-May-2000			25-May-2000	20-Jun-2000	18.50	1.28	18.39
48	–	20-Jun-2000		Down	21-Jun-2000	07-Jul-2000	17.50	0.76	17.34
	B	10-Jul-2000	Down		10-Jul-2000	19-Jul-2000	17.00	0.50	16.96
49	–	19-Jul-2000			20-Jul-2000	23-Aug-2000	16.50	1.53	16.51
50	–	23-Aug-2000			24-Aug-2000	20-Sep-2000	16.50	1.16	16.54
51	–	20-Sep-2000			21-Sep-2000	18-Oct-2000	16.50	1.16	16.60
52	–	18-Oct-2000			19-Oct-2000	22-Nov-2000	16.50	1.41	16.56
53	–	22-Nov-2000			23-Nov-2000	20-Dec-2000	16.50	1.21	16.38
54	–	20-Dec-2000			21-Dec-2000	17-Jan-2001	15.75	1.05	15.76
55	–	17-Jan-2001			18-Jan-2001	14-Feb-2001	15.25	1.13	15.19

Table 6 Interest rate decisions under Arminio Fraga (2001–2002)

Meeting	Type	Date	Bias used	Bias intended	Start	End	Selic Target	Selic (period)	Selic (average)
56	–	14-Feb-2001			15-Feb-2001	21-Mar-2001	15.25	1.30	15.20
57	–	21-Mar-2001			22-Mar-2001	18-Apr-2001	15.75	1.11	15.84
58	–	18-Apr-2001			19-Apr-2001	23-May-2001	16.25	1.45	16.30
59	–	23-May-2001			24-May-2001	20-Jun-2001	16.75	1.17	16.76
60	–	20-Jun-2001		Down	21-Jun-2001	18-Jul-2001	18.25	1.34	18.31
61	–	18-Jul-2001			19-Jul-2001	22-Aug-2001	19.00	1.74	18.96
62	–	22-Aug-2001			23-Aug-2001	19-Sep-2001	19.00	1.32	19.04
63	–	19-Sep-2001			20-Sep-2001	17-Oct-2001	19.00	1.32	19.07
64	–	17-Oct-2001			18-Oct-2001	21-Nov-2001	19.00	1.60	19.05
65	–	21-Nov-2001			22-Nov-2001	19-Dec-2001	19.00	1.39	19.05
66	–	19-Dec-2001			20-Dec-2001	23-Jan-2002	19.00	1.60	19.05
67	–	23-Jan-2002			24-Jan-2002	20-Feb-2002	19.00	1.25	19.05
68	–	20-Feb-2002			21-Feb-2002	20-Mar-2002	18.75	1.38	18.80
69	–	20-Mar-2002			21-Mar-2002	17-Apr-2002	18.50	1.28	18.45
70	–	17-Apr-2002			18-Apr-2002	22-May-2002	18.50	1.62	18.35
71	–	22-May-2002			23-May-2002	19-Jun-2002	18.50	1.26	18.07
72	–	19-Jun-2002		Down	20-Jun-2002	17-Jul-2002	18.50	1.35	18.40
73	–	17-Jul-2002			18-Jul-2002	21-Aug-2002	18.00	1.64	17.86
74	–	21-Aug-2002		Down	22-Aug-2002	18-Sep-2002	18.00	1.31	17.87
75	–	18-Sep-2002			19-Sep-2002	14-Oct-2002	18.00	1.18	17.90
76	E	14-Oct-2002			15-Oct-2002	23-Oct-2002	21.00	0.53	20.90
77	–	23-Oct-2002			24-Oct-2002	20-Nov-2002	21.00	1.44	20.90
78	–	20-Nov-2002			21-Nov-2002	18-Dec-2002	22.00	1.58	21.90
79	–	18-Dec-2002			19-Dec-2002	22-Jan-2003	25.00	2.05	24.90

the COPOM's monetary policy decisions have as their main objective the achievement of the inflation targets set by the National Monetary Council (CMN)."

Among the changes implemented by Arminio Fraga: Two days of meetings (starting in 2000; the rate decision is informed at the end of the 2nd day), and a short-lived attempt to start and end meetings earlier (from May-2002 to Aug-2003 meetings ended while the market was open; from Sep-2003 onwards, the decision is informed when the market is closed).

Also noteworthy is the pause between the easing cycle ending at meeting 55 and the tightening cycle starting at meeting 57. In fact, there is a strong autocorrelation between consecutive moves (the most probable move is one similar to the previous move).

The third group of decisions (Tables 7 and 8) is composed of the meetings held under Henrique Meirelles's mandate, coinciding with the period where Luís Inácio Lula da Silva was Brazil's President. In 2006 the frequency of the meetings changes from monthly to 8 per year (just like the FOMC). For the first time since 1986 we see the Selic rate in single digits (below 10). It stopped at 8.75%; why was this level significant?

There's a tax-free and government-guaranteed investment account in Brazil named "Poupança" ("Savings"), and until 2010 it payed 0.5% plus a variable rate - the "TR" or "Taxa Referencial" – per month. If the Selic dropped below 8.75%, returns after tax would be lower than the Poupança returns. To avoid a migration from Government Bonds to the Poupança, the government changed later the rules for these Savings, limiting the maximum amount invested and changing the rate from TR+0.5% per month to TR plus the lower of 0.5% per month or a percentage of the Selic rate.

The fourth group of decisions (Table 9) is composed of the meetings held under Alexandre Tombini's mandate, simultaneous with Dilma Rousseff's mandate as Brazil's President. Meeting 151 was historic: The Selic rate was lowered just after a meeting in which rates were raised. And the 8.75% floor was breached, with the Selic dropping to an all-time low of 7.25% in 2012. But this effort in lowering real interest rates was short-lived, with the Selic back to 11% in 2014, and after a brief pause, continuing to increase after the presidential elections.

1.1.3 The Brazilian Payment System (SPB): the end of the dual cash regime; CDI and Selic

Let's look at the week of 21/25-May-2001 (Table 10).

What is happening here? A dual cash regime. The CDI refers to banks receiving "checks" from other banks. In order for these checks to impact the reserve accounts at the Central Bank, these checks would have to wait one day to be cleared (this process was denominated "compensação"). So if one bank had a check at T+0, it could either give this check to another bank to receive another

Table 7 Interest rate decisions under Henrique Meirelles (2003–2005)

Meeting	Type	Date	Bias used	Bias intended	Start	End	Selic Target	Selic (period)	Selic (average)
80	–	22-Jan-2003			23-Jan-2003	19-Feb-2003	25.50	1.81	25.36
81	–	19-Feb-2003			20-Feb-2003	19-Mar-2003	26.50	1.68	26.30
82	–	19-Mar-2003		Up	20-Mar-2003	23-Apr-2003	26.50	2.16	26.32
83	–	23-Apr-2003			24-Apr-2003	21-May-2003	26.50	1.78	26.32
84	–	21-May-2003			22-May-2003	18-Jun-2003	26.50	1.87	26.27
85	–	18-Jun-2003			19-Jun-2003	23-Jul-2003	26.00	2.21	25.74
86	–	23-Jul-2003			24-Jul-2003	20-Aug-2003	24.50	1.74	24.32
87	–	20-Aug-2003			21-Aug-2003	17-Sep-2003	22.00	1.58	21.84
88	–	17-Sep-2003			18-Sep-2003	22-Oct-2003	20.00	1.81	19.84
89	–	22-Oct-2003			23-Oct-2003	19-Nov-2003	19.00	1.38	18.84
90	–	19-Nov-2003			20-Nov-2003	17-Dec-2003	17.50	1.28	17.32
91	–	17-Dec-2003			18-Dec-2003	21-Jan-2004	16.50	1.39	16.32
92	–	21-Jan-2004			22-Jan-2004	18-Feb-2004	16.50	1.21	16.30
93	–	18-Feb-2004			19-Feb-2004	17-Mar-2004	16.50	1.08	16.28
94	–	17-Mar-2004			18-Mar-2004	14-Apr-2004	16.25	1.13	16.09
95	–	14-Apr-2004			15-Apr-2004	19-May-2004	16.00	1.41	15.80
96	–	19-May-2004			20-May-2004	16-Jun-2004	16.00	1.11	15.79
97	–	16-Jun-2004			17-Jun-2004	21-Jul-2004	16.00	1.46	15.79
98	–	21-Jul-2004			22-Jul-2004	18-Aug-2004	16.00	1.17	15.83

continued

Table 7 Continued

Meeting	Type	Date	Bias used	Bias intended	Start	End	Selic Target	Selic (period)	Selic (average)
99	–	18-Aug-2004			19-Aug-2004	15-Sep-2004	16.00	1.12	15.90
100	–	15-Sep-2004			16-Sep-2004	20-Oct-2004	16.25	1.44	16.23
101	–	20-Oct-2004			21-Oct-2004	17-Nov-2004	16.75	1.11	16.71
102	–	17-Nov-2004			18-Nov-2004	15-Dec-2004	17.25	1.27	17.23
103	–	15-Dec-2004			16-Dec-2004	19-Jan-2005	17.75	1.63	17.74
104	–	19-Jan-2005			20-Jan-2005	16-Feb-2005	18.25	1.20	18.25
105	–	16-Feb-2005			17-Feb-2005	16-Mar-2005	18.75	1.37	18.75
106	–	16-Mar-2005			17-Mar-2005	21-Apr-2005	19.25	1.69	19.24
107	–	20-Apr-2005			22-Apr-2005	18-May-2005	19.50	1.35	19.51
108	–	18-May-2005			19-May-2005	15-Jun-2005	19.75	1.37	19.75
109	–	15-Jun-2005			16-Jun-2005	20-Jul-2005	19.75	1.80	19.73
110	–	20-Jul-2005			21-Jul-2005	17-Aug-2005	19.75	1.44	19.75
111	–	17-Aug-2005			18-Aug-2005	14-Sep-2005	19.75	1.37	19.74
112	–	14-Sep-2005			15-Sep-2005	19-Oct-2005	19.50	1.71	19.48
113	–	19-Oct-2005			20-Oct-2005	23-Nov-2005	19.00	1.60	18.98
114	–	23-Nov-2005			24-Nov-2005	14-Dec-2005	18.50	1.01	18.49
115	–	14-Dec-2005			15-Dec-2005	18-Jan-2006	18.00	1.66	18.00

Table 8 Interest rate decisions under Henrique Meirelles (2006–2010)

Meeting	Type	Date	Start	End	Selic Target	Selic (period)	Selic (average)
116	–	18-Jan-2006	19-Jan-2006	08-Mar-2006	17.25	2.11	17.26
117	–	08-Mar-2006	09-Mar-2006	19-Apr-2006	16.50	1.77	16.50
118	–	19-Apr-2006	20-Apr-2006	31-May-2006	15.75	1.69	15.72
119	–	31-May-2006	01-Jun-2006	19-Jul-2006	15.25	1.92	15.18
120	–	19-Jul-2006	20-Jul-2006	30-Aug-2006	14.75	1.64	14.67
121	–	30-Aug-2006	31-Aug-2006	18-Oct-2006	14.25	1.75	14.17
122	–	18-Oct-2006	19-Oct-2006	29-Nov-2006	13.75	1.43	13.67
123	–	29-Nov-2006	30-Nov-2006	24-Jan-2007	13.25	1.89	13.19
124	–	24-Jan-2007	25-Jan-2007	07-Mar-2007	13.00	1.36	12.93
125	–	07-Mar-2007	08-Mar-2007	18-Apr-2007	12.75	1.38	12.68
126	–	18-Apr-2007	19-Apr-2007	06-Jun-2007	12.50	1.59	12.43
127	–	06-Jun-2007	07-Jun-2007	18-Jul-2007	12.00	1.31	11.93
128	–	18-Jul-2007	19-Jul-2007	05-Sep-2007	11.50	1.51	11.43
129	–	05-Sep-2007	06-Sep-2007	17-Oct-2007	11.25	1.18	11.18
130	–	17-Oct-2007	18-Oct-2007	05-Dec-2007	11.25	1.40	11.18
131	–	05-Dec-2007	06-Dec-2007	23-Jan-2008	11.25	1.40	11.18
132	–	23-Jan-2008	24-Jan-2008	05-Mar-2008	11.25	1.18	11.18
133	–	05-Mar-2008	06-Mar-2008	16-Apr-2008	11.25	1.23	11.18
134	–	16-Apr-2008	17-Apr-2008	04-Jun-2008	11.75	1.41	11.63
135	–	04-Jun-2008	05-Jun-2008	23-Jul-2008	12.25	1.61	12.17
136	–	23-Jul-2008	24-Jul-2008	10-Sep-2008	13.00	1.70	12.92
137	–	10-Sep-2008	11-Sep-2008	29-Oct-2008	13.75	1.79	13.66

continued

Table 8 Continued

Meeting	Type	Date	Start	End	Selic Target	Selic (period)	Selic (average)
138	–	29-Oct-2008	30-Oct-2008	10-Dec-2008	13.75	1.53	13.65
139	–	10-Dec-2008	11-Dec-2008	21-Jan-2009	13.75	1.43	13.66
140	–	21-Jan-2009	22-Jan-2009	11-Mar-2009	12.75	1.57	12.66
141	–	11-Mar-2009	12-Mar-2009	29-Apr-2009	11.25	1.40	11.16
142	–	29-Apr-2009	30-Apr-2009	10-Jun-2009	10.25	1.12	10.16
143	–	10-Jun-2009	11-Jun-2009	22-Jul-2009	9.25	1.01	9.16
144	–	22-Jul-2009	23-Jul-2009	02-Sep-2009	8.75	0.99	8.65
145	–	02-Sep-2009	03-Sep-2009	21-Oct-2009	8.75	1.09	8.65
146	–	21-Oct-2009	22-Oct-2009	09-Dec-2009	8.75	1.09	8.65
147	–	09-Dec-2009	10-Dec-2009	27-Jan-2010	8.75	1.09	8.65
148	–	27-Jan-2010	28-Jan-2010	17-Mar-2010	8.75	1.09	8.65
149	–	17-Mar-2010	18-Mar-2010	28-Apr-2010	8.75	0.93	8.65
150	–	28-Apr-2010	29-Apr-2010	09-Jun-2010	9.50	1.04	9.40
151	–	09-Jun-2010	10-Jun-2010	21-Jul-2010	10.25	1.16	10.16
152	–	21-Jul-2010	22-Jul-2010	01-Sep-2010	10.75	1.21	10.66
153	–	01-Sep-2010	02-Sep-2010	20-Oct-2010	10.75	1.34	10.66
154	–	20-Oct-2010	21-Oct-2010	08-Dec-2010	10.75	1.34	10.66
155	–	08-Dec-2010	09-Dec-2010	19-Jan-2011	10.75	1.21	10.66

Table 9 Interest rate decisions under Alexandre Tombini

Meeting	Type	Date	Start	End	Selic Target	Selic (period)	Selic (average)
156	–	19-Jan-2011	20-Jan-2011	02-Mar-2011	11.25	1.27	11.17
157	–	02-Mar-2011	03-Mar-2011	20-Apr-2011	11.75	1.46	11.67
158	–	20-Apr-2011	21-Apr-2011	08-Jun-2011	12.00	1.49	11.92
159	–	08-Jun-2011	09-Jun-2011	20-Jul-2011	12.25	1.33	12.17
160	–	20-Jul-2011	21-Jul-2011	31-Aug-2011	12.50	1.40	12.42
161	–	31-Aug-2011	01-Sep-2011	19-Oct-2011	12.00	1.48	11.90
162	–	19-Oct-2011	20-Oct-2011	30-Nov-2011	11.50	1.21	11.40
163	–	30-Nov-2011	01-Dec-2011	18-Jan-2012	11.00	1.45	10.90
164	–	18-Jan-2012	19-Jan-2012	07-Mar-2012	10.50	1.30	10.40
165	–	07-Mar-2012	08-Mar-2012	18-Apr-2012	9.75	1.07	9.65
166	–	18-Apr-2012	19-Apr-2012	30-May-2012	9.00	0.99	8.90
167	–	30-May-2012	31-May-2012	11-Jul-2012	8.50	0.93	8.39
168	–	11-Jul-2012	12-Jul-2012	29-Aug-2012	8.00	1.06	7.89
169	–	29-Aug-2012	30-Aug-2012	10-Oct-2012	7.50	0.82	7.39
170	–	10-Oct-2012	11-Oct-2012	28-Nov-2012	7.25	0.88	7.14
171	–	28-Nov-2012	29-Nov-2012	16-Jan-2013	7.25	0.91	7.14
172	–	16-Jan-2013	17-Jan-2013	06-Mar-2013	7.25	0.90	7.12
173	–	06-Mar-2013	07-Mar-2013	17-Apr-2013	7.25	0.80	7.16
174	–	17-Apr-2013	18-Apr-2013	29-May-2013	7.50	0.82	7.40
175	–	29-May-2013	30-May-2013	10-Jul-2013	8.00	0.88	7.90
176	–	10-Jul-2013	11-Jul-2013	28-Aug-2013	8.50	1.13	8.40
177	–	28-Aug-2013	29-Aug-2013	09-Oct-2013	9.00	1.02	8.90
178	–	09-Oct-2013	10-Oct-2013	27-Nov-2013	9.50	1.22	9.40
179	–	27-Nov-2013	28-Nov-2013	15-Jan-2014	10.00	1.24	9.90
180	–	15-Jan-2014	16-Jan-2014	26-Feb-2014	10.50	1.18	10.40
181	–	26-Feb-2014	27-Feb-2014	02-Apr-2014	10.75	0.93	10.65
182	–	02-Apr-2014	03-Apr-2014	28-May-2014	11.00	1.53	10.90
183	–	28-May-2014	29-May-2014	16-Jul-2014	11.00	1.41	10.90
184	–	16-Jul-2014	17-Jul-2014	03-Sep-2014	11.00	1.45	10.90
185	–	03-Sep-2014	04-Sep-2014	29-Oct-2014	11.00	1.66	10.90
186	–	29-Oct-2014	30-Oct-2014	03-Dec-2014	11.25	1.05	11.15
187	–	03-Dec-2014	04-Dec-2014		11.75		

Table 10 Interest rates before the SPB

Date	SETA	Selic	CDI
21-May-2001	16.25	16.30	16.24
22-May-2001	16.25	16.30	16.25
23-May-2001	16.25	16.33	16.61
24-May-2001	16.75	16.77	16.72
25-May-2001	16.75	16.80	16.75

Table 11 Interest rates after the SPB

Date	SETA	Selic	CDI
15-Jul-2002	18.50	18.39	18.33
16-Jul-2002	18.50	18.39	18.35
17-Jul-2002	18.50	18.39	18.23
18-Jul-2002	18.00	17.89	17.89
19-Jul-2002	18.00	17.89	17.86

check at T+1 (with one day of CDI as interest - this was also known as ADM rates/trades, and trades registered at Cetip were settled in this way), or it could clear the check, receiving money on its reserve account at T+1 and therefore it would be able to lend that money at the Selic rate from T+1 to T+2.

With the introduction of the SPB (local acronym for "Brazilian Payment System") in April of 2002, the possibility of direct transfers was opened for the general public (for values larger than BRL 5,000.00), and banks now settled everything through their reserve accounts, ending this duality. This was reflected in the rates behavior (Table 11).

This reform also brought additional safety mechanisms for the financial system, as the Law 10214/2001 also gave legal support to systemically important clearings to conduct multilateral clearing and also to have precedence in the event of the failure of a participant. The combination of volatility and counterparty risk contributed to concentrate the interbank market into 3 clearings: Derivatives, FX (both controlled by BM&F) and Equities (CBLC, controlled by Bovespa). A 4th clearing (Government Bonds, also controlled by BM&F) never got enough volume. BM&F and Bovespa merged in 2008 and efforts to consolidate the clearings are ongoing.

Typically local hedge and mutual funds do not trade with credit limits; instead they trade futures, options and swaps guaranteed by the clearings.

The clearings were tested in 1999, when two banks (Marka and FonteCindam) were caught in the wrong side of the FX devaluation. In a controversial decision, the two banks were able to buy back contracts at a price lower than the market's price, limiting the amount owed to the CCP. Later, in 2008, no systemic issue happened at the CCP, although several companies that were caught short USD through OTC structured products found themselves in difficulties.

1.1.4 A new era? What has changed under Tombini? Coordination and communication, or more subtle changes?

In 2011, the worst of the 2008 crisis was over, and Brazil was growing with the government pumping credit into the system. There was a price though, as the IPCA was already approaching 6% over 12 months (it would close 2011 at exactly

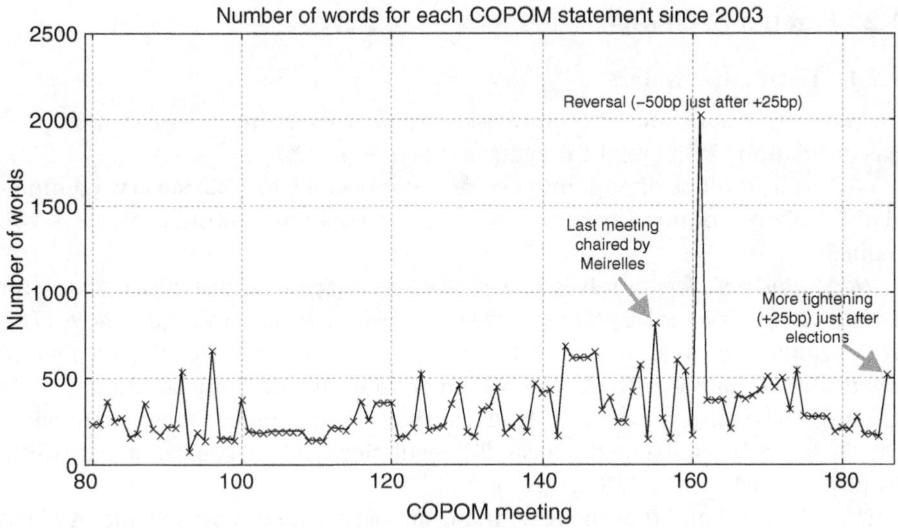

Figure 11 Words of each COPOM statement (not counting the votes tally) since 2003

6.50%; just 1bp more would force an official pronouncement by the Central Bank on why it had not fulfilled its duty). So it was quite surprising to see the COPOM do a 180 degrees turn at the end of Aug-2011, not only interrupting a tightening cycle (with the European crisis as the backdrop) but starting an easing cycle that would stop only when the SETA was at an unheard-of 7.25% level. Since 2002 there was not zig-zag in consecutive COPOM meetings.

As the market started doubting the commitment to inflation targeting (especially when the government started referring to the upper band of 6.5% as the target), it's not a surprise that the COPOM started struggling in its communication (Figure 11).

After this date, the market's projection for the IPCA (next 12 months) was higher by 0.25% on average in the following 2 years, increasing by an additional 0.60% since mid-2013. The expected IPCA for 2014 is close to the upper limit of the band (again). It was also not unusual to see the Central Bank dissent from the official pronunciations in one report, only to return to an alignment with government policy in the next report.

So the most puzzling behavior was really the decoupling of the interest rates set by the COPOM during the easing cycle and the inflation expectations, as those never got close to the 4.5% target again. The pause in the tightening cycle at the 2nd half of 2014 was not unprecedented (Meirelles started a tightening cycle one meeting later than expected, as rumors about his personal political projects swirled around, and paused in September and October of 2010).

1.2 Foreign Exchange

1.2.1 Testing the waters

By now the reader must be quite wary about this country ... devaluation ? Hyperinflation? What might they have invented in FX?

Well, you won't be disappointed – Brazil has been historically a very (commercially) isolated country, by means of arcane regulations, subsidies, taxes – you name it.

We should restrict ourselves to the 90s (for more into this history look for Emilio Garofalo's books: (*Cambio, Ouro e Divida Externa – De Figueiredo a FHC, 2007*) and (*Cambio no Brasil – As Peripécias da Moeda Nacional e da Política Cambial, 500 anos depois, 2000*)), which should give us some additional background for trading in Brazil. As a starting point, there's some material at the BCB (to be updated on local FX regulations is, of course, a necessity): http://www.bcb.gov.br/?EXCHANGE

There one will find that the Brazilian Real is a type A currency, so quotes are in Brazilian Reais per One US Dollar. This is not trivial, as sometimes stress methodologies will determine currencies devaluing against the dollar is US Dollar per currency terms: a 50% loss corresponds in fact to a 100% devaluation in quoted terms. Looking at some numbers:

If the USDBRL pair is quoted at 2.00 (BRL per USD), this is equivalent to 0.50 USD per BRL. A 50% loss in the USD per BRL quote will leave it at 0.25, which corresponds to a 4.00 BRL per USD quote, a devaluation of 100% as measured by the locals.

Examples of type B currencies include the Euro (EUR) and the British pound (GBP).

And how have the Real and its past incarnations fared against the dollar? Well, looking at series number 1 at the BCB's website (with data available since 1986) we find a puzzling chart (Figure 12).

We might need our logarithmic glasses again (Figure 13).

Now, where did we see these 1000 factors again? Yes, currency changes (Table 3). Adjusting the quotes by the conversion factors, we find it hard to see quotes before 1994 (Figure 14).

What is happening here? Where did we see these ramps? Maybe the chart for the overnight rates (Figure 4)? The daily CDI (up to 1994) looks remarkably similar to the rolling mean (over 21 business days) of the daily returns of USDBRL (Figure 15).

So over that period the realized trend seems to be determined by the overnight rate; as the (insert here the name of the currency at the time) was losing value, the almighty USD kept its value.

After the Real Plan, there's a brief period of BRL strength, followed by a period of almost zero return. We'll cover this on the next Section (1.2.2).

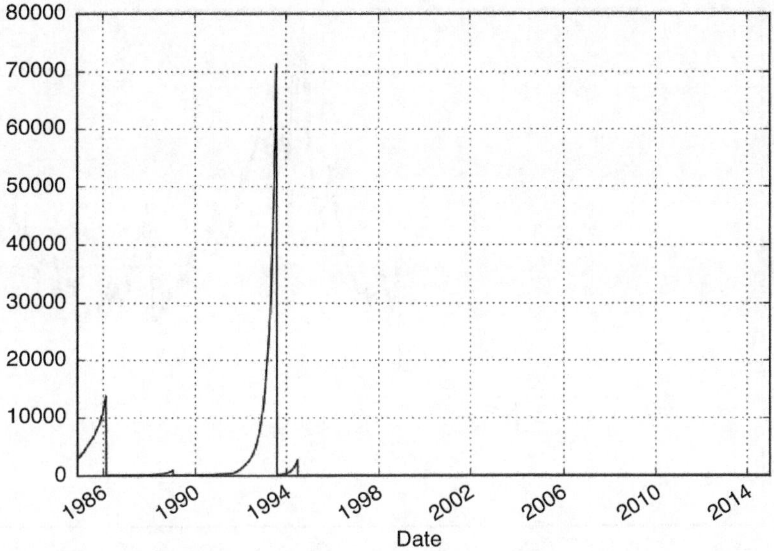

Figure 12 PTAX since 1986

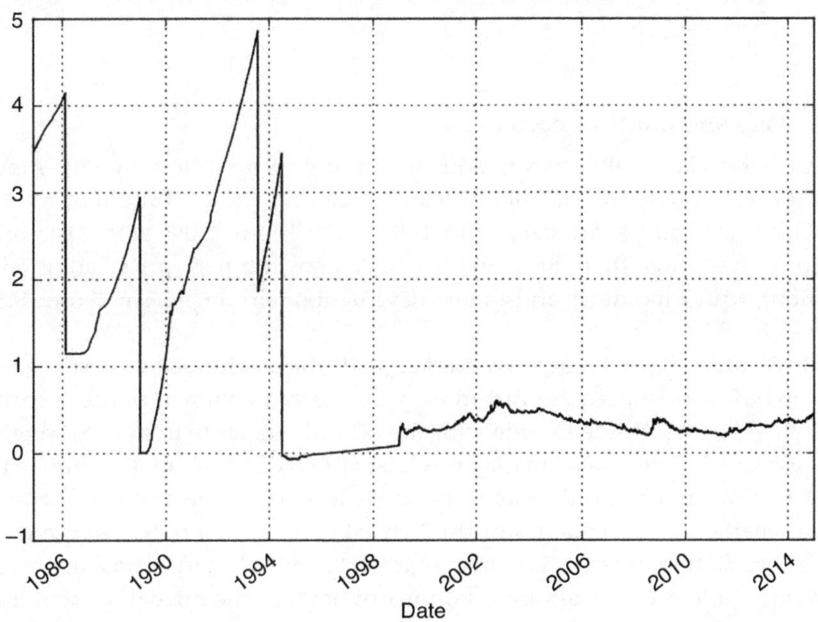

Figure 13 Log10(PTAX) since 1986

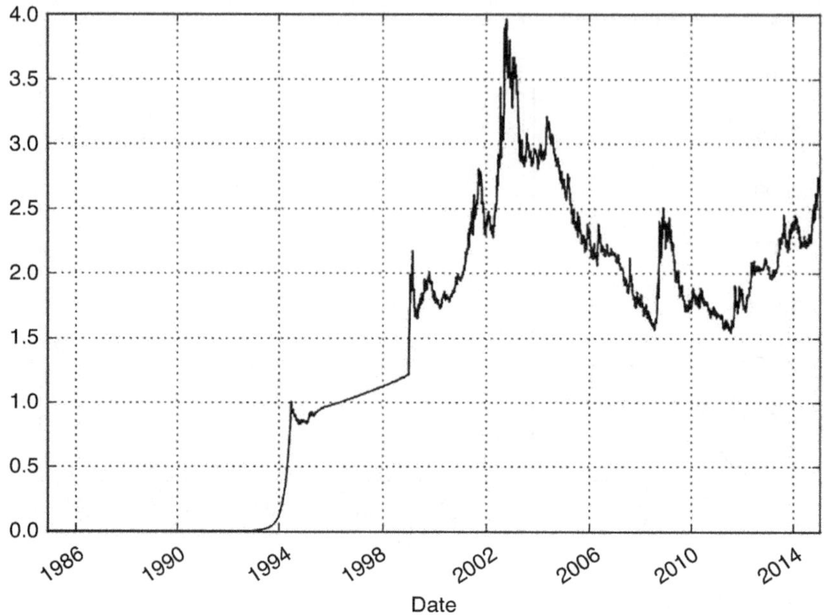

Figure 14 PTAX (adjusted) since 1986

1.2.2 Pegs and multiple currencies

The Cruzado Plan (1986) was famous for (trying to) fix prices by law. Among those prices ... yes, the USDBRL. It can be seen on the USDBRL returns chart (Figure 15) a small period starting in 1986 (from Feb to Nov) where the prices do not move. After that, Brazil returns to a crawling peg (prices adjusted by inflation), with a moratory and a maxi-devaluation (although a small one: 8.5%) in 1987.

In 1989 Brazil started a dual FX market, with the creation of the "Mercado de Câmbio de Taxas Flutuantes (Turismo)", which became known as the "floating" market, which stood side by side with the official market (where rates were still predetermined). The official market was later (1990) denominated "commercial".

But this was not the only way to trade FX in Brazil – there was, of course, a "black" market, a consequence of the Central Bank's monopoly and the draconian FX legislation. It was this market that the "floating" market was supposed to substitute. Gold was also an important instrument, as the price of gold in Brazil reflected the international market and a FX rate; in our case, the floating rate (informally, practiced by the BCB) or the black/parallel rate (when gold was sent illegally out of the country).

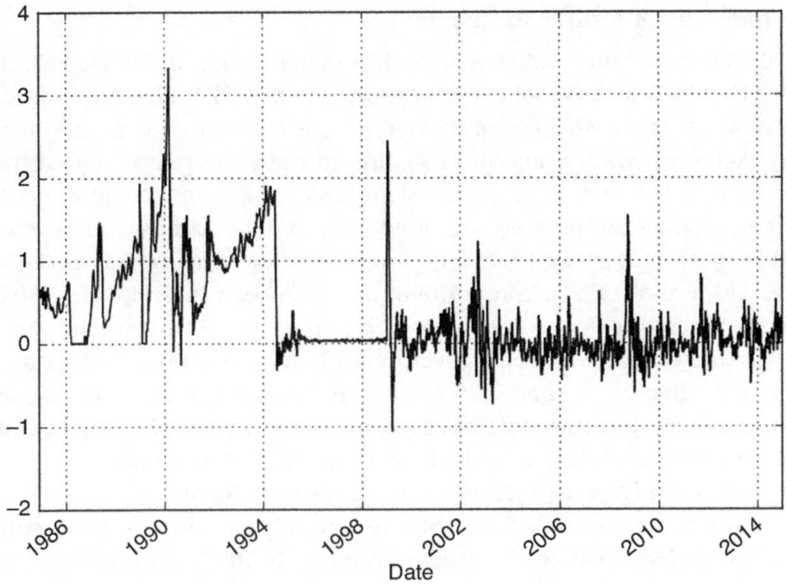

Figure 15 USDBRL % returns (rolling mean over 21 bd)

In 1990 the BCB itself enabled a gold vs USD trade (trading spot physical gold vs a future price set and settled in USD).

The Collor Plan (March 1990) started with a bang, confiscating most of the available money while adopting a free floating regime for FX. That didn't last long, with the Central Bank back to the market with a dirty floating regime; the Collor II plan (1991) tried to fix the USDBRL parity (after previously devaluing it 30%), but – not surprisingly – it didn't last long (2 months).

In Feb 1994 the URV was created, working as the index to rule them all (it was equivalent to 1 USD at the ask rate). This was preparation for the Real Plan, and at its inception we had 1 Real equal to 1 URV equal to 1 USD.

The dirty floating returned in Oct 1994, as the government, worried by the quick appreciation of the BRL (the parity went as low as 0.83 BRL per 1 USD), started buying at 0.83 and selling at 0.86 (an informal band).

A formal model of bands was officially adopted in March 1995 (0.86 vs 0.90). Those values would go up (in 1998 they were 1.12 vs 1.22), until the devaluation of 1999 (seen clearly in the chart) brought an end to the bands regime.

Although there was an adverse scenario in the background (the aftermath of the Russian crisis of 1998 made it harder to get credit and negatively impacted commodities prices), the substitution of Gustavo Franco by Francisco Lopes and the poorly conducted acceleration of the devaluation implied in the bands did not succeed.

1.2.3 Indexing of local instruments

With all the restrictions and challenges in buying (physical) US Dollars, it was expected that institutions that needed exposure to the USDBRL parity would look for other ways. The BM&F (Bolsa de Mercadorias e Futuros = Commodities and Futures Exchange) was created in 1986, and in the same year it started trading FX contracts (USD, DM, JPY). In the same way, swaps (much more like NDFs than traditional FX Swaps) were also used. Due to the volatility and uncertainty around interest rates at the time, a FX Swap could be structured as a NDF (USD Fixed vs BRL Fixed) or as a composite of a NDF and an IR Swap (USD Fixed vs BRL Float), where the floating leg was an accrual of the CDI overnight rate.

NTN-Ds and NBCEs were local government bonds issued by the Treasury and the BCB respectively, and their participation in the local government debt ranged from 10% to 30%; but their role has been filled now by the FX Swap operations conducted by the BCB. Just a residual exposure on NTN-As remains.

The PTAX is the FX rate of reference for those instruments.

The US Dollar futures traded at BVMF are currently the most liquid instrument to trade the USDBRL pair, leading the movements in the fx spot market.

1.2.4 Floating, ballast and hot air (on the different mechanisms to manage a floating currency)

Like a ship with a hole in the bottom, currencies sometimes needed a little help to stay afloat. Or sometimes the ship needs enough ballast (in most cases, reserves in strong foreign currencies) to keep it from capsizing.

If you're doing any monetary intervention, you have to ask yourself first: "Why bother?"

Assuming that there is a good answer (something like "It's not going to solve it but we are expected to do something"), the next question is: "How are we going to do it this time?"

Because, after all, your threat must be credible. Too many times emerging markets have started an intervention and the market just divided the available reserves by the size of the intervention, counted the days and said (with its money): "I call your bluff".

A country can keep the bands playing, if it has the means, but this was not the case with Brazil in 1999. Interventions in both spot and futures markets were common (although the interventions in the futures markets were not official), but the level of reserves was not as high as necessary to support the intervention's goals for enough time.

As we saw before, the 1999 devaluation was not exactly planned. One consequence was that the DOL futures were not prepared to follow such volatility, and the prices used for the daily margining process were somewhat delayed (Figure 16). One can also see the missing point on 25-Jan (exchange closed for the local holiday).

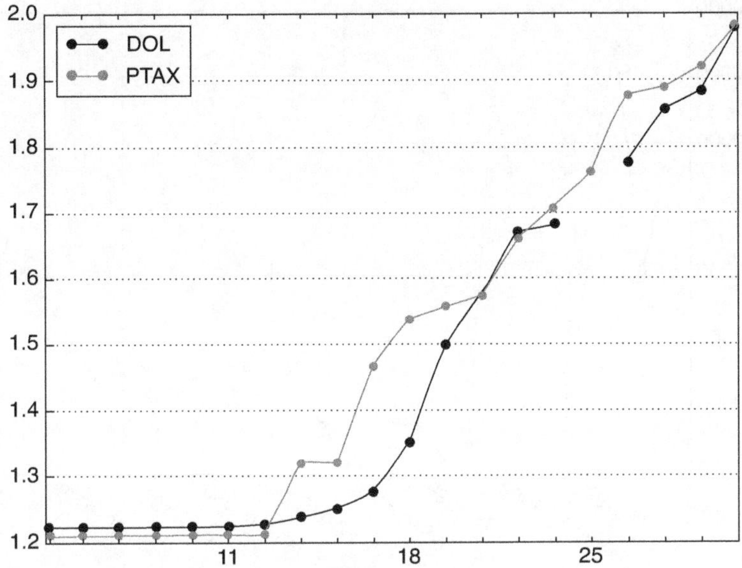

Figure 16 DOL x PTAX in Jan-1999

This pattern is also reflected in the number of contracts traded during that period (Figure 17).

Why is this interesting? Because with the Feb contract bound by the daily limits, trading at the maximum level permitted (figure), the fx spot market was trading higher (as reflected by the PTAX). Figure 18 shows how from 13-Jan to 19-Jan the contract got stuck at the maximum.

After the devaluation, at the end of 1999 the Central Bank resumed interventions in the market, although not in an organized way. A typical case happened in 21-Nov-2000, when Santander bought Banespa (a state bank privatized after being misused by former governors). The purchase price amounted to approximately USD 3.7 billions. Santander started to sell dollars on 20-Nov-2000 (a Monday), and on Tuesday the BCB announced that it would buy dollars up to USD 3 billion; estimates indicate that it bought USD 2.5 billion at 1.91 on this day.

Sales of US Dollars in the fx spot market were not the only weapons at the BCB's disposal; the government could also issue dollar-linked local government bonds (they represented about 20% of the local debt at the start of 2001).

In 2001 the government faced its share of problems (Argentina, 11 September, energy shortage crisis), but 2002 forced the BCB to reach in the bag of tricks. To avoid using currency futures (directly or indirectly), a new contract was developed, the SCC (a FX Swap cleared at BM&F, monthly at first and daily later). It

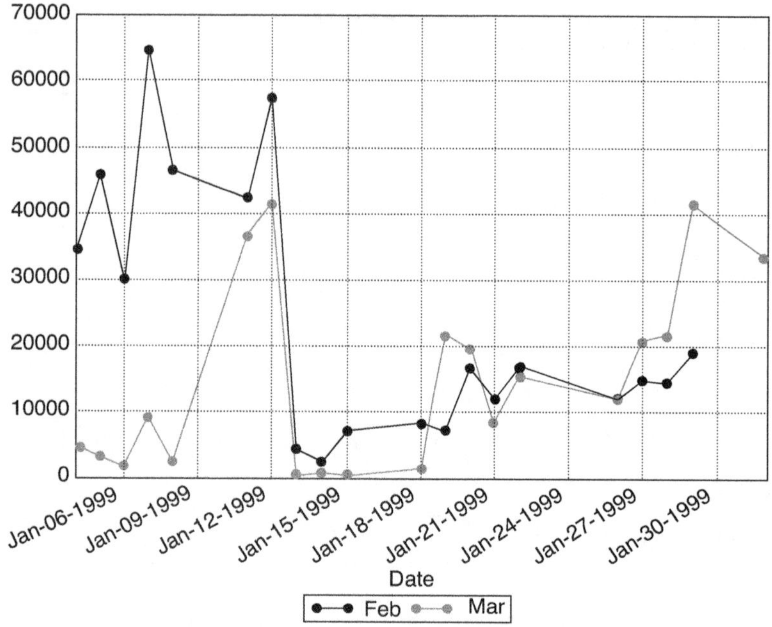

Figure 17 Contracts traded in DOL futures (expiries Feb. and Mar.) in Jan-1999

Date	SettPrice	Open	Last	High	Low	Trades	ContractsTraded
04-Jan-99	1,222.494	1,223.000	1,222.400	1,223.000	1,220.600	492	33,920
05-Jan-99	1,220.903	1,222.000	1,221.000	1,222.000	1,220.700	533	46,000
06-Jan-99	1,220.406	1,220.100	1,220.400	1,220.650	1,220.100	386	29,915
07-Jan-99	1,221.629	1,223.000	1,221.900	1,223.000	1,221.100	787	64,815
08-Jan-99	1,221.934	1,221.300	1,221.850	1,222.200	1,221.100	496	46,501
11-Jan-99	1,222.196	1,222.000	1,222.000	1,223.200	1,221.900	594	42,265
12-Jan-99	1,225.393	1,222.400	1,227.000	1,227.000	1,222.100	609	57,456
13-Jan-99	1,237.646	1,237.646	1,237.646	1,237.646	1,237.646	7	4,323
14-Jan-99	1,250.022	1,250.022	1,250.022	1,250.022	1,250.022	8	2,571
15-Jan-99	1,275.022	1,275.022	1,275.022	1,275.022	1,275.022	31	7,180
18-Jan-99	1,351.523	1,351.523	1,351.523	1,351.523	1,351.523	39	8,415
19-Jan-99	1,500.190	1,500.190	1,500.190	1,500.190	1,500.190	31	7,100
20-Jan-99	1,574.616	1,550.000	1,577.000	1,579.000	1,550.000	712	16,640
21-Jan-99	1,668.436	1,575.000	1,660.000	1,669.092	1,574.000	472	11,917
22-Jan-99	1,682.453	1,640.000	1,690.000	1,740.000	1,640.000	841	16,995
26-Jan-99	1,774.375	1,783.400	1,775.000	1,900.000	1,730.000	723	12,189
27-Jan-99	1,855.138	1,810.000	1,860.000	1,865.000	1,775.000	981	14,801
28-Jan-99	1,883.579	1,860.000	1,890.000	1,910.000	1,830.000	784	14,493
29-Jan-99	1,983.200	1,940.000	1,980.000	2,000.000	1,930.000	800	19,021

Figure 18 DOL prices (Feb-1999 expiry)

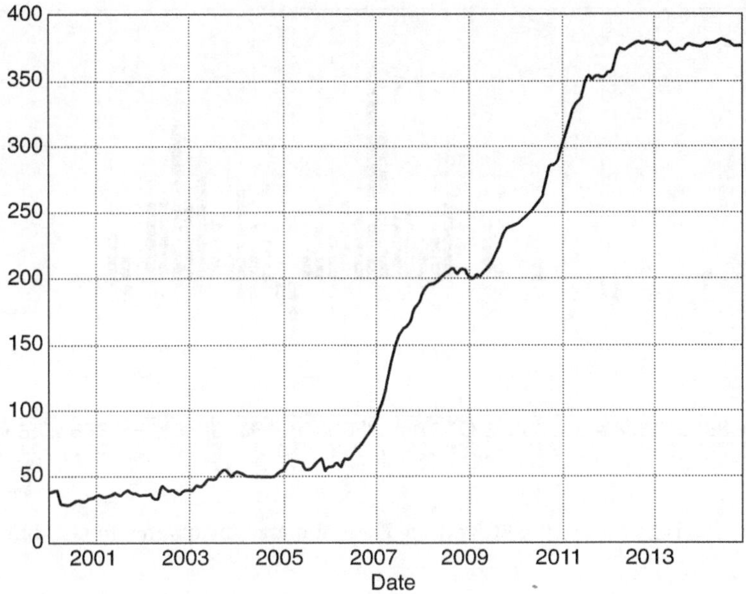

Figure 19 Reserves (liquidity) in USD billions

worked like a future, it walked like a future, it quacked like a future (especially after the daily margining), being very very similar to the existing DDI contract. The backdrop was not good, with the government candidate (José Serra) never really taking off. Other opposition candidates had strong starts, but faded, and Lula won at the end.

Even with Lula publishing an open letter promising to keep Brazil on the right track and avoid a debt moratory, markets were quite afraid. Even the FX Swaps could not prevent the BRL from reaching almost 4.0 and interest rates shooting up. More on 2002 in the next Subsection (1.2.5).

But after Lula kept the policies of the previous government mainly intact, with China bringing in demand for Brazilian exports, and with interest rates high, the flow of US Dollars into Brazil turned the BCB into a dollars buyer in 2004 (the "Reverse Swap Auctions"). One can see the rapid progress of the reserves since 2000 in Figure 19.

The period from 2004 to mid-2008 was marked by the attempts to stop the appreciation of the BRL, with derivatives, fx spot, and by letting the local dollar-denominated bonds expire without renewing them. But when the stress at the 2nd half of 2008 happened, the BCB was slow to react, letting the USDBRL reach 2.40 and allowing a 40% depreciation in one month. 2008 will be covered in

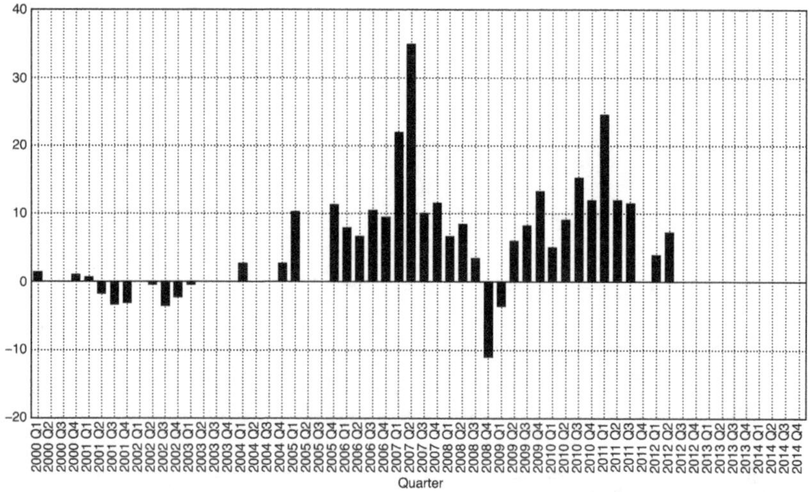

Figure 20 Interventions of the BCB on the FX Spot market by quarter, in USD billions

more detail in Subsection 1.2.6, but we can see how it represents the exception in the BCB's history of intervention in Figure 20.

Now, getting the data for the FX Spot interventions (at least the monthly totals) is relatively easy, since it impacts the reserves. Lines in USD impact more the availability of USD than the level of USDBRL, so they're not in the picture.

Getting data for the derivatives interventions is a bit more complicated. From 2002 to 2006 they're accessible directly on a web page (one for each month), even though the layout changes over time, and the header is not easily accessible in the 2nd half of 2006, making it hard to scrape the data. From 2007 on, you have to download a spreadsheet inside the monthly press communicate of the BCB's Trading Desk. Getting data from the exchange is not easier, and the information is incomplete (one will not know whether a particular contract is a normal or a reverse swap). An intervention that doesn't impact reserves is harder to track.

And another difference of the two types of intervention: Derivatives have an expiry date (and USD-denominated bonds also have it). So you can "issue" dollars that you don't have, but at some point they either expire (which has the opposite effect of the initial intervention) or they are rolled, postponing the day of reckoning. So if you're charting the effect of the intervention, you have to consider the date of the auction, the date of the fixing at the start, and the date of the fixing at the end. When rolling the existing stock, it is common to see a big difference between the date of the auction and the date of the fixing at the start.

So yes, getting all that data is important if you want to track the BCB's interventions in the derivatives market. The implied rate on the USD leg of the swap makes the FX risk at inception different than the FX risk at maturity, and clearly the values in BRL at inception will certainly be different than those at maturity.

Producing the chart of the derivatives interventions is left as an exercise for the reader, but the companion website will have it as well.

And the BCB was not the only currency warrior to pick up shield, sword and pen. Guido Mantega, Finance Minister, made headlines in Sep-2010 by declaring that "We're in the midst of an international currency war, a general weakening of currency. This threatens us because it takes away our competitiveness".

It is not in the scope of this book to track all the taxes imposed and suspended on the cash (Fixed Income, FX and Equities) markets, but we're delighted to discuss an interesting battle in the midst of this war: the IOF tax on derivatives imposed in July-2011.

Let's ask the usual questions: What, Who, When, Where, Why?

What: Decree 7536, dated 26-Jul-2011, instituted a tax (1% over the "adjusted notional value") on the acquisition, sale or expiry of derivatives contracts in which the payoff is influenced by the change in the FX rate and that result in an increase of the "net short exposure" compared with the previous day. After that: some definitions ("adjusted notional value", "net exposure"); the responsibility for calculating and collecting the tax is given to the institutions where the contracts are registered (BM&FBovespa and CETIP); exposures can be offset even if they're registered in different venues (BM&FBovespa typically with listed futures, CETIP with OTC trades between a bank and its customer); if the final net short position is lower than USD 10 millions, the 1% becomes zero. From now on BM&FBovespa will also be referred to as BVMF.

Who: This came quite out of the blue. Although there were some complaints that the futures were used for speculating against the BRL, and the government had taken some actions making it harder for foreign investors to trade futures locally (forbidding the acceptance of bank guarantees as margin, and taxing the FX trades used to buy government bonds (used then as margin). But it came from the Finance Ministry, with the BCB and the Federal Tax Service left to go over the details with the market.

When: Just after the BRL traded below 1.55 (on 25-Jul-2011) – this was the straw that broke the camel's back. So levels matter.

Where: Derivatives traded directly on the exchange which was indeed a novelty. It was common knowledge that the derivatives were more liquid and led the fx spot quote, but this was on a microstructure level. On longer timescales, there are other factors in consideration, mainly macroeconomic; and the interest rate differential is the main factor that attracted the flow. The government had put forward lots of taxes to make the carry trade less attractive, but the flows kept coming.

Why: To try to do something, to be seen doing something, and to threaten more actions. As mentioned before, credibility is everything when intervening.

Well, after the decree there were lots of questions and not a lot of answers. On subsequent meetings with the market, terms like maturity were replaced with more correct terms like fixing. Language is always important when defining contracts and taxes, after all – otherwise, why are there so many tax lawyers? It was now clear that the tax only applied to contracts where the goal was FX exposure against the BRL (crosses like USD x EUR, where the MTM itself had a FX exposure, were now clearly exempt; commodities derivatives, even though they typically had an FX component (reference prices are usually in USD) were also exempt.

Most importantly, Decree 7563, dated 15-Sep-2011, allowed fx delta hedging. One's FX exposure could change due to changes in market rates (a forward or an option are simple examples). If one is long a USD Call BRL Put, and the USDBRL parity goes up, the rebalancing of the position asks for a sale of USD. The Decree 7536 would tax that fx delta hedge trade, but Decree 7563 now explicitly made fx delta hedging possible.

In Mar-2012 Decree 7699 made the tax rate equal to zero for exporters, if the volume was compatible with the value exported.

In 2013, just after bringing down to zero the tax on the purchase of local government bonds by foreigners, the government capitulated and set the tax rate on the Derivatives IOF to zero as well (Decree 8027, 12-Jun-2013). Why? Because of a quick depreciation (Figure 21).

And so Brazil stumbles through new taxes and laws when its currency is strong, and weakens controls when it tumbles. For the last 3.5 years (mid-2011 to the end of 2014), the BRL has weakened, but the amount of the depreciation was similar to the devaluation implied on the forwards.

1.2.5 Paganism (on how to avoid conversion, and the history of offshore × onshore spreads)

Haven't we already talked about Brazil's FX legislation? Yes, we have. As the reader can imagine, conversion has not been big in the agenda of a country which many consider to be one of the less open economies of the world. Armies of Brazilians have been scouring shops in neighboring Paraguay and, most recently, in the USA, looking for items which could be bought in stores and sold at a profit in Brazil. Alas, your typical store in Europe or in the US won't accept BRL as payment – banks in Europe or in the US won't offer you an account in BRL in the same way they offer accounts in currencies like EUR or USD.

And things are not much better in Brazil. Buying and holding foreign currency was never easy, and at times forbidden or limited. If you had dollars, you were rich, and those dollars were a protection against inflation (remember the chart comparing the appreciation of the USD with inflation and interest rates), confiscation or other bad things that the government might think of.

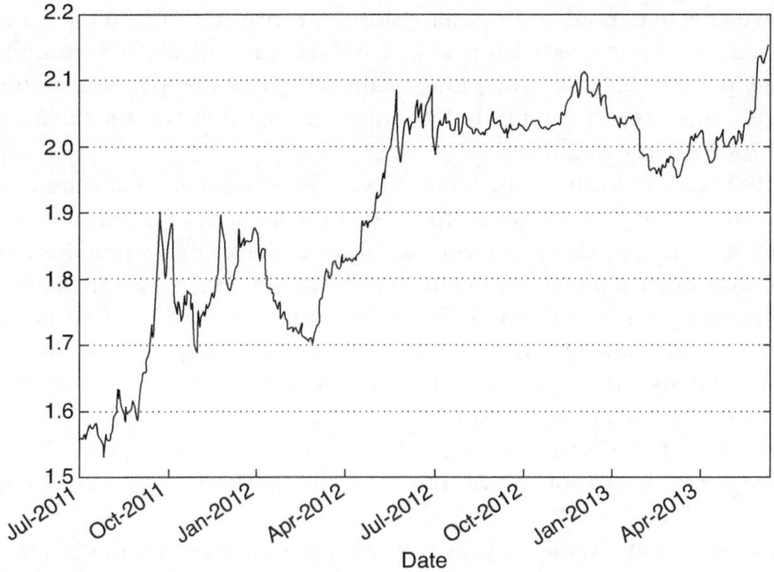

Figure 21 PTAX from 2011 to 2013

If you, as an investor, thought about investing in Brazil's capital markets directly, there was specific legislation governing how you could do it; the most recent example is Resolution 2689. It is common to see equities and fixed income using different accounts; also, when it comes to derivatives, exchange traded derivatives (futures) can be treated one way, and OTC derivatives another (especially for tax purposes).

It is not hard to see that there should be some (very important) differences between buying a bond issued offshore (in USD) and bringing money into Brazil (after opening an account in the local market) to buy a USD-indexed government bond; these are very different markets.

But, even with all these problems, the interest rates available in Brazil (both in BRL and also on the onshore USD-indexed instruments) always managed to bring in those looking for the classic carry trade or for the "arbitrage" of high rates in local USD-indexed instruments against cheaper USD offshore funding.

With the development of the NDF (non deliverable forward offshore) market, another opportunity like that appeared: Selling USD (buying BRL) offshore through NDFs and buying USD (selling BRL) onshore (hopefully matching maturities). In times like 1998 (July) and 2002 (1st half), these traded at single digits (expressed in % per year).

It all looked fine, money in the bank, etc, especially when you're a Brazilian and think that you have an informational edge (when in fact most of the time you have selective recall and tunnel vision). But reality seems to have a way of consciously trying to wreck our plans ... in both cases this NDF premium (NDF offshore quote – NDF onshore quote) went as high as 40% per year, testing risk appetites, stop losses and liquidity. The trigger in Aug 1998 was the Russian crisis, and in 2002 the rise of Lula.

The 2002 case was interesting, mainly because of the belief that rules wouldn't change within the current government – but what is the meaning of this? Up to 2002, the NDF premium was seen mainly as a convertibility premium; people were always worried about the definitions of the settlement rate in NDFs in the case something happened (the fallback fixing rates); the idea is to be able to follow what the market is pricing instead of what an entity like the government or a central bank would publish as the official settlement rate (see Argentina or Venezuela circa 2014 for example).

Settlement of the NDF meant receiving USD, clean and green. To ensure that, the party losing money over the life of the trade(s) would have to deposit collateral (in USD).

As for the onshore trade ... let's start with the tax that you might pay when sending money to Brazil. Why would you have to send money to Brazil? If you're opening a position in futures contracts at BVMF, you'll have to deposit margin (cash or securities). Cash will not receive any interest, so it's not a good option (unless taxes for buying bonds are higher than the expected interest). This is why most of the collateral deposited at BVMF is composed of government bonds.

So you now have added to your sovereign exposure, possibly paid taxes, and nothing has happened yet.

After you actually trade (buying USD), imagine that the BRL is weakening. We're talking about a time where Brazil's reserves could (and were) still be counted in terms of "days of intervention it can support before running out". As the daily margining happens, you're the happy owner of a bunch of BRL. Now, what do you do with it? Would you feel comfortable with that money in Brazil? Is the exchange increasing the initial margin?

Now, you've decided to send this money to your home country. Volatility is probably high, and spreads also. So on the next day there's a strengthening of the BRL, so you have to bring money in. This process is very likely to produce a lot of friction, inefficiency and costs, but it sounds better than increasing your sovereign exposure to a country that is, perhaps, unraveling.

Now, the previous paragraph is an optimist's view of the process. The pessimist would think about the credit risk involved in facing the exchange (basically exposure to big banks and local sovereign debt). He would also think that the settlement rate can be determined by the government to be lower than that practiced by the market. He would also worry that the FX rate used to send the money out might not be well matched with the rate used to price the futures.

All that was packaged into the NDF premium. In 2002 those NDFs did converge to the onshore settlement price, and there was much rejoicing.

After Lula continued the economical policies of his predecessor, and kept the market relatively untouched, the party started. High interest rates, and the FX appreciation that was a consequence of investment coming back to Brazil and the China/commodities boom, made the short USD long BRL forwards a very popular trade.

In fact, it was so popular that the demand for NDFs changed what was a convertibility premium to a negative (although small) spread. Since then, the spread has fluctuated according to demand and taxes. As convertibility seems no closer than it was 10 years ago, the NDF spread will be there in the market and in the models for some time still.

1.2.6 A bit of a fit (on the 2008 crisis)

Local corporates were very interested in the strength of the BRL from 2003 onwards. Exporters wanted hedges, and treasurers wanted bonuses. With a lot of companies hiring former traders, the aggressiveness of the trades put forth as "hedges" increased.

Some of the derivatives were sold together with loans, so the rates on the loans looked good. As for the derivatives: if the realized payoff was in favor of the company, nice work from the treasurer. If not, well, it was a hedge, wasn't it?

Popular derivatives were:

1. Series of forward starting options
2. Series of out-of-the-money USD calls
3. Target Redemption Forwards

The problem with the first product for the corporates became clear in May 2005, when the BRL depreciated by about 10%. Most of the previous monthly payoffs of the 1m USD calls were either zero or small. So, no big check was written, *but* in mid 2005, it was time to ask for the money. This product was not necessarily easy for the bank, as a simple analysis shows:

$$PremiumATMF(\%) \simeq 0.4 \cdot \sigma \cdot \sqrt{t} \tag{1}$$

For a 3 years trade, there would be 36 monthly options. Expressing the term of the trade as the number of months n (and therefore the numbers of monthly options), the sum of all the premia is:

$$TotalPremiumATMF(\%) \simeq n \cdot 0.4 \cdot \sigma \cdot \sqrt{\frac{1}{n}} = 0.4 \cdot \sigma \cdot \sqrt{n} \tag{2}$$

Showing that the bank has an incentive to transform one 3 years option into 36 monthly options.

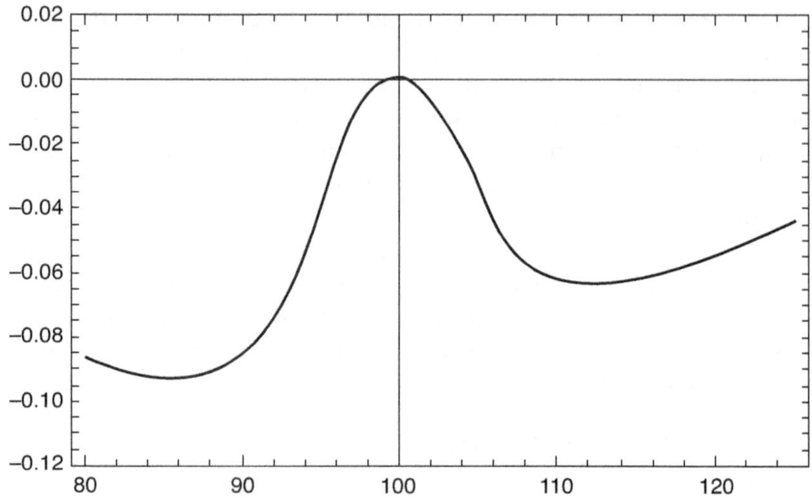

Figure 22 Gamma profile of hedged forward options

Vega scales up with the square root of time, and gamma scales down with the square root of time.

So 36 times the vega of a one month option is equal to six times the vega of a 3 years option.

And the gamma of a one month option is equal to six times the gamma of a 3 years option.

So the obvious hedge is selling a 3 years option with a notional equal to 6 times the notional of each monthly option: premia, vega and gamma are matched ... well, at least at inception they're matched.

But if there's a move in spot big enough, the gamma of the 1m option disappears quickly. The other 35 options contribute only with vega, not with gamma.

The resulting gamma profile is shown in Figure 22.

So, a simple pricing of the portfolio of forward starting options can give you a price related to a hedge that only works in certain states of the world; unfortunately, in the states of the world where the hedge doesn't work, you're short gamma when you've moved away from the current spot price (likely a high volatility scenario). How should the bank control for that? How to price this ongoing hedge? It is an interesting problem.

Back to the customer, he is likely to suffer realized losses from time to time, and there's also a MTM (mark-to-market) loss on the vega position of the options that are still forward starting.

The second product is more straightforward: just a series of OTM USD calls; the customer is less likely to suffer realized losses, depending on the moneyness and maturity of the options.

But the third product ... well, the consequences were pretty interesting.

At the end of 2007/beginning of 2008, a new product (but already known in other places) got hold of banks and corporates alike. The TARF (Target Redemption Forward) played on the theme of the continued appreciation of the BRL; the customer bought USD Puts and sold USD Calls (with the same strikes as the USD Puts) with maturities every month for a period like one year; in a typical trade the notional of the USD Calls would be twice the notional of the USD Puts. If the cumulative payoff of the USD Puts reaches or exceeds a target, the deal expires with this last payoff. Otherwise, the deal continues until TARF's maturity date.

With the strikes high enough, the BRL appreciation and with the interest rate differential increasing the moneyness of the longer dated USD Calls, there was an interesting situation: A positive PV (Present Value) for the bank (as calculated by whatever model each bank used) at inception, and happy customers receiving their 30 to 40 cents every 3 or 4 months. Until the BRL started to weaken in Aug/Sep-2008, from about 1.6–2.0. At this point there was both a lack of decisive action from the BCB and a moment in which each and every bank realized that the problem was really huge; this took USDBRL to 2.40 before the BCB intervened more decisively; October saw consecutive days in which limits were hit, both on the high and the low. In one particular day, the market was at the high limit (and probably trading higher at the OTC market) when the BCB intervened heavily, bringing the market from the upper limit to the lower limit in 45 minutes.

Even with a lot of volatility, all the trading was happening with a 2 handle, leaving a trail of destruction among corporates (and later at banks, when they were unable to collect all the receivables). Most notably, two big listed companies (Sadia and Aracruz) lost so much (hundreds of millions of dollars) that they had to be acquired.

Later, one of the problems identified was the fact that one bank could not assess correctly the risk of its customers, because customers were doing the same trades all over the market. The companies mentioned above had TARFs with approximately 10 banks. This led to the creation of CED, a central database of exposures populated by data from both BVMF and CETIP. This also helps the regulators to understand better the leverage of the system, something that it was unable to do previously (up to 2008, trades were registered in a way that was not helpful to the understanding of the structure).

2
We Mean Business

In the good old days, when the overnight rates were 2% a day, losing one day of interest in your calculation was a very serious business. Understanding how Brazil's Day Count calculations work, and knowing the different calendars, business days standards and fixings is critical for anyone using Brazilian financial instruments and references.

2.1 Calendars

2.1.1 Banking calendars and fixings

Most contracts where the underlying is a BRL fixed or float rate use frequently what's called business 252 day count basis (DCB). This DCB will be called BUS252 throughout this book. Since this DCB is computed in business days, the next natural question is: In which calendar is the number of business days computed? To answer this question, we have to look at the schedule for the two available floating interest rates indices for BRL denominated trades (CDI and Selic), and also at the FX Fixing (PTAX). They are published (on the same day or at the latest on the following business day) whenever it's a Brazilian national business day (see Table 12).

A calendar called CDI will be used throughout this book to take into account the Brazilian national holidays. This calendar will cover day count calculations done for Selic and CDI rates, and also any fixed exponential rate with BUS252 DCB.

If for some specific reason BCB is not able to publish the CDI or Selic fixing on a particular Brazilian national business day, then the previous available fixing will be repeated.

The next question is what is the start and end date for business days computation in BUS252 day count basis. It's defined as below:

Table 12 Holidays (partial)

Date	Holiday	CDI	PTAX
1-Jan	New Year's Day	N	N
Floating	Shrove Monday	N	N
Floating	Shrove Tuesday	N	N
Floating	Good Friday	N	N
21-Apr	Tiradentes' Day	N	N
1-May	Labour Day	N	N
Floating	Corpus Christi	N	N
7-Sep	Independence Day	N	N
12-Oct	Our Lady of Aparecida	N	N
2-Nov	All Souls' Day	N	N
15-Nov	Republic Day	N	N
25-Dec	Christmas Day	N	N

$\#BusDays_{t,T}$ is equal to the number of business days between date t inclusive and date T exclusive computed using a chosen calendar, which in most situations is the CDI calendar.

2.1.2 Trading and listed contracts

On the other hand, exchange traded contracts follow a different calendar for cash settlement of futures and options contracts and for trading days of exchange traded contracts. BVMF is headquartered in São Paulo, and is closed on São Paulo holidays (like 09-Jul) and on the last business day of December. To represent these holidays, a calendar called BMF will be used throughout this book. The calendar for the current year is published at http://www.bmfbovespa.com.br/pt-br/regulacao/calendario-do-mercado/calendario-do-mercado.aspx?idioma=pt-br#.

The 5 current holidays in the BMF calendar that are not in the CDI calendar are: 25-Jan, 09-Jul, 20-Nov, 24-Dec and the last business day of the year (typically 31-Dec).

We can represent the holidays with Table 13, with impacts not only on fixings but on daily volatility modeling as well.

2.1.3 New York, Rio, São Paulo – the FX combined calendar

There's another type of calendar that is used on FX related trades. A standard FX spot transaction of $\frac{BRL}{USD}$ currency pair, specifies that an amount in BRL and USD will be delivered in what's called the FX settlement date, which occurs on T+2 on a combined calendar of CDI with US national holidays. This combined calendar is frequently described in OTC contract term sheets as a calendar that checks if São Paulo, Rio de Janeiro and New York have regular bank activities to define its

Table 13 Holidays (total)

Date	Holiday	BVMF	CETIP	CDI	PTAX
1-Jan	New Year's Day	N	N	N	N
25-Jan	Sao Paulo's Foundation	N	Y	Y	Y
Floating	Shrove Monday	N	N	N	N
Floating	Shrove Tuesday	N	N	N	N
Floating	Ash Wednesday (1/2 day)	Y	Y	Y	Y
Floating	Good Friday	N	N	N	N
21-Apr	Tiradentes' Day	N	N	N	N
1-May	Labour Day	N	N	N	N
Floating	Corpus Christi	N	N	N	N
9-Jul	Constitutionalist Revolution	N	Y	Y	Y
7-Sep	Independence Day	N	N	N	N
12-Oct	Our Lady of Aparecida	N	N	N	N
2-Nov	All Souls' Day	N	N	N	N
15-Nov	Republic Day	N	N	N	N
20-Nov	Black Awareness Day	N	Y	Y	Y
24-Dec	Christmas Eve	N	Y	Y	Y
25-Dec	Christmas Day	N	N	N	N
Floating	Last Business Day of Year	N	Y	Y	Y

business days. In this book, we will use the notation of t_{FX} to represent the FX spot date calculated for a given date t.

2.1.4 Notation used for moving forward or backward business days in a specified calendar

In this book, the following notation will be used to move forward or backwards X business days in a BMF or CDI calendar:

$T+X$: from date T, it's assumed to be moving X business days in a CDI calendar.

$T+X^*$: from date T, it's assumed to be moving X business days in a BMF calendar. Please note the superscript $*$ on X to define the BMF calendar as the one to be applying the shift.

This notation will be very useful in many futures contract cashflow computations later in this book.

2.2 Interest rate fixings

2.2.1 Selic target

The Selic Target Rate (SETA) is not used directly in contracts (unlike the Fed Funds Rate). It is determined by the COPOM, as discussed previously, and it changes at scheduled or extraordinary meetings.

The SETA rate is officially published by the BCB and its history can be accessed either through the Temporal Series section of the BCB's site or directly from the COPOM section (there will be some code that scrapes data from the COPOM page available on the book's website).

The reader saw enough of the SETA in the chapter about Brazil's financial history, so we won't repeat the charts.

For modeling purposes, the main characteristics are:

1. Rates are multiples of 25 basis points.
2. Rates change by multiples of 25 basis points.
3. Almost all of the changes will happen on predetermined (and known) dates (exceptions: extraordinary COPOM meetings).
4. One should model the changes; the last time the level was relevant was in 2009/2010, when the floor of 8.75% was relevant because of the "Caderneta de Poupança" impact; since then, with new rules, this floor is not important anymore, and we're (at the time in which this book was written) still a long way from the floor.
5. Changes follow regimes (easing, tightening, observing/doing nothing).
6. Changes have autocorrelation.
7. The sign of the changes has an even stronger autocorrelation.

This screams transition probabilities, it begs for matrices! Well, at least for shorter maturities. Certainly those features will help to guide us later, in interpolation and option pricing model choices.

Meanwhile, there's space for one additional chart (the daily changes – Figure 23).

2.2.2 Selic

The Selic rate is officially published by the BCB (http://www.bcb.gov.br/pec/sdds/ingl/txselic_i.htm) and also through Sisbacen (the system used by the BCB to communicate with the market participants). It is defined as the adjusted average rate of one-day repos of non-specific government bonds registered at Selic, provided that participants are distinct. There are some statistical filters and a fallback (Circular 3671, 18-Oct-2013) allowing for its fixing as SETA – "residual base" (spread) if the base is lower than 50% of the average of the bases of the previous 5 days; in this case the residual base is the average of the spread in those 5 days.

It typically trades below the SETA (most recently the spread is close to 10bp), as shown in Figure 24.

There's some noise – the end of the year might see some distortion due to the lack of liquidity (addressed by the fallback), but overall you can model the

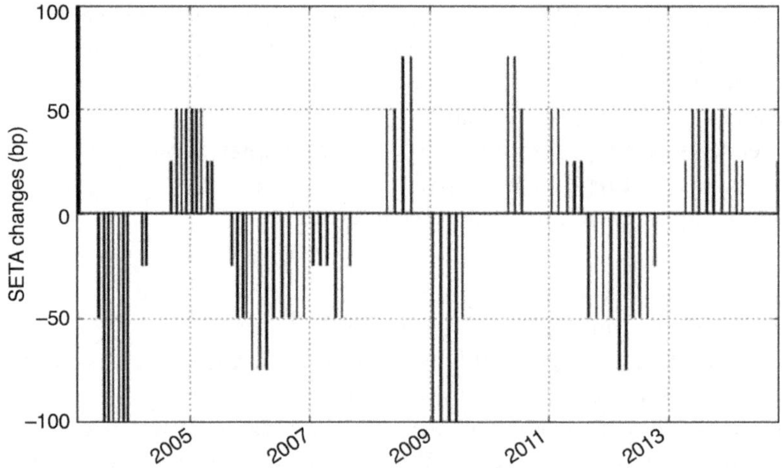

Figure 23 Daily changes in SETA

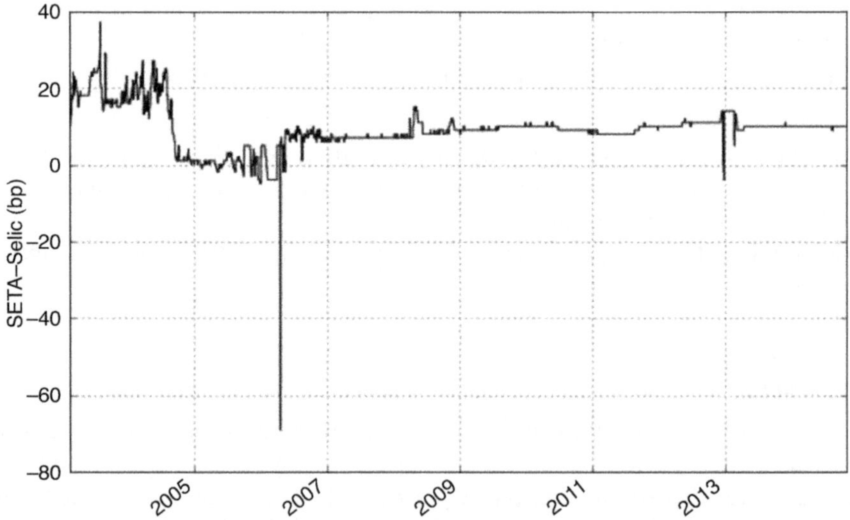

Figure 24 Spread SETA-Selic

changes of the Selic in the same way as you model the changes in the SETA (Figure 25).

Most of the volume will trade early in the day, synchronized with the settlement windows of the other cash markets (FX, bonds, equities).

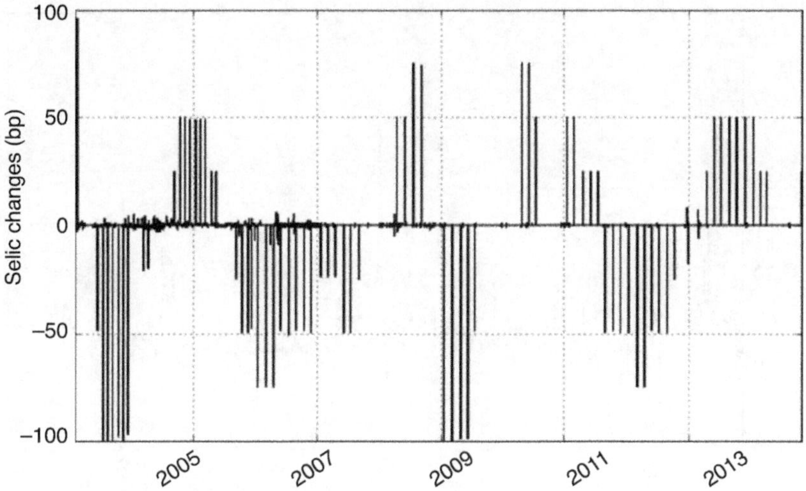

Figure 25 Daily changes in Selic

2.2.3 CDI

The CDI rate is published by CETIP (http://www.cetip.com.br/astec/series_v05/paginas/web_v05_template_informacoes_di.asp?str_Modulo=completo&int_Idioma=2&int_Titulo=6&int_NivelBD=2), but one can also find the historical series at the BCB's site.

We've already covered the creation of the SPB and the alignment between CDI and Selic, with changes driven by the changes in SETA now impacting both rates on the same day. The methodology was updated recently (http://estatisticas.cetip.com.br/astec/di_documentos/metodologia1_i1.htm), with lots of statistical filters, a special procedure for certain holidays and a fallback to a linear function of the Selic rate (it all comes back to the SETA in the end).

It is more noisy than the Selic (Figure 26 shows the spread between the Selic and the CDI):

But it still can be modeled similarly to the Selic, as shown by Figure 27.

The spread against the Selic (or against the SETA) did increase in 2012/2013, and the answer came with the BCB creating contracts indexed to the Selic instead of the CDI, and switching all of its FX derivatives auctions to one of the new contracts (the SCS).

One statistical analysis that can be performed to model the Selic-CDI spread is to look at the realized spread over a time window. In this way, we know the influence of simple spikes and holidays in the spread on longer contracts or trades, like a LFT government bond and a fixed x float (CDI) IR Swap.

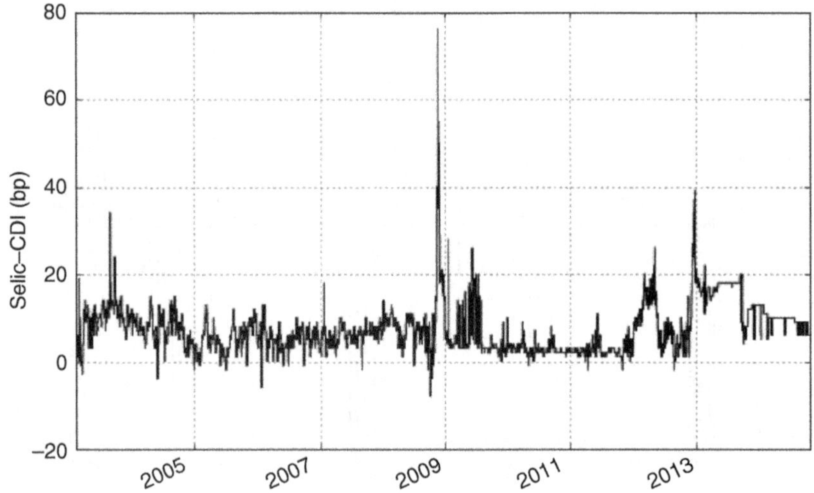

Figure 26 Spread between Selic and CDI

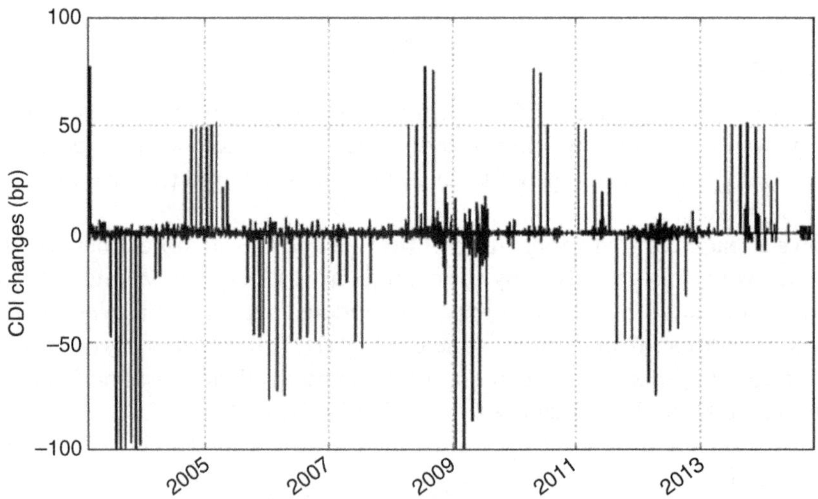

Figure 27 Daily changes in CDI

2.2.4 TJLP

TJLP stands for "Taxa de Juros de Longo Prazo" ("Long Term Interest Rate"). Now, in Brazil, long term once meant 3 months ... and this rate, established in 1994 as the main rate for BNDES loans (BNDES is the National Development Bank, known once as "hospital for companies" and now as the financing mechanism

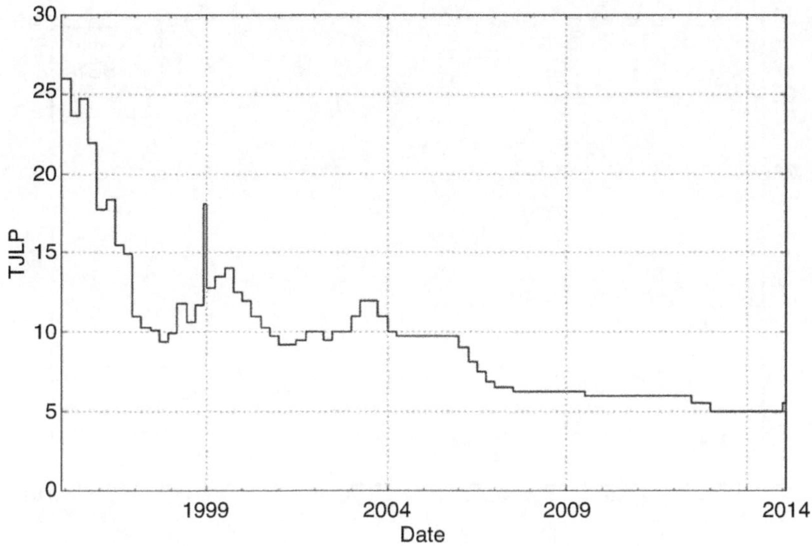

Figure 28 TJLP (monthly)

for the "national champions" policy), is fixed every 3 months (Figure 28). Originally it followed a formula (a function of inflation and a risk premium), but looking at its chart against a monthly average of the SETA (Figure 29), one might suspect it lost some of its correlation to other variables some time ago. In fact, borrowing at TJLP meant borrowing at a negative real rate. Recently it has also behaved like the SETA (increments are multiples of 25bp). Originally created as an alternative to the TR (see 2.2.5), it has a similar status as a rate without a liquid market.

Quite recently (Jan-2015) the government increased the TJLP to 5.5%, trying a difficult balancing act of ending subsidies without increasing too much the costs of the existing loans portfolio.

With all the political decisions that go into it, trade it at your own risk.

2.2.5 TR

Back in the 1985–95 period, high inflation led to a series of indexing mechanisms that, by passing though past inflation, kept everything going up in a never-ending race with the past. To change that, one of the ideas was the TR (Taxa Referencial), referencing projected inflation instead of past inflation.

As the reader can imagine, plotting this rate since 1991 yields a chart with one behavior up to 1994 and another after the Real Plan (Figure 30).

Looking at the rate from 2000 onwards (Figure 31), we see now that the rate is not much different than zero (it was actually zero for some time – see Figure 32).

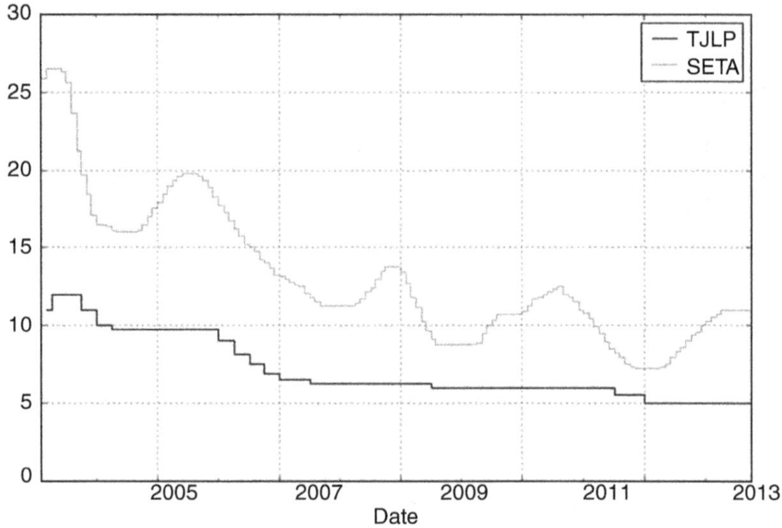

Figure 29 TJLP and SETA (monthly average)

As discussed before, the Savings accounts pay TR plus the lower of 0.5% per month or 70% of the Selic rate, and the banks can lend at TR + some rate on housing loans to match the liabilities. There's an option embedded in here, but it's not easy to capture this time value.

For more details (if one likes to trade with counterparties that have exposure to the TR), the page http://www.bcb.gov.br/pre/portalCidadao/indecon/poupanca.asp?idpai=PORTALBCB (in Portuguese) contains links to the savings rules, and how the TR is calculated (a function of the TBF, a rate derived from term deposits).

As of 2015, the TR is best seen as a spot mismatch and the coupons as a fixed cashflow (subject to some prepayment models).

2.3 Inflation fixings

2.3.1 IPCA

When discussing inflation indices in emerging markets, it is always worth remembering Goodhart's Law, which in the most popular form reads: "When a measure becomes a target, it ceases to be a good measure." One doesn't need to go further than Latin America to see the truth of this statement when applied to inflation indices, and even more when government debt depends on it.

The IPCA is the inflation index used by the COPOM in its inflation-targeting framework, and therefore is the most closely followed index. Because there's a

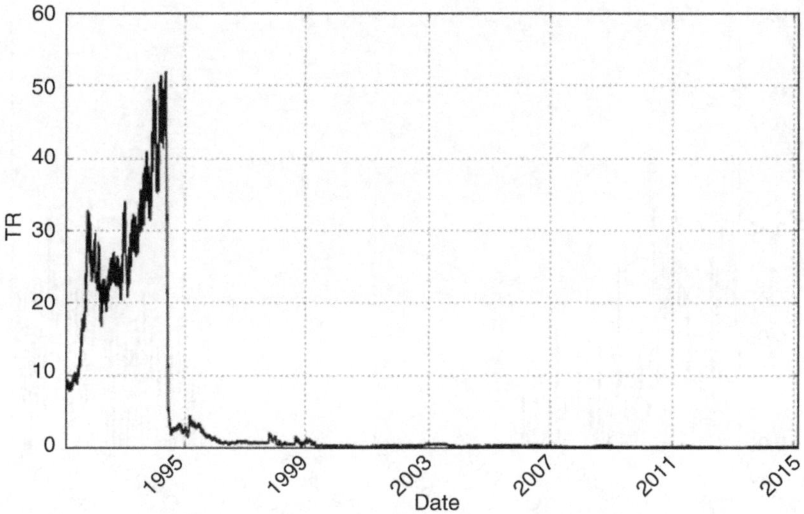

Figure 30 TR since 1991

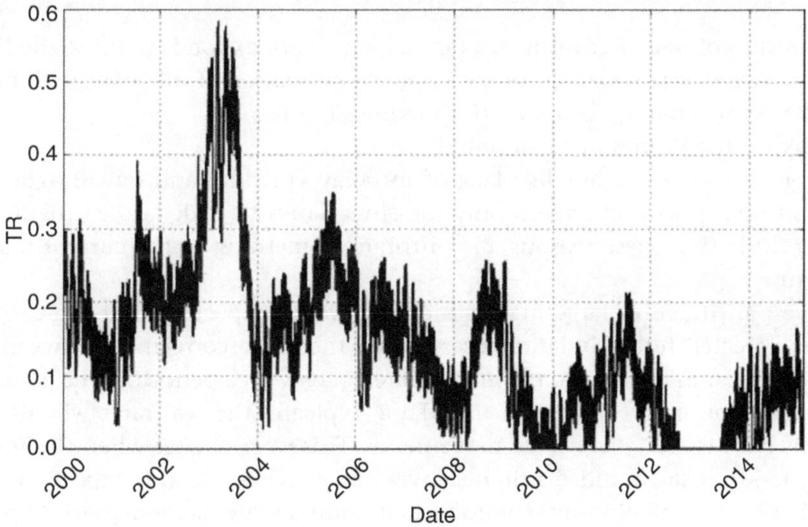

Figure 31 TR since 2000

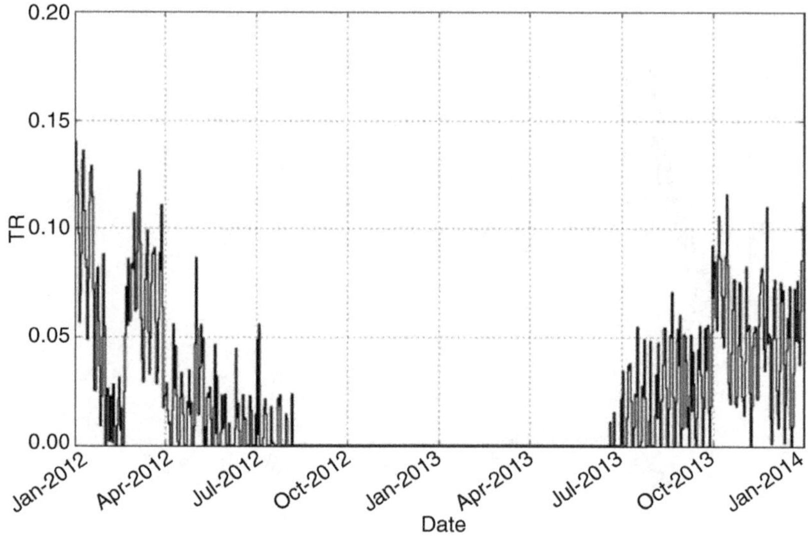

Figure 32 TR in 2012 and 2013

significant volume of government (and also corporate) bonds that use the IPCA as its index, there's a market for the implied expectation of the IPCA, with funds and banks also trading swaps (and sometimes futures).

Why are the futures not that liquid?

There are some reasons like lack of intraday volatility and unwillingness of banks to put prices on screens only for other banks to trade against them, and the truth is that these reasons all contribute something to the current market structure.

Given an inflation targeting regime, one would expect interest rates to rise when expected future inflation rises. Truly, there is a correlation between the moves of nominal rates and the moves of real rates over a period of time (stronger on a daily/monthly basis than intraday). Typically the real rates will rise (or fall) as 30% to 40% over large movements. This works better when the moves are somewhat large and distributed over some weeks. Do not expect to have good prices for inflation-linked products if nominal rates are moving 100bp in a single day.

Now, in the same way that once a famous fund manager in Brazil divided the Ibovespa into state-run companies that were losing market value and private sector companies that were doing Ok, one can look at the IPCA and separate it into prices directly affected by the government (e.g. energy, gasoline, etc. – the managed or supervised prices) and the free prices.

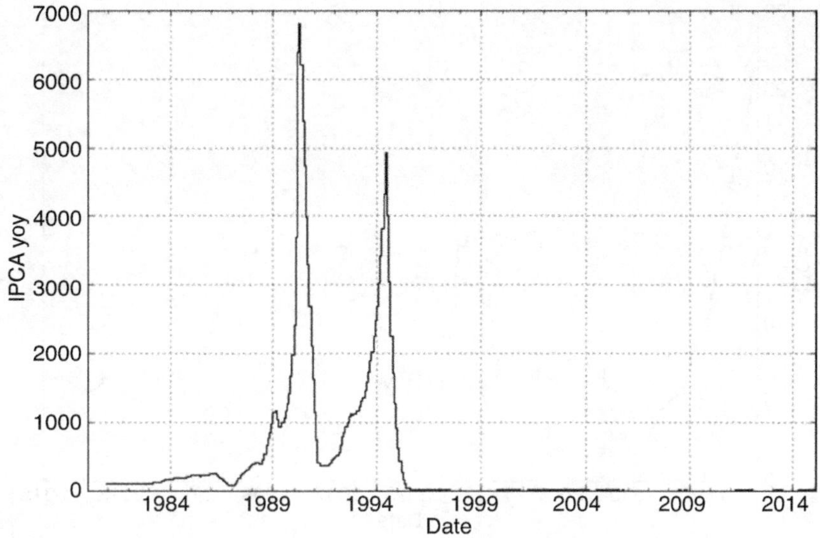

Figure 33 IPCA yoy since 1980

Looking at the time series since 1980 (Figure 33), we are not surprised to see that before 1994 inflation was quite high.

Things got better after the Real Plan (Figure 34).

Did we mention that the IPCA is run by the IBGE (http://www.ibge.gov.br/home/estatistica/indicadores/precos/inpc_ipca/defaultinpc.shtm)? The other inflation index covered in this book (the IGPM) is calculated by a private entity, but being from Latin America and having .gov in your website does not automatically disqualify your credibility (2 countries do not define a continent).

One can get past data at IBGE (see the calendar for publication here: http://www.ibge.gov.br/home/estatistica/pesquisas/indicadores.php) or at the BCB (Time Series by subject – Economic activity – Price indicators – Consumer price indices), including the components of the IPCA.

Although this is not a treaty in econometrics, it is worth outlining the components of the IPCA as seen by the BCB in its Inflation Report (http://www.bcb.gov.br/htms/relinf/port/2015/03/ri201503b7p.pdf): Free prices, inertia (rising from the dead), expectations (more and more disheartening), FX (just passing through), offer shock, and supervised prices. Knowing how these factors might change due to government decisions and due to seasonality (see Figure 36 for a monthly chart) is important when judging implied or breakeven inflation.

As this book is concerned with the near future (2015 up to the second edition), let's zoom to the most recent inflation behavior (Figure 36).

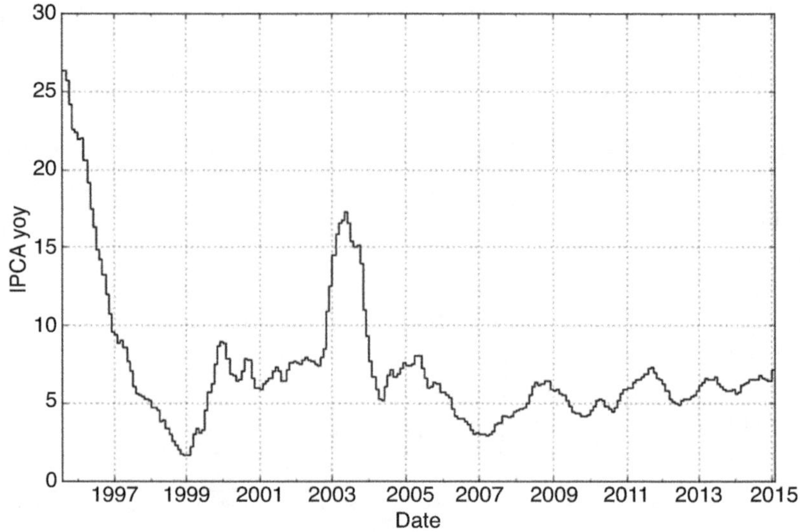

Figure 34 IPCA yoy after the Real plan

There is a V-shaped pattern common to each year, due to things like rising school prices at the beginning of the year, seasonality in crops, demand for travel, etc.

But the government can influence these monthly values a lot, as the recent examples (a discount in electricity prices that backfired and led to a big increase in those prices at the beginning of 2015; increases in gasoline prices; the delay of increases in bus fares in 2013) show.

What is the main worry now (2015)? The rise of inertia, as this can snowball into a lack of confidence that the Central Bank can bring inflation down. The latest Inflation Report shows that Expectations have risen from 0.48% in 2012 to 0.63% in 2013 to 0.70% in 2014.

2.3.2 IGP-M

Different source (Fundação Getúlio Vargas or FGV – private, not government), different prices and methodology, and a reputation of being a "known unknown" (rumors of leaked fixings). It is more sensitive to FX than the IPCA and it is more volatile, as seen in Figure 37.

The IGP-M has 60% coming from the IPA (Wholesale Price Index), 30% from the IPC (Consumer Price Index) and 10% from the INCC (National Index of Building Costs), and their recent behavior is shown in Figure 38. Please help in making this book so popular that the next edition will have color graphics.

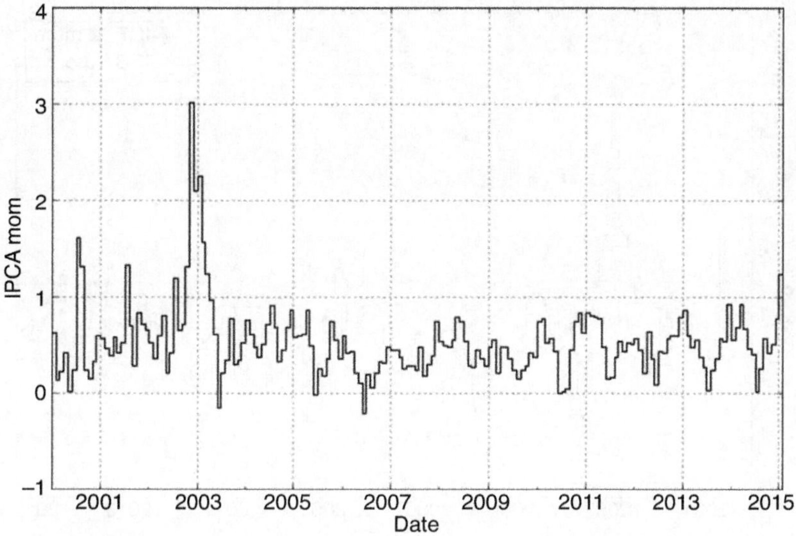

Figure 35 IPCA mom since 2000

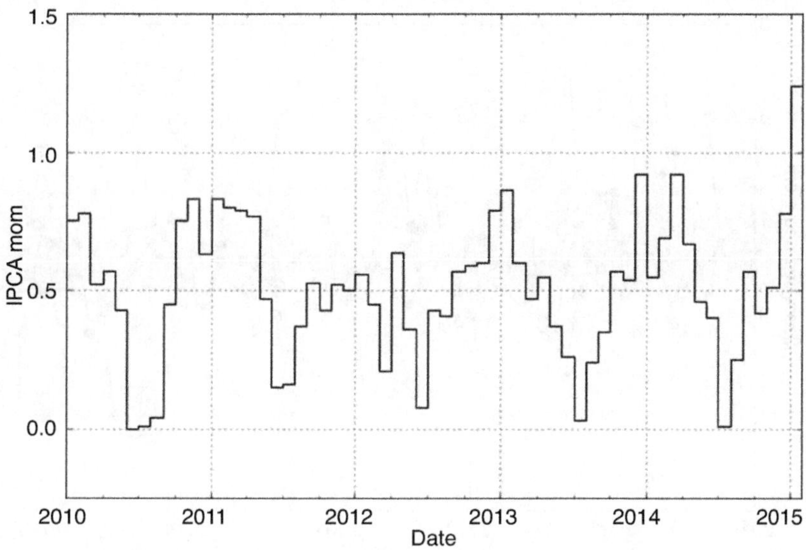

Figure 36 IPCA mom since 2010

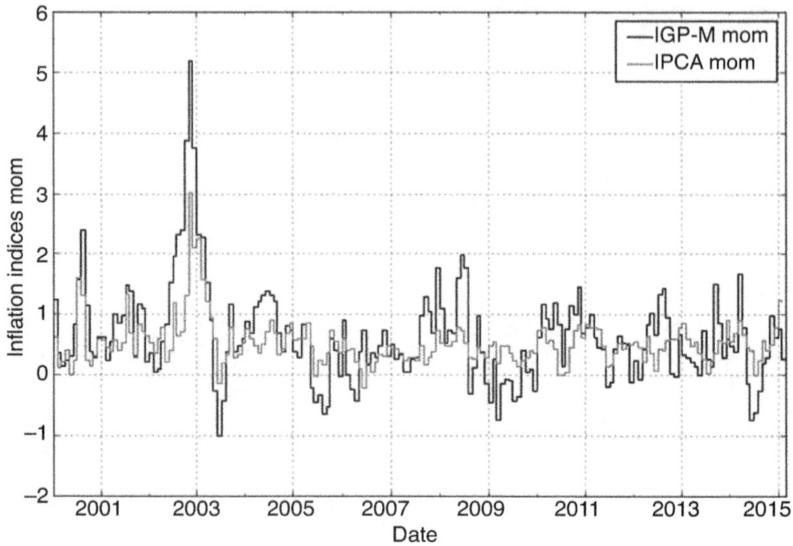

Figure 37 IGP-M mom compared with IPCA

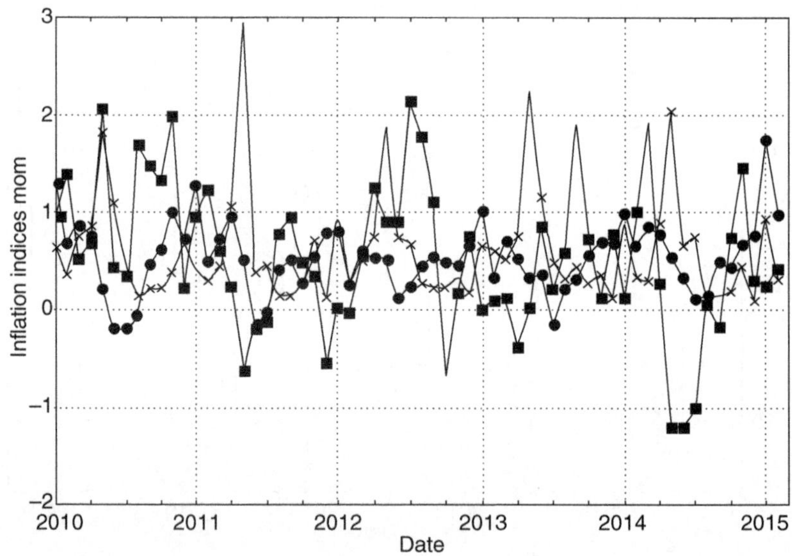

Figure 38 IGP-M components

It's less popular than the IPCA because: The COPOM looks at the IPCA, the IPCA is less volatile, more bonds are issued linked to the IPCA.

2.4 Foreign exchange fixings

2.4.1 PTAX

We've seen a chart of the PTAX before (Figure 12), and we'd rather save the space for some words (not one thousand though).

The PTAX has an interesting history as a fixing: although the market feared a government-induced failure of the PTAX reflecting the market (at least since the mid-nineties), this event never came to pass. But the main change (driven by the BCB) happened in 2011, and it could be seen as positive. Why?

Previously, the PTAX was defined as the weighted average of the standard FX Spot trades registered at Sisbacen (the system managed by the BCB where FX trades are registered). Since the weight was the notional of the trades, this seems like a good idea ... until you focus on the word "registered". The contracts registered could come from fx spot trades where one bank posted a price and another bank executed a trade against this price, but the probability of a registered trade belonging to this set is small. We'll look at this in more detail later (5.1), but it is enough to say that these kind of market-oriented trades (they can come from a Central Limit Order Book – CLOB) represent a small part of the trades registered.

This leaves the old methodology vulnerable to a simple manipulation:

1. Assume that a small number of participants would benefit from a lower PTAX on this particular date (e.g. there's a significant notional of open contracts with their fixing on this day).
2. At some time over the day, the currency will be traded at a price low enough (this could be just the usual randomness or a consequence of a concerted action by these participants).
3. When the price is low, trade a big notional of "casados" (Spot FX vs Futures) among the participants, and the Spot leg will increase the weight of this lower price in the PTAX calculation.
4. The participants distorted the VWAP (Volume Weighted Average Price) when compared with the TWAP (Time Weighted Average Price).
5. Even if the price returns to upper levels, this distortion will have helped them, at a relatively low cost (the "casado" has a negligible delta, and the mismatch risk has a relatively low volatility).

The BCB changed the methodology with the Circular 3506 (23-Sep-2010), establishing a dry run from Jan-2011 to Jun-2011 where the new rates would be published but not used; the new procedure would go live in 01-Jul-2011.

What is this new procedure? Two-way prices will be collected 4 times (at each collection, in a 2 minutes window randomly chosen within a 20 minutes centered at: 10h, 11h, 12h, 13h). For each of the four collections, an average of the bids and asks will be calculated. The PTAX (bid and ask) will each be the average of the four averages. And the ask price continues to be the one used for the fixings.

Another advantage is the time of the publication (just after the last collection, typically up to 13h30 local time), instead of really late in the day.

This alone should tell the reader who is interested in options that modeling the volatility of FX close to expiry is going to be interesting. There is a natural discontinuity between the O/N (overnight) implied volatility in the morning and at the close, just to start the fun. More on this later when we discuss FX options.

A simple trick to model this fixing mechanism (on a Monte Carlo simulation) is to consider each trading day as composed of 9 hours with continuous trading, sampled at each hour (from 9h to 18h), and a close-to-open (18h to 9h of the following day) "jump". In this case, just the observations at 10h, 11h, 12h and 13h would count towards the fixing. The volatility of the fixing intraday will decrease both by the reduction of the time of variability and by the averaging of the rates (after the 12h partial fix the unknown fixes – 13h – have only a 25% weight on the final fixing).

2.4.2 EMTA

At the Emerging Markets Trade Association, traders discuss and recommend standards for contracts, including (but not limited to) fixings, fallbacks and observability of the rates and their impact on events such as barriers and triggers (present in options such as knock-ins and knock-outs). For access to the documentation on the website, you must be a member.

For Brazil, there's always discussion about fallback fx fixings (as discussed above), with polls among dealers being a natural solution to lack of observability in an event. The difference in liquidity between spot and futures markets has also led the EMTA to publish recommendations for the observability of the currencies and the triggering of barriers and events, using the future and the casado instead of the less liquid spot (it is much easier to publish and trade an off-market rate on the spot market than in the futures market).

2.4.3 WMR

The WM/Reuters Closing Spot Rates service provides fixing spot rates for 160 currencies (21 trade currencies and 139 non-trade currencies; the reader must guess by now that Brazil is a non-trade currency); on the established hour, the snapshots of the quoted rates, taken from Reuters over a five-minute fix period, are extracted; medians for the bid and the ask are then calculated and subject to quality checks. Although some customers might ask for these rates in OTC contracts, they're not widely used.

2.4.4 Observability for barriers

As discussed above about EMTA, observability of the fx spot is defined as the observability of the relationship fx future – casado, with the future coming from the exchange and the casado coming from brokers. But there might be contracts (typically onshore and registered on the exchange) where the only variable accepted for verification is the PTAX. Why?

In the equities world, the exchange (BVMF) concentrates all the negotiation of the stocks and calculates the Ibovespa (and other indices) intraday; knowing the minimum and maximum of the prices for all the days (including the present day) and knowing that your sample is the whole population enables BVMF to determine whether a particular price level was reached/breached. Alas, this is not possible for FX (futures Ok but neither the FX Spot or the casado qualify).

2.5 The 3 Ts in FX option pricing: a more precise version of the Black Formula

In the financial literature, it's quite common to use only one time variable inside option and forward pricing formulas. This has been verifed, for instance, in *Options, Futures and Other Derivatives* (Hull, 2005). Our goal in this section is not to discuss the broad idea on how to price forward or option contracts, but rather on how to use a more precise version of the frequently used Black Formula to incorporate a better definition of the time variables used. We refer the reader unfamiliar with the Black formula to *Options, Futures and Other Derivatives* (Hull, 2005) to gain some basic knowledge. The Black Formula is also displayed on http://en.wikipedia.org/wiki/Black_model.

The extension of the Black Formula provided here will highlight the importance to distinguish 3 different times used for fx option pricing. The 3 times are described below as:

1. Time of volatility -> This is computed from today's date t until fx option expiry date T_{ex}.
2. Time of expected cashflow discounting -> This is computed from fx option price payment date t_{pay} to option payoff date T_{pay}.
3. Time of fx forward calculation ->This is computed from fx spot date t_{FX} to fx spot date obtained from fx fixing date (usually called settlement date) T_{Settle}

The idea is that when using a Black Formula, every time you find a term of $\sigma^2 \cdot T$, or $\sigma \cdot \sqrt{T}$, it means that you are really interested in the effective variance from today's date t until T_{ex}. So to be more explicit, in the more precise version of the Black Formula we will use $\sigma^2 \cdot T_{vol}$ or $\sigma \cdot \sqrt{T_{vol}}$ instead.

Going now to item 3, the fx forward price. The idea is to perform the cash and carry approach, but taking into account the fx spot settlement rule. Thus, to come up with a fx forward price for currency pair $\frac{CCY1}{CCY2}$, you need to borrow $CCY1$ only at t_{fx}, because this is the date where the fx spot transaction done at t will deliver the 2 currencies. Then you will pay interest in $CCY1$ until T_{Settle}, which is the fx spot date from the fx forward fixing date where the fx forward transaction will settle. Doing a fx spot transaction at t, will also enable you to exchange $CCY1$ to $CCY2$ units at date t_{fx}. So you earn interest on $CCY2$ by lending from t_{fx} to T_{Settle}. Following this approach, the no arbitrage price of a $\frac{CCY1}{CCY2}$ fx forward seen at t with settlement date at T_{Settle} is given by:

$$FXFWD_{t,T_{Settle}} = FX_t \cdot \frac{\left(1+R^{CCY1}_{t,t_{fx},T_{Settle}} \cdot \tau_{t_{fx},T_{Settle}}\right)}{\left(1+R^{CCY2}_{t,t_{fx},T_{Settle}} \cdot \tau_{t_{fx},T_{Settle}}\right)} \tag{3}$$

where,
$FXFWD_{t,T_{Settle}}$: is the $\frac{CCY1}{CCY2}$ fx forward price seen at t for settlement date T_{Settle}.
$R^{CCY1}_{t,t_{fx},T_{Settle}}$: is the rate you see at date t to borrow in $CCY1$ from fx spot date t_{fx} to settlement date T_{Settle}.
$R^{CCY2}_{t,t_{fx},T_{Settle}}$: is the rate you see at date t to lend in $CCY2$ from fx spot date t_{fx} to settlement date T_{Settle}.
$\tau_{t_{fx},T_{Settle}}$: is the day count fraction from t_{fx} to T_{Settle} in any convention compatible with rates $R^{CCY1}_{t,t_{fx},T_{Settle}}$ and $R^{CCY2}_{t,t_{fx},T_{Settle}}$.

So inside this more precise Black Formula, everytime you have a fx forward price, (3) will define the correct dates to obtain its value using the cash and carry argument.

Now going to item 2, the expected cashflow discounting. The expected payoff of the option has to be discounted from its payment date T_{pay} to the date you are paying the option premium t_{pay}. This would collapse to the following Black formula for a fx call option price c with a given notional of $CCY2$ called Not_{CCY2}:

$$c = Not_{CCY2} \cdot \left(FXFWD_{t,T_{Settle}} \cdot N(d1) - K \cdot N(d2)\right) \cdot P^{CCY1}_{t,t_{pay},T_{pay}} \tag{4}$$

with

$$d1 = \frac{ln\left(\frac{FXFWD_{t,T_{Settle}}}{K}\right) + 0.5 \cdot \sigma^2 \cdot T_{vol}}{\sigma \cdot \sqrt{T_{vol}}}.$$

$$d2 = \frac{ln\left(\frac{FXFWD_{t,T_{Settle}}}{K}\right) - 0.5 \cdot \sigma^2 \cdot T_{vol}}{\sigma \cdot \sqrt{T_{vol}}}.$$

$P^{CCY1}_{t,t_{pay},T_{pay}}$: the forward discount factor in CCY1 seen at date t from fx option premium payment date t_{pay} to fx option payoff date T_{pay}.
Not_{CCY2}: fx option Notional amount in $CCY2$ units.

$N(x) = \frac{1}{\sqrt{2 \cdot \pi}} \cdot \int_{-\infty}^{x} exp\left\{-\frac{1}{2} \cdot t^2\right\} \cdot dt$ is the cumulative distribution function of the standard normal distribution.

The put option formula would have the same corrections over its habitual formula found in textbooks like *Options, Futures and Other Derivatives* (Hull, 2005).

To illustrate this particular feature on the 3 different Ts, we decided to provide as an example the relevant dates for pricing as of 10-Jun-2014 of a fx listed option on BMF for $\frac{BRL}{USD}$ with maturity date on 1-Oct-2014. The first thing we have to find out is which date is the fx spot date for 10-Jun-2014. The answer, applying the $T+2$ settlement rule on a combined CDI and US calendar is 12-Jun-2014, as there are no holidays within the $T+2$ period on both calendars. The payment of the premium will occur on $T+1$ from trading date t in a BMF calendar. This date is 11-Jun-2014. The payment of the payoff will occur at $T+1$ in a BMF calendar of the contract's maturity date T, which is in this example 01-Oct-2014. Thus the payoff will be paid at 02-Oct-2014. The contract will fix its payoff based on PTAX published at $T-1$ from maturity date T in a CDI calendar, which is 30-Sep-2014. This is the FX Fixing Date T_{Fix}. The fx spot date from T_{Fix}, commonly known as settlement date will be at 02-Oct-2014. This is obtained with a $T+2$ rule in a combined fx spot calendar from T_{Fix}.

Thus, when using a Black Formula, the volatility period will be from t to T_{vol}, namely from 10-Jun-2014 to 30-Sep-2014. The fx forward price will be computed assuming the onshore curve for *BRL* and *USD* rates from fx spot date, which is 12-Jun-2014, to the settlement date, which is 02-Oct-2014. More details about the construction of the curves can be found later in the book. And finally the discounting of the payoff occurs from premium payment date 11-Jun-2014 to payoff payment date 02-Oct-2014.

3
Interesting BRL Interest Rates

3.1 3 months in the life of an IR Swap

Now, let's keep it simple at first. We'll start with a nice curve, almost flat, as seen in 01-Aug-2011 and shown in Figure 39.

But we are looking for a harmless 3-month swap, so let's zoom in Figure 40.

First of all, why only points in the chart? Are we lazy? Have we run out of ink? No, we still have a lot of ink to spill in our pursuit of interpolations, and before that we are not connecting these points. But there's one thing that we can already say: not all the points are equal. Let's look at Figure 39 again, but this time our markers and axes will be different (Figure 41).

Now the x-axis is in years, expressing the time to maturity for each contract, and the size (in points^2 <=> area) of each point is proportional to the contracts traded multiplied by the modified duration for each maturity (which is the equivalent RV01, or Real Value of 1 bp – here Real (BRL) is the local currency).

So over time we're going to give more weight to the points that have more liquidity.

Please accept for now that a swap is going to be priced using the DI futures.

So at inception a 3-month IR Swap will have the following characteristics:

Start Date: 01-Aug-2011

Maturity Date: 01-Nov-2011

Fixed Rate: 12.425% (equal to the rate in the DI1 maturing at the End Date)

Floating Rate: 100% of CDI (assume 100% as a default; later we will deal with percentages different than 100%)

BRL Notional: has same value for both legs at the Start Date; this could be a round number, or it could be calculated so that the value of the Fixed Leg at maturity is a round number. In our case, we'll opt for the latter. There are 64 business days from the Start Date to Maturity Date using the Bank Holidays (CDI) calendar (not the Trading Days calendar). The discount factor is then

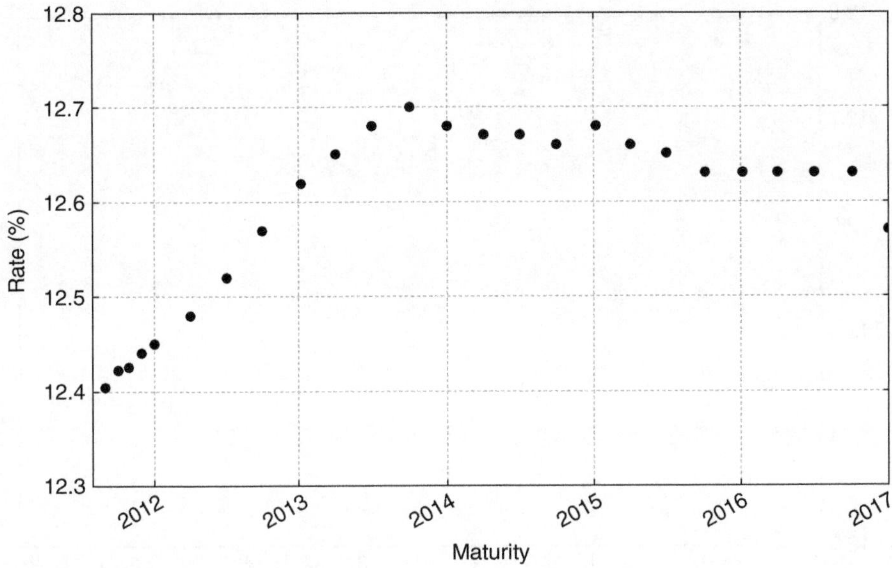

Figure 39 DI1 futures 01-Aug-2011

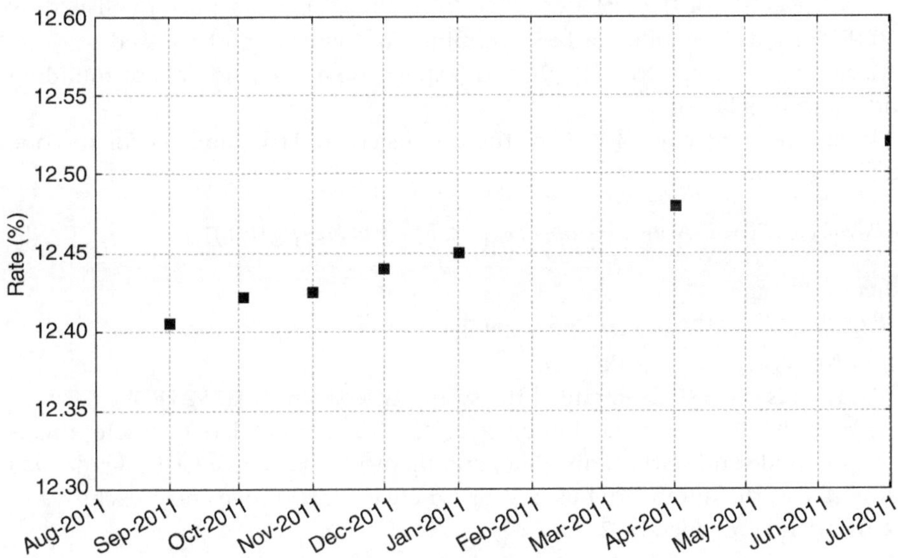

Figure 40 First DI1 futures 01-Aug-2011

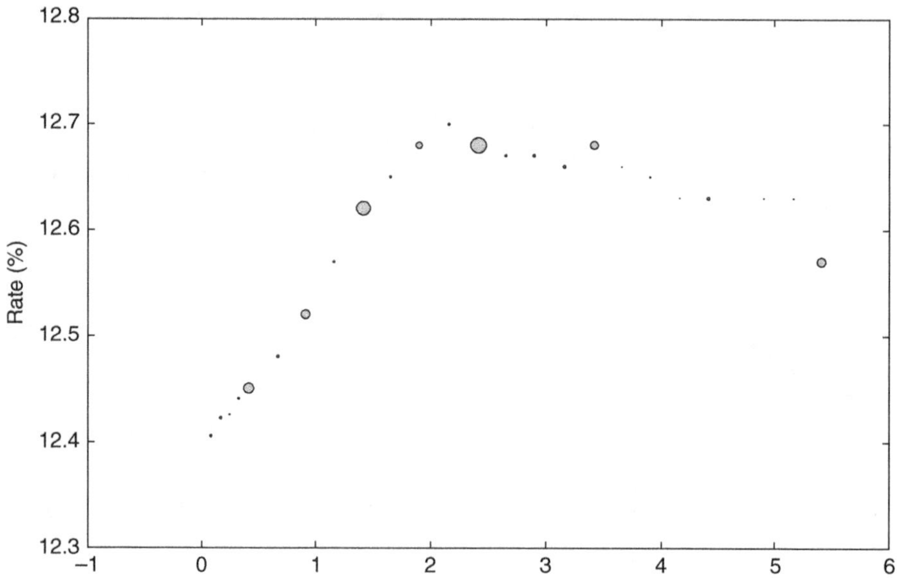

Figure 41 Weighted DI1s 01-Aug-2011

$\left(1+\frac{12.425}{100}\right)^{-\frac{64}{252}}$ or 0.970694 as reflected in the DI Unitary price published by BVMF. For a desired value of BRL 10 million at maturity on the Fixed Leg, the BRL Notional is equal to 9,706,942.10 (expect some discussion about rounding and truncating later).

Payoff: Let ϕ be equal to +1 for the one receiving Fixed and −1 for the one receiving Floating:

$$Payoff_{BRL}[T] = \phi \cdot Not_{BRL} \cdot \left(CapFac_{Fixed}(t,T) - CapFac_{Float}(t,T)\right) \tag{5}$$

where,

$Payoff_{BRL}[T]$: is the payoff in BRL paid at date T.

$CapFac_{Fixed}(t,T) = [1 + BRL_{Fixed}]^{\tau_{t,T}^{252}}$

BRL_{Fixed}: is the BRL fixed rate of the swap expressed in BUS252 DCB.

$\tau_{t,T}^{252}$: is the day count fraction between the first accrual date t (usually this is the swap trade and start accrual date) and maturity date T in a CDI calendar. It's computed as the number of business days between t inclusive and T exclusive in a CDI calendar divided by 252.

$CapFac_{Float}(t,T) = \prod_{T_i=t}^{T}\left[1 + CDI_{T_i}\right]^{\frac{1}{252}}$: is the product of overnight (O/N) capitalization factors from date t inclusive to date T exclusive. Thus, the last CDI fixing applied in the formula will be from $T-1$.

CDI_{T_i}: is the CDI fixings published at a particular date T_i.

How should we look at the swap during its brief but eventful life? Its present value, one could say.

Ok, let's write:

$$PV_t = (1 + DI_{t,T})^{-\tau_{t,T}^{252}} \cdot Payoff_{BRL}[T] \tag{6}$$

where,

PV_t: is the present value of the BRL Fixed Float swap seen at date t. Later in the book we will demonstrate why the PV is calculated based on (6).

$DI_{t,T}$: is the DI closing rate seen at date t for maturity date T (end date of the swap mentioned above).

But the PV can change from one day to another due to two factors: the DI rate $DI_{t,T}$ changes every day and the projected CDIs being different from the realized. There is also the accrual of the CDI to consider; one could have a big change today, no further changes in the market, but the PV will increase due to the accrual of the CDI (or the reduction of days in the discounting – in this case it's the same thing).

Let's try to find how to write PV_t as a function of the realized accrual, the difference between the realized and the projected (expected at inception) CDI and the difference between the DI rate and the one expected at inception.

We can define:

$$f(t,\tau,T) = \prod_{T_i=t}^{\tau} (1 + CDI_{T_i})^{\frac{1}{252}} \cdot \prod_{T_i=\tau}^{T} (1 + CDI_{T_i})^{\frac{1}{252}} \tag{7}$$

where,

t: is the swap start date.

τ: is a given pricing date. We are assuming that CDI hasn't been fixed yet for date τ.

T: is the swap maturity date.

$\prod_{T_i=t_x}^{t_y} [1 + CDI_{T_i}]^{\frac{1}{252}}$: is the product of overnight (O/N) capitalization factors from date t_x inclusive to date t_y exclusive. Later in this book we will explain why the product has been defined as exclusive for the last date, but we anticipate for the reader that a heavier notation would have to be adopted for formulas of Futures contract prices if the regular product definition were adopted.

By breaking down Equation (7), it can be seen that the first product involves only past CDI fixings and the second product involves future CDI projections given a yield curve. This breakdown helps to understand that we're going to deal with realized and unrealized fixings, and with comparisons between the expected path of the CDI at the Start Date and the realized CDI plus the

DI rate, which gives us a new projection for the future realizations of the CDI.

So the payoff at maturity can be written as:

$$Payoff = \phi \cdot Not_{BRL} \cdot (f(t,t,T) - f(t,T,T)) \tag{8}$$

So the Fixed Leg (payoff given by $f(t,t,T)$) is seen as a path of projected CDIs and the Floating Leg (payoff given by $f(t,T,T)$) is seen as the path of realized CDIs (which is fully known at maturity).

The PV at the time τ is written as:

$$PV_\tau = \phi \cdot Not_{BRL} \cdot \left(\frac{f(t,t,T) - f(t,\tau,T)}{f(\tau,\tau,T)} \right) \tag{9}$$

Dropping the Principal and looking at the PV of someone long the Fixed Leg:

$$PV_\tau = \left(\frac{f(t,t,T) - f(t,\tau,T)}{f(\tau,\tau,T)} \right) \tag{10}$$

Which we can rewrite as:

$$PV_\tau = \left(\frac{f(t,t,\tau)f(\tau,t,T)}{f(\tau,\tau,T)} - \frac{f(t,\tau,\tau)f(\tau,\tau,T)}{f(\tau,\tau,T)} \right) \tag{11}$$

Where the realized and unrealized parts get separated.

We want the realized accrual $f(t,\tau,\tau)$ to appear in the formula as a multiplier, so we'll write:

$$PV_\tau = \left(f(t,\tau,\tau) \cdot \frac{f(t,t,\tau)f(\tau,t,T)}{f(t,\tau,\tau) \cdot f(\tau,\tau,T)} - f(t,\tau,\tau) \cdot \frac{f(\tau,\tau,T)}{f(\tau,\tau,T)} \right) \tag{12}$$

Which is equivalent to:

$$PV_\tau = f(t,\tau,\tau) \left(\frac{f(t,t,\tau)f(\tau,t,T)}{f(t,\tau,\tau) \cdot f(\tau,\tau,T)} - 1 \right) \tag{13}$$

We want to monitor how the realized CDI $f(t,\tau,\tau)$ has differed from the projected CDI at the Start Date $f(t,t,\tau)$ up to τ. The ratio $\frac{f(t,\tau,\tau)}{f(t,t,\tau)}$ can be defined as the realized "drift", and it will be different from 1 if the CDI has drifted away from the expected path.

We also want to know how date τ expectations of future CDIs $f(\tau,\tau,T)$ differ from the expectations at the Start Date $f(\tau,t,T)$. The ratio $\frac{f(\tau,\tau,T)}{f(\tau,t,T)}$ can be viewed as the change (Delta) in unrealized MTM (mark-to-market) of the trade.

We then write the PV as:

$$PV_\tau = Accrual_{Realized} \cdot \left(\frac{\Delta MTM_{Unrealized}}{Drift_{Realized}} - 1 \right) \tag{14}$$

Now the need for a good interpolation is clear, since any methodology that presents an unrealistic CDI path will present a Drift very different from 1 after

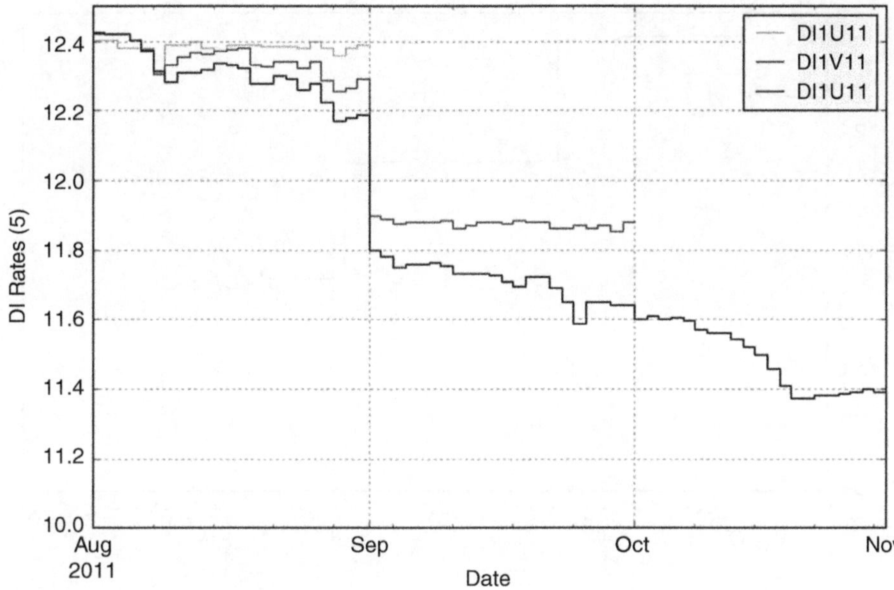

Figure 42 3 DIs maturing in our 3m window

some time; although this could be compensated by the unbalance at the change in MTM, it doesn't look like an interpolation that behaves in this way would be good.

We can look at our example for some guidance. The last COPOM meeting before the Start Date was in 20-Jul-2011, with a 25bp increase in the SETA, and the CDI reaching 12.40% on the following day. The CDI was 12.40% (give or take 1bp) throughout the rest of July and the whole of August. It would be reasonable to expect our interpolation to reflect that the CDI would be around 12.40% util the next COPOM meeting.

If we are lazy, we can rewrite (14) as:

$$PV_\tau = Accrual_{Realized} \cdot \left(\frac{f(t,t,T)}{Accrual_{Realized} \cdot f(\tau,\tau,T)} - 1 \right) \tag{15}$$

Which has the advantage of using as inputs just the accrual and the DI rates (easily available in the particular case of a swap maturing in the same as the DI1 Futures. In our particular case, it will be interesting to monitor the 3 DIs that expire within these 3 months (Figure 42).

One can see that the curve seems to have lost its flatness, becoming downward sloping (at least for the very short rates). Why? The CDI (following the SETA) went down, as Figure 43 shows.

The values for the Realized Accrual are shown in Figure 44.

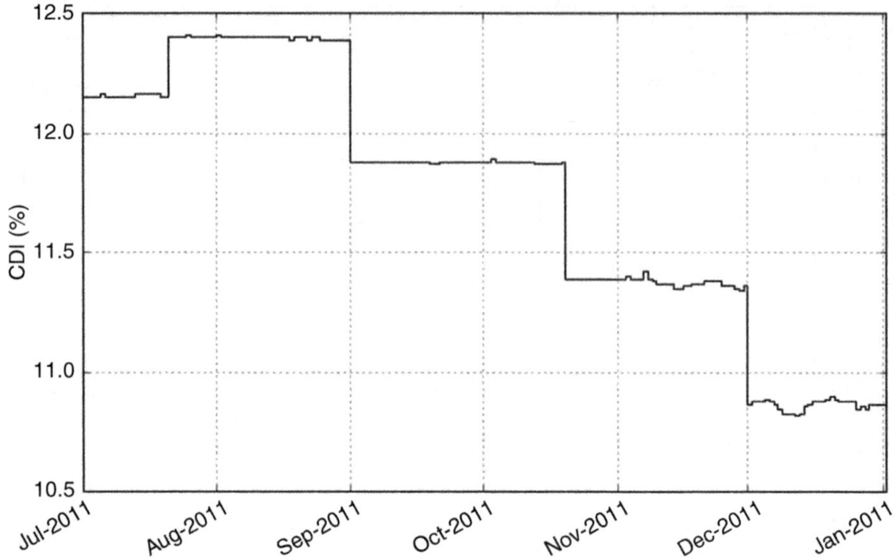

Figure 43 CDI for the 2nd half of 2011

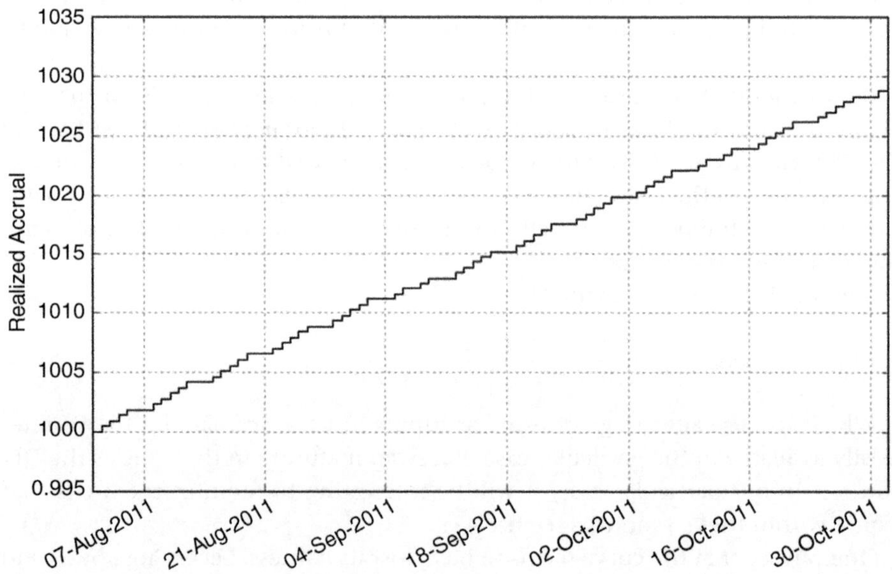

Figure 44 Realized Accrual for the 3m window

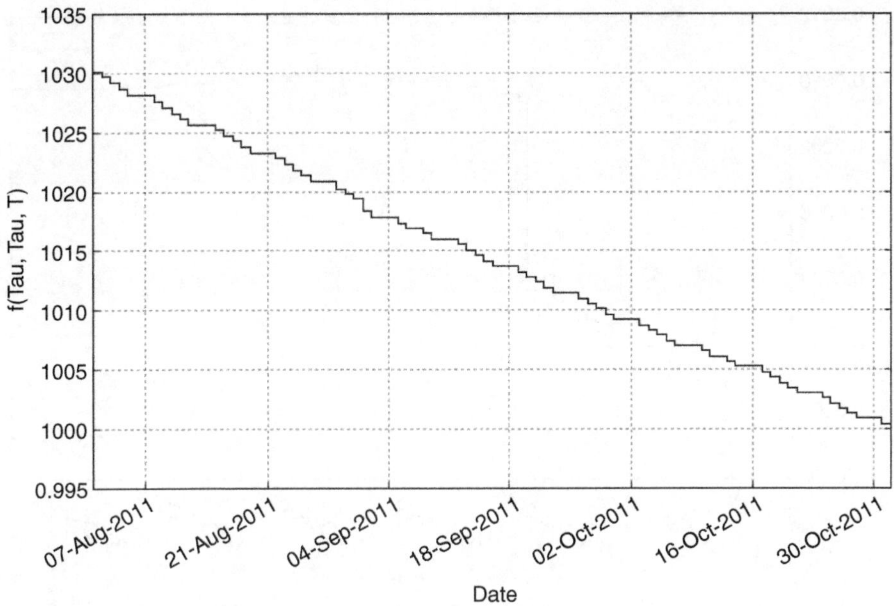

Figure 45 $f(\tau, \tau, T)$ for the 3m window

And the values for $f(\tau, \tau, T)$ are shown in Figure 45.

With all this data available, the PV over time is easy to calculate (Figure 46).

Without breaking the PV into its components, we can observe that $\Delta MTM_{Unrealized}$ component should converge to 1 as time passes and we approach the expiry, so at the end all of the changes in the PV (and therefore the Payoff) will come from the $Drift_{Realized}$ component. One could think that the Unrealized MTM is anticipating (or trying to anticipate) the future Realized Drift and, as time passes by, the unrealized becomes realized.

Knowing that, we can attribute all of the changes up to 01-Sep (one day after the 31-Aug COPOM meeting) to $\Delta MTM_{Unrealized}$, given that we knew that the CDI would be constant until 31-Aug (inclusive). The big jump in the PV happens at 01-Sep, and it is a reaction to the unexpected COPOM decision in 31-Aug; market rates fall as shown in Figure 42, and all this PV change is later transferred from unrealized to realized, as the DI rate for 01-Nov falls reflecting the changing weights of the higher CDI before the 19-Oct meeting relative to the lower CDI after this meeting (but without impacting significantly the PV - this rolling of the curve is an expected effect).

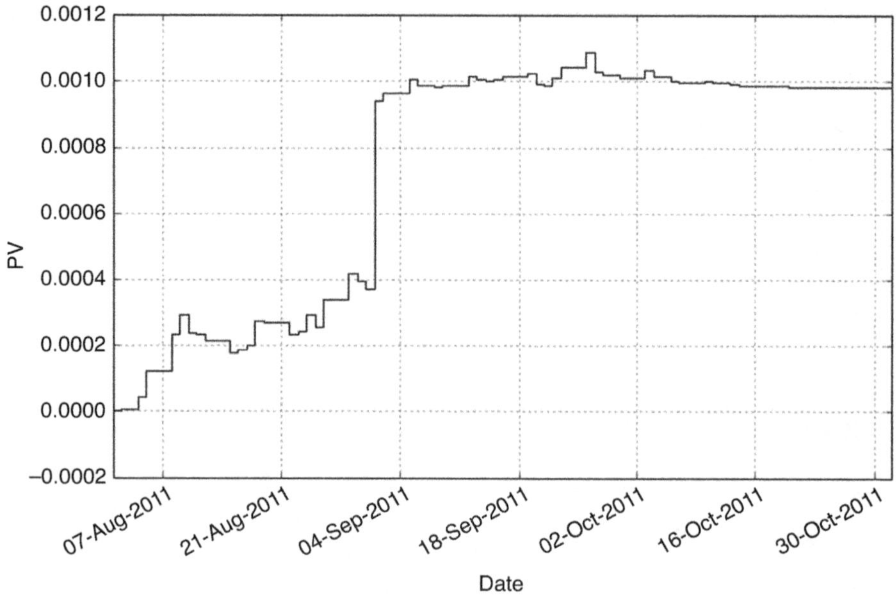

Figure 46 PV for the 3m IR Swap

3.2 3 months in the life of a DI Future

We have not discussed anything about margin calls and collateralization of the IR Swap yet. It is sufficient for now to think of the DIs as swaps that are repriced on a daily basis, with the daily change in the Unrealized MTM being paid/received in cash. So we can look first at the daily cashflows for 100 contracts, which should be equivalent to the IR Swap described above, and scale it in the same way (dividing by the Notional in BRL), as shown in Figure 47.

In order to compare the DI future with the swap, each cashflow must impact an account where one can borrow or lend at the CDI; the correct comparison would not look at the cumulative sum of the cashflows above, but it would calculate this cumulative sum with all cashflows brought to the relevant date by the CDIs between each date and today. More details about which CDIs to really use (considering the settlement dates) will be found later.

The cashflows of the daily margining process are not the only relevant cashflows though. Although Marcos left to Richard the hard task of explaining how the collateralization of swaps will influence their present value calculations, we can look now at how BVMF calculates the initial margin for futures: handcrafted scenarios, carefully chosen by diabolical minds to inflict maximum pain to a portfolio, historical scenarios (because history does not repeat itself, but rhymes)

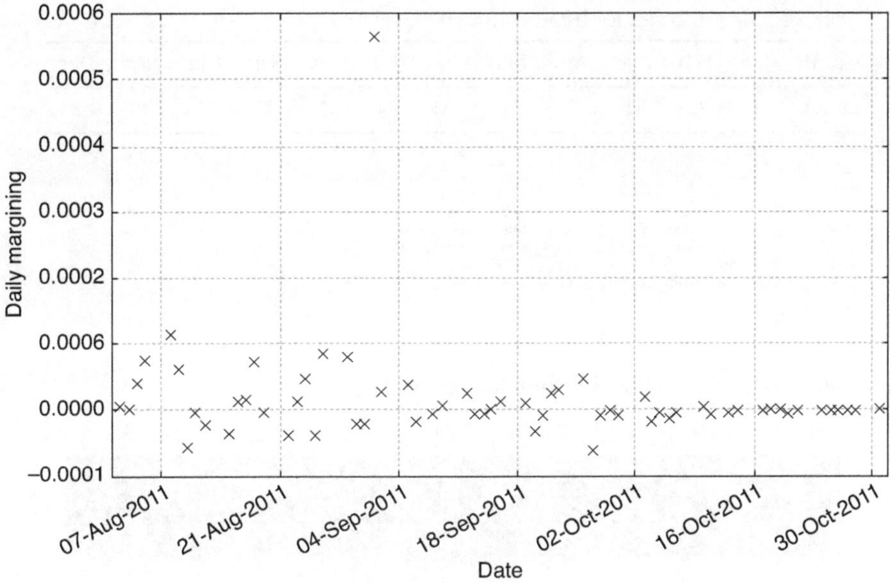

Figure 47 Daily cashflows for the DI

and scenarios generated through the magic of random numbers (Monte Carlo simulations). Each portfolio is then evaluated at each of these scenarios and the worst case for the customer is the initial margin.

If we assume a parallel shift is in the set of scenarios and it is (literally) the worst case scenario, the initial margin required will fall linearly over time.

If we assume a change in slope as the worst case scenario, it is not that hard to find that the margin will decrease with the square of time. Please hold this thought, as it will be useful in the future.

3.3 Explaining it all

There are currently 2 available exchange traded contracts related to BRL interest rate trading in Brazil. The first is called DI Futures and is the building block for the onshore BRL CDI interest rate curve construction. The second is the Selic Futures and its quotes are used to construct the Selic to CDI basis curve. Below is a summary of the 2 contracts:

- DI Futures -> The DI Future is a very liquid future contract. Its BVMF code starts with DI1 and then follows the letter + digits coding that represents the month and year of a particular contract. One example is DI1F21, that represents a DI Future for maturity at the first business day of the month F, which

Table 14 Month codes for listed contracts

Month	Jan	Feb	Mar	Apr	May	Jun	Jul	Aug	Sep	Oct	Nov	Dec
Letter	F	G	H	J	K	M	N	Q	U	V	X	Z

	Year												
Month	14	15	16	17	18	19	20	21	22	23	24	25	26
F		2,391,668	1,538,793	978,906	354,816	77,542	34,411	247,364	18,448	227,294	30,235	35,450	0
J		639,500	233,360	36,914	20,555	2,090	1,800	0					
M	227,309												
N	2,624,734	442,667	440,502	79,609	14,160	3,165	10,975	55	55	0	0		
Q	172,975												
U	42,468												
V	728,549	79,875	34,886	28,445	3,505	655	1,630	0					

Figure 48 DI1 Open interest as of 19th May of 2014

Commodity	Contract Months	Open Interest	Var.
OC1			
	N14	209,000	0
	V14	295,905	0
	F15	226,650	0
	J15	19,500	0
	N15	3,000	0
Total		754,055	0

Figure 49 Selic futures OC1 contract open interest on 19th of May 2014

maps to January, and year 2021 that is represented by the 2 last digits 21. Table 14 displays the current Futures Month Codes mapping:

To give an idea of the open interest in DI1 contracts, Figure 48 below displays this information broken down by contract code for 19th of May 2014.

The daily cashflow computation of a DI1 contract is a function of its previous and current BVMF closing prices and the CDI capitalization factor from previous business day in a BMF calendar to current day. More details on the calculation will be provided in the DI1 contract pricing subsection.

- Selic Futures -> This futures contract has been created recently, but so far the liquidity is still picking up, mostly as a hedge for SCS Futures (those will be detailed later in this book) and Government Bonds. Its BVMF code is OC1 followed by the standard month and year coding provided before. Figure 49 displays open interest information for the Selic Futures contracts. The initial idea from the exchange was to create a hedging mechanism for CDI to Selic basis and to allow market participants to bet in future monetary policy in a more direct way by having a derivative based on Selic future O/N rates as will be explained later. The other contract specifications were created to exactly mirror the ones defined in a DI1 contract.

Other relevant information about the BRL interest rate futures contracts can be summarized below:

1. They all have daily margin cashflow computed and paid only at BVMF calendar business days.
2. Margin cashflow computations are paid the next business day in a BVMF calendar, even the last cashflow computed at maturity date T.
3. The maturity date T is always at the first business day of the month in a BVMF calendar. BVMF has a specific code for each contract as mentioned before.
4. Other information like last contract trading date, margin requirements and assets eligible to meet margin requirements can be found at BVMF website.

In the offshore market, there is currently no exchange traded BRL interest rate market available. On the OTC side, the floating fixing indices available are Selic, CDI and Libor with a specified tenor for a particular currency. Even though it's common for Brazilian market participants to say just Libor rate, the correct specification of a Libor rate involves its currency and tenor. So when it's said simply Libor rate, it should be understood that it's a US Libor 3M rate. On the fixed side you can have BRL and USD Fixed rates for both onshore and offshore contracts, with BRL rates usually being defined in Bus252 DCB counted on CDI calendar and USD rates usually defined in Act360 or 30360 DCB. Any combination of Fixed-Float and cross currency swaps can be used given the available legs defined above, paying onshore or offshore. A BRL leg paying offshore has cashflows converted to USD based on an offshore FX Fixing (PTAX with fallback fx fixing to EMTA in an inconvertibility event). This occurs because BRL is not a deliverable currency outside Brazil. On the other hand, USD legs paying onshore have cashflows converted to BRL using an onshore FX Fixing, the PTAX exchange rate, defined as transaction PTAX800, option 5, closing quotation for settlement in 2 days. This occurs because inside Brazil, no payments can be done in USD, only in BRL.

2 interesting swaps that will have a section devoted to them are BRL Fixed-CDI Float swaps paying offshore in USD and USD Fixed-Float swaps paying onshore in BRL. Those trades are more complex to price and they require convexity adjustments. The main reason behind it is because they have their rate indices published onshore (CDI or Selic) but payoff occurs offshore or they have their index published offshore (US Libor for a specified tenor) but its payoff occurs

onshore. An example can be the BRL Fixed-CDI Float swap paying in USD offshore. The CDI fixings are published onshore. So the first idea is to forecast them based on the BRL onshore curve for pricing. However, since the payment is done offshore in USD, the payoff can be viewed as discounted by a BRL offshore discounting rate implied in $\frac{BRL}{USD}$ NDF prices. The difference between the forward CDI projections curve and the cashflow discounting curves generates a convexity correction on forward rates that needs to be applied for correct pricing.

3.4 A simple swap

In a Fixed BRL-Float CDI onshore zero coupon swap, the payoff is given by the following equation

$$Payoff_{BRL}[T] = Not_{BRL} \cdot \{CapFac_{Fixed}(t,T) - CapFac_{Float}(t,T)\}$$

For the above swap, it can be seen that usually the last CDI fixing occurs at one business day before maturity date T in a CDI calendar. Also, usually the payoff occurs at maturity date T.

The key differences that can be identified from regular G7 swaps are the daily compounding feature of the cashflows, and that rates are exponential rather than linear and expressed in BUS252 DCB. The daily cashflows follow a similar logic to any Libor rate related cashflow, where rate fixing is at the start of the accrual period and pays or compounds at the end of the accrual period.

3.5 A promising future – the DI1 Future

A DI1 contract closing price is always worth 100,000 BRL at maturity date T. As discussed before, its quotes are used to calibrate the onshore BRL CDI interest rate curve. The local market convention for trading a DI Futures is that market participants trade a number of contracts X and a DI rate $R_{t,T}$. One example would be a trader who buys 500 contracts for contract DIF21 at 10.00% DI rate. BVMF cash settlement mechanics works based on DI prices not DI rates. So in the previous example, first the exchange will convert the 10.00% traded DI rate to a DI price based on the following 2 step process:

$$CapFac_{t,T} = round\left((1+R_{t,T})^{\tau_{t,T}^{252}}, 7\right) \quad (16)$$

$$TP_t^T = round\left(\frac{100,000}{CapFac_{t,T}}, 2\right) \quad (17)$$

where,

$R_{t,T} = 10.00\%$ in the example.

TP_t^T: DI traded unitary price at date t for a DI contract with maturity date T.

$\tau_{t,T}^{252}$: is the day count fraction in Bus252 DCB between trading date t and DI maturity date T, which would be 4-Jan-2021 for DIF21 contract.

round(X, Y): rounds amount X in the Yth digit.

The second step executed by the exchange would be to convert the long position of 500 contracts traded to a short position of 500 DIF21 contracts. This is done because local market participants like to trade a DI contract in a way that if they are long a contract, they want to have positive P&L if DI rate $R_{t,T}$ moves up. However, because of the inverse relationship between TP_t^T and $R_{t,T}$ displayed in (17), a positive P&L when DI rates $R_{t,T}$ move up can only be obtained by a short position in traded price TP_t^T. To achieve that, the exchange converts all positions traded based on rate view to price view by inverting their quantity sign.

Another important topic to discuss is how the daily margin cashflows are computed and paid. The next equation demonstrates how daily cashflows are computed on trading date t

$$MCF_t^T = CP_t^T - TP_t^T \tag{18}$$

where

MCF_t^T: is the margin cashflow computed for date t for a DI future contract with maturity date T. Please bear in mind that the margin cashflow is computed at date t, but only paid the next business day in a BMF calendar.

CP_t^T: is the closing price (not the closing DI Rate) for DI Futures contract with maturity date T, published at t. For the reader's sake of clarity, it's assumed here the closing price to be published for a 100,000 contract face value. Figure 50 shows closing prices for DI1 contracts as of 19-May-2014.

TP_t^T: is the traded price at date t for a DI Futures contract with maturity date T.

The next equation demonstrates how daily cashflows are computed on any other given non trading date t_N:

$$MCF_{t_N}^T = CP_{t_N}^T - OP_{t_N}^T \tag{19}$$

where,

$OP_{t_N}^T$: is the t_N date opening price for DI Futures contract with maturity date T. The other variables have the same definition that was provided previously.

At any time a closing price CP_t^T may also be converted to an equivalent exponential closing rate $CR_{t,T}$ expressed in BUS252 DCB based on the following equation:

$$CR_{t,T} = \left(\frac{100,000}{CP_t^T}\right)^{\frac{1}{\tau_{t,T}^{252}}} - 1 \tag{20}$$

Commodity	Contract month	Previous settlement price (*)	Current settlement price	Variation	Settlement value per contract (R$)
DI1 - 1-day Interbank Deposits	M14	99,593.11	99,593.46	0.35	0.35
	N14	98,780.37	98,781.31	0.94	0.94
	Q14	97,851.01	97,851.30	0.29	0.29
	U14	97,009.87	97,010.18	0.31	0.31
	V14	96,135.02	96,141.98	6.96	6.96
	F15	93,570.98	93,576.90	5.92	5.92
	J15	91,099.48	91,107.88	8.4	8.4
	N15	88,553.57	88,582.35	28.78	28.78
	V15	85,902.13	85,947.21	45.08	45.08
	F16	83,424.93	83,476.48	51.55	51.55
	J16	81,020.75	81,105.35	84.6	84.6
	N16	78,657.15	78,735.06	77.91	77.91
	V16	76,315.14	76,415.88	100.74	100.74
	F17	74,161.15	74,251.47	90.32	90.32
	J17	71,988.87	72,112.43	123.56	123.56
	N17	69,967.24	70,067.95	100.71	100.71
	V17	67,859.88	67,985.79	125.91	125.91
	F18	65,934.10	66,022.46	88.36	88.36
	J18	64,083.36	64,168.18	84.82	84.82
	N18	62,225.22	62,303.61	78.39	78.39
	V18	60,391.28	60,481.30	90.02	90.02
	F19	58,668.52	58,767.99	99.47	99.47
	J19	57,040.30	57,129.60	89.3	89.3
	N19	55,433.59	55,509.52	75.93	75.93
	V19	53,770.18	53,837.19	67.01	67.01
	F20	52,206.52	52,261.48	54.96	54.96
	J20	50,702.74	50,739.83	37.09	37.09
	N20	49,264.61	49,285.99	21.38	21.38
	V20	47,779.12	47,819.58	40.46	40.46
	F21	46,381.38	46,438.51	57.13	57.13
	N21	43,739.47	43,797.19	57.72	57.72
	F22	41,183.66	41,227.80	44.14	44.14
	N22	38,790.76	38,848.90	58.14	58.14
	F23	36,511.37	36,569.39	58.02	58.02
	F24	32,323.77	32,328.48	4.71	4.71
	F25	28,546.06	28,601.65	55.59	55.59

Figure 50 DI1 Closing prices at 19th of May 2014

where,

$CR_{t,T}$: is the closing exponential DI rate seen at date t for a DI1 contract with maturity date T.

By looking at (19), it looks very similar to any kind of Futures contract cash-flow payments. But the difference lies on the procedure to obtain OP_t^T from the previous date closing price CP_{t-1}^{T}. It can be defined as:

$$OP_t^T = CP_{t-1^*}^T \cdot \prod_{T_i=t-1^*}^{t} [1+CDI_{T_i}]^{\frac{1}{252}} \tag{21}$$

where,

$CP_{t-1^*}^T$: is the closing price published by the exchange one business day previous than t in a BMF calendar.

$\prod_{t-1^*}^{t} [1+CDI_{T_i}]^{\frac{1}{252}}$: is the daily compounding of CDI capitalization factors from $t-1^*$ inclusive to t exclusive. It's worth pointing out again that $t-1^*$ is obtained by moving backwards from t in a BMF calendar.

As an example, let's say you want to obtain your opening price for 2-Jan-14. Moving this date one business day backwards in a BMF calendar yields 30-Dec-13, which is defined as $t-1^*$. But there are 2 CDI fixings available from 30-Dec-13 inclusive to 2-Jan-14 exclusive, which have as its publishing dates 30-Dec-13 and 31-Dec-13. This particular case with 2 CDI fixings required to convert $CP_{t-1^*}^T$ to OP_t^T justifies the formulation of (21) with a product term instead of a simple overnight CDI capitalization factor.

3.6 My first numéraire – a more mathematical framework for DI Futures (DI1)

This subsection will use the concepts of conditional expectations, probability measures and filtrations. It's assumed the existence of a probability space $(\Omega, \mathcal{F}, \mathbb{P})$, with Ω being a sample space, $\mathcal{F}$ being a sigma-algebra on Ω and $\mathbb{P}$ a probability measure on the measure space $(\Omega, \mathcal{F})$. We refer the reader who is not familiar with these stochastic calculus concepts to (Shreve, 2010) for a recap. The reader who's not interested in these concepts might skip directly to the end of this subsection where the key results will be discussed.

The DI1 contract, even though there's no closely related G10 interest rate contract traded, could be best described as a remaining maturity futures bond contract. As a Future contract, the DI1 Futures can enter or exit at no cost and its closing price is equal to 100,000 at maturity. We can use exactly this last boundary condition to state that:

$$FUT_{DI}(T,T) = 100{,}000 \tag{22}$$

where,

$FUT_{DI}(t,T)$ is the DI Future closing price seen at date t for maturity date T DI Future contract.

$FUT_{DI}(T,T)$ is the DI Future closing price seen at maturity date T, for a contract with maturity date on same date T.

As a future contract, we expect at date $T-1^*$, which is one business day backwards in a BMF calendar, that the last margin cashflow computed at date T to be equal to 0 in a risk neutral world. Also, this cashflow which is computed at time T, will only be paid at $T+1^*$, i.e, one business day forward in a BMF calendar. Combining (19), (21) and (22) and the statement above allows us to write the following equation:

$$\beta_{T-1^*} \cdot \mathbb{E}^{\mathbb{Q}^*}\left[\frac{FUT_{DI}(T,T) - FUT_{DI}(T-1^*,T) \cdot \prod_{T_i=T-1^*}^{T}\left[1+CDI_{T_i}\right]^{\frac{1}{252}}}{\beta_{T+1^*}} | \mathcal{F}_{T-1^*}\right] = 0 \tag{23}$$

where,

$\mathbb{E}^{\mathbb{Q}^*}$: is the expectation operator in the risk neutral measure $\mathbb{Q}^*$. This measure is associated with rolling O/N money market account $\beta_t = \prod_{T_i=t_0}^{t}\left[1+CDI_{T_i}\right]^{\frac{1}{252}}$,with $\beta_{t_0} = 1$ and t_0 being a hypothetical initial date for rolling the account. The choice of the expectation to be under $\mathbb{Q}^*$ and have CDI underlying inside numéraire is based on the fact that for derivatives pricing we are usually interested in payoff replication, and the DI1 Futures payoff could be replicated based on a strategy that involves trading in the CDI O/N market. Section 16.8.1 of *Interest Rate Modeling* (Andersen and Piterbarg, 2010) also highlights a similar money market account used as numéraire.

$\mathcal{F}_{T-1^*}$: is the filtration up to time $T-1^*$, which represents the information available up to time $T-1^*$ loosely speaking.

One way to see (23) is that inside the expectation you have the daily cashflow computed at date T, and that the term $\frac{\beta_{T-1^*}}{\beta_{T+1^*}}$ discounts this amount from cashflow payment date $T+1^*$ to pricing date $T-1^*$, which is the time we are taking the expectation in a risk neutral measure.

Using (22) into (23) yields:

$$\mathbb{E}^{\mathbb{Q}^*}\left[100{,}000 \cdot \frac{\beta_{T-1^*}}{\beta_{T+1^*}} | \mathcal{F}_{T-1^*}\right]$$
$$= \mathbb{E}^{\mathbb{Q}^*}\left[FUT_{DI}(T-1^*,T) \cdot \prod_{T_i=T-1^*}^{T}\left[1+CDI_{T_i}\right]^{\frac{1}{252}} \cdot \frac{\beta_{T-1^*}}{\beta_{T+1^*}} | \mathcal{F}_{T-1^*}\right] \tag{24}$$

Now let's focus on the term $\prod_{T_i=T-1^*}^{T}\left[1+CDI_{T_i}\right]^{\frac{1}{252}}$. Between $T-1^*$ and T, there may be 2 CDI fixings if between them there's a BMF holiday. In that case, the later CDI to be fixed is not F_{T-1^*} measurable and cannot be taken out of expectation. Only the first one could. However, the CDI market is very illiquid during those particular days and we will assume that the second CDI will be fixed with the same value as the previous published one. With this assumption we are turning the term $\prod_{T_i=T-1^*}^{T}[1+CDI_{T_i}]^{\frac{1}{252}}$ always F_{T-1^*} measurable. With this new assumption (24) can be rearranged as:

$$100,000 \cdot \mathbb{E}^{\mathbb{Q}^*}\left[\frac{\beta_{T-1^*}}{\beta_{T+1^*}}|\mathcal{F}_{T-1^*}\right]$$
$$= FUT_{DI}(T-1^*,T) \cdot \prod_{T_i=T-1^*}^{T}[1+CDI_{T_i}]^{\frac{1}{252}} \cdot \mathbb{E}^{\mathbb{Q}^*}\left[\frac{\beta_{T-1^*}}{\beta_{T+1^*}}|\mathcal{F}_{T-1^*}\right] \tag{25}$$

The equation above may be rewritten as:

$$FUT_{DI}(T-1^*,T) = \frac{100,000}{\prod_{T_i=T-1^*}^{T}[1+CDI_{T_i}]^{\frac{1}{252}}} \tag{26}$$

Going one business day backward in a BMF calendar for the previous cashflow, we may write that:

$$\beta_{T-2^*} \cdot \mathbb{E}^{\mathbb{Q}^*}\left[\frac{FUT_{DI}(T-1^*,T) - FUT_{DI}(T-2^*,T) \cdot \prod_{T_i=T-2^*}^{T-1^*}[1+CDI_{T_i}]^{\frac{1}{252}}}{\beta_T}|\mathcal{F}_{T-2^*}\right]$$
$$= 0 \tag{27}$$

Combining (26) and (27) and using again the assumptions that led us into (26) yields:

$$FUT_{DI}(T-2^*,T) = \mathbb{E}^{\mathbb{Q}^*}\left[\frac{FUT_{DI}(T-1^*,T)}{\prod_{T_i=T-2^*}^{T-1^*}[1+CDI_{T_i}]^{\frac{1}{252}}}|\mathcal{F}_{T-2^*}\right] \tag{28}$$

$$FUT_{DI}(T-2^*,T) = \mathbb{E}^{\mathbb{Q}^*}\left[\frac{100,000}{\prod_{T_i=T-2^*}^{T}[1+CDI_{T_i}]^{\frac{1}{252}}}|\mathcal{F}_{T-2^*}\right] \tag{29}$$

Repeating this procedure iteratively until pricing time t (current time) yields:

$$FUT_{DI}(t,T) = \mathbb{E}^{\mathbb{Q}^*}\left[\frac{100,000}{\prod_{T_i=t}^{T}[1+CDI_{T_i}]^{\frac{1}{252}}}|\mathcal{F}_t\right] \tag{30}$$

Looking at (30), we can see that the value of $FUT_{DI}(t,T)$, which is the current DI Future price (remember that originally the DI1 was traded as a price, not as a rate, and that $FUT_{DI}(t,T)$ is a price, not a rate), can be viewed as the expectation of 100,000 BRL discounted by future CDI O/N capitalization factors under the discrete risk neutral measure $\mathbb{Q}^*$, associated with numéraire $\prod_{T_i=0}^{t}[1+CDI_{T_i}]^{\frac{1}{252}}$.

For a long time DI Futures have been the best mechanism to trade expectations of future monetary policy, since the CDI rate was always very close to SETA. No relevant basis existed between CDI and Selic rates. Thus, there was no need to create a future contract where Selic rates were directly traded. But recently the basis became non negligible and the need for a Selic Futures contract was evident.

3.7 The still promising Future -> The Selic Futures (OC1)

As mentioned previously, this contract was created to enable market participants to bet more directly in future monetary policy, since the cashflow payments are based on Selic interest rate fixings, as opposed to CDI interest rate fixings in the DI1 contracts. Another interesting appeal would be to give market participants an instrument to hedge the CDI to Selic basis.

The Selic Futures contract has a BVMF code OC1 followed next by the month and digits usual coding. The mechanics of cashflow payments and trading are mirrored from DI1 contracts. The only difference is the reference interest rate index which is the Selic rate for cashflow computation. Cashflow payments are still computed as in (19), however it's the opening price calculation that's different from a DI1 contract and presented below:

$$OP_t^T = CP_{t-1^*}^T \cdot \prod_{T_i=t-1^*}^{t} [1 + Selic_{T_i}]^{\frac{1}{252}} \tag{31}$$

Following the same rationale, we can point out again that for any Futures contract there's no cost to enter or exit and that Selic Futures price is equal to 100,000 at maturity. Also, we expect at date $T-1^*$, that the last margin cashflow computed at date T will be equal to 0 in a risk neutral world. So now combining (19), (31) and (22), we can write the following cashflow present value equation at time $T-1^*$:

$$\beta_{\mathrm{T}-1^*}^S \cdot \mathbb{E}^{\mathbb{Q}^{\mathrm{X}}}\left[\frac{FUT_{Selic}(T,T) - FUT_{Selic}(T-1^*,T) \cdot \prod_{T_i=T-1^*}^{T}[1+Selic_{T_i}]^{\frac{1}{252}}}{\beta_{T+1^*}^S} | \mathcal{F}_{\mathrm{T}-1^*}\right]$$
$$= 0 \tag{32}$$

where,

$\mathbb{E}^{\mathbb{Q}^{\mathrm{X}}}$: is the expectation operator in the risk neutral measure $\mathbb{Q}^{\mathrm{X}}$. This measure is associated with rolling O/N money market account $\beta_t^S = \prod_{T_i=0}^{t}[1+Selic_{T_i}]^{\frac{1}{252}}$. For the Selic Futures case, the expectation is taken against a different probability measure than in the DI1 case. The rationale behind choosing this probability measure is the same as for DI1 contracts. It's about payoff replication. But now, the OC1 Futures contract could be replicated by trading in the Selic O/N market, not on the CDI O/N market like in DI1 Futures case.

By iterated conditioning plus assuming the same conditions as in the DI1 case, the Selic Futures price will be given by:

$$FUT_{Selic}(t,T) = \mathbb{E}^{\mathbb{Q}^X}\left[\frac{100,000}{\prod_{T_i=t}^{T}[1+Selic_{T_i}]^{\frac{1}{252}}}|\mathcal{F}_t\right] \quad (33)$$

By looking at (33), it can be seen that there are many similarities between $FUT_{Selic}(t,T)$ and $FUT_{DI}(t,T)$. The former is the expected value of 100,000 discounted by Selic O/N capitalization factors under a probability measure where its numéraire is $\beta_t^S = \prod_{T_i=0}^{t-1}[1+Selic_{T_i}]^{\frac{1}{252}}$. The latter is the expected value of the same 100,000, but now discounted by CDI O/N capitalization factors under a probability measure where $\beta_t = \prod_{T_i=0}^{t-1}[1+CDI_{T_i}]^{\frac{1}{252}}$ is its numéraire.

Also, now it's clearer why the Selic futures is a more direct way to bet on future monetary policy. Its price is a function of future Selic O/N rates, and doesn't incorporate Selic to CDI basis. As highlighted previously, the monetary policy affects directly SETA, which only has a small basis to the BCB published Selic rates which are the underlying for the Selic futures.

3.8 Pricing BRL interest rate futures

In the previous subsections, the price of OC1 and DI1 Futures contracts was expressed as 2 different expectations. Now it's time to solve them.

3.8.1 DI Future (DI1) pricing

In (30), the DI Futures price was expressed as an expectation. By choosing a more suitable probability measure, we will be able to calculate more precisely the DI Futures price $FUT_{DI}(t,T)$. Once again, the reader not familiar with change of probability measures can see that concept explained in (Shreve, 2010). Another book that might help the reader is *Interest Rate Models – Theory and Practice: With Smile, Inflation and Credit* (Brigo and Mercurio, 2006). Chapter 2 of this book has a change of numéraire toolkit that can be very useful for a first contact with this subject.

So starting again from (30):

$$FUT_{DI}(t,T) = \mathbb{E}^{\mathbb{Q}^*}\left[\frac{100,000}{\prod_{T_i=t}^{T}[1+CDI_{T_i}]^{\frac{1}{252}}}|\mathcal{F}_t\right] \quad (34)$$

Before performing the change of measure, it's necessary to introduce the following discount factor notation:

$P_{t,T}^{CDI}$ is the discount factor obtained in the CDI curve from start date t to final date T. The reader might ask then what's the CDI curve, but since it's constructed based on DI Futures quotes, it's like the dog biting it's own tail. We will revisit the CDI curve construction in the next subsection, but let's assume for now that a CDI curve exists and $P_{t,T}^{CDI}$ can be obtained.

The Radon-Nikodym derivative to change from the discrete O/N compounding risk neutral measure $\mathbb{Q}^*$, where the numéraire is $\beta_t = \prod_{T_i=0}^{t}\left[1+CDI_{T_i}\right]^{\frac{1}{252}}$, to the T forward measure $\mathbb{Q}_{\mathbb{CDI}}{}^{\mathrm{T}}$, where the numéraire is $P_{t,T}^{CDI}$ is given by:

$$\frac{d\mathbb{Q}^*}{d\mathbb{Q}_{\mathbb{CDI}}{}^{T}}|\mathcal{F}_{\mathrm{T}} = \frac{\beta_T}{\beta_t}\cdot\frac{P_{t,T}^{CDI}}{P_{T,T}^{CDI}} = \prod_{T_i=t}^{T}\left[1+CDI_{T_i}\right]^{\frac{1}{252}}\cdot P_{t,T}^{CDI} \tag{35}$$

where it was used the fact that $P_{T,T}^{CDI} = 1$. Performing the change of measure by plugging (35) into (34) yields:

$$FUT_{DI}(t,T) = \mathbb{E}^{\mathbb{Q}_{\mathbb{CDI}}^{\mathrm{T}}}\left[\frac{100{,}000}{\prod_{T_i=t}^{T}\left[1+CDI_{T_i}\right]^{\frac{1}{252}}}\cdot\frac{d\mathbb{Q}^*}{d\mathbb{Q}_{\mathbb{CDI}}{}^{T}}|_T|\mathcal{F}_{\mathrm{t}}\right] \tag{36}$$

$$FUT_{DI}(t,T) = 100{,}000\cdot\mathbb{E}^{\mathbb{Q}_{\mathbb{CDI}}^{\mathrm{T}}}\left[\frac{\prod_{T_i=t}^{T}\left[1+CDI_{T_i}\right]^{\frac{1}{252}}}{\prod_{T_i=t}^{T}\left[1+CDI_{T_i}\right]^{\frac{1}{252}}}\cdot P_{t,T}^{CDI}|\mathcal{F}_{\mathrm{t}}\right] \tag{37}$$

In (37) it can be seen that the CDI capitalization factor terms are cancelled inside the expectation. Also, $P_{t,T}^{CDI}$ is non-random at time t so it can be taken out of the expectation. This yields the final equation for the DI Futures price:

$$FUT_{DI}(t,T) = 100{,}000\cdot P_{t,T}^{CDI} \tag{38}$$

3.8.2 BRL onshore CDI curve construction

Based on (38), we can see a direct relationship of the DI Futures price to BRL onshore CDI curve discount factors. It's also common to trade and quote a DI Futures in rate terms, not in price. The conversion from traded rate to price was described a while ago in (16) and (17)

From (38) and (20) it follows that:

$$P_{t,T}^{CDI} = \frac{1}{\left(1+R_{t,T}^{CDI}\right)^{\frac{\tau_{t,T}}{252}}} \tag{39}$$

So given a DI Futures rate quote $R_{t,T}^{CDI}$, it can be converted to a BRL onshore CDI curve discount factor by applying (39). The next question is how to interpolate between DI Future maturity dates. Almost every market practitioner in the BRL market does a log-linear interpolation on the discount factors for a broken date. This feature is interesting because a log-linear interpolation on discount factors, keeps exponential O/N future CDI rates constant between DI Future maturity dates. Even though this is not true in reality, because O/N future CDI rates are pretty much constant between COPOM meeting dates and not DI Future maturity dates, this is still the most widely used interpolation method used for the CDI onshore curve among BRL market practitioners.

Below it will be demonstrated that log-linear interpolation on discount factors yield constant future CDI O/N exponential rates between DI Future maturity dates. Suppose that you have an array of DI Future maturity dates T_i, with i ranging from 1 to N, where N is the number of DI Futures used to construct the CDI onshore curve. Let's say we are interested in finding a discount factor for a date T_k, between date T_i and T_{i+1}. Log-linear interpolation will give us the following equation:

$$ln\left(P_{t,T_k}^{CDI}\right) = ln\left(P_{t,T_i}^{CDI}\right) + \frac{\tau_{T_i,T_k}^{252}}{\tau_{T_i,T_{i+1}}^{252}} \cdot \left(ln\left(P_{t,T_{i+1}}^{CDI}\right) - ln\left(P_{t,T_i}^{CDI}\right)\right) \tag{40}$$

The boundary conditions can be easily verified. When $\tau_{T_i,T_k}^{252} = 0$, then $T_k = T_i$ and you get the discount factor value at T_k equal to P_{t,T_i}^{CDI}. If $\tau_{T_i,T_k}^{252} = \tau_{T_i,T_{i+1}}^{252}$, then $T_k = T_{i+1}$ and the discount factor at T_k is equal to $P_{t,T_{i+1}}^{CDI}$.

Now let's turn our attention to how the exponential O/N future CDI rates behave in the log-linear interpolation on discount factors. Our starting point would be (40). Below we will demonstrate how to rearrange it with a bit of algebra to show our expected result:

$$P_{t,T_k}^{CDI} = P_{t,T_i}^{CDI} \cdot exp\left\{\frac{\tau_{T_i,T_k}^{252}}{\tau_{T_i,T_{i+1}}^{252}} \cdot ln\left(\frac{P_{t,T_{i+1}}^{CDI}}{P_{t,T_i}^{CDI}}\right)\right\} \tag{41}$$

$$P_{t,T_k}^{CDI} = P_{t,T_i}^{CDI} \cdot exp\left\{ln\left(\frac{P_{t,T_{i+1}}^{CDI}}{P_{t,T_i}^{CDI}}\right)^{\frac{\tau_{T_i,T_k}^{252}}{\tau_{T_i,T_{i+1}}^{252}}}\right\} \tag{42}$$

Then we can use the fact that $R_{t,T_i,T_{i+1}}^{CDI}$, which is the forward rate seen at t, from T_i to T_{i+1} on CDI onshore curve, can be used inside $\frac{P_{t,T_{i+1}}^{CDI}}{P_{t,T_i}^{CDI}}$ in (42).

$$\frac{P_{t,T_{i+1}}^{CDI}}{P_{t,T_i}^{CDI}} = \left(1 + R_{t,T_i,T_{i+1}}^{CDI}\right)^{-\tau_{T_i,T_{i+1}}^{252}} \tag{43}$$

Combining (43) and (42) yields:

$$P_{t,T_k}^{CDI} = P_{t,T_i}^{CDI} \cdot \left(1 + R_{t,T_i,T_{i+1}}^{CDI}\right)^{-\tau_{T_i,T_k}^{252}} \tag{44}$$

Thus another way to look at the CDI onshore curve discount factor for a broken date is to calculate the discount factor for the previous DI Future date of the curve and then use the forward CDI exponential rate $R^{CDI}_{t,T_i,T_{i+1}}$ to extra discount it for any extra business day from T_i to T_k. This is the proof that a log-linear interpolation on discount factors results in an O/N forward cdi onshore curve with flat exponential rates between DI Future dates.

3.8.3 Selic Future (OC1) pricing

Starting from the equation below:

$$FUT_{Selic}(t,T) = \mathbb{E}^{\mathbb{Q}^{\mathrm{X}}}\left[\frac{100{,}000}{\prod_{T_i=t}^{T}[1+Selic_{T_i}]^{\frac{1}{252}}}|\mathcal{F}_{\mathrm{t}}\right] \tag{45}$$

The idea will be very similar to the one applied for DI1 Futures contracts pricing. We will change from the probability measure $\mathbb{Q}^X$, where its numéraire is $\beta_t^S = \prod_{T_i=0}^{t-1}[1+Selic_{T_i}]^{\frac{1}{252}}$ to the Selic T forward measure $\mathbb{Q}_{\mathrm{Selic}}{}^{\mathrm{T}}$, where its numéraire is $P^{Selic}_{t,T}$. Again, we will assume the existence of a Selic BRL onshore curve where $P^{Selic}_{t,T}$ can be computed.

The Radon-Nikodym derivative to change from measure $\mathbb{Q}^X$ to measure $\mathbb{Q}_{\mathrm{Selic}}{}^{\mathrm{T}}$ is given by:

$$\frac{d\mathbb{Q}^X}{d\mathbb{Q}_{\mathrm{Selic}}{}^{T}}|_{F_{\mathrm{T}}} = \frac{\beta_T^S}{\beta_t^S}\cdot\frac{P^{Selic}_{t,T}}{P^{Selic}_{T,T}} = \prod_{T_i=t}^{T}[1+Selic_{T_i}]^{\frac{1}{252}}\cdot P^{Selic}_{t,T} \tag{46}$$

Plugging (46) into (45) yields:

$$FUT_{Selic}(t,T) = 100{,}000\cdot P^{Selic}_{t,T} \tag{47}$$

3.8.4 BRL onshore Selic spread curve construction

Currently the most liquid BRL interest rate Futures contract is still the DI1. Thus, it's common to see the CDI curve constructed as a parent curve and the Selic curve as a child spread curve. This way, trading a OC1 Futures contract will display 2 risks, one in a CDI curve, and another in a spread curve. Let's call the discount factors computed in this spread curve $P^{Selic*}_{t,T}$ that can be defined as:

$$P^{Selic*}_{t,T_i}\cdot P^{CDI}_{t,T_i} = P^{Selic}_{t,T_i} \tag{48}$$

The quotes used to calibrate $P^{Selic*}_{t,T}$ can be $R^{CDI}_{t,T}$ and $R^{Selic}_{t,T}$, which are the 2 rates quoted on DI1 and OC1 contracts respectively. Since the CDI to Selic basis spread is usually defined as the difference of the 2 rates, it could be constructed $P^{Selic*}_{t,T}$ by creating a spread curve that's composed of quotes $Quote_{T_i}$ for each maturity date T_i as below:

$$R^{Selic}_{t,T_i} - R^{CDI}_{t,T_i} = Quote_{T_i} \tag{49}$$

Given those quotes, the next step is to calculate R^{Selic}_{t,T_i} from $Quote_{T_i}$ since R^{CDI}_{t,T_i} is available in the already constructed CDI onshore curve. From R^{Selic}_{t,T_i}, it would be then calculated $P^{Selic}_{t,T}$ from:

$$P^{Selic}_{t,T} = \frac{1}{\left(1+R^{Selic}_{t,T_i}\right)^{\tau 252}} \tag{50}$$

Then, (48) would be applied to imply P^{Selic*}_{t,T_i} given the knowledge of P^{CDI}_{t,T_i} in the available CDI onshore curve. This way, it's possible to calculate for each maturity date T_i the value of P^{Selic*}_{t,T_i}. Again for broken dates, it may be applied a log-linear interpolation on discount factors of P^{Selic*}_{t,T_i} as in (40).

It's worth mentioning that P^{Selic*}_{t,T_i} is just an internal variable in the process. The quotes are still the linear spread of OC1 and DI1 future contract rates and interest rate risk will be computed by bumping that difference in rates defined in $Quote_{T_i}$ by let's say 1 basis point. So you would still have risk to the linear spread widening or tightening, even though the spread curve is internally multiplicative in the discount factors and defined by (48).

The reader may be asking why we are creating this whole process for a linear spread curve that could be constructed directly using rates as input. The issue usually arises when you work in the quant department of a bank that often is interested in having an homogeneous process for creating spread curves in a system. For USD offshore curves, the spread curves (Tenor basis and cross currency basis curves) are commonly designed this way. Thus, you would have to design spread curves in 2 different ways if the proposed approach is usually not followed.

3.9 Giving 110%

Some OTC contracts, usually swaps, have the floating BRL leg defined with a percentage applied to each of the daily fixings. The payoff is usually defined in the following way for a percentage of CDI X Fixed BRL swap:

$$Payoff_{BRL}[T] = Not_{BRL} \cdot \{CapFac_{Fixed}(t,T) - CapFac_{Float}(t,T)\}$$

This looks like the same onshore BRL Fixed X BRL Float payoff of the swap defined earlier for a 100% CDI case. However, the term $CapFac_{Float}(t,T)$ now uses a different daily compounding formula to accommodate a percentage of CDI applied to the O/N CDI accrued rate. Mathematically, $CapFac_{Float}(t,T)$ is defined for the percentage of CDI case as:

$$CapFac_{Float}(t,T) = \prod_{T_i=t}^{T} \left\{ \left[[1+CDI_{T_i}]^{\frac{1}{252}} - 1 \right] \cdot X + 1 \right\} \tag{51}$$

where,
X: is the percentage of CDI applied to the floating leg.

It's worth reinforcing that the percentage constant X is applied to the O/N CDI accrued rate $\left[1+CDI_{T_i}\right]^{\frac{1}{252}}-1$, and not on CDI annualized rate fixing directly like on:

$$CapFac_{Float}(t,T)=\prod_{T_i=t}^{T}\left[\left[1+CDI_{T_i}\cdot X\right]^{\frac{1}{252}}\right] \tag{52}$$

The 2 formulations result in different results and (51) should never be replaced ever with (52).

3.10 The CDI+Spread is a multiplicative spread

Other OTC swap contracts can be specified with a payoff based on a spread over the CDI to calculate the O/N capitalization factors. Frequently, market practitioners in Brazil call this other possible floating leg specification as CDI+Spread. However, as we will show, it's in fact a multiplicative spread to be applied to each one of the CDI O/N capitalization factors. The payoff for this floating leg is given by:

$$CapFac_{Float}(t,T)=\prod_{T_i=t}^{T}\left\{\left[1+CDI_{T_i}\right]^{\frac{1}{252}}\cdot\left[1+Spread\right]^{\frac{1}{252}}\right\} \tag{53}$$

3.11 How to price the 3 possible BRL Fixed X Float payoffs?

In this subsection, we will demonstrate how to price the 3 BRL Fixed X Float zero coupon swap payoffs discussed so far. The Fixed BRL leg on all of them is the same. It's the floating leg that differs among them, with the 100% CDI, the percentage of CDI and the CDI+Spread payoffs discussed previously.

3.11.1 100% CDI case

The payoff for a swap where the floating leg is based on 100% CDI is given by:

$$Payoff_{BRL}[T]=Not_{BRL}\cdot\left\{CapFac_{Fixed}(t,T)-CapFac_{Float}(t,T)\right\}$$

The expectation of the above payoff can be taken in the already mentioned risk-neutral daily compounding measure $\mathbb{Q}^*$, where the numéraire associated with it is $\beta_t=\prod_{T_i=0}^{t}\left[1+CDI_{T_i}\right]^{\frac{1}{252}}$.Thus,

$$PV_t^{BRL}=Not_{BRL}\cdot\beta_t\cdot\mathbb{E}^{\mathbb{Q}^*}\left[\frac{\left\{CapFac_{Fixed}(t,T)-CapFac_{Float}(t,T)\right\}}{\beta_T}|\mathcal{F}_t\right]$$

The interesting fact is that $\frac{\beta_T}{\beta_t} = CapFac_{Float}(t,T)$. Thus we could rearrange the above equation the following way:

$$PV_t^{BRL} = Not_{BRL} \cdot \beta_t \cdot \mathbb{E}^{\mathbb{Q}^*}\left[\frac{\{CapFac_{Fixed}(t,T)\}}{\beta_T}|\mathcal{F}_t\right] - Not_{BRL} \tag{54}$$

By using the Radon-Nikodym derivative specified in (35), we can change (6) to:

$$PV_t^{BRL} = Not_{BRL} \cdot P_{t,T}^{CDI} \cdot CapFac_{Fixed}(t,T) - Not_{BRL} \tag{55}$$

Equation (55) can be interpreted the following way. Its fixed BRL leg simply has its future value given by $Not_{BRL} \cdot CapFac_{Fixed}(t,T)$ which is a constant value. Since this BRL amount is paid at date T and we are pricing as of t, we should discount this future value amount by the cdi curve discount factor from t to T, which is $P_{t,T}^{CDI}$. On the other hand, the floating leg is at par at date t. This happens because you have to project the future CDI O/N capitalization factors and discount them with the same projections. So we are only left with the Notional in BRL as the present value of the floating leg.

If we are pricing the floating leg at t, but at the pricing time the CDI at t was already published, then the floating leg no longer prices at par. Now it's price is equal to:

$$PV_{Float}^{CDI} = Not_{BRL} \cdot (1 + CDI_t)^{\frac{1}{252}} \cdot P_{t,t+1}^{CDI} \tag{56}$$

So there's an O/N CDI interest rate risk on the floating leg because of the term $P_{t,t+1}^{CDI}$. If the cdi onshore curve is predicting the next CDI fixing at $t+1$, to be equal to its previous value at t, then the floating leg still prices at par though.

If pricing is done at a future date τ, without CDI O/N fixing being published at τ, the present value formula would be given by:

$$PV_\tau^{BRL} = Not_{BRL} \cdot P_{\tau,T}^{CDI} \cdot CapFac_{Fixed}(t,T) - Not_{BRL} \cdot CapFac_{Float}(t,\tau) \tag{57}$$

3.11.2 CDI+Spread case

Equation (53) describes the payoff in the case of a spread applied to O/N CDI capitalization factors. We can rearrange (53) to:

$$CapFac_{Float}(t,T) = \left\{\prod_{T_i=t}^{T} [1 + CDI_{T_i}]^{\frac{1}{252}}\right\} \cdot [1 + Spread]^{\tau_{t,T}^{252}} \tag{58}$$

Since $[1 + Spread]^{\tau 252}$ is now a constant, it can be taken out of the expectation, thus pricing for a CDI+Spread swap would be given by:

$$PV_t^{BRL} = Not_{BRL} \cdot P_{t,T}^{CDI} \cdot CapFac_{Fixed}(t,T) - Not_{BRL} \cdot [1 + Spread]^{\tau_{t,T}^{252}} \tag{59}$$

If the CDI fixing is already published, then the equation above would be adjusted according to the same idea in (56).

3.11.3 Percentage of CDI case

The payoff for this case is specified in (51). Most market practitioners in Brazil use a static rates model with no convexity corrections to price this payoff. This is a good assumption for many of the practical cases, but convexity corrections should be applied for trades with a percentage higher than 150% of CDI or longer than 5 years. Assuming static rates though, the present value of the swap will be given by:

$$PV_t^{BRL}$$

$$= Not_{BRL} \cdot P_{t,T}^{CDI} \cdot CapFac_{Fixed}(t,T) - Not_{BRL} \cdot \prod_{T_i=t}^{T} \left\{ \left[\frac{1}{P_{t,T_i,T_{i+1}}^{CDI}} - 1 \right] \cdot X + 1 \right\} \cdot P_{t,T}^{CDI} \tag{60}$$

where,

$P_{t,T_i,T_{i+1}}^{CDI}$: is the forward discount factor seen at date t from date T_i to date T_{i+1}.

4
BRL Interest Rate Market and Credit Risk

4.1 Historical spreads

We have discussed this a bit before, but our editor is paying us based on the number of words, so ... The glass half full person looks at the spreads among SETA, Selic and CDI and says that they do not change that much on a daily basis to really matter. The glass half empty person looks at 2012 and 2013 and says that something doesn't look right. And both will ask "Why the CDI is lower than the Selic"?

Anyway, one's main concern should be: How different can these rates get?

We can look at the daily differences as before (Figures 24 and 26), but how do those differences behave over time? Do they average out? In Figure 51 we look at the 3m (63 business days) moving window of the realized accrued annualized rate.

At this scale, we cannot see much. In Figure 52 we can see that interesting second half of 2011.

It seems that things are well behaved, but the next 6 months (Figure 53) show the CDI detaching itself from the Selic and going even lower.

The next 6 months are even more puzzling, with the spread decreasing and suddenly increasing again (Figure 54).

Please look carefully at Figure 55. One might never see this chart again for quite some time. Perhaps it's not a coincidence that the CDI was that far from the SETA just at the lowest level ever.

Looking at the spreads (please remember these spreads are those between the realized 3m accruals) directly (Figure 56), one could (at the time of these charts) assume that the Selic could be modeled as the SETA – 10bp. As for the CDI ... let's just say that there are contracts at BVMF using the Selic rate (created in 2013 – why? The mind wanders ...) that could replace those using the CDI, and all that is

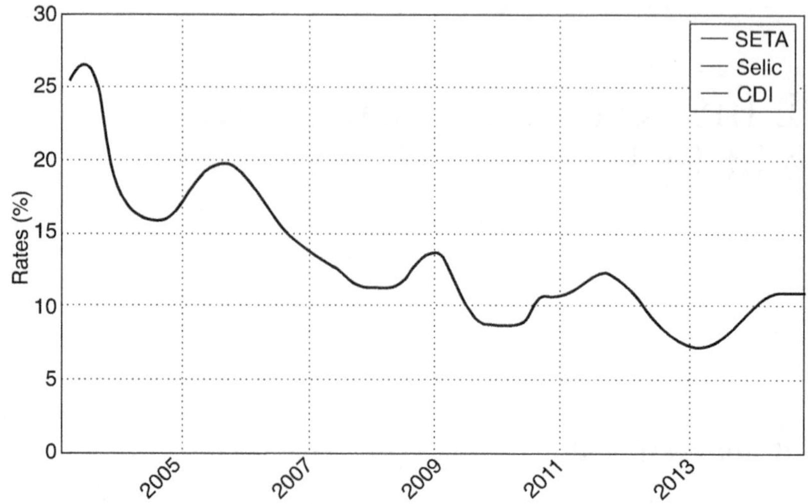

Figure 51 Annualized 3m "average" rates

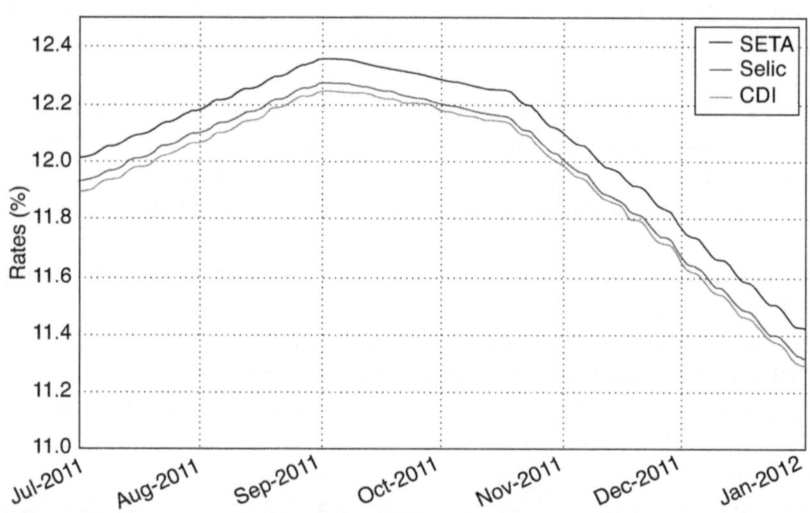

Figure 52 Annualized 3m "average" rates for the second half of 2011

needed for liquidity to migrate is perhaps a wink and a nod by some institutions. The BCB is already using one of these contracts (the SCS) in its FX interventions. So let's say that the CDI to Selic spread will be around 15bp for the foreseeable time.

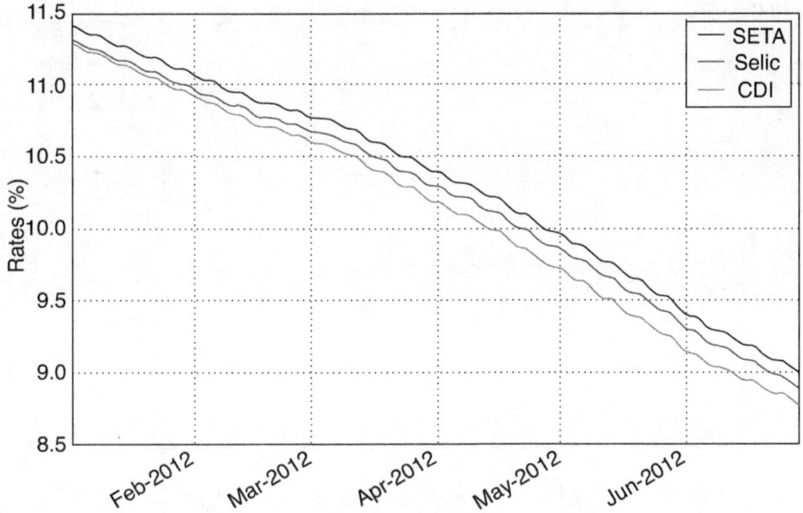

Figure 53 Annualized 3m "average" rates for the first half of 2012

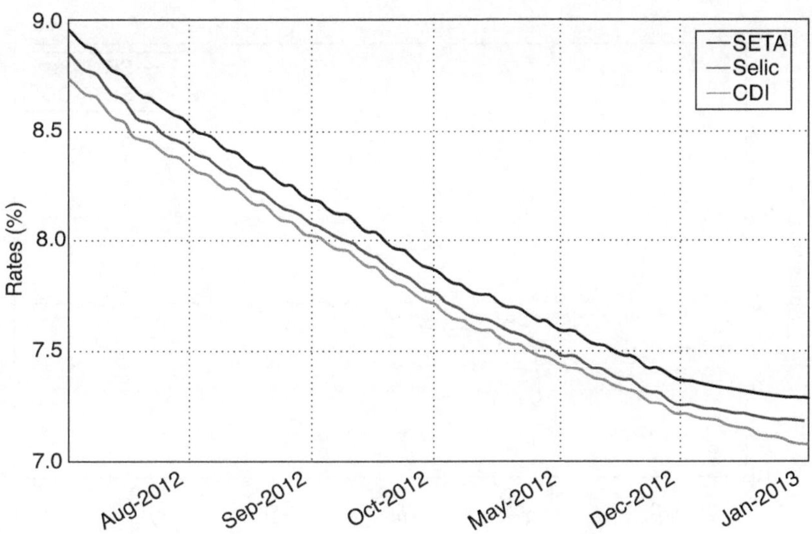

Figure 54 Annualized 3m "average" rates for the second half of 2012

4.2 The term structure of volatility

4.2.1 Slope

By now the reader must be tired of hearing about how the SETA changes by multiples of 25bp on known dates, etc. Now we're going to tackle how the term structure of dates changes daily.

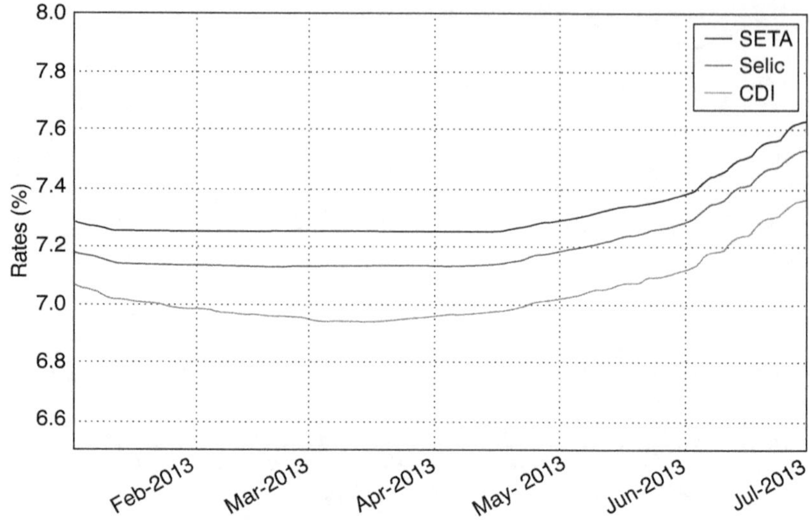

Figure 55 Annualized 3m "average" rates for the first half of 2013

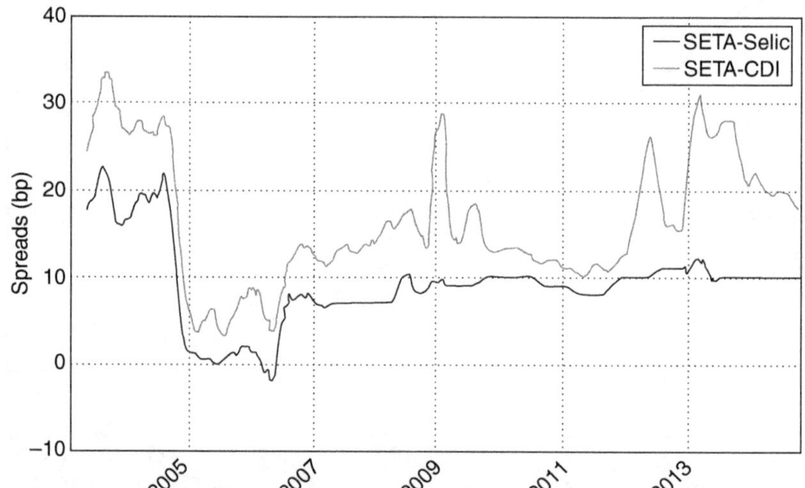

Figure 56 Spreads between the realized 3m accruals of SETA, Selic and CDI

A good example is what happened after the first round of the 2014 presidential elections in Brazil (Figure 57).

The close-to-close changes can be seen as absolute moves in basis points (Figure 58) or relative changes in % (Figure 59).

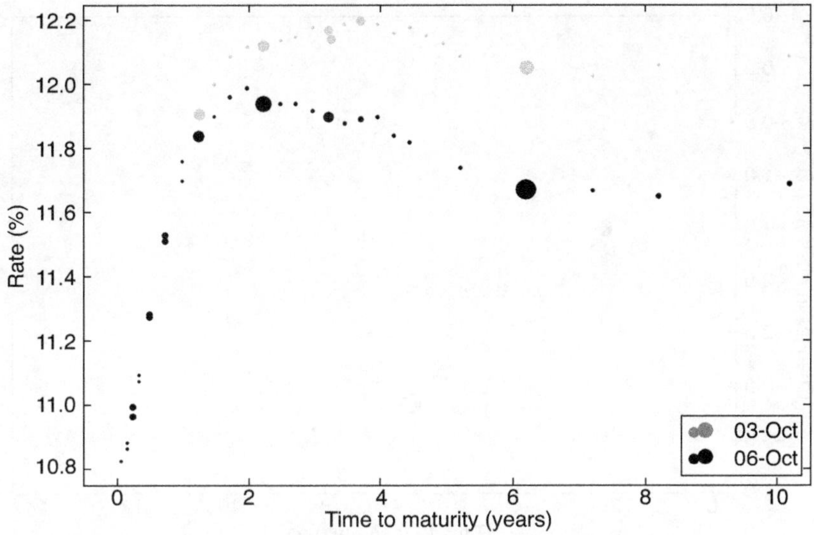

Figure 57 DI curve before and after the 1st round of the 2014 presidential elections

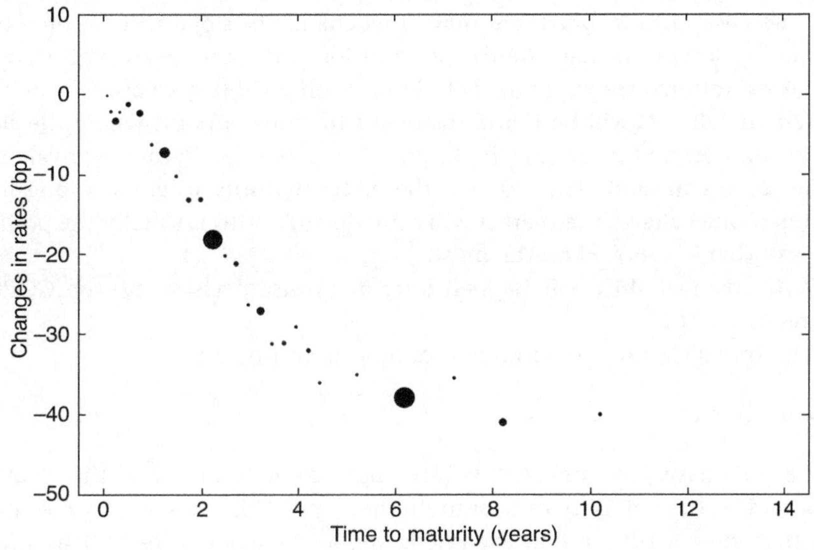

Figure 58 Absolute changes for the DI curve after the 1st round of the 2014 presidential elections

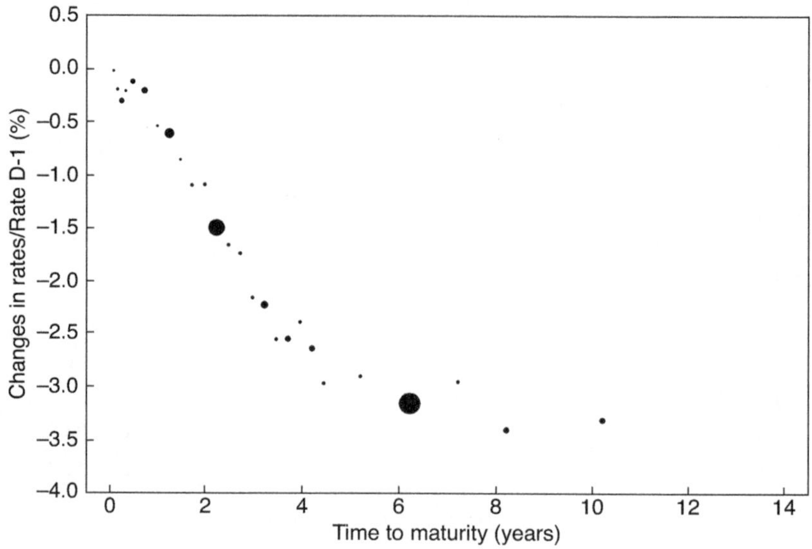

Figure 59 Relative changes for the DI curve after the 1st round of the 2014 presidential elections

Most (daily) market movements are not parallel shifts, they are changes in slope. Because rates in Brazil are high, this change in slope will at some time "saturate" – long term rates (both spot and forward) become so high that the curve does not increase anymore. Let's look at Jun-2014 (Figure 60).

Often an "elbow" will be found in these situations, a point where the slope decreases markedly (for 24-Jun this seems to be around 2.5 years, equivalent to the Jan-2016 contract). This often is the better maturity to enter a long fixed position if one believes the market will calm down, as this is usually the point in the curve that has moved up the most.

Often a parallel shift will happen after a surprise decision by the COPOM (Figures 61 and 62).

If we express the rates as a function of time according to:

$$r_t = \alpha + \beta \cdot t \tag{61}$$

On a daily basis most of the volatility might come from β, and the volatility of r would be the volatility of beta multiplied by t. This works up to the elbow. After that the volatility might even be lower, as the elbow goes back and forth in time (from 3 years to 2 years as the curve steepens, and back to 3 years as the market calms down). This can be modeled as:

$$r_t = \alpha + \beta \cdot Max\,(t, t_{elbow}) \tag{62}$$

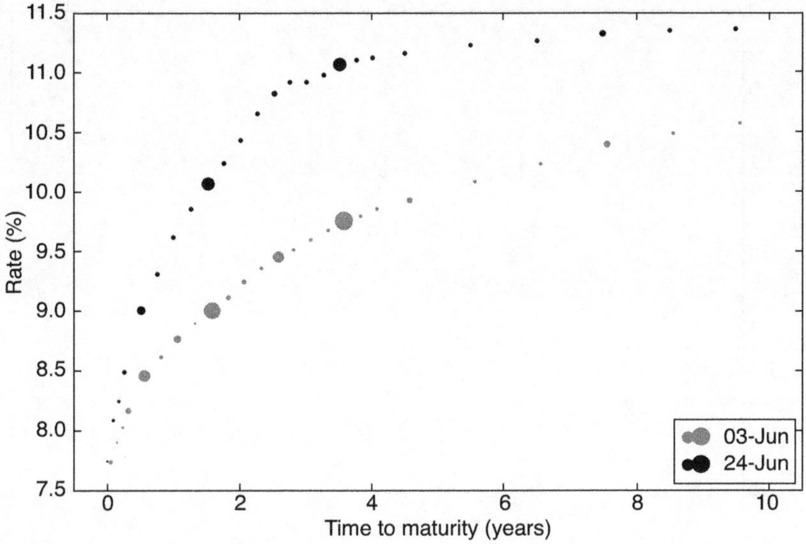

Figure 60 DI curve in Jun-2013

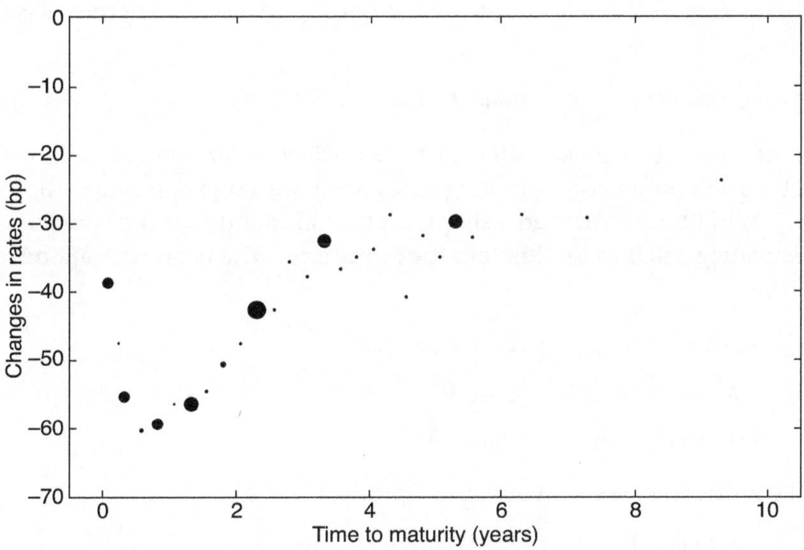

Figure 61 Changes in curve after the 31-Aug-2011 surprise

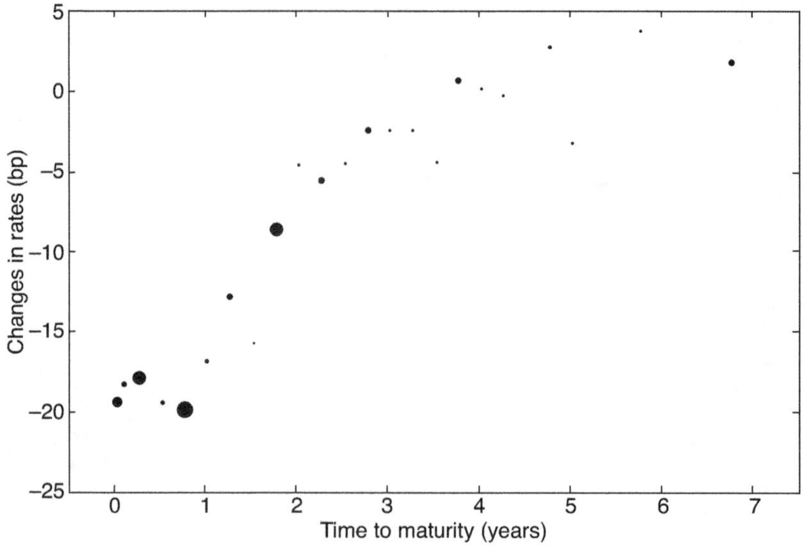

Figure 62 Changes in curve after the 17-Mar-2010 surprise

This works for a typical upward sloping curve such as the Jun-2013 curve. A curve such as the Oct-2014 curve is more challenging, as it is "articulated" at the elbow. A more complex model will be needed (basically another degree of freedom):

$$r_t = \alpha + \beta \cdot Max(t, t_{elbow}) + \lambda \cdot Max(t - t_{elbow}, t_\infty - t_{elbow}, 0) \tag{63}$$

And of course this linear behavior is just a first order approximation. Each linear term will have a corresponding curvature (with a sign opposite to the linear term). Ten to fifteen years ago a simple regression found that the curvature was approximately equal to −0.20 times the linear term. The parametrization would look like:

$$r_t = \alpha + \beta \cdot Max(t, t_{elbow}) + \gamma \cdot (Max(t, t_{elbow}))^2$$
$$+ \lambda \cdot Max(t - t_{elbow}, t_\infty - t_{elbow}, 0) + \tag{64}$$
$$+ \mu \cdot (Max(t - t_{elbow}, t_\infty - t_{elbow}, 0))^2 \tag{65}$$

And considering how the curvature typically behaved:

$$r_t = \alpha + \beta \cdot Max(t, t_{elbow}) - 0.2 \cdot \beta \cdot (Max(t, t_{elbow}))^2$$
$$+ \lambda \cdot Max(t - t_{elbow}, t_\infty - t_{elbow}, 0) - \tag{66}$$
$$- 0.2 \cdot \lambda \cdot (Max(t - t_{elbow}, t_\infty - t_{elbow}, 0))^2 \tag{67}$$

But this is not the best way to fit the curve – it's just a way to think how a curve moves (steepening and saturating, sometimes a parallel shift).

4.2.2 Covariance

Starting from the simplified model above, where rates are described as:

$$r_t = \alpha + \beta \cdot t \tag{68}$$

The variance of the rate is:

$$Var[r_t] = Var[\alpha] + 2 \cdot t \cdot Cov[\alpha, \beta] + t^2 \cdot Var[\beta] \tag{69}$$

And the covariance of the rates at times t_1 and t_2 is:

$$Cov\left[r_{t_1}, r_{t_2}\right] = Var[\alpha] + (t_1 + t_2) \cdot Cov[\alpha, \beta] + (t_1 \cdot t_2) \cdot Var[\beta] \tag{70}$$

There are some easy conclusions that the data allows us to take:

- Very short rates (up to the next COPOM) should have no volatility; and here one should consider the implied forward rates before calculating the changes, least one mistakes the carry with volatility
- By construction, correlation among rates with maturities close to each other should be high ($t_1 \approx t_2$); this is part of the problem with using spot rates, you end up with correlation matrices full of 80s and 90s, signifying nothing

The covariance matrix in this simplified case is:

$$\Sigma = \begin{bmatrix} Var\left[r_{t_1}\right] & Cov\left[r_{t_1}, r_{t_2}\right] \\ Cov\left[r_{t_1}, r_{t_2}\right] & Var\left[r_{t_2}\right] \end{bmatrix} = \begin{bmatrix} \sigma_1^2 & \sigma_{12} \\ \sigma_{12} & \sigma_2^2 \end{bmatrix} \tag{71}$$

4.2.3 Principal components

Calculating the eigensystem for the covariance matrix, we find the eigenvalues:

$$\lambda_{1,2} = \left(\frac{\sigma_2^2 + \sigma_1^2}{2}\right) \pm \sqrt{\left(\frac{\sigma_2^2 - \sigma_1^2}{2}\right) + \sigma_{12}} \tag{72}$$

And the eigenvectors:

$$v_{1,2} = \begin{bmatrix} \frac{1}{\sqrt{1+m_{1,2}^2}} \\ \frac{m_{1,2}}{\sqrt{1+m_{1,2}^2}} \end{bmatrix} \tag{73}$$

Where:

$$m_{1,2} = \left(\frac{\sigma_2^2 - \sigma_1^2}{2\sigma_{12}}\right) \pm \sqrt{\left(\frac{\sigma_2^2 - \sigma_1^2}{2\sigma_{12}}\right) + 1} \tag{74}$$

Substituting the formulas and considering $t_1 = 0$:

$$m_{1,2} = \left(\frac{2 \cdot t_2 \cdot \sigma_{\alpha\beta} + t_2^2 \cdot \sigma_\beta^2}{2 \cdot t_2 \cdot \sigma_{\alpha\beta} + 2 \cdot \sigma_\alpha^2}\right) \pm \sqrt{\left(\frac{2 \cdot t_2 \cdot \sigma_{\alpha\beta} + t_2^2 \cdot \sigma_\beta^2}{2 \cdot t_2 \cdot \sigma_{\alpha\beta} + 2 \cdot \sigma_\alpha^2}\right)^2 + 1} \tag{75}$$

$$\lambda_{1,2} = \sigma_\alpha^2 + \left(t_2 \cdot \sigma_{\alpha\beta} + \frac{1}{2} \cdot t_2^2 \cdot \sigma_\beta^2\right) \pm \sqrt{\left(t_2 \cdot \sigma_{\alpha\beta} + \frac{1}{2} \cdot t_2^2 \cdot \sigma_\beta^2\right)^2 + (t_2 \cdot \sigma_{\alpha\beta} + \sigma_\alpha^2)^2} \tag{76}$$

If the correlation between level and slope is zero $(\rho_{\alpha\beta} = 0)$:

$$m_{1,2} = \left(\frac{t_2^2 \cdot \sigma_\beta^2}{2 \cdot \sigma_\alpha^2}\right) \pm \sqrt{\left(\frac{t_2^2 \cdot \sigma_\beta^2}{2 \cdot \sigma_\alpha^2}\right)^2 + 1} \tag{77}$$

$$\lambda_{1,2} = \sigma_\alpha^2 + \left(\frac{1}{2} \cdot t_2^2 \cdot \sigma_\beta^2\right) \pm \sqrt{\left(\frac{1}{2} \cdot t_2^2 \cdot \sigma_\beta^2\right)^2 + (\sigma_\alpha^2)^2} \tag{78}$$

We can choose $t_2 = \sqrt{2}$ (which is close to 1.5 years), and then:

$$m_{1,2} = \left(\frac{\sigma_\beta^2}{\sigma_\alpha^2}\right) \pm \sqrt{\left(\frac{\sigma_\beta^2}{\sigma_\alpha^2}\right)^2 + 1} \tag{79}$$

$$\lambda_{1,2} = \left(\sigma_\alpha^2 + \sigma_\beta^2\right) \pm \sqrt{(\sigma_\alpha^2)^2 + \left(\sigma_\beta^2\right)^2} \tag{80}$$

Ok, algebra is nice, but what does this all mean?

- The bigger the difference between λ_2 and λ_1 , the bigger is the percentage of the total variance explained by the eigenvector v_1
- This difference is (after all the assumptions): $\lambda_1 - \lambda_2 = 2\sqrt{(\sigma_\alpha^2)^2 + \left(\sigma_\beta^2\right)^2}$
- The closer m_1 gets to 1, the more parallel v_1 gets; therefore, the lower the ratio $\frac{\sigma_\alpha}{\sigma_\beta}$, the more parallel is the first (and most important) eigenvector is
- The second eigenvector is always a rotation, because $m_2 = \left(\frac{\sigma_\beta^2}{\sigma_\alpha^2}\right) - \sqrt{\left(\frac{\sigma_\beta^2}{\sigma_\alpha^2}\right)^2 + 1} < 0$
- If m_1 is close to 1, m_2 is close to -1

But why are we discussing this? Just to make clear that the Principal Components methodology will, for the kind of covariance matrices usually found for spot rates, always return a parallel-like shift as the most important eigenvector and a rotation as the second. This even if the most relevant movements and volatility come from changes in the slope. It is as if a vector of changes of rates that corresponds to a change in slope is decomposed as a parallel "average" shift and a rotation centered at the average.

So please take care with the conclusions of applying Principal Components to Interest Rate movements. The article "Level-Slope-Curvature: Fact or Artifact" (Lord and Pelsser, 2008) is a good read on this matter.

4.3 Potential exposures

Earlier, we wrote (14):

$$PV = Accrual_{Realized} \cdot \left(\frac{\Delta MTM_{Unrealized}}{Drift_{Realized}} - 1 \right) \tag{81}$$

And this equation gives us some clues to the behavior of the potential exposure profile of an IR Swap.

At the inception of the trade (or close to it), both $Accrual_{Realized}$ and $Drift_{Realized}$ are equal (or very close) to 1. Therefore, any change in PV will come from $MTM_{Unrealized}$ and this risk can be easily modeled as a function of the shift of the relevant market rate r (in basis points) as:

$$\Delta MTM_{Unrealized} = -(PV_{FixedLeg}) \left(\frac{\tau_{t,T}^{252}}{1+r} \right) \left(\frac{1}{10000} \right) \Delta r \tag{82}$$

So the longer the maturity of the IR Swap, the riskier it is, because of the dependence of $\tau_{t,T}^{252}$ in the formula and also because Δr tends to increase with $\tau_{t,T}^{252}$ (we've stressed the importance of changes in slope in the dynamics of the DI curve throughout the book). This risk starts large and decreases with $\left(\tau_{t,T}^{252}\right)^2$, as it is substituted by the realized drift.

For this realized drift, a parallel shift between the projected and the realized CDI will translate into a linear growth with t as it goes from 0 to T.

How to build Potential Exposure profiles for an IR Swap? Don't worry, we are here to help you.

1. Start with the current term structure; for a simple example, consider 5 periods and a flat rate of 12%.
2. Have a good method for backing out your term structure for the forward rates (a good interpolation method); here it is easy to say that all forwards are 12%.
3. Guess what? What you want to guess is how each of those forward rates will move in the future; the interesting part is that there are two moving parts: the realized rates and the new market rates, with the realized rates influencing the market rates (if the realized rate is 13% in the first period it's hard to have the forward rate at 11% for the second period).
4. Build a new scenario starting today (time t), with good features like CDIs constant between COPOM meeting, autocorrelation of changes, etc. In our example, we'll build the scenario from the forward to the spot rates. Forwards will be {12.5%, 13.0%, 13.5%, 13.5%, 13.5%}.

5. Go forward in time using the scenario rates from t to τ (here τ is a future date, not the day count fraction term) as the realized CDIs (or the discrete changes close to it – you would expect the market to at least be within 25bp of the decision most of the time).
6. Now you can either use the existing scenario from τ to T or you can generate a new scenario (going back to 4), in both cases repeating the steps until reaching T.
7. You will end up with a matrix of n+2 rows (the original term structure, the stresses term structure at the inception, and a new scenario for each of the n periods.
8. At row j of this matrix, you should have $Max[0,j-2]$ realized rates and $n-Max[0,j-2]$ unrealized (forward) rates.
9. Run the functions above (PV and its 3 components) to calculate the PV at each date, and the Potential Exposure should be the maximum of the PV at all dates.
10. Run everything from 4. to 9. for all your scenarios.

That matrix structure is interesting, because now τ corresponds to a row in the matrix and also to the frontier between realized and unrealized rates. To make it easier to understand, Table 15 shows the matrix, and how the unrealized rates become realized rates (shown here with more decimal points).

Any case in which we would use $f(t_1,t,t_2)$ will look at the first row (scenario at trade inception); as we go forward in time,

For a bullet IR Swap, a set of at most 16 different scenarios (8 "up" and 8 "down") should be enough to look at the worst case scenarios for different maturities.

4.4 Zero curve: and the winner is ...

Let's finally look at different interpolation methods. We recommend "Interpolation Methods for Curve Construction" (Hagan and West, 2006) as a very good summary about this matter, and *Interest Rate Modeling* (Andersen and Piterbarg, 2010) is going to be the reference used in this chapter. But we would like to start by asking: What is the goal of an interpolation algorithm in finance?

The answer is: We want to price something (that doesn't have a price given by the market) as a function of other things (that have a price given by the market).

A simple parallel is to consider the problem of pricing an option. We have an option, the underlying asset and cash (borrowed and lent at the risk-free rate) – how much of asset and cash must we hold to minimize the risk of the portfolio? The answer depends on the dynamics chosen for the asset (for a geometric Brownian motion, this is expressed as the choice of volatility).

Table 15 Scenarios for potential exposures

Row	τ	r_{01}	r_{12}	r_{23}	r_{34}	r_{45}
Scenario at trade inception	t (not τ yet)	12.0%	12.0%	12.0%	12.0%	12.0%
Stressed scenario at inception	0 (=t)	12.5%	13.0%	13.5%	13.5%	13.5%
Stressed forward scenario	1	12.495%	13.0%	13.5%	13.5%	13.5%
Stressed forward scenario	2	12.495%	13.005%	13.5%	13.5%	13.5%
Stressed forward scenario	3	12.495%	13.005%	13.495%	13.5%	13.5%
Stressed forward scenario	4	12.495%	13.005%	13.495%	13.515%	13.5%
Stressed forward scenario	5 (=T)	12.495%	13.005%	13.495%	13.515%	13.505%

In our case, this becomes: We have a swap, a cash account borrowing and lending at CDI and several DI contracts – how much of each DI should we hold to minimize the risk of the portfolio?

Let's present the candidates:

4.4.1 Linear Interpolation (LI)

The first volume of *Interest Rate Modeling* (Andersen and Piterbarg, 2010) presents Linear Interpolation as "Piecewise Linear Yields" (6.2.1.1):

$$r(r_1,t_1,r_2,t_2,t) = r_1 + (r_2 - r_1) \cdot \frac{(t-t_1)}{(t_2-t_1)} \tag{83}$$

Main advantages: Simple to implement, local and bounded.

Wait, what do we mean by local? And by bounded?

Local means that the rate depends only on the two market rates that define the interval that contains the maturity t that defines r.

In mathematical terms:

$$r\left(\left[r_j\right],\left[t_j\right],t\right) = r(r_1,t_1,r_2,t_2,t) \tag{84}$$

Where:

$$t_1 = Max\left(\left[t_j\right] \mid t_j \le t\right) \tag{85}$$

And:

$$t_2 = Min\left(\left[t_j\right] \mid t_j \ge t\right) \tag{86}$$

Bounded means that the interpolated rate r will be within the interval defined by the two market rates above.

In mathematical terms:

$$r_1 \le r(r_1,t_1,r_2,t_2,t) \le r_2 \tag{87}$$

These are useful properties for a first, quick estimate; it leads to a number that is free of distortions caused by more complex models.

If we want to know the DIs portfolio at time t that hedges the swap, the procedure is simple:

$$\frac{\partial r}{\partial r_1} = \frac{(t_2-t)}{(t_2-t_1)} \tag{88}$$

$$\frac{\partial r}{\partial r_2} = \frac{(t-t_1)}{(t_2-t_1)} = 1 - \frac{(t_2-t)}{(t_2-t_1)} = 1 - \frac{\partial r}{\partial r_1} \tag{89}$$

And for the fixed leg of any swap or DI:

$$\frac{\partial PV}{\partial r} = -PV \cdot \frac{t}{(1+r)} \tag{90}$$

Therefore, for the portfolio:

$$\Pi = Swap + W_1 DI_1 + W_2 DI_2 \tag{91}$$

We should have:

$$\frac{\partial \Pi}{\partial r_1} = \frac{\partial \Pi}{\partial r_2} = 0 \tag{92}$$

And using the chain rule:

$$-PV \cdot \frac{t}{(1+r)} \cdot \frac{(t_2 - t)}{(t_2 - t_1)} - W_1 \cdot PV_1 \cdot \frac{t_1}{(1+r_1)} = 0 \tag{93}$$

$$W_1 = -\frac{PV}{PV_1} \cdot \frac{(1+r_1)}{(1+r)} \cdot \frac{t}{t_1} \cdot \frac{(t_2 - t)}{(t_2 - t_1)} \tag{94}$$

$$W_2 = -\frac{PV}{PV_{12}} \cdot \frac{(1+r_2)}{(1+r)} \cdot \frac{t}{t_2} \cdot \frac{(t - t_1)}{(t_2 - t_1)} \tag{95}$$

The implied one-day forward rates around t are not nice:

$$r_{fwd}(r_1, t_1, r_2, t_2, t) = \left(\frac{1 + r(r_1, t_1, r_2, t_2, t+\delta)}{1 + r(r_1, t_1, r_2, t_2, t)} \right)^{\frac{t}{\delta}} \cdot (1 + r(r_1, t_1, r_2, t_2, t+\delta)) - 1 \tag{96}$$

With:

$$\delta = \pm \frac{1}{252} \tag{97}$$

4.4.2 Flat Forward (FF)

The first volume of *Interest Rate Modeling* (Andersen and Piterbarg, 2010) presents Flat Forward as "Piecewise Flat Forward Rates" (6.2.1.2):

$$t \cdot \ln(1 + r(r_1, t_1, r_2, t_2, t)) = t_1 \cdot \ln(1+r_1) + (t_2 \cdot \ln(1+r_2) - t_1 \cdot \ln(1+r_1)) \cdot \frac{(t - t_1)}{(t_2 - t_1)} \tag{98}$$

Or also:

$$r(r_1, t_1, r_2, t_2, t) = (1+r_1)^{\frac{t_1}{t} \cdot \frac{(t_2 - t)}{(t_2 - t_1)}} \cdot (1+r_2)^{\frac{t_2}{t} \cdot \frac{(t - t_1)}{(t_2 - t_1)}} - 1 \tag{99}$$

Main advantages: Local and bounded. The locality makes it still relatively simple to implement.

$$\frac{\partial r}{\partial r_1} = \frac{(1+r)}{(1+r_1)} \cdot \frac{t_1}{t} \cdot \frac{(t_2 - t)}{(t_2 - t_1)} \tag{100}$$

$$\frac{\partial r}{\partial r_2} = \frac{(1+r)}{(1+r_2)} \cdot \frac{t_2}{t} \cdot \frac{(t - t_1)}{(t_2 - t_1)} \tag{101}$$

And:

$$W_1 = -\frac{PV}{PV_1} \cdot \frac{(t_2 - t)}{(t_2 - t_1)} \tag{102}$$

$$W_2 = -\frac{PV}{PV_{12}} \cdot \frac{(t - t_1)}{(t_2 - t_1)} \tag{103}$$

Which makes for an easier formula for cashflow mapping.

The implied one-day forward rates around t are constant in the interval defined by t_1 and t_2:

$$r_{fwd}(r_1, t_1, r_2, t_2, t) = \left(\frac{(1+r_2)^{t_2}}{(1+r_1)^{t_1}}\right)^{\frac{1}{t_2 - t_1}} - 1 \tag{104}$$

4.4.3 Cubic Spline (CS)

The first volume of *Interest Rate Modeling* (Andersen and Piterbarg, 2010) presents Cubic Spline as "C^2 Yield Curves: Twice Differentiable Cubic Splines" (6.2.3).

Instead of a formula, one has an algorithm, no locality and rates are not bounded. In fact, the sensitivity to small changes in the input is not desirable.

An application to local rates was published in "Interpolaçnao por Cubic Spline paraa Estrutura a Termo Brasileira" (Varga, 2000). But smoothness of forward rates is not our goal; in fact, our goal is quite opposite to that.

4.4.4 Which is better?

Although FF presents the constant one-day forwards that are characteristic of the local rates, there is one problem: they are changing at the wrong dates. They should be changing following the COPOM meetings, not at the maturity of the DIs (market points).

Is it possible to have an algorithm that works like the FF, but with changes at dates that are not market points?

4.5 Smooth operator

We thought you would never ask this question (well, in fact, we asked the question, but we are sure you were following us).

Let's start with a very simple case:

There's a DI contract maturing in 10 business days, a COPOM meeting in 20 business days, a DI contract maturing in 30 business days, a COPOM meeting in 40 business days, a DI contract maturing in 50 business days, a COPOM meeting in 60 business days, and so on.

Table 16 shows the simple procedure in this case (a "ladder"), with the symbol $\oplus$ denoting the composition of a spot rate r_i for t_i and a forward rate r_{ij} from i to j to arrive at a new spot rate r_j for t_j and the symbol $\ominus$ denoting the decomposition

Table 16 FFC algorithm (simple)

t	Δt	Mkt Rate	C or D?	Same Fwd?	Fwd	Spot	$\|rm - r\|$
t_1	t_{01}	rm_1	DI		$r_{01} = r_1$	$r_1 = rm_1$	0
t_2	t_{12}		COPOM	Yes	$r_{12} = r_{01}$	$r_2 = r_1 \oplus r_{12}$	
t_3	t_{23}	rm_3	DI		$r_{23} = r_3 \ominus r_2$	$r_3 = rm_3$	0
t_4	t_{34}		COPOM	Yes	$r_{34} = r_{23}$	$r_4 = r_3 \oplus r_{34}$	
t_5	t_{45}	rm_5	DI		$r_{45} = r_5 \ominus r_4$	$r_5 = rm_5$	0
t_6	t_{56}		COPOM	Yes	$r_{56} = r_{45}$	$r_6 = r_5 \oplus r_{56}$	

Table 17 FFC algorithm (simple, numeric)

t	Δt	Mkt Rate	C or D?	Same Fwd?	Fwd Inputs	Fwd	Spot	$\|rm - r\|$
t_1	t_{01}	rm_1	DI		$fi_1 = rm_1$	$r_{01} = fi_1$	$r_1 = r_{01}$	0
t_2	t_{12}		COPOM	Yes	$fi_2 = rm_1$	$r_{12} = r_{01}$	$r_2 = r_1 \oplus r_{12}$	
t_3	t_{23}	rm_3	DI		$fi_3 = rm_3$	$r_{23} = fi_3$	$r_3 = r_2 \oplus r_{23}$	0
t_4	t_{34}		COPOM	Yes	$fi_4 = rm_3$	$r_{34} = r_{23}$	$r_4 = r_3 \oplus r_{34}$	
t_5	t_{45}	rm_5	DI		$fi_5 = rm_5$	$r_{45} = fi_5$	$r_5 = r_4 \oplus r_{45}$	0
t_6	t_{56}		COPOM	Yes	$fi_6 = rm_5$	$r_{56} = r_{45}$	$r_6 = r_5 \oplus r_{56}$	

of a spot rate r_j for t_j into the forward rate r_{ij} from i to j given the spot rate r_i for t_i . These calculations follow the rules detailed on the description of the FF interpolation at 4.4.2.

Why do we have the last column there? Because we're preparing this algorithm to run numerically, without having to program a lot of ifs for each column.

What is the more efficient way of doing this? Let's add another column and look at Table 17.

What is the idea?

Run an algorithm that tries to find a set of values for the column "Fwd Inputs" such that the sum $\sum_k |rm_k - r_k|$ (where k moves through every time t_k where there is a market (DI) rate) is equal to zero. The logic of the COPOMs x DIs choice lies in the choice of k and also in the choice of keeping forwards the same until a COPOM meeting happens.

Now let's make things more complicated with Table 18.

Now we have a conundrum: How should we distribute the forward changes between the two COPOM meetings that lie within two DIs?

Let's rescue everything we discussed about the behavior of the SETA (and therefore the Selic and the CDI), mainly the autocorrelation of its changes and the idea of monetary policy cycles. The most probable value for the next SETA change is the last change. That suggests to us that the curve formed by the changes in the forward rates (by considering the curve only at the points where the forwards are supposed to change) should be as smooth as possible. So we will:

Table 18 FFC algorithm (complex)

t	Δt	Mkt Rate	C or D?	Same Fwd?	Fwd Inputs	Fwd	Spot	$\|rm-r\|$
t_1	t_{01}	rm_1	DI		$fi_1 = rm_1$	$r_{01} = fi_1$	$r_1 = r_{01}$	0
t_2	t_{12}		COPOM	Yes	$fi_2 = rm_1$	$r_{12} = r_{01}$	$r_2 = r_1 \oplus r_{12}$	
t_3	t_{23}	rm_3	DI		$fi_3 = rm_3$	$r_{23} = fi_3$	$r_3 = r_2 \oplus r_{23}$	0
t_4	t_{34}		COPOM	Yes	$fi_4 = rm_3$	$r_{34} = r_{23}$	$r_4 = r_3 \oplus r_{34}$	
t_5	t_{45}		COPOM		$fi_5 = rm_3$	$r_{45} = fi_5$	$r_5 = r_4 \oplus r_{45}$	
t_6	t_{56}	rm_6	DI		$fi_6 = rm_6$	$r_{56} = fi_6$	$r_6 = r_5 \oplus r_{56}$	0

Table 19 FFC algorithm (fit and curvature)

t	Δt	rm	C/D	Fwd	Spot	$\|rm-r\|$	ΔFwd	$\Delta(\Delta Fwd)$	$\|\Delta(\Delta(\Delta Fwd))\|$
t_1	t_{01}	rm_1	DI	r_{01}	r_1	0			
t_2	t_{12}		CO	r_{12}	r_2				
t_3	t_{23}	rm_3	DI	r_{23}	r_3	0	$d_3 = r_{23} - r_{12}$		
t_4	t_{34}		CO	r_{34}	r_4				
t_5	t_{45}		CO	r_{45}	r_5		$d_5 = r_{45} - r_{34}$	$dd_5 = d_5 - d_3$	
t_6	t_{56}	rm_6	DI	r_{56}	r_6	0	$d_6 = r_{56} - r_{45}$	$dd_6 = d_6 - d_5$	$\|ddd_6 = dd_6 - dd_5\|$

1. Calculate the changes of the forwards at the points where change is supposed to happen
2. Calculate the first and second differences of this curve
3. Minimize the sum of:
   a. The sum of the absolute values of these second differences together with
   b. The sum of the absolute values of the difference between market rates and calculated spot rates at the dates corresponding to (selected) DI contracts

We can see the structure at Table 19.

This can be implemented easily, even in Excel. One must take care in establishing the conditions for which the forward stays the same from one row to the other though.

Let's call this algorithm Flat Forward with COPOM meetings (FFC).

A more general implementation will deal with the following problems:

1. There is a CDI at the beginning of the table:
   a. It has a DI status, because if it precedes a DI the forward rate can change between the CDI and the DI, and if it precedes a COPOM the CDI will continue to be the forward rate
   b. Forward and Spot rates are considered given, CDI is a primary input
   c. It would not be part of the cells changed in the Goal Seek algorithm

2. There are two DIs without a COPOM in between:
   a. There is the potential for a change in forward rates not driven by a COPOM meeting
   b. There is the potential for a numerical problem, as the first of these DIs could be just one or two business days after a COPOM meeting (this is a more general problem, not limited to this situation)
   c. Solution: drop the first DI as redundant in the interpolation, use only the second (come back later and monitor the difference between market and calculated rates, but do not use it in the Goal Seek)
3. You're out of COPOM meetings:
   a. There are 8 meetings per year
   b. Typically (over the last few years) the calendar for the next year is published in June
   c. You can estimate the dates for the next year until these are published
   d. The curve can be interpolated as a FF curve after 2 years without too much risks of pricing and hedging it incorrectly
4. You have illiquid DI contracts that have bad prices
   a. This can be solved by ignoring these points as inputs for the Goal Seek algorithm (more on this later)
   b. Alternatively one could map those points as COPOM meetings if they have a maturity after 2 years
5. The algorithm is slow
   a. Make sure that you have a buffer between live rates and the inputs; in other words, freeze the inputs before running the algorithm
   b. If you're using Excel, do not have a lot of formulas in the same spreadsheet you're using (somewhat obvious, but still ...)

4.6 Sensitivities

4.6.1 Zero

An example of short rates interpolated with the 4 methods at 03-Jan-2011 is shown in Figure 63.

And the sensitivities of the rate in each of the interpolation methods chosen can be seen in two charts. Figure 64 shows the local interpolations (LI and FF) and Figure 65 shown the non-local interpolations. For each chart, each DI was bumped by 1bp, and the y axis shows by how much the 3m rate changed in basis points. Figure 64 shows how the 3m rate was a function of only the 3rd and the 4th contracts for the LI and FF interpolations.

Figure 65 shows how the 3m rate was a function of not only the 3rd and 4th contracts, but of other contracts as well.

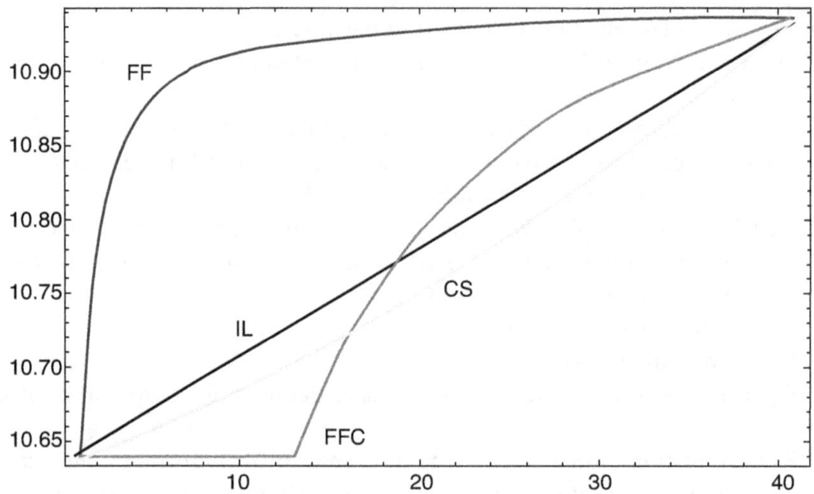

Figure 63 Interpolating short rates

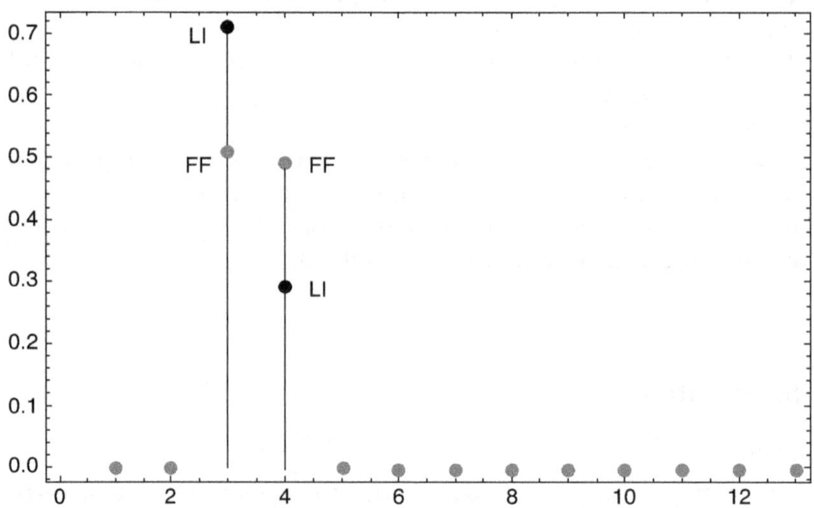

Figure 64 Sensitivities for local interpolations

4.6.2 Forward

For obvious reasons, not all interpolations will work well with mapping risks on forward rates instead of zero rates. To start, you must have forward rates that are reasonable, and therefore we refuse to print the forward rates of the CS interpolation. But a quick calculation should show an expected result: a rate at

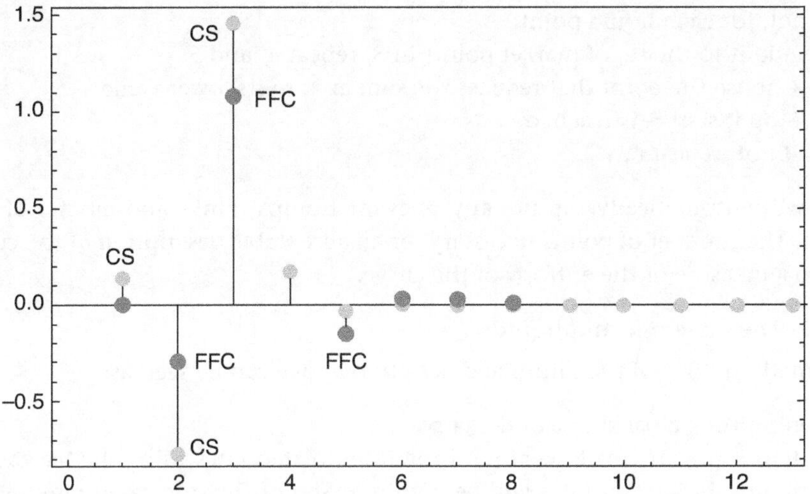

Figure 65 Sensitivities for non-local interpolations

time t should depend only on the forward rates r_{ij} for which $t_i \leq t$; the problem is that the last forward rate might depend on two or three DIs after t, as seen before. For the FF and the FFC we should have something like:

$$t \cdot \ln\left(1 + r(r_1, t_1, r_2, t_2, t)\right) = \sum_{k=1}^{n} \left(t_k^{fwd} \cdot \ln\left(1 + r_k^{fwd}\right)\right) \tag{105}$$

But the the last forward rate is worth only for a period of $t - t_1$, not the full t_n^{fwd}.

4.7 A framework for risk

4.7.1 Minimal description

Here the idea is simple: How should one describe the BRL curve? The best way seems to be:

1. In the beginning God created the CDI, and all was good
2. In the end God determined that all forward rates would look like the last spot rate
3. Interpolate the rates between both the CDI and the last rate using the FFC method (not given by God as the 11th Commandment, but it was close)
4. Calculate the sum of the absolute value of the difference between the calculated rates and the relevant (liquid) market rates
5. If this number is low enough to be acceptable, you have a minimal description (few rates and an algorithm)

6. If not, for each liquid point:
   a. Add it to the set of market points in 3, repeat 4. and 5.
   b. Choose the point that reduces the sum at 4. to its lower value
   c. Stop if step 5. is reached
   d. If not, repeat 6.

This will automatically capture any relevant humps, kinks and elbows of the curve. The number of points necessary for an acceptable description of the curve is also a measure of the entropy of the curve.

4.7.2 The envelope and liquidity risk

The methodology of the minimal description above can be seen as:

1. Determining a backbone of the curve.
2. Determining an envelope around the interpolated rates using the backbone; typically the market rates will be within ± 5bp of the calculated rate; bigger differences usually happen when a particular maturity is highly demanded (a particular flow is bigger than the liquidity provided by the market).

4.7.3 The first, the last and the ugly

Once you have determined the points necessary to describe the backbone, consider those as your first-order risks.

New trades should be mapped into these points first, as you weigh the tradeoff between mapping it to points closer to the trade but carrying higher execution costs or hedging the first-order movement risks by mapping to the backbone and (hopefully) paying less to execute your hedge.

This point seems trivial, but important: Not all points are equal. In order to be worth something, liquidity needs to be actionable, and not all points have the same depth of book, open contracts, volume traded. These points are the market; the other points may look like the market, but they are not the market. If you cannot execute a certain size without moving (a lot) this point, then you have become the market.

Keep monitoring the second-order risks; if you're getting too much of the same maturity, maybe this is becoming a new market point; otherwise, second-order risks from flow should be averaging out.

For an interesting time window to look at the emergence of new dynamics, look no further than the spread between the DIs maturing at Jan-2017 and Jan-2021 during 2014.

4.8 Trading forwards

Unfortunately there's no easy way of trading forward rates (no FRA like an eurodollar contract, no implied mechanism like the one at CME).

One has to trade calendar spreads, with a ratio that would cancel the risk up to the first date (an exercise left to the reader); these are mostly traded on the phone through a broker, and help to make trading the DI electronically hard (information out of the posted liquidity). These trades are typically crosses and can be detected in this way, with crosses responsible for about a quarter of the volume in recent years.

And of course the cost of trading a forward is the sum of trading two DIs. This is something that would benefit the market if changed (reduced).

4.9 Risk and P&L attribution

There are two ways of mapping risk and P&L for these products: Movements of the Spot rates or movements of the Forward rates. As discussed before, the problem with mapping risks to Spot rates (of course adjusting for the CDI carry before comparing the movements like BVMF does for the DI1 futures) is that there is usually too much correlation among the futures, and describing what happened when rates were up but not all of them at the same time is not necessarily very informative. An alternative is to decompose the sensitivity to a spot rate into sensitivities to forward rates, and map the changes of the forward rates. Both can be useful, and if you are trading some form of relative value play (one FRA against another) the forward mapping is probably what you're looking at and the most useful. Except for trades indexed to a percentage of the CDI very different from 100% and longer-dated, most of this risk is quite linear.

So P&L attribution will really be classified in market movements (that can be reconciled quite easily against sensitivities and movements of traded rates or implied forwards), the appreciation or carry of the positions (typically one CDI) and the cost of funding.

As for CVAs, FVAs and similar charges, they have arrived mainly at foreign banks, but with most of the exposure on futures there's not much going on in this market about the xVAs.

Another problem lies with bad data. It is too easy to just get all the DI1 prices from BVMF and call them "The Curve"; we know that sometimes rules and regulations do not leave too much choice about dismissing a price coming from an Exchange, but we'd rather focus on the behavior of the price of less liquid contracts during normal trading hours over a whole day or even week instead of marking a position based on an arbitrary price that is still subject to a qualitative filter applied by BVMF. In short: we would rather mark the curve using liquid points, a methodology and a provision on model risk than blindly accept all prices as equally liquid and informative, and (worse!) use them to interpolate other prices.

5
A Man With Two Clocks ... Foreign Exchange in Brazil

How to trade the currency in Brazil (if you can) and its derivatives (yes you can) and how each contract can be different (well, you can, but ...)

5.1 FX Spot

5.1.1 Who can trade it

Banks and financial entities like FX brokers, all authorized by the BCB. No mutual funds, not much diversity in this market. This is why this market is primarily an interbank market.

5.1.2 How, when and where to trade it

A bank could trade it through BVMF's screen, where banks can trade (almost) anonymously with settlement through BVMF's FX Clearing (margin needs to be deposited upfront).

But this is not a very liquid market. Otherwise, it will be traded either on a broker (by phone) or together with the DOL as part of the Casado. Chances are that FX flows will be first hedged with the DOL, and then throughout the day the mismatch will be managed by trading the Casado looking at the net position in both instruments.

Anyway, one can trade it from 9h to 16h30, and all trades must be registered at the BCB, not necessarily at the moment they were traded.

The standard trade is settled in both currencies two business days after the trade date, but here the business days are counted within a combined holidays calendar, as discussed in 2.1.3.

One can trade deliverable forwards for non standard D2 delivery on any of the 2 currencies as well, but most interbank activity is concentrated in the standard "D2D2" spot.

5.1.3 Observability

Given that tracking trades in real time is impossible (except at BVMF, but these represent a small part of the market), one is left either with published quotes of spot or with the DOL futures market and the Casado. As discussed before, when looking at whether a barrier was hit EMTA recommends looking at DOL–Casado instead of the spot, given how easy it is to trade at a certain level there by exhausting the little liquidity posted in its order book and then trading at the desired level. Because the order book for the DOL is deeper, more diverse and more liquid it is harder to do the same thing there (auction tunnels also help).

5.2 DOL

In this subsection, first we will describe the DOL contract details, quoting conventions and other useful information. Then we will discuss the maturity months in which the liquidity of DOL contracts is concentrated. The DR1 contract and the roll of the DOL contract mechanism will be discussed later. The next 3 topics will discuss the DOL contract payoff, its pricing, and why possibly the fx futures and fx spot prices might diverge. The last topic discusses the convexity correction that arises between fx forward and fx futures prices for long dated maturity contracts.

5.2.1 Contract details

The BVMF contract code for $\frac{BRL}{USD}$ FX Futures contract is DOL. The code for a single maturity contract is completed by adding the usual 3 characters that identifies its month and year. As an example, DOLF15 is the $\frac{BRL}{USD}$ FX Future contract with maturity month of January and year 2015. The exact maturity date is always the first business day of the maturity month in a *BMF* calendar, which is 2-Jan-2015 in the DOLF15 example. Each contract has a FX fixing date one business day in a *CDI* calendar prior to its maturity date. Its fixing source will be the PTAX FX rate published by Brazil Central bank. One contract is worth 50,000 *USD* based on a combination of a multiplier variable in its payoff set to 50 and its quoting convention that trades the $\frac{BRL}{USD}$ FX Futures value in $\frac{BRL}{1{,}000 \cdot USD}$ units. This contract settles daily in cash based on BVMF margin cashflow values. BVMF also requires its counterparty to post margin to cover possible unexpected daily cashflow payments.

5.2.2 Liquidity

The liquidity for a DOL contract is usually concentrated in the nearest maturity contract. Around the middle of the month, liquidity of DR1 contracts (that will be described below) increases and enables market participants to roll their positions from the nearest maturity contract to the one in the following month. The only case where liquidity of a DOL contract moves to the second nearest maturity contract is at fx fixing date which is one business day prior to maturity date in a *BMF* calendar.

As an example let's assume that today is 04-Mar-2015. The nearest maturity DOL contract is the J15 one, which has as its maturity date 01-Apr-2015. Trading will be liquid on the DOLJ15 contract until 31-Mar-2015, which is DOLJ15 FX fixing date. Around 15-Mar-2015, the liquidity of the DR1 strategy will also increase. At 31-Mar-2015, the DOL contract with largest liquidity will be the May 2015 DOLK15 contract.

5.2.3 DR1 and the roll

The demand for DR1 contracts exist mostly because there are market participants wanting to roll the nearest maturity DOL contract into a DOL contract on the second nearest maturity. However, the DR1 strategy allows market participants to trade simultaneously any given pair of DOL contracts. The BVMF code is DR1 followed by 3 characters to represent the first DOL contract maturity and followed after by other 3 additional characters to identify the second DOL contract maturity. As an example, DR1F15J15 is a DR1 strategy that the first maturity contract is a DOLF15 and the second maturity contract is a DOLJ15.

If one is long Q number of DR1F15J15 contracts it means he's long Q contracts of DOLJ15 and short Q contracts of DOLF15. This strategy is quoted as the forward points differential between the first maturity DOL contract and the second one and the quotation is in $\frac{BRL}{1{,}000 \cdot USD}$ units, exactly like in DOL contracts. Let's assume that a market participant traded a DR1F15J15 with a price of P. The first maturity DOL contract price will be equal to the last traded price executed at the moment the trade is registered at the exchange. For now, it will be assumed this price to be equal to P_{Last}. The second maturity DOL contract price will be equal to $P_{Last} + P$, which represents the first maturity DOL contract price plus the DR1 traded forward points P.

5.2.4 Payoff of DOL contract

The margin cashflow for one $\frac{BRL}{USD}$ FX Future contract at BVMF on trading date t is given by:

$$MCF_t^T = M \cdot \left(CP_t^T - TP_t^T\right) \tag{106}$$

where

MCF_t^T: is the margin cashflow computed in *BRL* currency for date t for a $\frac{BRL}{USD}$ FX Future contract with maturity date T. Please bear in mind that the margin cashflow is computed at date t, but only paid the next business day in a *BMF* calendar.

CP_t^T: is the closing price for $\frac{BRL}{USD}$ FX Future contract with maturity date T, published by BVMF at t in $\frac{BRL}{1{,}000 \cdot USD}$ units. At the FX fixing date, $CP_{T-1}^T = PTAX_{T-1} \cdot 1{,}000$.

TP_t^T: is the traded price at date t for a $\frac{BRL}{USD}$ FX Future contract with maturity date T in $\frac{BRL}{1{,}000 \cdot USD}$ units.

M: is the multiplier, currently set to 50.

The next equation demonstrates how daily cashflows are computed on any other given non trading date t_N:

$$MCF_t^T = M \cdot \left(CP_{t_N}^T - CP_{t_{N-1*}}^T \right) \tag{107}$$

where,

$CP_{t_{N-1*}}^T$: is the t_{N-1*} closing price for a $\frac{BRL}{USD}$ FX Future contract with maturity date T, which is one business day previous to date t_N in a *BMF* calendar.

It's worth noting that the quoting convention of CP_t^T and TP_t^T in $\frac{BRL}{1{,}000 \cdot USD}$ units together with multiplier $M = 50$ effectively corresponds that one contract is worth 50,000 *USD* Notional. Therefore, the DOL contract could be also viewed as:

$$MCF_t^T = 50{,}000 \cdot \left(FXFUT_{t,T}^{ON} \left[\frac{BRL}{USD} \right] - FXFUT_{t-1*,T}^{ON} \left[\frac{BRL}{USD} \right] \right) \tag{108}$$

where,

$FXFUT_{t,T}^{ON}\left[\frac{BRL}{USD}\right]$: is the $\frac{BRL}{USD}$ FX Future price, seen at date t with maturity date at T. The superscript *ON* refers to onshore because there's also a CME FX Future contract that will be specified with a superscript *OFF*. We assume here also that the futures price $FXFUT_{t,T}^{ON}\left[\frac{BRL}{USD}\right]$ is not scaled by 1,000 as BVMF publishes it and its unit is $\frac{BRL}{USD}$.

5.2.5 Pricing a DOL contract based FRC, DI's, nearest maturity FXFUT and CASADO quotes

Section 6 will describe the FRC strategy and, a bit later, Section 5 will detail how the CASADO trade works. With those 2 missing ingredients we can proceed to price DOL contracts based on a model, either because they have a long maturity and are not liquid and their price should be coming from other instruments or simply because even for the liquid ones we could be willing to calculate its risk, which should be coming from a model anyway. Therefore we ask the reader to wait a bit until Section 6 to have the pricing model for DOL contracts derived.

5.2.6 Apples and oranges

One must always remember that DOL and Spot FX are not interchangeable. Figure 66 shows how in 2002 the typical sawtooth behavior of the Casado was disrupted by the demand for "real" USD to pay debts that were not being rolled because of the uncertainty brought by the perspective of the election of the opposition's candidate.

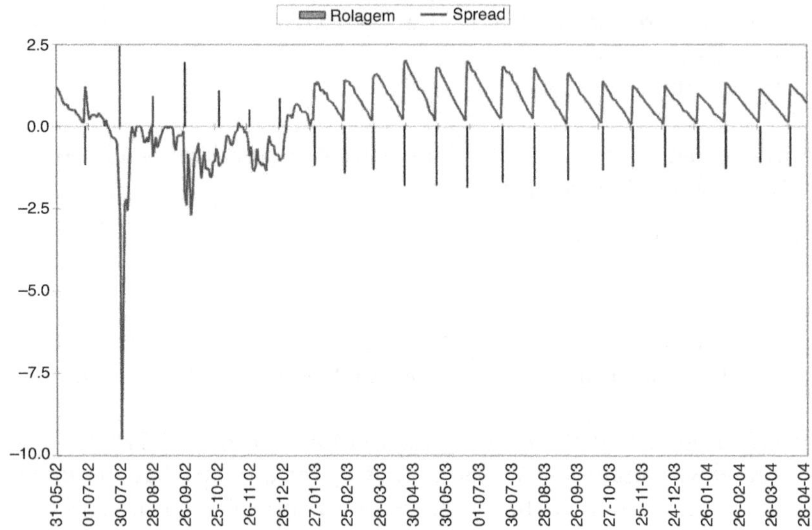

Figure 66 Behavior of the roll DR1 and casado (spread) from 2002 to 2004

One can see how the roll ("Rolagem" in the chart, shown as the bars marking the difference between the second future and the first future on the day before the last business day of each month) and the Casado ("Spread" in the chart, shown as the continuous line) inverted in July 2002 (values in %). This corresponds to a quite high Cupom Cambial.

But the DOL must settle at the PTAX. If most of the time the changes in the DOL are limited by the exchange, on the last 3 business days of the month it is free to pursue the spot price (as discussed before when describing the 1999 devaluation).

5.2.7 Convexity corrections

It's known that Futures and Forward prices may display a non negligible convexity correction for long dated maturity contracts. Since this is true for any Futures contract, the DOL contract certainly displays a convexity correction to a FX forward price for long dated maturity contracts.

The liquidity of DOL long dated maturity contracts is small but anyone interested in trading them should not overlook the convexity correction term. The reason for the convexity correction can be justified loosely speaking in terms of the replicating strategy of a long dated maturity DOL contract with a FX forward contract. The FX Forward contract discounts the expected payoff to compute its PV and the FX Future doesn't. Therefore, their FX Delta is not the same and different Notional amounts of both contracts have to be traded in order to be FX Delta neutral. However, this replication is not static and dynamic hedging should be conducted in order to hedge the portfolio containing the FX Future and its FX Forward hedge at all times. The dynamic hedging or FX Delta rebalancing is a function of the covariance of the *BRL* cdi onshore discount factor with the FX forward price. So for short dated maturity contracts, the *BRL* cdi discount factor volatility is small and the convexity correction is negligible. But not for long dated maturity contracts. This topic will be revisited later in this book, with a complete derivation of the convexity correction value.

5.3 Forward points strategies

In this subsection we will discuss the 2 forward points strategies. The first is called FRP which allows market participants to hedge the PTAX to FX Spot fixing risk at BVMF. The second is called CASADO and allows market participants to trade the forward points between the FX spot rate and most liquid FX Future DOL contract in BVMF.

5.3.1 FRP

Most of the FX linked trades in Brazil have the PTAX fx rate published by Brazil Central Bank as their fx fixing source. But, as we will demonstrate later in this book, pricing for any of those fx linked trades is usually done based on the current FX spot value. Because of this fact, at fixing date the market participant who holds a position in any one of those trades face a FX Fixing risk, as the contract will have its payoff based on PTAX value but pricing until its publication is done using the current fx spot rate.

The FRP contract is a strategy created by BVMF exactly to overcome the fx fixing risk on fixing date. This can be accomplished because the FRP strategy allows market participants to enter a DOL contract fx future price by the PTAX fx rate value multiplied by 1,000 plus a traded forward point value in $\frac{BRL}{1{,}000 \cdot USD}$ units. There are 2 possibilities to choose the PTAX rate date that will determine the fx future price to enter the DOL contract. FRP0 determines the FX future DOL contract traded price with trading date's t PTAX value by:

$$TP_t^T = PTAX_t \cdot 1{,}000 + FRP0_{Rate} \tag{109}$$

where,

TP_t^T: is the DOL contract traded price done at date t for maturity date T, derived from FRP0 formula above.

$PTAX_t$: is the PTAX fx rate published by Brazil Central Bank at trading date t.

$FRP0_{Rate}$: is the FRP0 traded quote, expressed in $\frac{BRL}{1{,}000 \cdot USD}$ units which is the same quoting convention for the DOL contract.

The FRP1 strategy is a bit different. It allows market participants to enter one business day after trading date t in a BMF calendar into a DOL contract with its traded price computed as $PTAX_{t+1^*}$ plus the traded forward points value $FRP1_{Rate}$. The formula for the DOL contract traded price would be given by:

$$TP^T_{t+1^*} = PTAX_{t+1^*} \cdot 1,000 + FRP1_{Rate} \tag{110}$$

where,

$TP^T_{t+1^*}$: is the DOL contract traded price, only computed at date $t+1_{BMF}$ for a maturity date T DOL contract, derived from FRP1 formula above.

$PTAX_{t+1^*}$: is the PTAX fx rate published by Brazil Central Bank one business day after trading date t in a BMF calendar.

$FRP1_{Rate}$: is the FRP1 traded quote, expressed in $\frac{BRL}{1,000 \cdot USD}$ units which is the same quoting convention for the DOL contract.

5.3.2 "Casado"

As discussed before, the Casado is a trade in which one counterparty sells DOL and buys USD through a FX Spot trade, with the other counterparty buys DOL (through a cross trade at BVMF) and sells USD through the same FX Spot trade. Typically the FX Spot will settle at the FX Clearing at BVMF.

There are two main differences between the Casado and the FRP. The first is that they (obviously) have different consequences, as the FRP is only a derivatives trade and the Casado is a delivery of USD against a derivative. The second is that the Casado's price will be relatively unchanged over the course of a normal day, but the FRP will change as it is anchored on the PTAX, not the Spot.

5.4 FX Future crosses

BVMF has a large list of FX Future contracts that are considered fx crosses. The list includes $\frac{BRL}{AUD}$, $\frac{BRL}{CAD}$, $\frac{BRL}{CHF}$, $\frac{BRL}{JPY}$, $\frac{BRL}{GBP}$, $\frac{BRL}{NZD}$, $\frac{BRL}{CNY}$, $\frac{BRL}{TRY}$, $\frac{BRL}{CLP}$, $\frac{BRL}{MXN}$, $\frac{BRL}{EUR}$ and $\frac{BRL}{ZAR}$. Assuming the contract's non BRL currency to be called CCY, all of those contracts construct the $\frac{BRL}{CCY}$ FX Fixing for the last margin cashflow payment as a function of 2 fx fixings. One is the PTAX FX fixing that covers the $\frac{BRL}{USD}$ piece of the cross. The other is a WMR fx rate fixing of $\frac{CCY}{USD}$ or $\frac{USD}{CCY}$, depending on the quoting convention for the currency pair composed of USD and CCY. In case the WMR fx fixing is published in $\frac{USD}{CCY}$ units, then the $\frac{BRL}{CCY}$ cross fx fixing is constructed as a multiplication of PTAX and $\frac{USD}{CCY}$ WMR fx fixing. In case the WMR is published as $\frac{CCY}{USD}$ units, then the $\frac{BRL}{CCY}$ cross fx fixing is constructed as a division of PTAX and $\frac{USD}{CCY}$ WMR fx fixing. The exception to this rule is the $\frac{USD}{EUR}$ fx fixing source for $\frac{BRL}{EUR}$ FX Futures contracts which is published by European Central Bank (ECB) and not WMR.

Both fx fixing dates are the same. It's one day prior to the contract's maturity date in a CDI calendar. At that day always the PTAX fx fixing will be available, but the WMR might not be. If the WMR fixing is not available, then it looks for the previous day where WMR fx fixing was available for currency pair $\frac{CCY}{USD}$ and that is not a holiday in CDI calendar as well.

Regarding contract size, it varies upon currency pair. For a GBP contract, one contract is worth 35,000 *GBP* Notional. For a CHF contract, one contract is worth 50,000 *CHF* Notional and for a *JPY* contract, one contract is worth 5,000,000 *JPY* Notional. For all currency pair contracts listed above the maturity date is the first business day of the contract month in a *BMF* calendar and margin cashflows computed by the exchange are paid the next business day in a *BMF* calendar.

5.4.1 Payoff

The margin cashflow for any $\frac{BRL}{CCY}$ FX Future cross contract at BVMF on trading date t is given by:

$$MCF_t^T = M \cdot \left(CP_t^T - TP_t^T\right) \tag{111}$$

where

MCF_t^T: is the margin cashflow computed in *BRL* currency for date t for a $\frac{BRL}{CCY}$ FX Future cross contract with maturity date T.

CP_t^T: is the closing price for $\frac{BRL}{CCY}$ FX Future cross contract with maturity date T, published by BVMF at t in $\frac{BRL}{1{,}000 \cdot CCY}$ units. The exception is the $\frac{BRL}{JPY}$ FX Future cross contract that's quoted in $\frac{BRL}{100{,}000 \cdot JPY}$. At the FX fixing date $T-1$, $CP_{T-1}^T = PTAX_{T-1} \cdot \frac{CCY}{USD} \cdot 1{,}000$ or $CP_{T-1}^T = PTAX_{T-1} \cdot \frac{USD}{CCY} \cdot 1{,}000$, depending on the quoting convention of the currency pair that involves *USD* and *CCY* currencies. The exception is again the $\frac{BRL}{JPY}$ FX Future cross contract that computes its closing price at FX Fixing date $T-1$ by $CP_{T-1}^T = PTAX_{T-1} \cdot \frac{CCY}{USD} \cdot 100{,}000$.

TP_t^T: is the traded price at date t for a $\frac{BRL}{CCY}$ FX Future cross contract with maturity date T in $\frac{BRL}{1{,}000 \cdot CCY}$ units, except the $\frac{BRL}{JPY}$ cross contract.

M: is the multiplier, which is different for most of the contracts.

The next equation demonstrates how daily cashflows are computed on any other given non trading date t_N:

$$MCF_t^T = M \cdot \left(CP_{t_N}^T - CP_{t_{N-1*}}^T\right) \tag{112}$$

where,

$CP_{t_{N-1*}}^T$: is the t_{N-1*} date closing price for a $\frac{BRL}{CCY}$ FX Future cross contract with maturity date T, which is one business day previous to date t_N in a *BMF* calendar.

5.4.2 Pricing and hedging

Assume that we want to price a fx future cross contract for a given currency *CCY*. In the same way as it was mentioned in the DOL contract subsection, any futures contract price display convexity corrections to the forward price. In the case of FX Future Cross contracts at BVMF it's no different and its price should display convexity corrections to FX forward cross values for long dated maturity contracts. But here we focus on short dated fx futures crosses contracts with negligible convexity corrections to a FX FWD price for same maturity. Given that assumption and assuming that a futures contract is expected to have no expected gain or loss, since it doesn't cost anything to enter the contract, yields the following risk neutral expected futures price:

$$\mathbb{E}^{\mathbb{Q}^*}\left[MCF_t^T|\mathcal{F}_t\right]=\mathbb{E}^{\mathbb{Q}^*}\left[M\cdot\left(CP_t^T-TP_t^T\right)|\mathcal{F}_t\right]=0 \tag{113}$$

Since TP_t^T is the traded futures price and it's a constant it yields:

$$\mathbb{E}^{\mathbb{Q}^*}\left[CP_t^T|\mathcal{F}_t\right]=TP_t^T \tag{114}$$

given the filtration up to trading time t, earlier than closing time t.

Now assuming that the expected closing futures price CP_t^T at end of day is modeled by a forward price

$$FXFWD_{t,T-1_{FX1}}^{ON}\left[\frac{BRL}{USD}\right]\cdot FXFWD_{t,T-1_{FX2}}^{OFF}\left[\frac{USD}{CCY}\right]=CP_t^T \tag{115}$$

where,

$FX1$: settlement rule applied for $\frac{BRL}{USD}$ currency pair.

$FX2$: settlement rule applied for a generic $\frac{USD}{CCY}$ currency pair.

$FXFWD_{t,T-1_{FX1}}^{ON}[\frac{BRL}{USD}]$: is the FX FWD onshore for currency pair $\frac{BRL}{USD}$ seen at date t with FX Fixing date at $T-1$ and settlement date at $T-1_{FX1}$.

$FXFWD_{t,T-1_{FX2}}^{OFF}[\frac{USD}{CCY}]$: is the FX FWD offshore for currency pair $\frac{USD}{CCY}$ seen at date t with FX Fixing date at $T-1$ and settlement date at $T-1_{FX2}$.

(115) states that the trade price you should enter the CCY fx future cross contract is given by the product of the onshore $\frac{BRL}{USD}$ fx forward by the offshore $\frac{USD}{CCY}$ fx forward. Many market participants in Brazil like to adopt a different route. They create a CCY onshore curve calibrated to the following equation:

$$FXFWD_{t,T-1_{FX1}}^{ON}\left[\frac{BRL}{USD}\right]\cdot FXFWD_{t,T-1_{FX2}}^{OFF}\left[\frac{USD}{CCY}\right]=FXFWD_{t,T-1_{FX1}}^{ON}\left[\frac{BRL}{CCY}\right] \tag{116}$$

The left hand side of (116) has a model given by the product of 2 fx forward prices and will yield 2 FX Risks (for currency pair $\frac{BRL}{USD}$ and $\frac{USD}{CCY}$) and 4 yield curve risks (CDI curve, cupom, USD libor and ccy libor). But all 4 yield curve risks are computed on liquid curves and are hedgeable. The following equation describes better the yield curve risk management when breaking down the fx forwards as a fx spot times the ratio of 2 discount factors given by the no arbitrage argument.

$$\frac{BRL}{USD}[t]\cdot\frac{P_{t_{FX1},T-1_{FX1}}^{USB}}{P_{t_{FX1},T-1_{FX1}}^{CDI}}\cdot\frac{USD}{CCY}[t]\cdot\frac{P_{t_{FX2},T-1_{FX2}}^{CCY}}{P_{t_{FX2},T-1_{FX2}}^{USD}}=\frac{BRL}{CCY}[t]\cdot\frac{P_{t_{FX1},T-1_{FX1}}^{CCY}}{P_{t_{FX1},T-1_{FX1}}^{CDI}} \tag{117}$$

where,
$\frac{CCY1}{CCY2}[t]$: is the fx spot rate for currency pair $\frac{CCY1}{CCY2}$ seen at date t.
USB: is the cupom cambial curve that will be calibrated in Section 6.

On the other hand, the right hand side of (117) has a model that will yield 1 FX risk for currency pair $\frac{BRL}{CCY}$ directly. But it will yield 2 yield curve risks. One for CDI curve which is liquid, but the other for a non hedgeable CCY onshore curve calibrated based on (117). A concrete example is when you assume that $CCY = EUR$, in that case (117) is changed to

$$\frac{BRL}{USD}[t] \cdot \frac{P^{USB}_{t_{FX1},T-1_{FX1}}}{P^{CDI}_{t_{FX1},T-1_{FX1}}} \cdot \frac{USD}{EUR}[t] \cdot \frac{P^{EUR}_{t_{FX2},T-1_{FX2}}}{P^{USD}_{t_{FX2},T-1_{FX2}}} = \frac{BRL}{EUR}[t] \cdot \frac{P^{EUB}_{t_{FX1},T-1_{FX1}}}{P^{CDI}_{t_{FX1},T-1_{FX1}}} \tag{118}$$

In the particular EUR FX Future case, it's quite common to see market participants creating an onshore EUR curve (EUB) calibrated to (118) which is unhedgeable, instead of using a model that breaks down the yield curve risk into the more liquid 4 yield curves (cdi curve, cupom curve, USD libor curve and EUR libor curve) which yields in better risk management.

5.4.3 Convexity corrections

In the same way as it was mentioned in the DOL contract subsection, any futures contract price display convexity corrections to the forward price. In the case of FX Future Cross contracts at BVMF it's no different and its price should display convexity corrections to FX forward cross values for long dated maturity contracts.

But there's another convexity correction term for FX Futures cross contracts at BVMF. It's based on the fact that PTAX is an onshore fx fixing but the WMR (or ECB for the EUR contract case) is an offshore fx fixing. So the replicating strategy for a FX Future cross contract at BVMF involves trading for long dated maturity contracts a $\frac{BRL}{USD}$ FX Forward and a $\frac{USD}{CCY}$ FX Forward. The first FX Forward hedge has to be executed onshore (and hedge is usually done in DOL contract) while the second offshore in order to mitigate the fx fixing source risk. Because the second hedge is done offshore and it's a FX Forward contract, it will be discounted by an offshore discount factor. But the FX Future Cross contract doesn't discount the payoff because it pays daily. One could see the difference of hedging being discounted offshore to FX Future Cross trade not being discounted in a 2 step process. The difference of the hedge being discounted offshore to an equivalent FX Forward Cross contract discounted onshore, and this same contract convexity to FX Futures that are not discounted at all and was already discussed. Here we focus more on the first convexity term, that could be viewed as an additional convexity on top of the regular Futures X Forward convexity just because one FX Fixing is WMR and requires offshore hedging.

6
And the Even More Interesting USD Onshore Interest Rates ...

6.1 3 months in the life of a FX Swap

It should be similar to the previous section on the life of an IR Swap (3.1), but now there's an additional risk factor (FX).

6.2 3 months in the life of a DDI Future

It should be similar to the previous section on the life of a DI Future (3.2), but now there's an additional risk factor (FX).

6.3 Explaining it all

USD onshore interest rate products are sometimes viewed as a big question mark by financial market newcomers. Even people with some experience sometimes struggle to fully understand the calibration of the USD onshore interest rate curve. What instruments are liquid on the short end and on the long end? What's the difference of a clean and dirty USD onshore interest rate and what drives it? Should we adopt T+0 or T+2 as the spot date for our USD onshore interest rate curve? One of the biggest motivations of this book is to try to make the comprehension of this topic more straightforward.

The USD onshore interest rate curve is called inside Brazil the "cupom cambial" curve. We will call it simply the cupom curve throughout this book to shorten the notation.

The basic building block for its construction are the FRA DE CUPOM Futures. They have decent liquidity, mostly for contracts with maturity month being January. In the short end, usually until the first FX Future available contract, the cupom curve is implied from FX Futures, *Casado* and the BRL onshore interest rate curve. Below is a summary of the 3 USD onshore interest rate contracts that are exchange traded and have been traded for the last 5 years:

- DDI Futures -> As a FRA de CUPOM future contract is in reality one short and long position in a DDI Future contract, it can be viewed as the most important contract for cupom curve construction. The only issue is that the DDI Future when traded as a single future, and not part of the FRA de CUPOM strategy, has very low liquidity. This happens mostly because it's referenced on past PTAX values for cashflow computation, and is thus viewed as an instrument that trades a "dirty" cupom rate. This particular fact will be explained in the DDI pricing subsection. The BVMF code for those contracts is DDI followed by the month and year code. Figure 67 displays open interest for DDI contracts on 19th of May 2014.
- SCC Futures -> this was the contract used by Brazil Central Bank to intervene in the fx derivatives market until 27-Mar-2013. It's payoff is very similar to the one in DDI Futures contract, except for an O/N extra carry of the computed daily margin that will be explained in more detail later in its pricing subsection. Its BVMF code is DCO followed by the previously explained month and year code.
- SCS Futures -> Very similar to the SCC contract, but with daily cash flows computed based on Selic rate instead of CDI. Its BVMF code is SCS followed by the previously explained month and year code. The recent demand on this contract was mostly driven by Brazil Central Bank, who chose this contract as the recent mechanism, more precisely after 31-May-2013 until the time this book was written, to try to keep the $\frac{BRL}{USD}$ fx spot rate within the range that the institution thought was good for the country.

6.4 The DDI Futures (DDI) -> Why they were designed this way?

DDI stands for Dollar DI. It's a contract with a closing price always worth 100,000 at maturity date T. But since there's a multiplier of 0.5 points per contract, the DDI contract is viewed currently as a contract where its closing price will be 50,000 USD at maturity considering the multiplier. This matches the USD notional amount per contract of a $\frac{BRL}{USD}$ FX Futures contract, which is also set to 50,000 USD considering its quoting convention and multiplier. In both cases the change was introduced after the 1999 devaluation.

It's traded in a similar way as the DI1 Futures, based on a DDI rate $R^C_{t,T}$, that later is converted to a traded price TP^T_t by exchange as below:

$$TP^T_t = \frac{100,000}{\left(1 + R^C_{t,T} \cdot \tau^{Act360}_{t,T}\right)} \tag{119}$$

where,

$R^C_{t,T}$: is the DDI traded linear rate expressed in Act360 DCB. The superscript C stands for cupom cambial.

Commodity	Contract Months	Open Interest	Var.
DDI			
	M14	464,298	7,544
	N14	393,304	17,900
	Q14	166,380	2,330
	U14	107,150	1,370
	V14	278,831	300
	F15	444,480	4,760
	J15	194,040	-100
	N15	69,479	400
	V15	61,898	1,500
	F16	133,086	-4,500
	J16	63,054	1,300
	N16	43,259	340
	V16	28,270	440
	F17	70,480	560
	J17	19,710	0
	N17	22,017	980
	V17	26,997	0
	F18	48,582	-100
	J18	15,088	-200
	N18	14,287	-200
	V18	31,710	200
	F19	25,015	0
	J19	8,925	0
	N19	8,575	0
	V19	13,705	-100
	F20	56,466	0
	N20	9,960	0
	F21	53,295	0
	N21	510	0
	F22	37,470	0
	F23	18,740	0
	F24	20,070	0
	F25	3,600	0
	F26	10	0
Total		2,952,741	34,724

Figure 67 DDI Futures contracts open interest on 19 May 2014

$\tau_{t,T}^{Act360} = \frac{(T-t)}{360}$: is the day count fraction in Act360 DCB between trading date t and DDI contract maturity date T.

Similarly to DI1 contracts, long positions in rate are converted to short positions in DDI price by the exchange, because the market convention is to quote DDI contract in a rate perspective.

The DDI contract's margin cashflow computation formula differs slightly from (19), and is displayed below for one contract on trading date t:

$$MCF_t^T = \left(CP_t^T - TP_t^T\right) \cdot PTAX_{t-1} \cdot M \tag{120}$$

And for any given non trading date t_N:

$$MCF_{t_N}^T = \left(CP_{t_N}^T - OP_{t_N}^T\right) \cdot PTAX_{t_N-1} \cdot M \tag{121}$$

where, $MCF_{t_N}^T$, $CP_{t_N}^T$ and $OP_{t_N}^T$ were previously described in the DI1 Futures subsection and play the same role for the DDI contract. The other 2 variables are defined as:

$PTAX_{t-1}$: the PTAX FX rate published at $t-1$, i.e., moving one day backwards in a CDI calendar from t. PTAX FX rate is defined in BVMF's contracts as:

"The exchange rate variation, measured by the exchange rate of Brazilian Reals (R$) per U.S. Dollar for cash delivery, traded in the foreign exchange market, pursuant to the provisions of Resolution No. 3265/2005 of the National Monetary Council (CMN), calculated and published by the Central Bank of Brazil (BACEN) through SISBACEN, transaction PTAX800, option "5," closing offered quotation, for settlement in two days, utilizing the maximum of six decimal places, also published by BACEN with the denomination "closing PTAX," pursuant to Communication 10742, of February 17, 2003."

M: points per contract multiplier currently defined as 0.5 for DDI contracts.

There are 2 major differences from formula (121) and (19). Inside Brazil, all bank accounts can only carry BRL. Thus, there was a need in (121) to convert the difference of closing price and opening price, which is in USD, for an USD interest rate denominated contract like DDI, to BRL units. This is done by the multiplication of the difference of closing and opening prices by $PTAX_{t-1}$. The reader may be asking himself why to use the PTAX value published from the previous day in a CDI calendar. Why not use the one published at the same computation date t?

When the contract was created a long time ago, the PTAX was published after the $\frac{BRL}{USD}$ fx spot market was closed around 5:30 São Paulo time. So the exchange didn't use the PTAX from the same day, since this procedure would require them to only start their end of day marking and cashflow computation process when

PTAX was published. In fact, it makes the contract easier to trade, since knowing the initial FX rate enables you to trade only the USD-linked interest rate.

This particular point will be revisited later in the book, where new simpler payoffs will be suggested by the authors with the intention to bring more foreign investors to the USD onshore interest rate market. Currently, most of FRA de CUPOM liquidity is driven by a daily call that happens at 4:00 pm São Paulo time. Away from this call hours, it has unfortunately very little liquidity.

Another key difference from DI1 contracts to DDI contracts is the conversion from $CP^T_{t-1^*}$ to OP^T_t. In DI1 contracts, $CP^T_{t-1^*}$ is accrued one business day forward in a BMF calendar using the CDI Fixings, which is one of the 2 choices we have available in Brazil for O/N BRL interest rate. But there are no O/N USD interest rate fixings available to do the same sort of accrual for the DDI contracts. To circumvent this issue, the exchange proposed the following formula to convert $CP^T_{t-1^*}$ to OP^T_t:

$$OP^T_t = CP^T_{t-1^*} \cdot \frac{\prod_{T_i=t-1^*}^{t} \left[1+CDI_{T_i}\right]^{\frac{1}{252}}}{\frac{PTAX_{t-1}}{PTAX_{t-1}(t-1^*)}} \qquad (122)$$

where,

$PTAX_{t-1}$: is obtained by looking at the PTAX FX Fixing published one business day previous to t in a CDI calendar.

$PTAX_{t-1}(t-1^*)$: is obtained in a 2 step process. First it goes one business day backward in a BMF calendar as proposed in the outer parenthesis. This is the step1 date. Then it looks for the PTAX FX Fixing published one previous day in a CDI calendar from the step1 date. This 2 step process is not clear in BMF documentation inside the contract termsheet, available at the BVMF website. However, after some telephone calls and e-mails exchanged with the team from the exchange, it was found that rule (122) works to convert closing to opening prices for any given date and that follows the procedure currently executed by the exchange in dates where there's a BMF holiday.

In a particular case, if you have a regular day that doesn't have any holidays adjacent to t, which is the cashflow computation date, then (122) may be written with a lighter notation as:

$$OP^T_t = CP^T_{t-1} \cdot \frac{\left[1+CDI_{t-1}\right]^{\frac{1}{252}}}{\frac{PTAX_{t-1}}{PTAX_{t-2}}} \qquad (123)$$

In the authors opinion, the rationale used by the exchange for the above closing to opening price formula was to expect loosely speaking the following:

$$\mathbb{E}\left[\frac{PTAX_{t-1}}{PTAX_{t-2}} | \mathcal{F}_{t-2}\right] = \frac{\left[1+CDI_{t-1}\right]^{\frac{1}{252}}}{\left[1+O/N^{USD}_{t-1} \cdot \frac{1}{252}\right]} \qquad (124)$$

where,

O/N_{t-1}^{USD}: is the implied O/N USD onshore interest rate fixing based on (123), fictitiously published at date $t-1$.

$\mathbb{E}$: is a loosely speaking expectation, without any formal mention to a probability measure.

By plugging (124) into (123) would yield that:

$$OP_t^T = CP_{t-1}^T \cdot \left[1 + O/N_{t-1}^{USD} \cdot \frac{1}{252}\right] \tag{125}$$

By looking at (125), the authors believe that BVMF would have accomplished to create a synthetic O/N USD onshore interest rate fixing implied in the term $\frac{[1+CDI_{t-1}]^{\frac{1}{252}}}{\frac{PTAX_{t-1}}{PTAX_{t-2}}}$. The key assumption used though is if indeed (124) is valid. The answer is no as the expectation of $\frac{PTAX_{t-2}}{PTAX_{t-1}}$ involves in reality a cash and carry strategy from fx spot dates. Considering no holidays to ease the notation, let's assume that the fx spot date from $t-2$ falls on t and for $t-1$ falls on $t+1$. With this assumption the expected value of the ratio $\frac{PTAX_{t-1}}{PTAX_{t-2}}$, could be formulated as:

$$\mathbb{E}\left[\frac{PTAX_{t-1}}{PTAX_{t-2}} | \mathcal{F}_{t-2}\right] = \frac{[1+CDI_t]^{\frac{1}{252}}}{\left[1+O/N_t^{USD} \cdot \frac{1}{252}\right]} \tag{126}$$

Please note that under the no holidays assumption, CDI and O/N^{USD} dates obtained from the cash and carry strategy would be for date t. However, $t-1$ was the date required to cancel the CDI_{t-1} in the numerator of (124) to just yield the expected carry of previous closing price CP_{t-1}^T based on O/N_{t-1}^{USD} as proposed in (125).

This mismatch of CDI dates will be revisited later in this book and its effect in the cupom curve construction will be demonstrated.

6.5 The mathematical derivation of a DDI contract price

This subsection relies on the concepts of conditional expectations, probability measures and filtrations. We refer the reader who is not familiar with these stochastic calculus concepts to (Shreve, 2010) for a recap. Readers who are not interested might skip directly to the end of this subsection where the key results are discussed.

Similarly to the DI1 contracts, there's a boundary condition at maturity date T that forces the closing price at that date to be 100,000.

$$FUT_{DDI}(T,T) = 100,000 \tag{127}$$

where,

$FUT_{DDI}(t,T)$ is the DDI Future closing price seen at date t for maturity date T.

$FUT_{DDI}(T,T)$ is the DDI Future closing price seen at maturity date T, for a contract with maturity date on same date T.

As the DDI is a future contract, it is expected at date $T-1^*$, which represents one business day backwards in a BMF calendar, that the last margin cashflow computed at date T to be equal to 0 in a risk neutral world. Also, this cashflow which is computed at time T , will only be paid at $T+1^*$, which is one business day forward in a BMF calendar. Combining (121), (122) and (127) and the statement above allows us to write the following equation:

$$\beta_{T-1^*}\mathbb{E}^{\mathbb{Q}^*}\left[\left(FUT_{DDI}(T,T)-\frac{FUT_{DDI}(T-1^*,T)}{\frac{\frac{PTAX_{T-1}}{PTAX_{T-1(T-1^*)}}}{\prod_{T_i=T-1^*}^{T}\left[1+CDI_{T_i}\right]^{\frac{1}{252}}}}\right)\cdot\frac{PTAX_{T-1}\cdot M}{\beta_{T+1^*}}|\mathcal{F}_{T-1^*}\right]=0 \tag{128}$$

All terms above have been previously defined in this book. Using (127) into (128), and noticing that the term $PTAX_{T-1}\cdot M$ is non zero because both $PTAX_{T-1}$ and M are positive quantities, so that only the term inside parenthesis in the numerator must be zero to hold (128) true yields:

$$\mathbb{E}^{\mathbb{Q}^*}\left[100{,}000\cdot\frac{\beta_{T-1^*}}{\beta_{T+1^*}}|\mathcal{F}_{T-1^*}\right]$$
$$=\mathbb{E}^{\mathbb{Q}^*}\left[FUT_{DDI}(T-1^*,T)\cdot\frac{\prod_{T_i=T-1^*}^{T}\left[1+CDI_{T_i}\right]^{\frac{1}{252}}}{\frac{PTAX_{T-1}}{PTAX_{T-1(T-1^*)}}}\cdot\frac{\beta_{T-1^*}}{\beta_{T+1^*}}|\mathcal{F}_{T-1^*}\right] \tag{129}$$

Here again we will make the assumption that $\prod_{T_i=T-1^*}^{T}\left[1+CDI_{T_i}\right]^{\frac{1}{252}}$ is always F_{T-1^*}measurable, by assuming the CDI published in a BMF holiday equal to its previous published value. With this new assumption (129) can be arranged as:

$$100{,}000\cdot\mathbb{E}^{\mathbb{Q}^*}\left[\frac{\beta_{T-1^*}}{\beta_{T+1^*}}|\mathcal{F}_{T-1^*}\right]$$
$$=FUT_{DDI}(T-1^*,T)\cdot\frac{\prod_{T_i=T-1^*}^{T}\left[1+CDI_{T_i}\right]^{\frac{1}{252}}}{\frac{PTAX_{T-1}}{PTAX_{T-1(T-1^*)}}}\cdot\mathbb{E}^{\mathbb{Q}^*}\left[\frac{\beta_{T-1^*}}{\beta_{T+1^*}}|\mathcal{F}_{T-1^*}\right] \tag{130}$$

The equation above may be rewritten as:

$$FUT_{DDI}(T-1^*,T) = \frac{100{,}000}{\frac{\prod_{T_i=T-1^*}^{T}\left[1+CDI_{T_i}\right]^{\frac{1}{252}}}{\frac{PTAX_{T-1}}{PTAX_{T-1}(T-1^*)}}} \tag{131}$$

Going one business backward in a BMF calendar for the previous cashflow, we may write that:

$$\beta_{T-2^*} \cdot \mathbb{E}^{\mathbb{Q}^*}\left[\frac{FUT_{DDI}(T-1^*,T) - FUT_{DDI}(T-2^*,T) \cdot \frac{\prod_{T_i=T-2^*}^{T-1^*}\left[1+CDI_{T_i}\right]^{\frac{1}{252}}}{\frac{PTAX_{T-1}(T-1^*)}{PTAX_{T-1}(T-2^*)}}}{\beta_T} \Big| \mathcal{F}_{T-2^*}\right]$$

$$= 0 \tag{132}$$

Combining (131) and (132) and using the assumptions that led us into (131) again yields:

$$FUT_{DDI}(T-2^*,T) = \mathbb{E}^{\mathbb{Q}^*}\left[\frac{FUT_{DDI}(T-1^*,T)}{\frac{\prod_{T_i=T-2^*}^{T-1^*}\left[1+CDI_{T_i}\right]^{\frac{1}{252}}}{\frac{PTAX_{T-1}(T-1^*)}{PTAX_{T-1}(T-2^*)}}} \Big| \mathcal{F}_{T-2^*}\right] \tag{133}$$

Rearranging a bit the above equation yields:

$$FUT_{DDI}(T-2^*,T) = \mathbb{E}^{\mathbb{Q}^*}\left[\frac{PTAX_{T-1}}{PTAX_{T-1}(T-2^*)} \cdot \frac{100{,}000}{\prod_{T_i=T-2^*}^{T}\left[1+CDI_{T_i}\right]^{\frac{1}{252}}} \Big| \mathcal{F}_{T-2^*}\right] \tag{134}$$

Repeating this procedure iteratively until pricing time t (current time) yields:

$$FUT_{DDI}(t,T) = \mathbb{E}^{\mathbb{Q}^*}\left[\frac{PTAX_{T-1}}{PTAX_{t-1}} \cdot \frac{100{,}000}{\prod_{T_i=t}^{T}\left[1+CDI_{T_i}\right]^{\frac{1}{252}}} \Big| \mathcal{F}_t\right] \tag{135}$$

6.5.1 DDI Future pricing

By looking at (135), the first thing that can be noticed is that we can use the Radon-Nikodym derivative, previously presented in (35), to change the expectation to the probability measure $\mathbb{Q}^{T}_{\mathrm{CDI}}$, which has as its numéraire $P^{CDI}_{t,T}$. This change of probability measure will cancel the term $\prod_{T_i=t}^{T}[1+CDI_{T_i}]^{\frac{1}{252}}$ inside the expectation and the DDI futures price $FUT_{DDI}(t,T)$ can be rewritten as:

$$FUT_{DDI}(t,T) = \mathbb{E}^{\mathbb{Q}^{T}_{CDI}}\left[\frac{PTAX_{T-1}}{PTAX_{t-1}} \cdot \frac{100{,}000}{\prod_{T_i=t}^{T}[1+CDI_{T_i}]^{\frac{1}{252}}} \cdot \frac{d\mathbb{Q}^*}{d\mathbb{Q}_{CDI}}^{T}|_T|\mathcal{F}_t\right] \tag{136}$$

Plugging (35) into (136) yields:

$$FUT_{DDI}(t,T) = \frac{100{,}000 \cdot \mathrm{P}^{CDI}_{t,T}}{\mathrm{PTAX}_{t-1}} \cdot \mathbb{E}^{\mathbb{Q}^{T}_{CDI}}[PTAX_{T-1}|\mathcal{F}_t] \tag{137}$$

Now the only remaining question is how to calculate $\mathbb{E}^{\mathbb{Q}^{T}_{CDI}}[PTAX_{T-1}|\mathcal{F}_t]$. This answer can be partially answered intuitively. The cash and carry argument would suggest that the expected value of $PTAX_{T-1}$ is equal to today's date t $\frac{BRL}{USD}$ onshore fx forward rate for a contract that has $PTAX_{T-1}$ as the FX Fixing source and settlement date at $T-1_{FX}$. We will call this variable $FXFWD^{ON}_{t,T-1_{FX}}[\frac{BRL}{USD}]$, where the superscript ON designates it's an onshore fx forward value, and the subscript $t, T-1_{FX}$ represents that it's a fx forward with settlement at date $T-1_{FX}$, seen at date t.

But more precisely, under which probability measure is the cash and carry argument valid?

To answer this question we require the knowledge of a stochastic calculus theorem. This theorem is fully explained in stochastic calculus books and the interested reader may refer to Section 9.2, theorem 9.2.2 of (Shreve, 2010) for a complete derivation. Basically, this theorem states that given an asset S_t and a numéraire N_t, the asset discounted by this numéraire $\frac{S_t}{N_t}$ is a martingale under the probability measure N associated with numéraire N_t. For the readers unfamiliar with some stochastic calculus definitions, a martingale asset would have as its expected value in a future time its current value. Mathematically:

$$\mathbb{E}^{N}\left[\frac{S_T}{N_T}|\mathcal{F}_t\right] = \frac{S_t}{N_t} \tag{138}$$

Now going back to our initial question. We are interested in calculating $\mathbb{E}^{\mathbb{Q}^{T}_{CDI}}[PTAX_{T-1}|\mathcal{F}_t]$. The term $PTAX_{T-1}$ can be replaced by $FXFWD^{ON}_{T-1,T-1_{FX}}$, which is the value of a fx forward rate seen at date $T-1$ with settlement date $T-1_{FX}$, because a fx forward rate collapses to its fx fixing value at fixing date. Thus we need to calculate $\mathbb{E}^{\mathbb{Q}^{T}_{CDI}}\left[FXFWD^{ON}_{T-1,T-1_{FX}}\left[\frac{BRL}{USD}\right]|\mathcal{F}_t\right]$.

On the other hand, the cash and carry argument using fx settlement rules tells us that that:

$$FXFWD^{ON}_{t,T-1_{FX}}\left[\frac{BRL}{USD}\right] = \frac{BRL}{USD}[t] \cdot \frac{P^{USB}_{t,t_{FX},T-1_{FX}}}{P^{CDI}_{t,t_{FX},T-1_{FX}}} \tag{139}$$

where,
$\frac{BRL}{USD}[t]$: is the $\frac{BRL}{USD}$ fx spot rate observed at date t.
$P^{USB}_{t,t_{FX},T-1_{FX}}$: is the USD onshore forward discount factor seen at today's date t and calculated from fx spot date t_{FX} to the fx spot date obtained from $T-1$, which is $T-1_{FX}$, also called the settlement date.

The USD onshore interest rate curve hasn't been constructed yet, but let's assume it's available so that we can express the $FUT_{DDI}(t,T)$ as a function of it. The code that has been chosen to specify the USD onshore interest rate curve is *USB*. US are the first 2 letters of *USD* and *B* would be the first letter of Brazil, to designate that the curve is onshore. This way we can differentiate the onshore USD interest rate curve labeled *USB*, from the USD offshore interest rate curve labeled *USD*.

By looking at (139), it can be seen that $FXFWD^{ON}_{t,T-1_{FX}}[\frac{BRL}{USD}]$ must be a martingale under the probability measure associated with $P^{CDI}_{t,t_{FX},T-1_{FX}}$ as its numéraire. This result can be verified given the knowledge of the previously described stochastic calculus theorem, as $P^{CDI}_{t,t_{FX},T-1_{FX}}$ plays the role of N_t and $\frac{BRL}{USD}[t]\cdot\frac{P^{USB}_{t,t_{FX},T-1_{FX}}}{P^{CDI}_{t,t_{FX},T-1_{FX}}}$, plays the role of $\frac{S_t}{N_t}$. By the martingale property then:

$$\mathbb{E}^{\mathbb{Q}^{T_{FX}}_{CDI}}\left[FXFWD^{ON}_{T-1,T-1_{FX}}[\frac{BRL}{USD}]|\mathcal{F}_t\right]$$

$$=FXFWD^{ON}_{t,T-1_{FX}}[\frac{BRL}{USD}]=\frac{BRL}{USD}[t]\cdot\frac{P^{USB}_{t,t_{FX},T-1_{FX}}}{P^{CDI}_{t,t_{FX},T-1_{FX}}} \tag{140}$$

where,
$\mathbb{E}^{\mathbb{Q}^{T_{FX}}_{CDI}}$: is the expectation under a probability measure $\mathbb{Q}^{T_{FX}}_{CDI}$, associated with $P^{CDI}_{t,t_{FX},T-1_{FX}}$ as its numéraire.

But we are interested in calculating on the other hand $\mathbb{E}^{\mathbb{Q}^{T}_{CDI}}[FXFWD^{ON}_{T-1,T-1_{FX}}[\frac{BRL}{USD}]|\mathcal{F}_t]$. How different can it be the 2 expectations, under $\mathbb{Q}^{T}_{CDI}$ and $\mathbb{Q}^{T_{FX}}_{CDI}$, given that the numéraires are respectively $P^{CDI}_{t,T}$ and $P^{CDI}_{t,t_{FX},T-1_{FX}}$ and its values are almost the same numerically? The correct mathematical answer is that a convexity correction should be performed to calculate $\mathbb{E}^{\mathbb{Q}^{T}_{CDI}}\left[FXFWD^{ON}_{T-1,T-1_{FX}}[\frac{BRL}{USD}]|\mathcal{F}_t\right]$, since $FXFWD^{ON}_{t,T-1_{FX}}[\frac{BRL}{USD}]$ is not a martingale under the probability measure $\mathbb{Q}^{T}_{CDI}$. However this convexity correction is negligible and considered to be 0, since it's a function of the discount factor volatility difference of $P^{CDI}_{t,t_{FX}}$ and $P^{CDI}_{T,T-1_{FX}}$, which is reasonably small and could be considered as 0. The proof is omitted here, but can be verified with a change of numéraire approach that can be studied also in chapter 9 of (Shreve, 2010). Using this last assumption, it will be considered that:

$$\mathbb{E}^{\mathbb{Q}^{T}_{CDI}}\left[FXFWD^{ON}_{T-1,T-1_{FX}}\left[\frac{BRL}{USD}\right]|\mathcal{F}_t\right]$$
$$= FXFWD^{ON}_{t,T-1_{FX}}\left[\frac{BRL}{USD}\right] = \frac{BRL}{USD}[t]\cdot\frac{P^{USB}_{t,t_{FX},T-1_{FX}}}{P^{CDI}_{t,t_{FX},T-1_{FX}}} \tag{141}$$

And then we can finally derive the DDI futures price $FUT_{DDI}(t,T)$ as:

$$FUT_{DDI}(t,T) = \frac{100{,}000\cdot \mathrm{P}^{\mathrm{CDI}}_{\mathrm{t,T}}}{\mathrm{PTAX}_{\mathrm{t-1}}}\cdot\frac{BRL}{USD}[t]\cdot\frac{P^{USB}_{t,t_{FX},T-1_{FX}}}{P^{CDI}_{t,t_{FX},T-1_{FX}}} \tag{142}$$

Rearranging a bit (142) to analyze the above equation in the next paragraph:

$$FUT_{DDI}(t,T) = 100{,}000\cdot P^{USB}_{t,t_{FX},T-1_{FX}}\cdot\frac{\frac{BRL}{USD}[t]}{\mathrm{PTAX}_{\mathrm{t-1}}}\cdot\frac{P^{CDI}_{t,t_{FX}}}{P^{CDI}_{t,T,T-1_{FX}}} \tag{143}$$

By observing (143), it can be seen that there's a correspondence between a DDI Future contract price $FUT_{DDI}(t,T)$ to today's date t forward discount factor in the USD onshore (USB) interest rate curve from date t_{fx} to date $T-1_{FX}$, namely $P^{USB}_{t,t_{FX},T-1_{FX}}$. However, to imply $P^{USB}_{t,t_{FX},T-1_{FX}}$ from $FUT_{DDI}(t,T)$, you also need the CDI curve to provide you the calculation for the term $\frac{P^{CDI}_{t,t_{FX}}}{P^{CDI}_{t,T,T-1_{FX}}}$. This term is generated exactly because of the CDI dates mismatch that we mentioned in the previous subsection that arose because of the cashflow computation formula proposed by BVMF.

But the most important term inside (143) is the ratio $\frac{\frac{BRL}{USD}[t]}{\mathrm{PTAX}_{\mathrm{t-1}}}$. Given that the current value of $\frac{BRL}{USD}[t]$ can be substantially different than yesterday's PTAX value $PTAX_{t-1}$, the DDI contract is quoted with what's called by market practitioners a "dirty" interest rate. This can be seen by looking at the following equation:

$$FUT_{DDI}(t,T) = \frac{100{,}000}{\left(1+R^{C}_{t,T}\cdot\tau^{Act360}_{t,T}\right)} \tag{144}$$

where,

$R^{C}_{t,T}$: is the DDI dirty rate calculated from date t to date T in Act360 DCB.

$\tau^{Act360}_{t,T}$: is the day count fraction in Act360 DCB from date t to date T.

On an extreme case, let's assume that $\frac{BRL}{USD}[t]$ is greater than $PTAX_{t-1}$ by 5%. Thus the ratio $\frac{\frac{BRL}{USD}[t]}{\mathrm{PTAX}_{\mathrm{t-1}}}$ is equal to 1.05. Considering a DDI contract that has a maturity date T close to today's date t, like for instance the first open contract available, we could as an approximation consider that $P^{USB}_{t,t_{FX},T-1_{FX}}$ to be equal to 1. Considering also $\frac{P^{CDI}_{t,t_{FX}}}{P^{CDI}_{t,T,T-1_{FX}}}$ to be equal to 1 would make the right-hand side of (143) greater than 100,000. The only way that we could make $FUT_{DDI}(t,T)$ greater than 100,000 by looking at (144) is if we consider the possibility of the traded DDI dirty rate $R^C_{t,T}$ to be negative. So in an extreme situation, the quoted DDI rate for short dated maturity contracts can even be negative and the cause of it is the term $\frac{\frac{BRL}{USD}[t]}{\mathrm{PTAX}_{t-1}}$.

Because of this specific feature, market participants usually avoid trading the DDI contract as a stand alone contract. To circumvent this issue, BVMF created another Future contract called FRA de CUPOM.

6.6 It takes two (DDI contracts) to (con)tango -> The FRA de CUPOM strategy (FRC)

To circumvent the problem that DDI Future contracts trade a "dirty" rate, BM&F has created the FRA de cupom contracts. Its contract code begins with FRC and is then followed by the usual letter and digits code that represents the month and year of the contract. Those contracts were specified in such a way that it enables the market participants to trade a USD onshore forward rate through a long position in a T_2 maturity date DDI contract together with a short position in a T_1 maturity date DDI contract, with $T_2 > T_1$. The T_1 maturity date contract is called the basis month DDI contract and T_1 is always the next available DDI contract. The exception to this rule occurs one business day in a BMF calendar prior to the last FX Fixing date for the next available FX Futures contract, when the basis month of FRC contract changes to the second available DDI contract. As an example, suppose we are at 17-Jul-2014, the next available FX Futures contract is DOLQ14. It's last FX Fixing is based on $PTAX_{t-1}$ from 01-Aug-2014, which is 31-Jul-2014. So the basis month T_1 for any FRC contract will be DDIQ14 until one business day prior to 31-Jul-2014 in a BMF calendar, which is 30-Jul-2014. At this date, the FRC basis contract will be DDIU14, which is the September DDI contract.

The T_1 maturity DDI number of contracts $q1^*$ will be calculated based on the traded number of FRC contracts $q2$ by:

$$q1 = q2 \cdot P^K(T_1, T_2) \tag{145}$$

$$q1^* = round(q1, 0) \tag{146}$$

and

$$P^K(T_1, T_2) = \frac{1}{1 + R_{FRC} \cdot \tau^{Act360}_{T_1,T_2}} \tag{147}$$

where,

R_{FRC}: is the traded FRC rate.

$\tau^{Act360}_{T_1,T_2}$: is the day count fraction between T_1 and T_2 in Act360 convention.

$round(q1,0)$: rounds the calculated $q1$ quantity to the nearest unit.

It's been previously discussed that a long position in a FRC contract for maturity date T_2 generates a long position in a DDI contract for maturity date T_2 plus a short position in a DDI contract for the basis month T_1. However, there's only one traded FRC rate. So how will the 2 DDI contract traded rates be generated based on a single traded FRC rate? The basis month DDI contract traded rate R^C_{t,T_1} will be equal to the closing DDI rate for the same T_1 maturity date contract. Thus, the short dated contract is guaranteed to have a 0 cashflow at trade date. On the other hand, the T_2 maturity date contract traded rate R^C_{t,T_2} will be calculated by:

$$R^C_{t,T_2} = \frac{\left[\left(1+R^C_{t,T_1}\cdot\tau^{Act360}_{t,T_1}\right)\cdot\left(1+R_{FRC}\cdot\tau^{Act360}_{T_1,T_2}\right)-1\right]}{\tau^{Act360}_{t,T_2}} \tag{148}$$

where,

R^C_{t,T_2}: is the computed T_2 maturity date contract DDI traded rate.
R^C_{t,T_1}: is the basis month maturity date DDI contract traded rate.

Now that the contractual information for FRC contracts has been described, it's time to demonstrate how to price them.

6.6.1 FRC Future pricing

As any other future contract, we expect that the cashflows computed at trade date t are zero for this contract. We already know that by construction the basis month DDI contract will have its traded rate defined equal to that contract closing rate. Therefore, the cashflow will always be 0 at trade date for the basis month contract. Given that information, we just have to focus now on the T_2 maturity date DDI contract cash flow to be 0 as well. Thus,

$$FUT_{DDI}(t,T_2) - FUT_{DDI}(t,T_1)\cdot P^K(T_1,T_2) = 0 \tag{149}$$

(149) tells us that the T_2 maturity date DDI contract closing price $FUT_{DDI}(t,T_2)$ needs to be equal to the computed T_2 maturity date DDI traded price $FUT_{DDI}(t,T_1)\cdot P^K(T_1,T_2)$. Plugging (143) into (149) yields:

$$100{,}000\cdot\frac{\frac{BRL}{USD}[t]}{\text{PTAX}_{t-1}}\cdot P^{CDI}_{t,t_{FX}}\cdot\left(\frac{P^{USB}_{t,t_{FX},T_2-1_{FX}}}{P^{CDI}_{t,T_2,T_2-1_{FX}}} - \frac{P^{USB}_{t,t_{FX},T_1-1_{FX}}}{P^{CDI}_{t,T_1,T_1-1_{FX}}}\cdot P^K(T_1,T_2)\right) = 0 \tag{150}$$

The only way (150) could be zero is if the term inside parenthesis is equal to zero.

$$\left(\frac{P^{USB}_{t,t_{FX},T_2-1_{FX}}}{P^{CDI}_{t,T_2,T_2-1_{FX}}} - \frac{P^{USB}_{t,t_{FX},T_1-1_{FX}}}{P^{CDI}_{t,T_1,T_1-1_{FX}}}\cdot P^K(T_1,T_2)\right) = 0 \tag{151}$$

Rearranging (151) a bit yields:

$$P^K(T_1,T_2) = \frac{P^{USB}_{t,t_{FX},T_2-1_{FX}}}{P^{USB}_{t,t_{FX},T_1-1_{FX}}} \cdot \frac{P^{CDI}_{t,T_1,T_1-1_{FX}}}{P^{CDI}_{t,T_2,T_2-1_{FX}}} \tag{152}$$

In (152), the term $\frac{P^{USB}_{t,t_{FX},T_2-1_{FX}}}{P^{USB}_{t,t_{FX},T_1-1_{FX}}}$ can be simplified to $P^{USB}_{t,T_1-1_{FX},T_2-1_{FX}}$, which is the forward discount factor on USD onshore interest rate curve *USB*. Plugging that information in (152) yields:

$$P^K(T_1,T_2) = P^{USB}_{t,T_1-1_{FX},T_2-1_{FX}} \cdot \frac{P^{CDI}_{t,T_1,T_1-1_{FX}}}{P^{CDI}_{t,T_2,T_2-1_{FX}}} \tag{153}$$

The first important feature of (153) is that the FRC price $P^K(T_1,T_2)$ is no longer a function of $\frac{\frac{BRL}{USD}[t]}{PTAX_{t-1}}$ as the DDI contract was. Therefore, it's a contract where market participants trade a "clean" cupom rate as opposed to the "dirty" rate traded on DDI contracts.

6.6.2 Handling a FRC trade before BVMF publication of the first DDI closing price

As we have seen previously, a FRC contract gets converted into 2 DDI contracts at the end of the day by the exchange. However, the 2 DDI contract traded rates are linked to the closing T_1 maturity date DDI rate that's only published by BVMF at the end of the day. So how can we manage the risk of a FRC position realtime during trade date?

The solution to this question can be implemented by booking the 2 DDI contracts instead of the FRC right away. With knowledge of FRC number of contracts traded $q2$, the T_2 maturity date number of DDI contracts will be $q2$ as well. But the tricky part is how to book the traded rate R^C_{t,T_2}. Based on (148), we can see that R^C_{t,T_2} won't be fixed until end of day, since it changes based on R^C_{t,T_1}. This variable, on the other hand, can be computed based on (143) together with (144), until it get's finally published by BVMF at the end of the day.

For the T_1 maturity date DDI contract, things are slightly easier. Its number of contracts are computed through (145) and (146) and it's known with only knowledge of the FRC traded rate and the number of FRC contracts traded. Its traded rate will also depend on R^C_{t,T_1} like for the T_2 maturity date DDI case and can be computed during the day based on the same procedure.

We reinforce here that the 2 DDI contracts traded rates derived from the FRC contract will be computed and varying based on market data changes before BVMF publishes its T_1 maturity date DDI closing rates. Thus, when computing any interest rate onshore risk to those contracts, there must be a mechanism to also bump their traded rates based on the market data change predicted by the model equations in (143) and (144).

Finally, at the end of the day there must be a fixing procedure of the DDI traded rates derived from FRC contracts. This procedure will set the DDI traded rates to a constant value and they should stop being computed based on the model equations mentioned above.

6.7 Calibration of the cupom curve

As we have previously mentioned, the long end of the *USB* (cupom) curve is calibrated to FRC contract quotes. The short end is calibrated to DI1 contracts, $\frac{BRL}{USD}$ FX Future contract for the FRC basis month and $Casado_t$ quotes. The FRC contract provides a way to trade a "clean" forward rate after the basis month. So our definition of short end of the curve and long end is basically driven by the FRC basis month contract. The cupom curve is calibrated after the basis month contract with the FRC quotes and before with, DI1 contracts, $\frac{BRL}{USD}$ FX Future contract for the FRC basis month and *Casado* quotes.

6.7.1 Calibration of the cupom curve on the short end

For the short end of cupom curve, it's assumed that there's no basis, also called convexity, between the price of a FRC basis month $\frac{BRL}{USD}$ FX Future contract and the price of a $\frac{BRL}{USD}$ onshore FX Forward contract, both having the same FX Fixing date. The notation used in this subsection follows below:

$FXFUT^{ON}_{t,T_1-1_{FX}}[\frac{BRL}{USD}]$: is the FRC basis month $\frac{BRL}{USD}$ FX Future price, seen at date t with settlement date at $T_1 - 1_{FX}$. T_1 is considered the FRC basis month maturity date . The superscript *ON* refers to onshore because there's also a CME FX Future contract that will be specified with a superscript *OFF* to denote that it's offshore and different than the BVMF one. We assume here also that the futures price is not scaled by 1,000 as BVMF publishes its.

$FXFWD^{ON}_{t,T_1-1_{FX}}[\frac{BRL}{USD}]$: is the previously defined $\frac{BRL}{USD}$ onshore FX Forward price seen at date t with settlement date at $T_1 - 1_{FX}$.

The zero convexity assumption of $FXFUT^{ON}_{t,T_1-1_{FX}}[\frac{BRL}{USD}]$ and $FXFWD^{ON}_{t,T_1-1_{FX}}[\frac{BRL}{USD}]$ will be revisited later in this book and will be considered to be negligible for the FRC basis month maturity date. It was defined previously that the no arbitrage cash and carry argument provides us the following equation:

$$FXFWD^{ON}_{t,T_1-1_{FX}}\left[\frac{BRL}{USD}\right] = \frac{BRL}{USD}[t] \cdot \frac{P^{USB}_{t,t_{FX},T_1-1_{FX}}}{P^{CDI}_{t,t_{FX},T_1-1_{FX}}} \tag{154}$$

Using the zero basis assumption of $FXFUT^{ON}_{t,T_1-1_{FX}}[\frac{BRL}{USD}]$ and $FXFWD^{ON}_{t,T_1-1_{FX}}[\frac{BRL}{USD}]$ enables us to rewrite (154) as:

$$FXFUT^{ON}_{t,T_1-1_{FX}}\left[\frac{BRL}{USD}\right] = \frac{BRL}{USD}[t] \cdot \frac{P^{USB}_{t,t_{FX},T_1-1_{FX}}}{P^{CDI}_{t,t_{FX},T_1-1_{FX}}} \tag{155}$$

The value of fx spot rate $\frac{BRL}{USD}[t]$ is implied on $FXFUT^{ON}_{t,T_1-1_{FX}}[\frac{BRL}{USD}]$ price and the $Casado_t$ quote by:

$$FXFUT^{ON}_{t,T_1-1_{FX}}\left[\frac{BRL}{USD}\right] - Casado_t = \frac{BRL}{USD}[t] \tag{156}$$

Assuming also that a calibrated onshore BRL CDI curve is available to us enables us to imply the forward cupom discount factor seen at date t, from fx spot date t_{fx} to settlement date $T_1 - 1_{FX}$, namely $P^{USB}_{t,t_{FX},T_1-1_{FX}}$ by:

$$P^{USB}_{t,t_{FX},T_1-1_{FX}} = \frac{FXFUT^{ON}_{t,T_1-1_{FX}}[\frac{BRL}{USD}]}{\frac{BRL}{USD}[t]} \cdot P^{CDI}_{t,t_{FX},T_1-1_{FX}} \tag{157}$$

If we are interested in expressing $P^{USB}_{t,t_{FX},T_1-1_{FX}}$, only in terms of liquid instruments we should use (156) to substitute $\frac{BRL}{USD}[t]$ by $FXFUT^{ON}_{t,T_1-1_{FX}}[\frac{BRL}{USD}] - Casado_t$. The next equation shows this other possible formulation which is better for risk management purposes, as will be explained later in this book.

$$P^{USB}_{t,t_{FX},T_1-1_{FX}} = \frac{FXFUT^{ON}_{t,T_1-1_{FX}}[\frac{BRL}{USD}]}{FXFUT^{ON}_{t,T_1-1_{FX}}[\frac{BRL}{USD}] - Casado_t} \cdot P^{CDI}_{t,t_{FX},T_1-1_{FX}} \tag{158}$$

6.7.2 Calibration of the cupom curve on the long end

Now let's focus on the calibration of the portion of cupom curve based on FRC quotes. Our starting point will be Equations (153) and (147). By looking at (147), it can be seen that given a FRC quote R_{FRC}, it can be converted to a FRC price $P^K(T_1, T_2)$. Assuming a calibrated CDI onshore interest rate curve to be available, the term $\frac{P^{CDI}_{t,T_1,T_1-1_{FX}}}{P^{CDI}_{t,T_2,T_2-1_{FX}}}$ can also be computed. Given the FRC quote and the calibrated CDI onshore curve, (153) could be inverted to imply the cupom forward discount factor seen at date t with start date $T_1 - 1_{FX}$ and end date $T_2 - 1_{FX}$, namely $P^{USB}_{t,T_1-1_{FX},T_2-1_{FX}}$.

$$P^{USB}_{t,T_1-1_{FX},T_2-1_{FX}} = P^K(T_1, T_2) \cdot \frac{P^{CDI}_{t,T_2,T_2-1_{FX}}}{P^{CDI}_{t,T_1,T_1-1_{FX}}} \tag{159}$$

One important feature is that the calibrated forward discount factor $P^{USB}_{t,T_1-1_{FX},T_2-1_{FX}}$ is not based on T_1 and T_2 dates like the FRC quote, but instead is based on $T_1 - 1_{FX}$ and $T_2 - 1_{FX}$. Refreshing the notation again, $T_1 - 1$ and $T_2 - 1$ are the FX Fixing dates for FX Futures contracts with maturity date at T_1 and T_2, and the *FX* subscript on $T_1 - 1_{FX}$ and $T_2 - 1_{FX}$ applies a fx settlement rule from the fixing dates, which shift those dates 2 business dates in a combined CDI and US holiday calendar. Because of this particularity, the cupom curve is often called a T+2 curve, since its curve spot date is obtained applying a fx settlement rule.

Another important fact is that even though the process to calibrate $P^{USB}_{t,T_1-1_{FX},T_2-1_{FX}}$ is not as easy as it was for calibrating a curve like the CDI curve based on DI1 contracts for example, pricing a $\frac{BRL}{USD}$ onshore FX Forward contract, with fixing date on the same date as a T_2 maturity date BVMF FX Future contract, could be derived only with knowledge of basis month DOL contract quote, the FRC rate between T_1 and T_2 and DI1 rates for T_1 and T_2 contracts. No interpolation would be required or a CDI or cupom curve to be calibrated. The proof for this statement can be constructed starting from the cash and carry argument used to price $FXFWD^{ON}_{t,T_1-1_{FX}}[\frac{BRL}{USD}]$. It will lead to:

$$FXFWD^{ON}_{t,T_2-1_{FX}}\left[\frac{BRL}{USD}\right] = \frac{BRL}{USD}[t] \cdot \frac{P^{USB}_{t,t_{FX},T_2-1_{FX}}}{P^{CDI}_{t,t_{FX},T_2-1_{FX}}} \tag{160}$$

$FXFWD^{ON}_{t,T_2-1_{FX}}[\frac{BRL}{USD}]$ can also be constructed using the cash and carry argument from $FXFWD^{ON}_{t,T_1-1_{FX}}[\frac{BRL}{USD}]$.

$$FXFWD^{ON}_{t,T_2-1_{FX}}\left[\frac{BRL}{USD}\right] = FXFWD^{ON}_{t,T_1-1_{FX}}\left[\frac{BRL}{USD}\right] \cdot \frac{P^{USB}_{t,T_1-1_{FX},T_2-1_{FX}}}{P^{CDI}_{t,T_1-1_{FX},T_2-1_{FX}}} \tag{161}$$

Now we could use the zero convexity assumption of (155) to change in (161) $FXFWD^{ON}_{t,T_1-1_{FX}}[\frac{BRL}{USD}]$ to $FXFUT_{t,T_1-1_{FX}}[\frac{BRL}{USD}]$. Thus:

$$FXFWD^{ON}_{t,T_2-1_{FX}}\left[\frac{BRL}{USD}\right] = FXFUT_{t,T_1-1_{FX}}\left[\frac{BRL}{USD}\right] \cdot \frac{P^{USB}_{t,T_1-1_{FX},T_2-1_{FX}}}{P^{CDI}_{t,T_1-1_{FX},T_2-1_{FX}}} \tag{162}$$

The cupom forward discount factor $P^{USB}_{t,T_1-1_{FX},T_2-1_{FX}}$ was calibrated using (159). By plugging (159) into (162) yields:

$$FXFWD^{ON}_{t,T_2-1_{FX}}\left[\frac{BRL}{USD}\right] = FXFUT_{t,T_1-1_{FX}}\left[\frac{BRL}{USD}\right] \cdot \frac{P^K(T_1,T_2)}{P^{CDI}_{t,T_1-1_{FX},T_2-1_{FX}}} \cdot \frac{P^{CDI}_{t,T_2,T_2-1_{FX}}}{P^{CDI}_{t,T_1,T_1-1_{FX}}} \tag{163}$$

The term $\frac{1}{P^{CDI}_{t,T_1-1_{FX},T_2-1_{FX}}} \cdot \frac{P^{CDI}_{t,T_2,T_2-1_{FX}}}{P^{CDI}_{t,T_1,T_1-1_{FX}}}$ can be calculated as:

$$\frac{1}{P^{CDI}_{t,T_1-1_{FX},T_2-1_{FX}}} \cdot \frac{P^{CDI}_{t,T_2,T_2-1_{FX}}}{P^{CDI}_{t,T_1,T_1-1_{FX}}} = \frac{1}{P^{CDI}_{t,T_1,T_2}} \tag{164}$$

Plugging (164) into (163) yields:

$$FXFWD^{ON}_{t,T_2-1_{FX}}\left[\frac{BRL}{USD}\right] = FXFUT_{t,T_1-1_{FX}}\left[\frac{BRL}{USD}\right] \cdot \frac{P^K(T_1,T_2)}{P^{CDI}_{t,T_1,T_2}} \tag{165}$$

Plugging now (147) and (39) into (165) yields:

$$FXFWD^{ON}_{t,T_2-1_{FX}}\left[\frac{BRL}{USD}\right]=FXFUT_{t,T_1-1_{FX}}\left[\frac{BRL}{USD}\right]\cdot\frac{1}{1+R_{FRC}\cdot\tau^{Act360}_{T_1,T_2}}\cdot\frac{\left(1+R^{CDI}_{t,T_2}\right)^{\tau^{252}_{t,T_2}}}{\left(1+R^{CDI}_{t,T_1}\right)^{\tau^{252}_{t,T_1}}} \tag{166}$$

Recalling that R_{FRC} is the FRC quote for a contract with maturity date T_2 and R^{CDI}_{t,T_1} and R^{CDI}_{t,T_2} are the DI1 quotes for contracts with maturity dates T_1 and T_2 respectively, proves our previous statement that pricing a $\frac{BRL}{USD}$ onshore FX Forward contract, with fixing date on the same date as a T_2 maturity date BVMF FX Future contract , could be derived only with knowledge of the basis month DOL quote, the FRC rate between T_1 and T_2 and DI1 rates for T_1 and T_2 contracts.

Another important question to be asked is why the calibration only produces forward discount factors? Don't we ever have to use a discount factor that discounts until pricing date t? The answer is no, as all USD onshore tradable instruments that produce a USD linked cashflow have to be paid in BRL. Therefore their future expected cashflows need to be converted by a $\frac{BRL}{USD}$ FX forward price to a BRL expected payoff that is subsequently discounted until computation date t in a BRL onshore curve. So in the limit at FX Fixing date, you only need to convert the cashflow by the fx forward at t_{FX}.

6.8 How to compute cupom interest rate risk?

In the previous section we described how to calibrate the cupom curve forward discount factors $P^{USB}_{t,T_1-1_{FX},T_j-1_{FX}}$, for T_j being the maturity date for a particular FRC contract. Assuming we have N available FRC contracts, we could calibrate $N+1$ forward discount factors for a cupom curve, being N calibrated in the long end using FRC quotes with a calibrated CDI onshore curve, and 1 in the short end with DI1 quotes, *Casado* and the FRC basis month $\frac{BRL}{USD}$ FX Futures contract price. What's very frequent among market practitioners is to construct a cupom curve, based on the combination of the short and long end cupom forward discount factors $P^{USB}_{t,t_{fx},T_1-1_{FX}}$ and $P^{USB}_{t,T_1-1_{FX},T_j-1_{FX}}$ to obtain $P^{USB}_{t,t_{fx},T_j-1_{FX}}$ through:

$$P^{USB}_{t,t_{fx},T_j-1_{FX}}=P^{USB}_{t,t_{fx},T_1-1_{FX}}\cdot P^{USB}_{t,T_1-1_{FX},T_j-1_{FX}} \tag{167}$$

The next step would be to compute $R^{USB}_{t,t_{fx},T_j-1_{FX}}$, also called the "clean" cupom rate, which is a non tradable equivalent cash deposit rate seen at t, for start date t_{fx} and end date T_j-1_{FX} by:

$$R^{USB}_{t,t_{fx},T_j-1_{FX}}=\left(\frac{1}{P^{USB}_{t,t_{fx},T_j-1_{FX}}}-1\right)\cdot\frac{1}{\tau^{Act360}_{t_{FX},T_j-1_{FX}}} \tag{168}$$

This procedure would enable us to compute the $N+1$ quotes, for each $R^{USB}_{t,t_{fx},T_j-1_{FX}}$, associated with the $N+1$ forward discount factors of the calibrated cupom curve. However, all computed "clean" cupom rates $R^{USB}_{t,t_{fx},T_j-1_{FX}}$ are not tradable as mentioned above. Therefore, they shouldn't be the selected instrument used for cupom curve interest rate risk computation. In G10 market, interest rate risk is computed with respect to hedgeable (or tradable) instruments. That feature is desired because it could tell you which amount of the liquid instruments you would have to hold in order to hedge your portfolio against that particular interest rate risk metric. Nonetheless, it's still quite frequent to observe market practitioners in Brazil computing cupom risk based on the unhedgeable "clean" cupom rates.

Based on the argument presented above, the correct cupom risk computation methodology should be based on its liquid instruments, which are the FRC liquid quotes, the *Casado*$_t$ quote and the FRC basis month $\frac{BRL}{USD}$ FX Futures contract. The risk obtained from this procedure would now be meaningful, and a trader could go directly to the market to execute his hedge by trading the liquid instruments.

Another weird result of using interest rate with respect to cupom "clean" rates $R^{USB}_{t,t_{fx},T_j-1_{FX}}$, is that if you trade a FRC contract, you would end up having BRL CDI curve interest rate risk. This can be verified by looking at (153), which is shown below again to highlight this particular issue:

$$P^K(T_1,T_2) = P^{USB}_{t,T_1-1_{FX},T_2-1_{FX}} \cdot \frac{P^{CDI}_{t,T_1,T_1-1_{FX}}}{P^{CDI}_{t,T_2,T_2-1_{FX}}}$$

The FRC contract price $P^K(T_1,T_2)$ is a function of $P^{USB}_{t,T_1-1_{FX},T_2-1_{FX}} = \frac{P^{USB}_{t,t_{FX},T_2-1_{FX}}}{P^{USB}_{t,t_{FX},T_1-1_{FX}}}$, which ends up being a function of "clean" rates $R^{USB}_{t,t_{fx},T_1-1_{FX}}$ and $R^{USB}_{t,t_{fx},T_2-1_{FX}}$. But the term $\frac{P^{CDI}_{t,T_1,T_1-1_{FX}}}{P^{CDI}_{t,T_2,T_2-1_{FX}}}$ exists and results in BRL CDI curve interest rate risk no matter what.

On the other hand, it's quite obvious that using the FRC quote as the instrument to represent interest rate risk would yield only risk on the same FRC contract.

Another good example is the already mentioned $\frac{BRL}{USD}$ FX Forward onshore $FXFWD^{ON}_{t,T_2-1_{FX}}[\frac{BRL}{USD}]$ contract with same FX Fixing date as the T_2 maturity date FX Future. As demonstrated in the previous subsection in (166), its price is a function of only liquid instruments. So having an interest rate risk computation methodology based on shifting liquid instruments would naturally only yield risk to the very same instruments. On the other hand, shifting the cupom "clean" rates would require the pricing to be based on:

$$FXFWD^{ON}_{t,T_2-1_{FX}}\left[\frac{BRL}{USD}\right]=\frac{BRL}{USD}[t]\cdot\frac{P^{USB}_{t,t_{FX},T_2-1_{FX}}}{P^{CDI}_{t,t_{FX},T_2-1_{FX}}}$$

And the term $P^{CDI}_{t,t_{FX},T_2-1_{FX}}$ would require interpolation and would result in residuals of risk being displayed in adjacent tenors to the T_1 and T_2 in BRL CDI interest rate curve.

Another interesting fact is that a shift in $Casado_t$ or $FXFUT^{ON}_{t,T_1-1_{FX}}[\frac{BRL}{USD}]$ quote would recalibrate the implied cupom forward discount factor $P^{USB}_{t,t_{FX},T_1-1_{FX}}$ through:

$$P^{USB}_{t,t_{FX},T_1-1_{FX}}=\frac{FXFUT^{ON}_{t,T_1-1_{FX}}\left[\frac{BRL}{USD}\right]}{FXFUT^{ON}_{t,T_1-1_{FX}}\left[\frac{BRL}{USD}\right]-Casado_t}\cdot P^{CDI}_{t,t_{FX},T_1-1_{FX}}$$

So there's a bit of interest rate risk coming from FX related quotes $Casado_t$ and $FXFUT^{ON}_{t,T_1-1_{FX}}[\frac{BRL}{USD}]$ as well, and not only from FRC contract quotes.

6.9 Interpolation choices for the cupom curve

In this subsection, we will discuss the 3 most used interpolations methods for cupom curve. 2 of those methods are very similar and perform a log-linear interpolation on forward discount factors $P^{USB}_{t,t_{FX},T_j-1_{FX}}$, but one does it log-linear in business days and the other log-linear in calendar days. The other interpolation is log-linear also, but in fx forward prices space.

6.9.1 Log-linear interpolation of cupom curve forward discount factors curve in business days

This interpolation method will set as knots the $N+1$ forward discount factors $P^{USB}_{t,t_{FX},T_j-1_{FX}}$ obtained in the cupom curve calibration. Similarly as for the CDI onshore curve calibration, it will be assumed we are interested in finding a discount factor for a date T_k, between knot dates T_i-1_{FX} and $T_{i+1}-1_{FX}$. Subsequently, the following equations will be used:

$$ln\left(P^{USB}_{t,t_{FX},T_k}\right)=ln\left(P^{USB}_{t,t_{FX},T_i-1_{FX}}\right)+\frac{\tau^{252}_{T_i-1_{FX},T_k}}{\tau^{252}_{T_i-1_{FX},T_{i+1}-1_{FX}}}\cdot\left(ln\left(P^{USB}_{t,t_{FX},T_{i+1}-1_{FX}}\right)-ln\left(P^{USB}_{t,t_{FX},T_i-1_{FX}}\right)\right) \quad (169)$$

$$P^{USB}_{t,t_{FX},T_k}=exp\left\{ln\left(P^{USB}_{t,t_{FX},T_k}\right)\right\} \quad (170)$$

6.9.2 Log-linear interpolation of cupom curve forward discount factors curve in calendar days

In this method, the knots of the curve are the same as in the method above. The only difference will be that day count fractions are computed based on Act360 DCB instead of BUS252. Therefore the interpolation equations are:

$$ln\left(P^{USB}_{t,t_{FX},T_k}\right) = ln\left(P^{USB}_{t,t_{FX},T_i-1_{FX}}\right) + \frac{\tau^{Act360}_{T_i-1_{FX},T_k}}{\tau^{Act360}_{T_i-1_{FX},T_{i+1}-1_{FX}}} \cdot \left(ln\left(P^{USB}_{t,t_{FX},T_{i+1}-1_{FX}}\right)\right.$$
$$\left. -ln\left(P^{USB}_{t,t_{FX},T_i-1_{FX}}\right)\right) \quad (171)$$

And (170) would be used again to invert the natural logarithm function.

6.9.3 Log-linear interpolation of cupom curve in FX forward prices

Here again the log-linear interpolation could be done in business days or in calendar days. One can be constructed from the other by just changing the day count fraction in the same interpolation formula. However, the available days to be counted should be obtained using the combined CDI and US holidays calendar, because that's where the fx market is based to compute its fx forward settlement dates. Assuming we also have $N+1$ knot dates which are again $T_i - 1_{FX}$ and $T_{i+1} - 1_{FX}$ yields the following equations:

$$ln\left(FXFWD^{ON}_{t,T_k}\left[\frac{BRL}{USD}\right]\right) = ln\left(FXFWD^{ON}_{t,T_i-1_{FX}}\left[\frac{BRL}{USD}\right]\right) + \frac{\tau^{252FX}_{T_i-1_{FX},T_k}}{\tau^{252FX}_{T_i-1_{FX},T_{i+1}-1_{FX}}} \cdot \quad (172)$$
$$\cdot\left(ln\left(FXFWD^{ON}_{t,T_{i+1}-1_{FX}}\left[\frac{BRL}{USD}\right]\right)\right.$$
$$\left. -ln\left(FXFWD^{ON}_{t,T_i-1_{FX}}\left[\frac{BRL}{USD}\right]\right)\right) \quad (173)$$

where,

$\tau^{252FX}_{T_i,T_j}$: is the day count fraction between T_i and T_j in a BUS252 DCB that counts business days in a combined CDI and US holidays calendar.

There's no clear evidence for the authors that one method should be better than the others and investigating with historical market data which method produces PnL closer to zero with smaller standard deviation for a portfolio consisting on broken dates $\frac{BRL}{USD}$ fx forwards could be a good way to try to investigate this in the future.

Hey, before you go on with the rest of the formulas, let's talk about New Year's Eve. Not the day itself, but that last business day of the year, that one that is a trading holiday. The IOF on Derivatives introduced in 2011 brought home a problem: how do you look at this fixing? You might get yourself paying a tax because a long position matured on 31-Dec and your traded hedge matured on 30-Dec. To avoid this situation, every year an explicit communication from the BCB determines that the PTAX of that last business day will be equal to the the PTAX of the previous day. Why not implement this for all holidays where only BVMF is closed? Because this is the only situation where the holiday is near the last fixing date for the listed FX contracts.

Because you, our reader, is clearly a smart person (you bought this book, after all), the image of a diagonal line going up forever that was associated with this interpolation is now replaced with a broken diagonal (up until 30-Dec, equal for 30-Dec and 31-Dec, and then up again). Some minutes (maybe hours - go to a bar, a pub, anywhere, but get out of the office) of fun are expected as the trader, the quant and the poor soul who will have to implement this model discuss whether to treat this as a feature, an exception, a bug, something permanent, something that will change only when the BCB publishes the yearly communication, ... you get the idea (you are smart after all).

These little gems make Brazilian models famous around the world for their uniqueness (although other Brazilian models are also famous as well).

6.10 The SCC contract

The SCC contract is defined as a cross currency swap contract with daily resets but in reality it works essentially as a USD linked Futures contract very similar to DDI. It was introduced in 2002 as an alternative to currency intervention by the BCB (as discussed before), but the government had said before it would not intervene in the futures markets; therefore, a swap with periodic margining was introduced. The period started as monthly, changing to daily later. So as a general rule in this book, this contract will be also referred as a future contract even though its contract specification might say that it's a swap.

There are 2 main differences for the daily cashflow computations of SCC and DDI contracts:

- There's no multiplier in cashflow computation formula as there was for a DDI contract. A SCC contract is for face value of 50,000 USD at maturity date. In essence that doesn't change much as the 100,000 face value DDI is later multiplied by 0.5, but there's a difference in units of closing prices published. For the SCC, published prices are 50,000 USD based and for DDI they are 100,000 based.
- The daily cashflow equation for a SCC contract is given by

$$MCF_t^T = \left(CP_t^T - OP_t^T\right) \cdot PTAX_{t-1} \cdot \prod_{T_i=t}^{t+1^*} \left(1 + CDI_{T_i}\right)^{\frac{1}{252}} \tag{174}$$

So there's an accrual of the DDI contract cashflow formula by the term $\prod_{T_i=t}^{t+1^*}(1+CDI_{T_i})^{\frac{1}{252}}$. The rationale behind this term is that the cashflow is paid only the next business day in a BMF calendar. Thus the term $\prod_{T_i=t}^{t+1^*}(1+CDI_{T_i})^{\frac{1}{252}}$ is supposed to cancel the present value effect that will discount the expected cashflow by the same term.

The conversion from closing price of the previous BMF date to opening price is also given by (122) and doesn't change from the DDI contract to the SCC one.

6.11 The mathematical derivation and pricing of a SCC contract price

Since the cashflow computation is very similar to DDI contract case besides the accrual term $\prod_{T_i=t}^{t+1^*}(1+CDI_{T_i})^{\frac{1}{252}}$, the SCC futures price will be derived similarly to the way that the DDI futures price was derived. The first equation to be used is the boundary condition at maturity date:

$$FUT_{SCC}(T,T) = 50{,}000 \tag{175}$$

The cashflow computation expected value is slightly different than (128), but only because of the accrual term $\prod_{T_i=t}^{t+1^*}(1+CDI_{T_i})^{\frac{1}{252}}$ and (175). Again, as a futures contract, it's expected to have a 0 expected cashflow computed at maturity date T. The equation below is constructed using all those details:

$$\beta_{T-1^*}\cdot\mathbb{E}^{\mathbb{Q}^*}\left[\frac{\left(FUT_{SCC}(T,T) - FUT_{SCC}(T-1^*,T)\cdot\dfrac{\prod_{T_i=T-1^*}^{T}\left[1+CDI_{T_i}\right]^{\frac{1}{252}}}{\frac{PTAX_{T-1}}{PTAX_{T-1}(T-1^*)}}\right)\cdot PTAX_{T-1}}{\beta_{T+1^*}\cdot\left(\prod_{T_i=T}^{T+1^*}(1+CDI_{T_i})^{\frac{1}{252}}\right)^{-1}}|\mathcal{F}_{T-1^*}\right]$$
$$=0 \tag{176}$$

Again, the terms $PTAX_{T-1}$, $\prod_{T_i=T}^{T+1^*}(1+CDI_{T_i})^{\frac{1}{252}}$ and $\frac{\beta_{T+1^*}}{\beta_{T-1^*}}$ are positive quantities, and to impose (176) to be zero we need that:

$$\mathbb{E}^{\mathbb{Q}^*}\left[50{,}000\cdot\frac{\beta_{T-1^*}}{\beta_{T+1^*}}|\mathcal{F}_{T-1^*}\right]$$
$$= \mathbb{E}^{\mathbb{Q}^*}\left[FUT_{SCC}(T-1^*,T)\cdot\frac{\prod_{T_i=T-1^*}^{T}\left[1+CDI_{T_i}\right]^{\frac{1}{252}}}{\frac{PTAX_{T-1}}{PTAX_{T-1}(T-1^*)}}\cdot\frac{\beta_{T-1^*}}{\beta_{T+1^*}}|\mathcal{F}_{T-1^*}\right] \tag{177}$$

It can be seen that (177) is very similar to (129), being the only difference the face value amount of 100,000 for the DDI case and 50,000 for the SCC case. This enables us to use the same pricing equation for the SCC contract than the one used for DDI in (143) with the face value adjustment as below:

$$FUT_{SCC}(t,T) = 50,000 \cdot P^{USB}_{t,t_{FX},T-1_{FX}} \cdot \frac{\frac{BRL}{USD}[t]}{\mathrm{PTAX_{t-1}}} \cdot \frac{P^{CDI}_{t,t_{FX}}}{P^{CDI}_{t,T,T-1_{FX}}} \tag{178}$$

6.12 The SCS contract - a modern, but exotic, cousin

The SCS contract is also defined as a cross currency swap contract with daily resets but can be also be viewed as a Futures contract very similar to SCC. The only difference among the 2 contracts is the BRL interest rate fixing index associated to it which is Selic for SCS instead of CDI for the SCC contract. The cashflow computation formula for SCS contracts is displayed below:

$$MCF^T_t = \left(CP^T_t - OP^T_t\right) \cdot PTAX_{t-1} \cdot \prod_{T_i=t}^{t+1^*} (1 + Selic_{T_i})^{\frac{1}{252}} \tag{179}$$

Again as in the SCC contract case there's an accrual of the contract cashflow formula, but as stated above the reference interest rate index is Selic.

The conversion from closing price of the previous BMF date to opening price is not given by (122) anymore as we need to change the CDI by the Selic index in this formula also. This is shown in the equation below:

$$OP^T_t = CP^T_{t-1} \cdot \frac{\prod^{t}_{T_i=t-1^*} \left[1 + Selic_{T_i}\right]^{\frac{1}{252}}}{\frac{PTAX_{t-1}}{PTAX_{t-1}(t-1^*)}} \tag{180}$$

The SCS contract was introduced together with the OC1, within a coordinated push to introduce listed contracts using Selic instead of CDI at a time in which the spread between both was too wide.

6.13 The mathematical derivation of a SCS contract price

The only difference between the cashflow computation of a SCC contract and the SCS one is the change from the CDI index to Selic. Again we have a 50,000 USD face value for one contract which gives us the following boundary condition:

$$FUT_{SCS}(T,T) = 50,000 \tag{181}$$

As done previously in the OC1 contracts, the risk neutral expectation used to calculate the SCS contract price is the one which has $\beta^S_t = \prod^{t-1}_{T_i=0} \left[1 + Selic_{T_i}\right]^{\frac{1}{252}}$ as its numéraire. As a future contract, we again expect the value of the computed cashflow at maturity date T to be equal to 0. Using (181) and the above statement yields:

$$\beta^{S}_{T-1^*}\cdot\mathbb{E}^{\mathbb{Q}^{\mathbb{X}}}\left[\frac{\left(50,000-FUT_{SCS}(T-1^*,T)\cdot\frac{\prod_{T_j=T-1^*}^{T}\left[1+Selic_{T_i}\right]^{\frac{1}{252}}}{\frac{PTAX_{T-1}}{PTAX_{T-1(T-1^*)}}}\right)\cdot PTAX_{t-1}}{\beta^{S}_{T+1^*}\left(\prod_{T_j=T}^{T+1^*}\left(1+Selic_{T_i}\right)^{\frac{1}{252}}\right)^{-1}}|\mathcal{F}_{T-1^*}\right]$$
$$=0 \tag{182}$$

Again, the terms $PTAX_{T-1}\cdot\prod_{T_j=T}^{T+1^*}(1+Selic_{T_i})^{\frac{1}{252}}$ and $\frac{\beta_{T+1^*}}{\beta_{T-1^*}}$ are positive quantities, and to impose (182) to be zero we need that:

$$\mathbb{E}^{\mathbb{Q}^{\mathbb{X}}}\left[50,000\cdot\frac{\beta^{S}_{T-1^*}}{\beta^{S}_{T+1^*}}|\mathcal{F}_{T-1^*}\right]$$
$$=\mathbb{E}^{\mathbb{Q}^{\mathbb{X}}}\left[FUT_{SCS}(T-1^*,T)\cdot\frac{\prod_{T_j=T-1^*}^{T}\left[1+Selic_{T_i}\right]^{\frac{1}{252}}}{\frac{PTAX_{T-1}}{PTAX_{T-1(T-1^*)}}}\cdot\frac{\beta^{S}_{T-1^*}}{\beta^{S}_{T+1^*}}|\mathcal{F}_{T-1^*}\right] \tag{183}$$

The equation above may be rewritten as:

$$FUT_{SCS}(T-1^*,T)=\frac{50,000}{\frac{\prod_{T_j=T-1^*}^{T}\left[1+Selic_{T_i}\right]^{\frac{1}{252}}}{\frac{PTAX_{T-1}}{PTAX_{T-1(T-1^*)}}}} \tag{184}$$

Going one business backward in a BMF calendar for the previous cashflow, we may write that:

$$\beta^{S}_{T-2^*}\cdot\mathbb{E}^{\mathbb{Q}^{\mathbb{X}}}\left[\frac{FUT_{SCS}(T-1^*,T)-FUT_{SCS}(T-2^*,T)\cdot\frac{\prod_{T_j=T-2^*}^{T-1^*}\left[1+Selic_{T_i}\right]^{\frac{1}{252}}}{\frac{PTAX_{T-1(T-1^*)}}{PTAX_{T-1(T-2^*)}}}}{\beta^{S}_{T}}|\mathcal{F}_{T-2^*}\right]$$
$$=0 \tag{185}$$

Combining (184) and (185) and using the assumptions that led us into (184) again yields:

$$FUT_{SCS}(T-2^*,T)=\mathbb{E}^{\mathbb{Q}^{\mathbb{X}}}\left[\frac{\frac{FUT_{SCS}(T-1^*,T)}{\prod_{T_i=T-2^*}^{T-1^*}\left[1+Selic_{T_i}\right]^{\frac{1}{252}}}}{\frac{PTAX_{T-1}(T-1^*)}{PTAX_{T-1}(T-2^*)}}|\mathcal{F}_{T-2^*}\right] \tag{186}$$

Rearranging a bit the above equation yields:

$$FUT_{SCS}(T-2^*,T)=\mathbb{E}^{\mathbb{Q}^{\mathbb{X}}}\left[\frac{PTAX_{T-1}}{PTAX_{T-1}(T-2^*)}\cdot\frac{50{,}000}{\prod_{T_i=T-2^*}^{T}\left[1+Selic_{T_i}\right]^{\frac{1}{252}}}|\mathcal{F}_{T-2^*}\right] \tag{187}$$

Repeating this procedure iteratively until pricing time t (current time) yields:

$$FUT_{SCS}(t,T)=\mathbb{E}^{\mathbb{Q}^{\mathbb{X}}}\left[\frac{PTAX_{T-1}}{PTAX_{t-1}}\cdot\frac{50{,}000}{\prod_{T_i=t}^{T}\left[1+Selic_{T_i}\right]^{\frac{1}{252}}}|\mathcal{F}_t\right] \tag{188}$$

6.14 SCS Future pricing

By looking at (188), the first thing that can be noticed is that we can use the Radon-Nikodym derivative, previously presented in (46), to change the expectation to the probability measure $\mathbb{Q}_{\text{Selic}}{}^{T}$, which has as its numéraire $P_{t,T}^{Selic}$. This change of probability measure will cancel the term $\prod_{T_i=t}^{T}[1+Selic_{T_i}]^{\frac{1}{252}}$ inside the expectation and the SCS futures price $FUT_{SCS}(t,T)$ can be rewritten as:

$$FUT_{SCS}(t,T)=\mathbb{E}^{\mathbb{Q}_{\text{Selic}}{}^{T}}\left[\frac{PTAX_{T-1}}{PTAX_{t-1}}\cdot\frac{50{,}000}{\prod_{T_i=t}^{T}\left[1+Selic_{T_i}\right]^{\frac{1}{252}}}\cdot\frac{d\mathbb{Q}^{\mathbb{X}}}{d\mathbb{Q}_{\text{Selic}}{}^{T}}|T|\mathcal{F}_t\right] \tag{189}$$

Plugging (46) into (189) yields:

$$FUT_{SCS}(t,T)=\frac{50{,}000\cdot \mathrm{P}_{\mathrm{t,T}}^{\mathrm{Selic}}}{\mathrm{PTAX}_{\mathrm{t-1}}}\cdot\mathbb{E}^{\mathbb{Q}_{\text{Selic}}{}^{T}}\left[PTAX_{T-1}|\mathcal{F}_t\right] \tag{190}$$

A closer look at (190) unfortunately points to us that to derive the SCS futures price $FUT_{SCS}(t,T)$ won't be as simple as it was to derive the SCC futures price $FUT_{SCC}(t,T)$. The complication lies in the computation of the term $\mathbb{E}^{\mathbb{Q}_{\text{Selic}}{}^{T}}[PTAX_{T-1}|\mathcal{F}_t]$ as in the DDI or SCC futures price derivation, it was required to compute an expectation under a different probability measure. The term to be computed was $\mathbb{E}^{\mathbb{Q}_{\text{CDI}}^{T}}[PTAX_{T-1}|\mathcal{F}_t]$ instead.

In DDI future pricing subsection, we showed how to compute $\mathbb{E}^{\mathbb{Q}_{CDI}^{T}}[PTAX_{T-1}|\mathcal{F}_t]$ with just one assumption that had a negligible impact on pricing. First, it was used the fact that $PTAX_{T-1}$ could be replaced by $FXFWD^{ON}_{T-1,T-1_{FX}}[\frac{BRL}{USD}]$ inside the expectation, because the FX Forward price at expiry date collapses to its fx fixing value, in our particular case $PTAX_{T-1}$. Then, one stochastic calculus theorem was shown demonstrating that $FXFWD^{ON}_{t,T-1_{FX}}[\frac{BRL}{USD}]$ was a martingale under the the probability measure associated with $P^{CDI}_{t,t_{FX},T-1_{FX}}$ as numéraire. But pricing of the DDI contract required us to compute the expectation of $PTAX_{T-1}$ under the probability measure $\mathbb{Q}^{T}_{CDI}$, associated with numéraire $P^{CDI}_{t,T}$, which was different than $P^{CDI}_{t,t_{FX},T-1_{FX}}$ to validate the martingale property. However, $P^{CDI}_{t,T}$ is always sufficiently close to $P^{CDI}_{t,t_{FX},T-1_{FX}}$ and the convexity adjustment required to adjust for this difference can be considered to be negligible. All those facts allowed us to compute the required expectation as below:

$$\mathbb{E}^{\mathbb{Q}_{CDI}^{T}}\left[FXFWD^{ON}_{T-1,T-1_{FX}}\left[\frac{BRL}{USD}\right]|\mathcal{F}_t\right]=\frac{BRL}{USD}[t]\cdot\frac{P^{USB}_{t,t_{FX},T-1_{FX}}}{P^{CDI}_{t,t_{FX},T-1_{FX}}}$$

Now we need, on the other hand, to compute $\mathbb{E}^{\mathbb{Q}_{Selic}{}^{T}}[PTAX_{T-1}|\mathcal{F}_t]$. We can also substitute $PTAX_{T-1}$ by $FXFWD^{ON}_{T-1,T-1_{FX}}[\frac{BRL}{USD}]$ inside the expectation. $FXFWD^{ON}_{t,T-1_{FX}}[\frac{BRL}{USD}]$ is still a martingale under the probability measure associated with $P^{CDI}_{t,t_{FX},T-1_{FX}}$ as numéraire. However, now we need the compute the expectation under the probability measure $\mathbb{Q}_{Selic}{}^{T}$, which has $P^{Selic}_{t,T}$ as its numéraire. We can't use now the assumption that $P^{Selic}_{t,T}$ is close enough to $P^{CDI}_{t,t_{FX},T-1_{FX}}$ so that convexity adjustments are negligible. Specially for SCS contracts with a long maturity date. In that case, $P^{Selic}_{t,T}$and $P^{CDI}_{t,t_{FX},T-1_{FX}}$ values will be even more distant.

To finish the pricing derivation we need another stochastic calculus theorem called the Girsanov Theorem, summarized below.

Consider the stochastic differential equation:

$$dX_t=f(X_t)\cdot dt+\sigma(X_t)\cdot dW_t \tag{191}$$

under $\mathbb{P}$. Define a new measure $\mathbb{P}^*$ by:

$$\frac{d\mathbb{P}^*}{d\mathbb{P}}|_{\mathcal{F}_t}=exp\left\{-\frac{1}{2}\cdot\int_0^t Y_s^2\cdot ds+\int_0^t Y_s\cdot dW_s\right\} \tag{192}$$

and

$$dW_t^*=-Y_t\cdot dt+dW_t \tag{193}$$

Is a Brownian Motion under $\mathbb{P}^*$.

The more interested reader is referred again to (Shreve, 2010) for a full derivation of the theorem.

Let's assume that we have the following constant volatility geometric Brownian motion stochastic differential equation for $FXFWD^{ON}_{T-1,T-1_{FX}}[\frac{BRL}{USD}]$

$$dFXFWD^{ON}_{t,T-1_{FX}}\left[\frac{BRL}{USD}\right] = FXFWD^{ON}_{t,T-1_{FX}}\left[\frac{BRL}{USD}\right] \cdot \sigma_{FXFWD} \cdot dW^{T_{CDI}}_{1_t} \tag{194}$$

where,

σ_{FXFWD}: is a constant volatility for the $\frac{BRL}{USD}$ onshore FX forward value.

$W^{T_{CDI}}_{1_t}$: is a Brownian motion under the probability measure $\mathbb{Q}^{T}_{CDI}$, associated with numéraire $P^{CDI}_{t,T}$.

The Radon-Nikodym derivative to move from measure $\mathbb{Q}^{T}_{\mathbb{CDI}}$ to measure $\mathbb{Q}_{\text{Selic}}{}^{T}$ is given by:

$$\frac{d\mathbb{Q}^{T}_{\text{Selic}}}{d\mathbb{Q}^{T}_{\mathbb{CDI}}}|\mathcal{F}_{T} = \frac{d\mathbb{Q}^{T}_{\text{Selic}}}{d\mathbb{Q}_{\text{Selic}}} \cdot \frac{d\mathbb{Q}_{\mathbb{CDI}}}{d\mathbb{Q}^{T}_{\mathbb{CDI}}} = \frac{\beta^{S}_{T}}{\beta^{S}_{t}} \cdot \frac{1}{P^{Selic}_{t,T}} \cdot \frac{\beta_{t}}{\beta_{T}} \cdot P^{CDI}_{t,T} \tag{195}$$

Defining,

$$\frac{\beta_{T}}{\beta_{t}} \cdot \frac{\beta^{S}_{t}}{\beta^{S}_{T}} = \frac{\beta^{S*}_{T}}{\beta^{S*}_{t}} \tag{196}$$

and recalling that the CDI to Selic spread discount factor P^{Selic*}_{t,T_i} was defined as:

$$P^{Selic*}_{t,T_i} \cdot P^{CDI}_{t,T_i} = P^{Selic}_{t,T_i}$$

enables us to rewrite (195) as:

$$\frac{d\mathbb{Q}^{T}_{\text{Selic}}}{d\mathbb{Q}^{T}_{\mathbb{CDI}}}|\mathcal{F}_{T} = \frac{\beta^{S*}_{t}}{\beta^{S*}_{T}} \cdot \frac{1}{P^{Selic*}_{t,T_i}} \tag{197}$$

Now, let's assume that P^{Selic*}_{t,T_i} follows a HJM type diffusion like the one defined below:

$$\frac{dP^{Selic*}_{t,T}}{P^{Selic*}_{t,T}} = r^{Selic^*}_{t} \cdot dt - \sigma^{t}_{P^{Selic*}_{t,T}} \cdot dZ_{t} \tag{198}$$

with,

$$dW^{T_{CDI}}_{1_t} \cdot dZ_{t} = \rho^{Selic^*}_{FX} \cdot dt \tag{199}$$

where,

$\rho^{Selic^*}_{FX}$: is the correlation of FXFWD variable $FXFWD^{ON}_{t,T-1_{FX}}[\frac{BRL}{USD}]$ and CDI to Selic spread continuously compounded rate $r^{Selic^*}_{t}$.

$\sigma^{t}_{P^{Selic*}_{s,T}}$: is HJM type instantaneous volatility for the already defined Selic to CDI spread discount factor term $P^{Selic*}_{t,T}$ seen at date t for maturity date T.

Z_t: is a Brownian motion under the probability measure $\mathbb{Q}_{\text{Selic}}$, that has β_t^S as its numéraire.

Using the Cholesky decomposition enables us to express dZ_t as a combination of independent Brownian Motions $dW_{1_t}^{T_{CDI}}$ and $dW_{2_t}^{T_{CDI}}$ under probability measure $\mathbb{Q}_{CDI}^{\text{T}}$ as:

$$dZ_t = \rho_{FX}^{Selic^*} \cdot dW_{1_t}^{T_{CDI}} + \sqrt{1 - \left(\rho_{FX}^{Selic^*}\right)^2} \cdot dW_{2_t}^{T_{CDI}} \tag{200}$$

By plugging (200) into (198) yields:

$$\frac{dP_{t,T}^{Selic*}}{P_{t,T}^{Selic*}} = r_t^{Selic^*} \cdot dt - \sigma_{P_{t,T}^{Selic*}}^t \cdot \left(\rho_{FX}^{Selic^*} \cdot dW_{1_t}^{T_{CDI}} + \sqrt{1 - \left(\rho_{FX}^{Selic^*}\right)^2} \cdot dW_{2_t}^{T_{CDI}}\right) \tag{201}$$

By plugging (201) into (197) and with some HJM and stochastic calculus algebra, we can rewrite (197) as an exponential martingale as proposed below:

$$\frac{d\mathbb{Q}_{\text{Selic}}{}^{\text{T}}}{d\mathbb{Q}_{\text{CDI}}^{\text{T}}} |\mathcal{F}_{\text{T}} = exp\left\{-\frac{1}{2} \cdot \int_t^T \left(\sigma_{P_{s,T}^{Selic*}}^s\right)^2 \cdot ds\right\} \cdot \tag{202}$$

$$\cdot exp\left\{\int_t^T \left(\sigma_{P_{s,T}^{Selic*}}^s\right) \cdot \left(\rho_{FX}^{Selic^*} \cdot dW_{1_s}^{T_{CDI}} + \sqrt{1 - \rho_{FX}^{Selic^* 2}} \cdot dW_{2_s}^{T_{CDI}}\right)\right\} \tag{203}$$

Applying the Girsanov theorem we can define a Brownian motion $W_{1_t}^{T_{Selic}}$ under the probability measure $\mathbb{Q}_{\text{Selic}}{}^{\text{T}}$ as:

$$dW_{1_t}^{T_{Selic}} = -\rho_{FX}^{Selic^*} \cdot \sigma_{P_{t,T}^{Selic*}}^t \cdot dt + dW_{1_t}^{T_{CDI}} \tag{204}$$

Plugging (204) into (194) yields:

$$dFXFWD_{t,T-1_{FX}}^{ON}\left[\frac{BRL}{USD}\right]$$

$$= FXFWD_{t,T-1_{FX}}^{ON}\left[\frac{BRL}{USD}\right] \cdot \sigma_{FXFWD} \cdot \left(dW_{1_t}^{T_{Selic}} + \rho_{FX}^{Selic^*} \cdot \sigma_{P_{t,T}^{Selic*}}^t \cdot dt\right) \tag{205}$$

Finally, by plugging (205) into (190) yields:

$$FUT_{SCS}(t,T) = \frac{50{,}000 \cdot \text{P}_{\text{t,T}}^{\text{Selic}}}{\text{PTAX}_{\text{t}-1}} \cdot \text{FXFWD}_{\text{t,T}-1_{\text{FX}}}^{\text{ON}}\left[\frac{\text{BRL}}{\text{USD}}\right]$$

$$\cdot \exp\left\{\sigma_{FXFWD} \cdot \rho_{FX}^{Selic^*} \cdot \sigma_{P_{t,T}^{Selic*}}^t \cdot \tau_{t,T-1}\right\} \tag{206}$$

After a bit of algebra we can rewrite it in a format better suited to be compared with a DDI or SCC contract price:

$$FUT_{SCS}(t,T) = \frac{50{,}000 \cdot \mathrm{P}^{\mathrm{Selic}}_{\mathrm{t,T}}}{\mathrm{PTAX}_{\mathrm{t-1}}} \cdot \frac{BRL}{USD}[t] \cdot \frac{P^{USB}_{t,t_{FX},T-1_{FX}}}{P^{CDI}_{t,t_{FX},T-1_{FX}}}$$
$$\cdot\, exp\left\{\sigma_{FXFWD} \cdot \rho^{Selic^*}_{FX} \cdot \sigma^{t}_{P^{Selic*}_{t,T}} \cdot \tau_{t,T-1}\right\}$$

$$FUT_{SCS}(t,T) = FUT_{DDI}(t,T) \cdot P^{Selic*}_{t,T} \cdot exp\left\{\sigma_{FXFWD} \cdot \rho^{Selic^*}_{FX} \cdot \sigma^{t}_{P^{Selic*}_{t,T}} \cdot \tau_{t,T-1}\right\} \tag{207}$$

By looking at (205), it can be observed now that the dynamics of $FXFWD^{ON}_{t,T-1_{FX}}[\frac{BRL}{USD}]$ under the probability measure $\mathbb{Q}^{\mathrm{T}}_{\mathrm{Selic}}$ has a drift based on the covariance of $P^{Selic*}_{t,T}$ and $FXFWD^{ON}_{T-1,T-1_{FX}}[\frac{BRL}{USD}]$. If the rate spread of CDI to Selic $r^{Selic*}_{s,T}$ has positive (negative) correlation to $FXFWD^{ON}_{T-1,T-1_{FX}}[\frac{BRL}{USD}]$, then we should have a positive (negative) drift of $FXFWD^{ON}_{t,T-1_{FX}}[\frac{BRL}{USD}]$ under $\mathbb{Q}^{\mathrm{T}}_{\mathrm{Selic}}$.

This was the missing information required to price a SCS contract and it should be noted that if the covariance of $FXFWD^{ON}_{t,T-1_{FX}}[\frac{BRL}{USD}]$ and $P^{Selic*}_{s,T}$ is non negligible, then the price of a SCS contract is model dependent as observed in (207). Particularly, in the above SCS price derivation, we chose to use a volatility constant geometric Brownian motion for $FXFWD^{ON}_{t,T-1_{FX}}[\frac{BRL}{USD}]$ and a HJM type process for $P^{Selic*}_{t,T}$ to arrive at a first order convexity adjustment on the price without having to deal with complex models.

Also, from (207), 2 particular aspects can be noticed when pricing a SCS Futures contract. One is the expected result that its price should depend on the CDI to Selic spread discount factor $P^{Selic*}_{t,T}$ when compared to the SCC or DDI Futures price. The other aspect tells us that it's not possible to replicate or hedge statically a SCS Futures position, with DDI (or SCC), DI and Selic Futures positions. Thus, a dynamic hedging strategy needs to put in place, which results in the convexity term $\exp\left\{\sigma_{\mathrm{FXFWD}} \cdot \rho^{\mathrm{Selic}^*}_{\mathrm{FX}} \cdot \sigma^{\mathrm{t}}_{\mathrm{P}^{\mathrm{Selic*}}_{\mathrm{t,T}}} \cdot \tau_{\mathrm{t,T-1}}\right\}$.

One may argue that historically, the correlation of the CDI to Selic O/N spread with the components of the $\frac{BRL}{USD}$ fx forward onshore value, namely the fx spot rate $\frac{BRL}{USD}[t]$, $P^{CDI}_{t,T}$ and $P^{USB}_{t,T}$ is not statistically different than 0. Therefore, the convexity adjustment would be close to 0. However, even if one believes this to be true, still it would be required to dynamically hedge a SCS Futures with a DDI, DI and Selic Future contracts. This dynamic hedging strategy should produce an expected total P&L close to 0, but there may be periods with positive and negative P&L from carrying the dynamic hedge through time. A trader that doesn't want to generate this P&L volatility in his book could still charge a bit to enter into a SCS contract.

Another important fact is that the convexity adjustment is dependent on 2 terms that are a function of time. First is the obvious day count fraction term

$\tau_{t,T-1}$. The other is $\sigma^{t}_{p^{Selic*}_{t,T}}$ that is a discount factor volatility. Since a discount factor has a pull to par (in this case 1) effect, similarly to what occur to bond prices, then the volatility of a discount factor can be viewed to be a linear function of time. Therefore, for SCS maturities shorter than 3M, the convexity adjustment should be small, regardless of a correlation value.

6.15 Forward starting SCS contracts

In the previous subsection it was mentioned that a SCS Futures contract is already quite complex. Market participants in Brazil, however, trade forward starting SCS contracts. Much alike the DDI, the SCS future contract trades a "dirty" rate. And the idea of trading it forward starting is exactly one way to overcome this issue and trade a "clean" rate instead.

However, one complication is regarding registering those contracts at BVMF. Currently all SCS traded contracts for the same maturity date are aggregated under the same BVMF code. BVMF has a file that distinguishes them by a field called Position Date, which indicates what's the starting date of the SCS contract.

Usually banks develop a system for computing future contracts analytics and P&L based on contract codes, and since the contract codes are the same for SCS contracts with different start dates, this generates a lot of problems for the banks. The usual aggregation of positions with same code cannot happen, as the information regarding Position Date would be lost which is relevant for P&L and risk management purposes.

Regarding pricing formulas for the SCS contracts that have start dates in the future, the basic SCS formulas derived in (190) can be used replacing date t by t_{start}, recalling that t is the trading date and t_{start} is now a new variable to designate the forward starting date. Also, the FX spot to yesterday's PTAX ratio term will not be present justifying trading a "clean" rate, similarly to what happens with FRC contracts.

6.16 A much simpler alternative to FRC contracts

As you can see, Section 6 is pretty extensive. This happens mostly because the USD linked onshore interest rate future contracts, like DDI, FRC, SCC and SCS, are somehow complex to understand. Maybe even a bit more for a market participant based outside Brazil. Those contracts have margin cashflows formulated in a non trivial way, at least when compared to similar interest rate future contracts for G10 currencies. We also highlighted many issues with them that prevent perhaps the liquidity of these contracts to grow. As pointed out previously, the FRC, which is the most liquid USD linked interest rate future contract, trades mostly during the day driven by a call that happens daily at around 4pm São Paulo time.

Summarizing the issues mentioned previously for the current USD linked contracts, the DDI future contract trades a dirty cupom rate and because of that it has very small liquidity when traded as a single contract and not part of the FRC strategy. The FRC strategy itself, trades a clean forward cupom rate, but is at the end of the day converted to 2 DDI future contracts, which have complex and non standard margin cashflow formulas for the market participant based outside brazil which is used to other interest rate future contracts offered on other market exchanges. The SCC and SCS contracts are mostly traded with Brazil Central Bank as counterparty and currently the SCS future is the elected one by BCB to intervene in FX derivatives market. But, as we have previously demonstrated, its price is model dependent, at least for longer maturity dates.

The limitations previously discussed lead us to question ourselves if there's an alternative to the FRC formulation, which could be simpler and closer to what market participants have outside Brazil. The authors believe the answer is yes and propose a contract constructed similarly to an Eurodollar Futures contract. It would trade, as the FRC strategy, a forward clean cupom rate, would not require a conversion to 2 DDI at the end of the day and don't involve complex margin cashflow formulas. As a matter of fact, the margin cashflows could be extremely simple and given by:

$$MCF_t = \left(L_{t,T_1,T_2} - L_{t-1,T_1,T_2}\right) \cdot \tau_{T_1,T_2}^{Act360} \cdot PTAX_t \tag{208}$$

where,

L_{t,T_1,T_2}: is the new proposed contract closing rate published at date t by BVMF for a contract that trades a forward rate between T_1 and T_2 dates. At maturity date T_1, L_{T_1,T_2} would be implied from closing BVMF FX Future prices for T_1, Casado and DI closing rates. Or a deposit rate needs to be created and used as a fixing source for this contract playing a similar role that US Libor 3M rate plays for Eurodollar Futures.

This contract could pay at date t_{FX} the margin cashflow computed at date t. This way it would take into account the fact that $PTAX_t$, as a proxy for fx spot rate to convert cashflows, is a valid rate to convert cashflows from BRL to USD only at date t_{FX}. However, the exchange could have some complications to settle the margin payments based on t_{FX}, which could be a holiday in a BMF calendar and because of this fact the exchange would be closed.

Therefore, the authors think that margin cashflows could be paid the same way as any current BVMF future contract, which is one business day forward in a BMF calendar, still without affecting much the pricing of this hypothetical contract.

6.17 A BRL Float or Fixed X USD onshore Fixed swap

Usually, one key difference on the specification of a BRL Float or Fixed X USD onshore Fixed swap is how to convert the BRL leg Notional (USD leg Notional) into the USD onshore leg Notional (BRL leg Notional) at the start of the trade. If it's done using $\frac{BRL}{USD}[t]$, which is the fx spot rate seen at pricing time, then the swap is called a clean swap, as it doesn't reference any previous fx fixing for converting Notionals. However, as we have seen previously, the fx spot rate $\frac{BRL}{USD}[t]$, is obtained from the subtraction of first available contract $\frac{BRL}{USD}[t]$ FX Future rate $FXFUT^{ON}_{t,T-1_{FX}}[\frac{BRL}{USD}]$ and $Casado_t$ value. The liquidity of $Casado_t$ is not the same as $FXFUT^{ON}_{t,T-1_{FX}}[\frac{BRL}{USD}]$ though, and the 2 counterparties entering the swap sometimes could have some problems to agree on the fx spot rate used to convert Notionals at the start of the trade. To circumvent the issue of agreeing on the fx spot rate, sometimes a BRL Float or Fixed X USD onshore Fixed swap uses $PTAX_{t-1}$ as the FX Fixing used to convert the BRL leg Notional into USD or vice-versa. When this happens, the swap is said to be trading a dirty USD onshore fixed rate, in a similar way that occurs with DDI Futures contracts.

6.17.1 Coupon payoff specification

Assuming a clean swap that has N coupons and a BRL Fixed rate, the T_{i-th} coupon payoff in BRL is defined as:

$$\begin{aligned} Cpn_{T_i}[BRL] &= Not_{BRL} \cdot \left((1+R_{BRL})^{\tau^{Bus252}_{T_{i-1},T_i}} - 1 \right) \\ &\quad - \frac{Not_{BRL}}{\frac{BRL}{USD}[t]} \cdot \left(R_{USB} \cdot \tau^{Act360}_{T_{i-1},T_i} \right) \cdot PTAX_{T_i-1} \end{aligned} \tag{209}$$

where

Cpn_{T_i}: is the coupon payoff for T_{i-th} coupon assumed to be paid at time T_i.

R_{BRL}: is the exponential BRL fixed rate defined in BUS252 DCB.

R_{USB}: is the linear USB(cupom) fixed rate defined in Act360 DCB.

$\frac{Not_{BRL}}{\frac{BRL}{USD}[t]} = Not_{USD}$: is the Notional of USD leg converted from BRL Notional based on fx spot rate seen at time t , $\frac{BRL}{USD}[t]$.

$PTAX_{T_i-1}$: usually the USD onshore leg has its payoff converted to BRL by the PTAX published one business day prior to coupon payment date T_i in a CDI calendar.

The dirty version of the above payoff would simply use a past FX Fixing in (209) to substitute the definition of $Not_{USD} = \frac{Not_{BRL}}{PTAX_{t-1}}$.

6.17.2 Coupon pricing

The present value of the T_{i-th} coupon of a clean BRL Fixed swap can be calculated by:

$$PV_t = P^{CDI}_{t,T_i} \cdot \mathbb{E}^{\mathbb{Q}^{T_i}_{CDI}}[\mathrm{Cpn}_{T_i}[\mathrm{BRL}]|\mathcal{F}_t]$$

$$PV_t = P^{CDI}_{t,T_i} \cdot Not_{BRL} \cdot \left((1+R_{BRL})^{\tau^{Bus252}_{T_{i-1},T_i}} - 1 \right) + \tag{210}$$

$$(-1)P^{CDI}_{t,T_i} \cdot \frac{Not_{BRL}}{\frac{BRL}{USD}[t]} \cdot \left(R_{USB} \cdot \tau^{Act360}_{T_{i-1},T_i}\right) \cdot FXFWD^{ON}_{t,T_i-1_{FX}}\left[\frac{BRL}{USD}\right] \tag{211}$$

It's worth mentioning that inside $FXFWD^{ON}_{t,T_i-1_{FX}}[\frac{BRL}{USD}]$, there's a forward discount factor term $P^{CDI}_{t_{FX},T_i-1_{FX}}$ that doesn't cancel perfectly the discounting term P^{CDI}_{t,T_i} because the payment date is T_i. That's why to be really accurate when pricing a contract, the lag between payment dates and fx settlement dates need to be taken into account. Also, we used again the approximation that $\mathbb{E}^{\mathbb{Q}^{T_i}_{CDI}}\left[\mathrm{FXFWD}^{ON}_{T_i-1,T_i-1_{FX}}[\frac{BRL}{USD}]|\mathcal{F}_t\right] = \mathrm{FXFWD}^{ON}_{t,T_i-1_{FX}}[\frac{BRL}{USD}]$, since the convexity adjustment is negligible as discussed in the previous subsections.

We used a fixed BRL leg in this subsection, but a floating leg could be used as well, as the main purpose was to describe the usual dates and definitions for the USD onshore leg of the swap, since the BRL fixed or floating leg mechanics have been discussed in this book's previous subsections.

7
Too Many Options?

After describing the methodology to construct the majority of the required yield curves for the onshore Brazilian market, it's possible now to move one step forward in the complexity level and talk about IR and FX options in the onshore market.

Currently there are 2 IR options available at BVMF. The first is called DI Future option and is a product where you have the option to enter at a future time T_1 into a DI Futures contract with maturity date T_2 . Since you can only exercise at expiry date T_1, it's an European option and it's deliverable, meaning that upon exercise you enter a DI Future contract and there's no cash being settled upon exercise.

The second interest rate option available is called IDI option, it's also European but cash settled at its maturity date T. There are also 2 strategies called VTF and VID that allow market participants to enter into a delta hedged DI Future option or IDI option contract, respectively. The delta hedge amount is given in DI Future contracts and the amount of contracts given for delta hedge is calculated by the exchange through a formula that will be discussed later in more detail.

Regarding IDI options, we will discuss the construction of all 3 different indices used as their underlying, being 2 related to CDI index compounding and one to Selic. The next topic discusses the IDI option payoff, including some algebra transformations that are useful to trade it in terms of a fixed Notional in BRL, which is more frequent in the OTC market, or based on a quantity of contracts, which happens more often when traded through BVMF exchange. The next subsection gives an example of how to trade IDI options to bet in future monetary policy.

The following subsections enter into IDI options pricing based on different assumptions of its underlying. First, an IDI options Black pricer is derived considering the IDI index as it's main underlying. It's explained later that this method has some drawbacks, the most evident being the limitation to compute the Vega risk in a uniform way across different maturities for IDI options. To circumvent this issue, a second model and its associated Black pricer are proposed where the underlying is the realized rate between trading date and maturity date.

The next subsection tries to explain how to fit the 2 most frequent volatility surfaces shapes that are found in the Brazilian IR options market. For the smile shaped volatility surface, the SABR model is proposed. For the smirk shaped volatility surface, a discrete tree model is proposed that only allows the CDI or Selic O/N rate to jump between Brazil Central Bank meeting dates, since no stochastic volatility model would be able to fit a smirk shaped volatility surface.

Still regarding interest rate options, in case 2 market participants want to trade a particular strike not provided in current listed options at BVMF they could register the trade at CETIP which covers the OTC market in Brazil. Some brokers also provide other payoffs like digital IDI options which will be constructed based on a strategy containing a combination of options. Also discussed will be the limitation that diffusive models have to price IDI options, especially the digital IDI options that are strongly dependent of the jumpy nature of Selic rate between Brazil Central Bank meeting dates.

The subsequent subsection discusses the pricing of IDI options under a HJM model. Another interesting subsection will discuss how to calculate a historical volatility of an IDI option, imagining that the only data available to you are DI Futures historical closing rates. We will show that this computation is far from trivial and justifies an extra subsection to expose what the authors believe is the correct methodology.

The last IDI options subsection explains what IDI option exotic payoffs are proposed to corporate companies to hedge floating debt issued indexed by CDI. The difficulties to price those type of options will be presented and 2 models will be proposed to price them. The drawbacks of each model will be discussed also.

Regarding DI Future options, its first dedicated section will cover the basic trading information for this contract and the contract codes defined by BVMF to trade them. The next subsection transforms the DI Future option payoff into a zero coupon swaption payoff. In the next subsection the most usual trading strategies where DI Future options are used are discussed. A swaption Black pricer for DI Future options is created in the next subsection. However, it's not capable of generating a volatility smile, therefore the next subsection discusses how to use the SABR model in order to generate it. The next subsections derives DI Future option pricing formulas under HJM and BGM models. Finally, a method to compute DI Future options historical implied volatility is suggested.

On the FX side, there are currently 2 types of listed options at BVMF. One is a regular European vanilla listed $\frac{BRL}{USD}$ FX option which is cash settled, meaning that upon exercise you don't enter into a $\frac{BRL}{USD}$ fx spot trade but only cash settle the agreed payoff of the option. The other is a listed option with daily margining, where the only difference compared with the previous FX listed option product is that it has daily margin calls based on the difference of BVMF published option prices on 2 consecutive days. However, the option based on daily margin never really traded like the exchange was foreseeing and currently there's very little open interest on it. There are also FX option strategies to trade delta-hedged FX options. VTC is the strategy that consists in a $\frac{BRL}{USD}$ FX delta hedged regular vanilla listed option and VCA is the strategy to trade a delta hedged $\frac{BRL}{USD}$ FX option with daily margining. Again, different amounts of BVMF delta hedge calculated to the ones based on known models that produce a volatility smile will be compared.

Finally, there's also an over-the-counter (OTC) version of the regular FX option to cover strikes that are not traded in the exchange to better suit a particular market participant need which are registered at CETIP, as in the interest rate options case.

7.1 IDI options

IDI options are a popular way to bet in future monetary policy using the interest rate options market. As will be explained in more detail later, the underlying of this option is the IDI index and the payoff for an IDI option is based on the IDI index value at maturity date T. The link of IDI options payoff to future monetary policy decisions can be explained by the fact that the IDI index at a future value depends on future CDI or Selic O/N rates. Those rates are strongly linked to future Selic target O/N rates, which are driven finally by monetary policy decisions.

7.1.1 IDI options available indices and compounding methodology

There are currently 2 IDI indices defined. The first is called IDI2003 and its base date is 02-Jan-2003. The second one is called IDI2009 and its base date is 02-Jan-2009. Both these indices were set to 100,000 points at base date and they compound every business day in CDI calendar based on the CDI O/N published fixing for that same date. The procedure is defined as below:

$$IDI_t = IDI_{BaseDate} \cdot \prod_{T_i=Basedate}^{t} (1+CDI_{T_i})^{\frac{1}{252}} \tag{212}$$

It's worth mentioning again that the notation of the compounding product operator above uses the Basedate inclusive and date t exclusive like used throughout this book.

After 2009, the IDI2003 compounded value was considered already too high and BVMF thought that it could boost back again liquidity of IDI options by reducing the contract size of an IDI option contract. However, the IDI index value at trade date was exactly the equivalent BRL Notional of one contract. Thus, to reduce the contract size, a decrease of IDI index value was required. The way BVMF achieved this was by creating a new IDI index for IDI options, now with a base date on 02-Jan-2009. For example, at 02-Jan-2009, the IDI2003 index value was 246,277.82 and the IDI2009 index was set to 100,000. This means that for the same IDI option, the option premium that a market participant would have to pay would be reduced approximately by 2.5 times for the same amount of contracts if done based on IDI2009 instead of IDI2003 index. This also means that there's a big chance that from time to time BVMF would have to create other indices, in order to set their values back to 100,000 to increase liquidity again.

There's also another index used for IDI options based on Selic O/N compounding instead of CDI. It's called ITC2012 and its base date is 02-Jan-2012 and it was also set with a value of 100,000 at base date. Its compounding formula is:

$$ITC_t = ITC_{BaseDate} \cdot \prod_{T_i=Basedate}^{t} (1+Selic_{T_i})^{\frac{1}{252}} \tag{213}$$

7.1.2 IDI options payoff and other contractual information

For an IDI option with maturity date T, the BRL payoff is given by:

$$Payoff_{T+1^*} = Q \cdot M \cdot max\left(cp \cdot [IDI_T - K], 0\right) \tag{214}$$

where,

Q: is the quantity of contracts.

M: M is a multiplier of points for an IDI index, currently set to 1.

$max(A,B)$: is the operator that computes the maximum value of A and B.

cp: variable to define if it's a call or put option. It's equal to 1 if it's a call and equal to -1 if it's a put.

IDI_T: is the IDI (or ITC) index value at maturity date T. It's worth mentioning that the last CDI or Selic fixing occurs at $T-1$. This is consistent with the definition we use for $\prod_{T_i=t}^{T}(1+CDI_{T_i})^{\frac{1}{252}}$ throughout the book, where it's inclusive on start accrual date t and exclusive on end accrual date T.

K: the IDI option strike.

$Payoff_{T+1^*}$: the payoff of the IDI option that occurs at $T+1^*$, which is one business day after maturity date T in a BMF calendar.

Sometimes market participants want to rearrange (214) to trade an IDI option based on a BRL Notional instead of number of contracts. To achieve that, we have to redefine the IDI option strike in rate units instead of index units by:

$$K = IDI_t \cdot (1+R_K)^{\tau_{t,T}^{Bus252}} \tag{215}$$

Plugging (212) and (215) into (214) yields:

$$Payoff_{T+1^*} = Q \cdot M \cdot IDI_t \cdot max\left(cp \cdot \left[\prod_{T_i=t}^{T} (1+CDI_{T_i})^{\frac{1}{252}} - (1+R_K)^{\tau_{t,T}^{Bus252}}\right], 0\right) \tag{216}$$

In our notation, IDI_t is the IDI spot value at date t. It can be seen from (216) that the quantity $Q \cdot M \cdot IDI_t$ plays the role of a BRL Notional, since the term $max\left(cp \cdot \left[\prod_{T_i=t}^{T}(1+CDI_{T_i})^{\frac{1}{252}} - (1+R_K)^{\tau_{t,T}^{Bus252}}\right], 0\right)$ has as its basic components BRL floating and fixed rate capitalization factors. Using this argument we can rewrite (216) as:

$$Payoff_{T+1^*} = Not_{BRL} \cdot max\left(cp \cdot \left[\prod_{T_i=t}^{T}(1+CDI_{T_i})^{\frac{1}{252}} - (1+R_K)^{\tau_{t,T}^{Bus252}}\right], 0\right) \quad (217)$$

where,

Not_{BRL}: is the IDI option BRL Notional.

R_K: is the IDI option equivalent strike rate obtained through (215).

Using (217) is the way that market participants, usually in the OTC market, agree on an IDI option payoff written in terms of a BRL Notional. They prefer to trade this way because sometimes they have loans or swaps where the underlying is CDI and are based on a BRL Notional. For those trades, (217) provides an easy way to enter into an option contract to hedge the swap or loan on the required BRL Notional amount directly.

On the contractual side, all listed options are defined at BVMF by a series, which is effectively a code that defines the option details like maturity date, exercise price, underlying asset and if it's a call or put option. Series codes are constructed based on a methodology that can be found at http://www.bmfbovespa.com.br/pt-br/regulacao/regulamentos-e-normas/procedimentos-operacionais/derivativos/codigo-de-negociacao-de-opcoes.aspx?idioma=pt-br. The idea is that the first 3 letters of a series represent the underlying asset, so for IDI options it would be IDI. The fourth letter would represent the maturity month of the contract. Fifth and sixth characters would represent the year. Seventh character represents if it's a call or put, being call represented by C and put by P. The last 6 digits would represent the strike. So IDIJ17C250000 represents an IDI call option for maturity date 2-Jan-17 (J17) with strike 250,000.

Other contractual information like assets accepted as collateral for the daily margin calls and operational costs are documented at BVMF website.

7.1.3 IDI options common trading strategies

As mentioned previously, IDI options can allow market participants to bet on future monetary policy. The best way to try to describe this process is with an example.

Imagine a market participant that thinks that there will be a hike of 50 bps on the O/N Selic target rate in the next BCB COPOM meeting. Let's assume this 50 bps hike in Selic O/N target rates turns out to be translated perfectly into a 50 bps hike in CDI O/N rate. Other assumptions required for this example are that the current CDI O/N rate is 10% and that the current IDI index is at 120,000 points. Regarding dates, it will be assumed that there are 15 business days in a CDI calendar to BCB COPOM meeting date and 40 business days in a CDI calendar to IDI option maturity date. Given that the market is predicting no hikes, the CDI O/N rate will be kept constant on at 10% for the remaining 40 business days until IDI option maturity date. Under this scenario, the IDI index at maturity date would be:

$$IDI_T = 120,000 \cdot (1+10\%)^{\frac{40}{252}} = 121,829.2$$

On the other hand, for the market participant that believes there will be a 50 bps hike, his forecast of IDI index at maturity date is:

$$IDI_T = 120,000 \cdot (1+10\%)^{\frac{15}{252}} \cdot (1+10.50\%)^{\frac{25}{252}} = 121,884.1$$

By entering an IDI call option with strike at 121,829, the market participant that believes a 50 bps hike will happen is expecting to exercise the option at maturity date and make a profit. If that expectation is not realized and CDI O/N rate remains at 10% he only loses the upfront premium paid.

Usually the future monetary policy bets are done through option strategies, as combinations of calls and puts with different strikes to compose a suitable payoff in the scenario that a particular market participant is forecasting. This combination of calls and puts can produce any kind of payoff graphs, like collars, call or put spreads and other similar strategies.

7.1.4 A simple Black pricing formula for an IDI option assuming the IDI index as its main underlying

Let's suppose we are interested in pricing an IDI option based on CDI O/N rate (we will discuss IDI options based on the Selic index later in this section). Assuming that the IDI forward value follows a geometric Brownian motion stochastic process like below:

$$dIDI_{t,T} = IDI_{t,T} \cdot \sigma_{IDI} \cdot dW_t^{T_{CDI}} \tag{218}$$

where,

$IDI_{t,T}$: is the IDI forward value seen at date t for an IDI option with maturity date T. It's computed by $IDI_{t,T} = \frac{IDI_t}{P_{t,T}^{CDI}}$.

σ_{IDI}: is the IDI index forward value constant volatility.

$W_t^{T_{CDI}}$: is a Brownian motion under the probability measure $\mathbb{Q}_{\mathbb{CDI}}^{\mathbb{T}}$, associated with numéraire $P_{t,T}^{CDI}$.

One could interpret the IDI index as a common financial index, like an equity index for example. If that path is followed, then we could obtain a Black pricer for a call IDI option by:

$$c = Q \cdot M \cdot \left(IDI_{t,T} \cdot N(d1) - K \cdot N(d2)\right) \cdot P_{t,t+1^*,T+1^*}^{CDI} \tag{219}$$

with

c: IDI call option premium to be paid at $t+1^*$, which is one business day in a BMF calendar after trading date t.

$$d1 = \frac{ln\left(\frac{IDI_{t,T}}{K}\right)+0.5\cdot\sigma_{IDI}^2\cdot T_{vol}}{\sigma_{IDI}\cdot\sqrt{T_{vol}}}$$

$$d2 = \frac{ln\left(\frac{IDI_{t,T}}{K}\right)-0.5\cdot\sigma_{IDI}^2\cdot T_{vol}}{\sigma_{IDI}\cdot\sqrt{T_{vol}}}$$

$P^{CDI}_{t,t+1^*,T+1^*}$: the forward discount factor in BRL onshore CDI curve seen at date t from option premium payment date $t+1^*$ to payoff payment date $T+1^*$. Discounting of payoff is done from $T+1^*$ because IDI option payoff occurs one business day in BMF calendar after maturity date T. Option premium payment occurs one business day in BMF calendar after trading date t like mentioned above.

T_{vol}: has to be in the same units as σ_{IDI}. As an example, if σ_{IDI} is defined in Bus252 DCB, then T_{vol} has to be computed as the number of business days between t date inclusive and maturity date T exclusive. One key thing to always remember is that the important quantity is $\sigma_{IDI}^2 \cdot T_{vol}$, which is the effective variance computed from t to T of the IDI forward value Brownian motion. Therefore, σ_{IDI} and T_{vol} have to always be in compatible units.

The equivalent IDI option put would be computed by:

$$p = Q\cdot M\cdot\left(K\cdot N(-d2) - IDI_{t,T}\cdot N(-d1)\right)\cdot P^{CDI}_{t,t+1^*,T+1^*} \tag{220}$$

where,

p: IDI put option premium.

The proofs to derive (219) and (220) are omitted in this book, but can be verified at Chapter 9 of (Shreve, 2010). Theorem 9.4.2 of (Shreve, 2010) describes the Black-Scholes-Merton option pricing with random interest rates, assuming an underlying that follows an SDE like in (218). The results are not identical because in our case we are using the fact that payment dates of option premium and payoff occur one business day after t and T respectively in a BMF calendar. In (Shreve, 2010), he assumes they occur at the same date, thus some cancellation of terms occurs in his formula.

One key point that we wanted to emphasize here is that to use the IDI index as a pure index with no interest rate connection is not the best route to take in the authors opinion. The first drawback is that the IDI index is in reality a function of interest rates, therefore one could argue that an arbitrage free interest rate model like HJM would provide better dynamics and therefore better hedging. In fact, we will show that using a HJM model to price IDI options helps to understand a lot from its nature, but also has its own drawbacks, as it will be discussed later in this book.

The second drawback is that the IDI index forward value implied volatility σ_{IDI} could be very small for short maturity IDI options. Typical values for a 1M option can be around 0.1% . On the other hand, for a 3Y IDI option, typical values of σ_{IDI} would be around 2.5%. Intuitively, it makes sense that the IDI forward value volatility is approximately linear with time to maturity, as the main underlying of the IDI index is the daily compounding capitalization factor of CDI (or Selic on IDI options based on ITC) O/N rates until option maturity date. So as time passes, the number of fixings remaining reduce linearly with time. The fact that σ_{IDI} is intuitively linear with time creates a problem for volatility risk computation. Usually the Vega of an IDI call option is computed by:

$$Vega = c_{\sigma_{Up}} - c_{Base}$$

where,

Vega: is the volatility sensitivity of an option.

$c_{\sigma_{Up}}$: is the price of an IDI call option shifting the implied volatility input of the Black formula by a predetermined shift size.

c_{Base}: is the IDI call option base (non-shifted) price.

The key question here is which volatility shift size to adopt for IDI options Vega calculation across different maturities. Clearly, it cannot be a common 1% shift, which is adopted usually for other assets, since a 1% shift in a 1M IDI option would represent a very large shift. On the other hand a 1% shift for a 3Y IDI option would be reasonable. Thus, a common approach to calculate Vega risk for IDI options across different maturity dates is tricky when treating the IDI index as a regular financial index and not recommended.

7.1.5 How to fit a volatility smile for an IDI option assuming the IDI index as its main underlying

Market participants that assume the IDI index as the main underlying for an IDI option usually adopt a parametric form to fit its volatility surface. The volatility surface is usually constructed based on Strike X Volatility X Maturity Date, but could be obtained also through Delta X Volatility X Maturity Date. Parametric forms usually adopted are cubic splines, quadratic polynomials and other polynomial and spline variations commonly used for FX or equity markets.

Those methods won't be discussed in depth because the authors believe that assuming the IDI index as the main underlying for IDI options is not the best approach.

7.1.6 A simple Black pricing formula assuming the IDI index equivalent realized interest rate as the underlying

The idea of this subsection is to try to change the underlying of the IDI option into an interest rate format so that the same volatility shift used to compute Vega risk could be used across different maturity dates.

We start from the same payoff of an IDI option given by:

$$Payoff_{T+1^*} = Q \cdot M \cdot IDI_t \cdot max\left(cp \cdot \left[\prod_{T_i=t}^{T} (1+CDI_{T_i})^{\frac{1}{252}} - (1+R_K)^{\tau_{t,T}^{252}}\right], 0\right) \quad (221)$$

Let's assume that the capitalization factor of CDI O/N exponential rates can be defined in terms of a realized interest rate variable by:

$$\prod_{T_i=t}^{T} (1+CDI_{T_i})^{\frac{1}{252}} = 1 + R_{t,T}^* \cdot \tau_{t,T}^{252} \quad (222)$$

where,

$R_{t,T}^*$: is the realized linear (not exponential) rate from date t to date T. Please bear in mind that this is a realized rate, that can only be computed at date $T-1$ when all the relevant CDI O/N fixings for IDI option pricing have been already published, in the same way that $\prod_{T_i=t}^{T} (1+CDI_{T_i})^{\frac{1}{252}}$ is only fully known also at time $T-1$.

Let's also redefine the term $(1+R_K)^{\tau_{t,T}^{Bus252}}$ in terms of a linear strike rate instead of exponential by:

$$(1+R_K)^{\tau_{t,T}^{Bus252}} = 1 + R_{K_L} \cdot \tau_{t,T}^{252} \quad (223)$$

where,

R_{K_L}: is a linear strike rate obtained from IDI option strike value K and IDI index spot value IDI_t .

By plugging (222) and (223) into (221) yields:

$$Payoff_{T+1^*} = Q \cdot M \cdot IDI_t \cdot \tau_{t,T}^{252} \cdot max\left(cp \cdot \left[R_{t,T}^* - R_{K_L}\right], 0\right) \quad (224)$$

Assuming that the realized rate $R_{t,T}^*$ is lognormally distributed enables us to use a Black formula based on interest rates to compute an IDI option price. This is exactly what was needed to overcome the issue of computing Vega risk based on the IDI index forward value as the underlying, as now the underlying is an interest rate and Vega risk can be computed with the same shift size, typically 1%, across all maturity dates.

But there's still one remaining variable that we have to compute in order to use the Black formula. What's the forward value of $R_{t,T}^*$ that will be input to the Black formula? We can answer this with the following equations:

$$\mathbb{E}^{\mathbb{Q}^{\mathrm{T}}_{\mathrm{CDI}}}\left[\prod_{T_i=t}^{T} (1+CDI_{T_i})^{\frac{1}{252}} | \mathcal{F}_t\right] = \mathbb{E}^{\mathbb{Q}^*}\left[\prod_{T_i=t}^{T} (1+CDI_{T_i})^{\frac{1}{252}} \cdot \frac{d\mathbb{Q}^{\mathrm{T}}_{\mathrm{CDI}}}{d\mathbb{Q}^*} | \mathcal{F}_t\right] \quad (225)$$

$$\frac{d\mathbb{Q}^{\mathrm{T}}_{\mathrm{CDI}}}{d\mathbb{Q}^*} = \frac{1}{P_{t,T}^{CDI} \cdot \prod_{T_i=t}^{T} (1+CDI_{T_i})^{\frac{1}{252}}} \quad (226)$$

By plugging (226) and (222) into (225) yields:

$$\mathbb{E}^{\mathbb{Q}^{\mathrm{T}}_{\mathrm{CDI}}}\left[1+R^{*}_{t,T}\cdot\tau^{Bus252}_{t,T}|\mathcal{F}_t\right]=\frac{1}{P^{CDI}_{t,T}}=1+R^{L}_{t,T}\cdot\tau^{252}_{t,T} \tag{227}$$

where,

$R^{L}_{t,T}$: is a linear rate from date t to date T obtained from CDI onshore curve calibrated discount factor $P^{CDI}_{t,T}$.

Finally,

$$\mathbb{E}^{\mathbb{Q}^{\mathrm{T}}_{\mathrm{CDI}}}\left[R^{*}_{t,T}|\mathcal{F}_t\right]=R^{L}_{t,T} \tag{228}$$

Therefore, the forward value of $R^{*}_{t,T}$ is $R^{L}_{t,T}$ and the Black formula used to price an IDI call option is:

$$c=Q\cdot M\cdot IDI_t\cdot\tau^{252}_{t,T}\left(R^{L}_{t,T}\cdot N(d1_R)-R_{K_L}\cdot N(d2_R)\right)\cdot P^{CDI}_{t,t+1^*,T+1^*} \tag{229}$$

where, $d1_R=\dfrac{ln\left(\frac{R^{L}_{t,T}}{R_{K_L}}\right)+0.5\cdot\sigma_R^2\cdot T_{vol}}{\sigma_R\cdot\sqrt{T_{vol}}}$

$$d2_R=\frac{ln\left(\frac{R^{L}_{t,T}}{R_{K_L}}\right)-0.5\cdot\sigma_R^2\cdot T_{vol}}{\sigma_R\cdot\sqrt{T_{vol}}}$$

σ_R: is the realized rate $R^{*}_{t,T}$ implied volatility.

The IDI put option would be given by:

$$p=Q\cdot M\cdot IDI_t\cdot\tau^{Bus252}_{t,T}\left(R_{K_L}\cdot N(-d2_R)-R^{L}_{t,T}\cdot N(-d1_R)\right)\cdot P^{CDI}_{t,t+1^*,T+1^*} \tag{230}$$

7.1.7 Is the IDI option smiling at you now?

In the previous subsection we arrived at Black-Scholes equations for an IDI option based on a lognormal distribution assumption on the realized linear rate $R^{*}_{t,T}$. However, IDI options implied volatility surface sometimes generate a smile shape, usually for longer than 3M expiries, and sometimes generate a smirk or smile shape, usually for shorter than 3M expiries which have 1 or 2 Central Bank meeting dates until expiry date. Therefore the lognormal assumption of $R^{*}_{t,T}$ must be changed in order to fit the implied volatilities observed in the IDI options market.

In case one is interested in generating a volatility smile, market participants often use the SABR stochastic volatility model. This model was proposed by Hagan, Kumar, Lesniewski and Woodward in "Managing Smile Risk" (Hagan, Kumar, Lesniewski and Woodward, 2002). The basic equations of this model are:

$$dF=\alpha\cdot F^{\beta}\cdot dW_1$$

$$d\alpha=\nu\cdot\alpha\cdot dW_2$$

$$dW_1\cdot dW_2=\rho\cdot dt$$

where,

F: is a forward value. In our particular case of IDI options, F will be substituted by $R^*_{t,T}$ in the SABR stochastic differential equations above and in the implied volatility definition below.

β: is a constant elasticity parameter. When $\beta = 1$, F stochastic differential equation is a geometric Brownian Motion. If $\beta = 0$, it's an arithmetic Brownian Motion.

α: is the instantaneous volatility of F.

ν: is the volatility of α, sometimes also called the vol-of-vol parameter.

ρ: is the correlation of F and α.

dW_1 and dW_2: are correlated Brownian Motions under the T forward measure. On the specific case of IDI options, they will be Brownian motions under the probability measure $d\mathbb{Q}^T_{\mathbb{CDI}}$.

Using perturbation techniques, the authors of "Managing Smile Risk" (Hagan, Kumar, Lesniewski and Woodward, 2002) managed to price an European option with a Black pricer, where its implied volatility input is a function of the SABR parameters α, β, ν and ρ given by:

$$\sigma_b(K,F) = \frac{\alpha}{(F\cdot K)^{\frac{(1-\beta)}{2}}\left\{1+\frac{(1-\beta)^2}{24}\cdot log^2\frac{F}{K}+\frac{(1-\beta)^4}{1920}log^4\frac{F}{K}+\ldots\right\}}\cdot\left(\frac{z}{x(z)}\right)\cdot \tag{231}$$

$$\cdot\left\{1+\left[\frac{(1-\beta)^2}{24}\cdot\frac{\alpha^2}{(FK)^{1-\beta}}+\frac{1}{4}\cdot\frac{\rho\beta\nu\alpha}{(FK)^{\frac{(1-\beta)}{2}}}+\frac{2-3\rho^2}{24}\nu^2\right]t_{ex+\ldots}\right\} \tag{232}$$

where,

$$z = \frac{\nu}{\alpha}(FK)^{\frac{(1-\beta)}{2}}\cdot log\frac{F}{K} \tag{233}$$

$$x(z) = log\left\{\frac{\sqrt{1-2\rho z+z^2}+z-\rho}{1-\rho}\right\} \tag{234}$$

In the case of IDI options, the Black pricer specified in (229) will have the input σ_R substituted by $\sigma_b(K,F)$ defined above. For the fit of SABR parameters α, β, ν and ρ to the IDI options volatility surface, usually it's chosen a process where β is considered to be 1, and the other parameters could be fit with a numerical procedure, with a constraint of ρ being in the range $[-1,1]$, $\alpha > 0$ and $\nu > 0$.

7.1.8 Or is it smirking?

If the IDI option volatility surface produces a smirk, then any type of stochastic volatility model won't be able to fit it. Stochastic volatility models like SABR are only able to reproduce a smile or a skew shaped volatility surface. In the case of a smirk, then the essence of the model is inappropriate, mostly because the jumpy nature of the the realized forward rate $R^*_{t,T}$ is more significant than the diffusive behavior of it. This is what drives that shape of volatility surface.

For IDI options with short term maturity dates that display the smirk type volatility shape, a discrete tree model that jumps between Central Bank meeting dates would be more suitable, even though its calibration is far from trivial. The next subsection will propose a model to enable market participants to fit the smirk shaped volatility smile. Other interesting literature related to this topic is *Pricing Interest Rate Derivatives Under Monetary Policy Changes* (Dario and Avellaneda, 2012).

Another complication in this setup is the concept of delta hedging. In this discrete tree model, it doesn't make sense to calculate the delta hedge of an IDI option by finite differences method by shifting the forward rate by 1 basis point and recalculating the IDI option price. In this setup, there are many possible paths for the O/N CDI rate, but either it stays constant between Central Bank meeting dates, or it shifts by multiples of 25 basis points. Under this situation, what seems to be more reasonable in terms of delta hedging is an approach where you try to solve the quantity of DI Futures that would be held in order to minimize the variance of the portfolio of IDI options plus hedge across all different possible paths.

7.1.9 A discrete tree model that could fit the smirk volatility surface shape for IDI options

The idea is to model the CDI O/N rate as a process where it remains constant between Central Bank meetings. After each Central Bank meeting (COPOM), the CDI O/N rate can jump in multiples of 25 bps. Here we are assuming that the CDI O/N rate basis to Selic O/N rates driven by Brazil Central Bank meetings is constant and not stochastic. In *Pricing Interest Rate Derivatives Under Monetary Policy Changes* (Dario and Avellaneda, 2012), it was proposed a method in which this assumption can be relaxed.

The model can be understood as a tree model (Stefan Andreev and Carlos Fuertes were main contributors to the development of this model), where we can specify all possible paths for the CDI rate. The CDI O/N rate is assumed to jump only in multiples of 25 bps and big jumps are extremely unlikely (for example jumps of more than ±150 bps), thus we could restrict ourselves to a finite set of possible paths.

There is strong dependence on the evolution of the CDI rate on what the Brazil Central Bank did in past COPOM meeting, therefore the evolution of the rate is *non-Markovian*. This means that the tree is non-recombining.

In order to price instruments, we follow the standard procedure of using a risk neutral probability distribution and obtain prices by averaging payoffs over all possible paths using this distribution,where we use as numéraire the IDI spot value IDI_t.

$$\frac{C_t}{IDI_t} = \mathbb{E}^{\mathbb{Q}^*}\left[\frac{C_T}{IDI_T}|\mathcal{F}_t\right] = \sum_{\omega} p(\omega)\frac{C_T(\omega)}{IDI_T(\omega)} \tag{235}$$

where:

ω is the set of paths.

$p(\omega)$ is the risk neutral probability of the corresponding path.

$C_T(\omega)$ and $IDI_T(\omega)$ are the values of the payoff of the IDI options and DI futures used in the calibration process and the IDI spot value, respectively, given path ω at time T.

It will not be assumed any parametric form for the distribution $p(\omega)$. We will infer it from market prices of instruments (DI futures and IDI options). From Equation (235), we can see that if the payoffs are independent of the path probabilities, this reduces to a linear system for $p(\omega)$ of the form

$$c_i = \sum_j A_{ij} p_j \tag{236}$$

for a given payoff matrix A_{ij}.

The problem with Equation (236) is that the rank of matrix A_{ij} is lower than the number of $p(\omega)$, therefore there is not a unique solution but many (if any). We have to specify which solution of (236) we want to pick with additional criteria. The market is incomplete because the risk neutral martingale measure is not unique and the exact replication of contingent claims is not possible.

The entropic distance between two discrete probability distributions, P and Q, also known as Kullback-Leibner divergence, is given by

$$H(P|Q) = \sum_k p_k \ln \frac{p_k}{q_k} \tag{237}$$

One possibility to arrive at a unique solution to our calibration problem (236) is to start with some *a priori* probability distribution $q(\omega)$ and solve the problem

$$\begin{aligned} &\min_P H(P|Q) \\ s.t.\ & c_i = \textstyle\sum_j A_{ij} p_j \end{aligned} \tag{238}$$

This is a convex problem with a unique solution.

One can prove that the problem (238) corresponds to the problem of utility maximization of a exponential utility function, more concretely, (238) is the Legendre dual problem of utility maximization of the exponential family.

(238) can be rewritten as the following min-max problem (Lagrange dual)

$$\min_{\lambda_i} \max_P \left\{ -H(P|Q) + \sum_i \lambda_i \left(\sum_j A_{ij} p_j - c_i \right) \right\} \tag{239}$$

which can be further rewritten as:

$$\min_{\lambda_i}\left\{\ln Z(\lambda) - \sum \lambda_i c_i\right\} \tag{240}$$

with

$$Z(\lambda) = \sum_k q_k \exp\left(-\sum \lambda_j A_{ji}\right) \tag{241}$$

$$p_k = \frac{q_k}{Z}\exp\left(-\sum \lambda_j A_{ji}\right) \tag{242}$$

This way we have performed a huge dimensional reduction of our problem at hand. Instead of minimizing over p_i, we only have to solve for problem (240) over the parameter space, λ_k, which has the same dimension as the number of market instrument prices that we start with c_i.

7.1.10 Delta hedging IDI options under the discrete tree model

Finding a delta hedging strategy for an IDI option under the discrete tree model is a bit different than the usual Greek type approach. In incomplete markets there is no perfect replication and you will be always left with a residual PnL. Hence, in an incomplete market, you have to choose an additional criterion to select the best hedge.

A hedging strategy is given by a series of Δ_{t_i} with

$$C(\omega_{t_{i+1}}) = \Delta_{t_i} X(\omega_{t_{i+1}}) + B(\omega_{t_{i+1}}) \tag{243}$$

where $X(\omega_{t_{i+1}})$ is the price of the hedging securities and B is the value of the money market account. In our example $X(\omega_{t_{i+1}})$ would be a DI Futures and B would be the amount of cash used to buy the IDI option. Δ_{t_i} can then be interpreted as the number of units of the DI Futures that you hold to hedge the IDI option at time t_i.

When perfect hedging is not possible, one natural criteria is to minimize the variance under the risk neutral probability of the residual P&L given the set of paths.

$$\min_{\Delta_{t_i}} Var^P\left[C(\omega_{t_{i+1}}) - \Delta_{t_i} X(\omega_{t_{i+1}}) - B(\omega_{t_{i+1}})\right] \tag{244}$$

In the case of complete markets it reduces to the usual perfect replication scheme.

The solution of eq. (244) is given by the linear regression of $C(\omega_{t_{i+1}})$ over $X(\omega_{t_{i+1}})$, that is

$$\Delta_{t_i} = \frac{Cov(C(\omega_{t_{i+1}}), X(\omega_{t_{i+1}}))}{Var(X(\omega_{t_{i+1}}))} \tag{245}$$

7.1.11 Delta hedging IDI options under the SABR model

In "Managing Smile Risk" (Hagan, Kumar, Lesniewski and Woodward, 2002), it's derived delta hedging formulas for 2 possible parametrization modes using the SABR model. The first mode assumes $\sigma_b(K,F) = \sigma_B(K,F,\alpha,\beta,\rho,\nu)$. In this mode, α which is the instantaneous volatility is kept constant when F moves. The second parametrization assumes $\sigma_b(K,F) = \sigma_B(K,F,\alpha(\sigma_{ATM},F),\beta,\rho,\nu)$. In this mode, α is a function of F and is recalibrated in order to maintain σ_{ATM} constant after a move by F. Applying the chain rule for differentiation results in the following formula to compute the delta hedging quantity under the first parametrization mode:

$$\Delta = \frac{dc}{dF} = \frac{\partial c}{\partial F} + \frac{\partial c}{\partial \sigma_B} \cdot \frac{\partial \sigma_B(K,F,\alpha,\beta,\rho,\nu)}{\partial F}$$

It's worth mentioning again that for IDI options specifically, σ_B is substituted by σ_R in (229).

In the SABR setup, usually differentiation occurs with finite differences. So $\frac{\partial f}{\partial a}$ is approximated by $\frac{f(a+\delta)-f}{\delta}$ for any function $f(a)$ applying a shift δ to the variable a. The first term $\frac{\partial c}{\partial F}$ is similar to just a Black-Scholes type of delta quantity, since it doesn't correct for the fact that implied volatility σ_B may be a function of F. The second term $\frac{\partial c}{\partial \sigma_B} \cdot \frac{\partial \sigma_B(K,F,\alpha,\beta,\rho,\nu)}{\partial F}$ is a correction to the previously mentioned term. The second parametrization mode yields another extra term. In that setup delta hedging is computed by:

$$\Delta = \frac{dc}{dF} = \frac{\partial c}{\partial F} + \frac{\partial c}{\partial \sigma_B} \cdot \frac{\partial \sigma_B(K,F,\alpha,\beta,\rho,\nu)}{\partial F} + \frac{\partial \sigma_B(K,F,\alpha,\beta,\rho,\nu)}{\partial \alpha} \cdot \frac{\partial \alpha(\sigma_{ATM},F)}{\partial F} \quad (246)$$

The last term $\frac{\partial \sigma_B(K,F,\alpha,\beta,\rho,\nu)}{\partial \alpha} \cdot \frac{\partial \alpha(\sigma_{ATM},F)}{\partial F}$ is another correction in order to maintain σ_{ATM} constant when F moves. This term is always zero when $\beta = 1$ in the SABR model. Therefore, if β value is chosen to be 1, then there's only one possible parametrization after all.

Regarding which choice is best for parametrization, it really depends how you think the volatility surface moves when your underlying moves. This is one of the focal points of "Managing Smile Risk" (Hagan, Kumar, Lesniewski and Woodward, 2002).

Another correction that was later observed within the SABR model was pointed out in "Hedging Under the SABR Model" (Bartlett, 2006). Loosely speaking, it was noticed that in average the instantaneous volatility α changes when F moves because SABR is a stochastic volatility model with α and F respective Brownian Motions being correlated through ρ. Mathematically, the delta hedging proposed by Bartlett is:

$$\Delta = \frac{dc}{dF} = \frac{\partial c}{\partial F} + \frac{\partial c}{\partial \sigma_B} \cdot \frac{\partial \sigma_B(K,F,\alpha,\beta,\rho,\nu)}{\partial F} + \frac{\partial \sigma_B(K,F,\alpha,\beta,\rho,\nu)}{\partial \alpha} \cdot \frac{\partial \alpha}{\partial F}$$

$$\Delta = \frac{dc}{dF} = \frac{\partial c}{\partial F} + \frac{\partial c}{\partial \sigma_B} \cdot \frac{\partial \sigma_B(K,F,\alpha,\beta,\rho,\nu)}{\partial F} + \frac{\partial \sigma_B(K,F,\alpha,\beta,\rho,\nu)}{\partial \alpha} \cdot \frac{\rho \cdot \nu}{F^{\beta}} \quad (247)$$

Chapter 12 of *The SABR/LIBOR Market Model: Pricing, Calibration and Hedging for Complex Interest-Rate Derivatives* (Rebonato, McKay and White, 2009) discusses in depth the aspects of delta hedging in the SABR model. It creates replicating portfolios of an option based on each of the 3 delta hedging terms in (247) and then plots the histogram of realized P&L for each one of the strategies.

7.1.12 IDI options pricing under HJM model

In a HJM model based on the BRL CDI onshore calibrated curve, the forward rate is the underlying and it's defined by:

$$f_{t,T} = -\frac{\partial lnP_{t,T}^{CDI}}{\partial T} \tag{248}$$

It's assumed that a HJM model has the following dynamics for the forward rate $f_{t,T}$ under the real-world probability measure $\mathbb{P}$:

$$df_{t,T} = \alpha_{t,T} \cdot dt + \sigma_{t,T} \cdot dW_t \tag{249}$$

where,

$\alpha_{t,T}$: is the drift of the forward rate $f_{t,T}$ under the real-world probability measure $\mathbb{P}$.

$\sigma_{t,T}$: is the instantaneous volatility of $f_{t,T}$.

W_t: is a Brownian Motion under $\mathbb{P}$.

The no-arbitrage condition states that a HJM model can be defined by the equation below under the BRL CDI onshore risk neutral probability measure $\mathbb{Q}^{\mathrm{CDI}}$, associated with numéraire $\beta_t^C = exp\left\{\int_0^t r_s \cdot ds\right\}$, with r_t being the continuously compounded CDI onshore rate in the money market account:

$$df_{t,T} = \sigma_{t,T} \cdot \left(\int_t^T \sigma_{t,u} \cdot du\right) \cdot dt + \sigma_{t,T} \cdot dW_t^{CDI} \tag{250}$$

where,

W_t^{CDI}: is now a Brownian Motion under the probability measure $\mathbb{Q}^{\mathrm{CDI}}$.

The derivation of the equation above can be found at chapter 10 of *Stochastic Calculus for Finance II: Continuous-Time Models* (Shreve, 2010), more precisely in Section 10.3 which covers the HJM model. In the same chapter it's also presented the stochastic differential equation for the discount zero coupon bond, obtained by applying Ito's Lemma on (250) with the function $P_{t,T} = exp\left\{-\int_t^T f_{t,s} \cdot ds\right\}$. In our specific example for IDI options, we will have the discount zero coupon bond derivation substituted and applied to the discount factor term $P_{t,T}^{CDI}$:

$$dP_{t,T}^{CDI} = r_t \cdot P_{t,T}^{CDI} \cdot dt - \left(\int_t^T \sigma_{t,u} \cdot du\right) \cdot P_{t,T}^{CDI} \cdot dW_t^{CDI} \tag{251}$$

Using Ito's Lemma again on (251) with the natural logarithmic function yields:

$$dln\left(P_{t,T}^{CDI}\right)=\left(r_t-\frac{1}{2}\cdot\left(\int_t^T\sigma_{t,u}\cdot du\right)^2\right)\cdot dt-\int_t^T\sigma_{t,u}\cdot du\cdot dW_t^{CDI} \tag{252}$$

Integrating both sides of (252) yields:

$$\int_t^T dln\left(P_{t,T}^{CDI}\right)=\int_t^T\left(r_s-\frac{1}{2}\cdot\left(\int_s^T\sigma_{s,u}\cdot du\right)^2\right)\cdot ds-\int_t^T\left(\int_s^T\sigma_{s,u}\cdot du\right)\cdot dW_s^{CDI}$$

$$ln\left(P_{T,T}^{CDI}\right)-ln\left(P_{t,T}^{CDI}\right)=\int_t^T\left(r_s-\frac{1}{2}\cdot\left(\int_s^T\sigma_{s,u}\cdot du\right)^2\right)\cdot ds-\int_t^T\left(\int_s^T\sigma_{s,u}\cdot du\right)\cdot dW_s^{CDI}$$

$$ln\left(P_{t,T}^{CDI}\right)=-\int_t^T\left(r_s-\frac{1}{2}\cdot\left(\int_s^T\sigma_{s,u}\cdot du\right)^2\right)\cdot ds+\int_t^T\left(\int_s^T\sigma_{s,u}\cdot du\right)\cdot dW_s^{CDI}$$

Exponentiating both sides of the equation above yields:

$$P_{t,T}^{CDI}=exp\left\{-\int_t^T\left(r_s-\frac{1}{2}\cdot\left(\int_s^T\sigma_{s,u}\cdot du\right)^2\right)\cdot ds+\int_t^T\left(\int_s^T\sigma_{s,u}\cdot du\right)\cdot dW_s^{CDI}\right\} \tag{253}$$

Using the fact that the Radon-Nikodym derivative to change from probability measure $\mathbb{Q}^{\mathbb{CDI}}$ to $\mathbb{Q}^*$ is given by:

$$\frac{d\mathbb{Q}^*}{d\mathbb{Q}^{\mathbb{CDI}}}=\frac{\prod_{T_i=t}^{T}\left(1+CDI_{T_i}\right)^{\frac{1}{252}}}{exp\left\{\int_t^T r_s\cdot ds\right\}} \tag{254}$$

It can be rearranged as:

$$exp\left\{\int_t^T r_s\cdot ds\right\}=\prod_{T_i=t}^{T}\left(1+CDI_{T_i}\right)^{\frac{1}{252}}\cdot\frac{d\mathbb{Q}^{\mathbb{CDI}}}{d\mathbb{Q}^*}=\frac{IDI_T}{IDI_t}\cdot\frac{d\mathbb{Q}^{\mathbb{CDI}}}{d\mathbb{Q}^*} \tag{255}$$

Next we can plug (255) into (253) to arrive at the value of the IDI index at a future time T by:

$$IDI_T=\frac{IDI_t}{P_{t,T}^{CDI}}\cdot exp\left\{\frac{1}{2}\cdot\int_t^T\left(\int_s^T\sigma_{s,u}\cdot du\right)^2\cdot ds+\int_t^T\left(\int_s^T\sigma_{s,u}\cdot du\right)\cdot dW_s^*\right\} \tag{256}$$

It's worth mentioning that in (256) we changed the Brownian Motion back to W_s^*, because we changed the probability measure affected by the term $\frac{d\mathbb{Q}^{\mathbb{CDI}}}{d\mathbb{Q}^*}$ inside (255).

Taking a closer look at the equation $\frac{IDI_t}{IDI_T} = \frac{1}{\prod_{T_i=t}^{T}\left(1+CDI_{T_i}\right)^{\frac{1}{252}}}$, it tells us that it must be a martingale under the BRL CDI O/N rolling money market account probability measure $\mathbb{Q}^*$, where its numéraire is $\beta_t = \prod_{T_i=0}^{t}(1+CDI_{T_i})^{\frac{1}{252}}$. Again, we used the stochastic calculus theorem that was introduced in Section 6 of this book and we refer again to Shreve (2010) for further details. Indeed rearranging (256) yields:

$$\frac{IDI_t}{IDI_T} = P_{t,T}^{CDI} \cdot exp\left\{-\frac{1}{2} \cdot \int_t^T \left(\int_s^T \sigma_{s,u} \cdot du\right)^2 \cdot ds - \int_t^T \left(\int_s^T \sigma_{s,u} \cdot du\right) \cdot dW_s^*\right\} \tag{257}$$

And,

$$\mathbb{E}^{\mathbb{Q}^*}\left[\frac{IDI_t}{IDI_T}|\mathcal{F}_t\right] = P_{t,T}^{CDI} \tag{258}$$

This corroborates the fact we presented early in the book in the DI1 Future section, which states that the expected value of $\frac{1}{\prod_{T_i=t}^{T}\left(1+CDI_{T_i}\right)^{\frac{1}{252}}}$ under $\mathbb{Q}^*$ must be equal to the BRL CDI onshore discount factor $P_{t,T}^{CDI}$. The only thing we are adding here is a twist of the equations to make more evident its use as an IDI option payoff.

The proof of (258) can be constructed based on the fact that the exponential of a normally distributed random variable has as its average $exp\left\{+\frac{1}{2} \cdot \sigma^2\right\}$, where σ is the volatility of the normal random variable. Since the differential of a Brownian motion is normally distributed, the integral of it would be a sum of normally distributed variables, which is also normally distributed and the variance would be equal to $\int_t^T \left(\int_s^T \sigma_{s,u} \cdot du\right)^2 \cdot ds$ in our specific case.

Another interesting result is that the IDI forward value seen at date t for maturity date T, namely $IDI_{t,T}$, must be a martingale under the probability measure $\mathbb{Q}_{\mathbb{CDI}}^{\mathrm{T}}$, which has as its numéraire $P_{t,T}^{CDI}$. This can be verified because $IDI_{t,T} = \frac{IDI_t}{P_{t,T}^{CDI}}$, so it must be a martingale under the measure associated with numéraire $P_{t,T}^{CDI}$. Taking a look at (256), we can see that the IDI forward value $IDI_{t,T}$ is not a martingale under the BRL CDI O/N rolling money market account that has $\prod_{T_i=0}^{t}(1+CDI_{T_i})^{\frac{1}{252}}$ as its numéraire. This can be verified in the equation below:

$$IDI_T = IDI_{t,T} \cdot exp\left\{\frac{1}{2} \cdot \int_t^T \left(\int_s^T \sigma_{s,u} \cdot du\right)^2 \cdot ds + \int_t^T \left(\int_s^T \sigma_{s,u} \cdot du\right) \cdot dW_s^*\right\} \tag{259}$$

But changing IDI_T dynamics to the BRL CDI T forward probability measure $\mathbb{Q}^{\mathrm{T}}_{\mathbb{CDI}}$ yields:

$$\frac{d\mathbb{Q}^{\mathrm{T}}_{\mathbb{CDI}}}{d\mathbb{Q}^*} = \frac{IDI_t}{IDI_T} \cdot \frac{1}{P_{t,T}}$$

$$= exp\left\{ -\frac{1}{2} \cdot \int_t^T \left(\int_s^T \sigma_{s,u} \cdot du \right)^2 \cdot ds - \int_t^T \left(\int_s^T \sigma_{s,u} \cdot du \right) \cdot dW_s^* \right\} \tag{260}$$

Applying Girsanov theorem,

$$dW_t^{T_{CDI}} = dW_t^* + \left(\int_t^T \sigma_{t,u} \cdot du \right) \cdot dt \tag{261}$$

By plugging (261) into (259) yields:

$$IDI_T = IDI_{t,T} \cdot exp\left\{ -\frac{1}{2} \cdot \int_t^T \left(\int_s^T \sigma_{s,u} \cdot du \right)^2 \cdot ds + \int_t^T \left(\int_s^T \sigma_{s,u} \cdot du \right) \cdot dW_t^{T_{CDI}} \right\} \tag{262}$$

And,

$$\mathbb{E}^{\mathbb{Q}^{\mathrm{T}_{CDI}}} \left[IDI_T | \mathcal{F}_t \right] = IDI_{t,T} \tag{263}$$

which proves the fact that the IDI forward is a martingale under the probability measure $\mathbb{Q}^{\mathrm{T}}_{\mathbb{CDI}}$. To be clearer, the reader may use the fact that $IDI_T = IDI_{T,T}$, which means that the IDI spot value at date T will be equal to its forward value for maturity date T, seen at same date T.

Now that we derived the IDI forward value HJM dynamics in (262), we are ready to price an IDI option. The IDI option payoff was again defined as:

$$Payoff_{T+1^*} = Q \cdot M \cdot max\left(cp \cdot [IDI_T - K], 0 \right) \tag{264}$$

It's worth mentioning one more time that the option premium payment occurs at date $t+1^*$, and option payoff occurs at date $T+1^*$. Thus the selected probability measure used for pricing is the one which has as its numéraire $P^{CDI}_{t,t+1^*,T+1^*}$. However, we will also assume that:

$$\mathbb{E}^{\mathbb{Q}^{\mathrm{T+1*CDI}}} \left[IDI_T | \mathcal{F}_t \right] = IDI_{t,T} \tag{265}$$

where,

$Q^{\mathrm{T+1*CDI}}$: is the probability measure that has as its numéraire $P^{CDI}_{t,t+1^*,T+1^*}$.

This assumption is used because the numéraires $P^{CDI}_{t,t+1^*,T+1^*}$ and $P^{CDI}_{t,T}$ are approximate the same and they display negligible volatility in its difference in any model. Therefore, only a negligible convexity is really needed by performing the required change of probability measure. This results in the following IDI option pricing equation:

$$PV_{t+1^*} = Q \cdot M \cdot P^{CDI}_{t,t+1^*,T+1^*} \cdot E^{\mathbb{Q}^{\mathrm{T+1*CDI}}} \left[max\left(cp \cdot [IDI_T - K], 0\right) | \mathcal{F}_t \right] \tag{266}$$

Under the HJM model IDI_T is lognormally distributed under the probability measure $Q^{\mathrm{T+1*CDI}}$ given the assumption above, so Black Formulas can be applied to yield the final IDI option price under the HJM model as:

$$c = Q \cdot M \cdot (IDI_{t,T} \cdot N(d1_{HJM}) - K \cdot N(d2_{HJM})) \cdot P^{CDI}_{t,t+1^*,T+1^*} \tag{267}$$

where,

$$d1_{HJM} = \frac{ln\left(\frac{IDI_{t,T}}{K}\right) + 0.5 \cdot \sigma^2_{IDI_{Black}} \cdot T_{vol}}{\sigma_{IDI_{Black}} \cdot \sqrt{T_{vol}}}$$

$$d2_{HJM} = \frac{ln\left(\frac{IDI_{t,T}}{K}\right) - 0.5 \cdot \sigma^2_{IDI_{Black}} \cdot T_{vol}}{\sigma_{IDI_{Black}} \cdot \sqrt{T_{vol}}}$$

and

$$\sigma^2_{IDI_{Black}} \cdot T_{vol} = \int_t^T \left(\int_s^T \sigma_{s,u} \cdot du \right)^2 \cdot ds$$

The put would be priced as:

$$p = Q \cdot M \cdot (K \cdot N(-d2_{HJM}) - IDI_{t,T} \cdot N(-d1_{HJM})) \cdot P^{CDI}_{t,t+1^*,T+1^*} \tag{268}$$

All IDI option pricing equations presented so far in this section are very similar. They are all Black-Scholes type of equations based on an underlying. The first had the assumption that the IDI index was the underlying. The second that the realized rate was the underlying. Only the third uses an interest rate model (HJM) to fully derive the IDI option pricing in a consistent arbitrage free way.

Moreover, if you really believe the HJM model dynamics, it can be used to price DI Future options and IDI options with the same model. Thus, one could try to look at relative value trades between the 2 option markets if this model achieves good fit to calibrate both volatility smiles.

It also tells us something very interesting about the IDI option Black implied volatility. The term $-\int_t^T \sigma_{t,u} \cdot du$ represent the discount factor volatility of $P^{CDI}_{t,T}$ under the HJM model. To obtain an IDI option implied volatility, you have to integrate again this quantity from computation date t to option maturity date T. However, $P^{CDI}_{t,T}$ as a discount factor has a pull to 1 effect moving date t towards maturity date T. Just as a curiosity, let's suppose that the instantaneous forward rate dynamics follows a simpler constant volatility model than HJM given by:

$$df_{t,T} = \mu \cdot dt + \sigma \cdot dW^{CDI}_t \tag{269}$$

The Black Effective Variance for an IDI option will be given by:

$$\sigma^2_{IDI_{Black}} \cdot T_{vol} = \int_t^T \left(\int_s^T \sigma \cdot du \right)^2 \cdot ds$$

$$\sigma^2_{IDI_{Black}} \cdot T_{vol} = \int_t^T (\sigma \cdot (T - s))^2 \cdot ds$$

$$\sigma^2_{IDI_{Black}} \cdot T_{vol} = \sigma^2 \cdot \int_t^T (T - s)^2 \cdot ds$$

$$\sigma_{IDI_{Black}} = \sigma \cdot \frac{T_{Vol}}{\sqrt{3}} \tag{270}$$

It is noticeable that a $\sqrt{3}$ factor appears in (270), since the discount factor instantaneous volatility in a constant volatility HJM model would be equal to $\sigma \cdot T_{Vol}$, but that would be linearly reduced each day after a CDI O/N fixing occurs. This result can be also considered a consequence of the pull to 1 effect on discount factor term $P^{CDI}_{t,T}$.

The main drawback however of the HJM model for IDI options pricing is its inability to fit the IDI options volatility smirk observed sometimes for options expiring in the short term, typically up to 3M. As discussed previously, in that particular situation, the nature of the CDI O/N forward rates are much more jumpy than diffusive and no diffusive model can fit a smirk shaped smile.

Also, for IDI options with maturity greater than 3M, usually the volatility curve implied from market prices is a smile or skew, not a smirk anymore. But a one factor HJM model can't produce a smile. Even if extending it to a multi-factor HJM model it would only be possible to generate a bit of a skew, but still it's not enough to fit perfectly the implied volatility hockey stick shaped smile observed in the market in an accurate manner.

7.1.13 IDI options historical volatility computation – how to price an IDI option if only the DI Futures market was liquid?

Imagine that you have only historical data of the DI Futures market. How would you compute an IDI option historical volatility? As demonstrated in the previous subsection, the HJM model is a very good starting point to look at in order to try to come back with an answer for that question.

In this subsection, we will reformulate the IDI option implied volatility under a HJM model into a discrete daily version of it, by approximating the integrals over continuous time into discrete sums over a 1 business day in CDI calendar period. Below follows this derivation:

$$\sigma^2_{IDI_{Black}} \cdot T_{vol} = \int_t^T \left(\int_s^T \sigma_{s,u} \cdot du \right)^2 \cdot ds$$

$$\sigma^2_{IDI_{Black}} \cdot T_{vol} = \int_t^T \left(\sigma_{P^{CDI}_{s,T}}(s)\right)^2 \cdot ds$$

$$\sigma^2_{IDI_{Black}} \cdot T_{vol} = \sum_{T_i=t}^{T-1} \left[\left(\sigma_{P^{CDI}_{T_i,T}}(T_i)\right)^2 \cdot \frac{1}{252}\right]$$

$$\sigma_{IDI_{Black}} = \sqrt{\frac{\sum_{T_i=t}^{T-1}\left[\left(\sigma_{P^{CDI}_{T_i,T}}(T_i)\right)^2 \cdot \frac{1}{252}\right]}{T_{Vol}}} \tag{271}$$

For each T_i, the discount factor volatility $\sigma_{P^{CDI}_{T_i,T}}(T_i)$ will be estimated by a time series of the historical CDI curve and later (271) will be applied to arrive at $\sigma_{IDI_{Black}}$, which is the IDI option implied volatility in unitary price units. But often the market practitioner is interested in obtaining the volatility σ_R of the realized rate $R^*_{t,T}$, which is more meaningful to compare it with other IDI options maturity date implied volatilities. In order to obtain σ_R, we will first compute an at-the-money forward (ATMF) IDI option price with our historical estimate of $\sigma_{IDI_{Black}}$, and then imply the volatility σ_R by root searching it on (229) with same input IDI option price. The full procedure follows below:

1. Compute the number of business days $BD_{t,T} = K$ between your IDI option pricing date t (usually today's date) and your IDI option expire date T. Define loop variables $i = 1$ and $j = 0$ to start the process. T_i will loop on historical dates and j will reduce the tenor of the discount factor underlying P_{T_i,T_i+K-j}. When $j = K-1$ you will be calculating a one business day discount factor P_{T_i,T_i+1}.
2. Define the start date (T_1) and end date (T_n) to construct your DI Futures historical time series and a business days window called *window*. For every i-th date of the historical time series, construct a discount factor time series P_{T_i,T_i+K-j} until $i = n$.
3. From 2 construct a log return time series of P_{T_i,T_i+K-j} . After this operation your first result will be at the second date of your historical time series because the log return needs 2 dates to calculate one value.
4. Estimate the instantaneous volatility of the discount factor P_{T_i,T_i+K-j} by taking the standard deviation of the time series obtained in 3 in a rolling window of size *window*. Now our time series of instantaneous volatilities estimates starts at $T_1 + 1 + window$. Save these estimates in a vector V_1.
5. Increase j by 1 and repeat steps 2 to 4 until $j = K-1$. Each one of the $K-1$ Vectors V_j obtained at the end of step 4 will be used to construct a matrix M with $K-1$ columns and $n - window - 1$ rows. Each column of matrix M can be understood as rolling instantaneous volatilities estimates of discount factors P_{T_i,T_i+K-j}. The last column of M is a vector containing rolling instantaneous volatility estimates of one business discount factors. The first column contains

estimates of discount factors with K business days as its underlying tenor. Let's assume the elements of the matrix M to be defined as $m_{i,j}$.

6. For every i-th row of M, calculate historical IDI option vol as $\sigma_{IDI_{Black}}(i) = \sqrt{\frac{\sum_{j=1}^{K-1}\left[\left(m_{i,j}\right)^2 \cdot \frac{1}{252}\right]}{T_{Vol}}}$
7. For every value of $\sigma_{IDI_{Black}}(i)$ time series computed in 6, compute ATMF BS price c through (219). Compute afterwards ATMF vol $\sigma_R(i)$ with the realized rate as underlying of the BS pricer. To accomplish that, it's needed to root search $\sigma_R(i)$ on (229) with same input IDI option price c.
8. Plot $\sigma_R(i)$ obtained in 7 which is the IDI option implied volatilities based on realized rate lognormal assumption.

7.1.14 IDI Digital Options – limitations and applicability

Currently many market participants bet in future monetary policy through combinations of IDI call and put options. The most usual strategies used are IDI call and put spreads. However, this is not the most correct way to bet precisely in future monetary policy. A digital option would be a better vehicle to accomplish that. On the other hand, BVMF and CETIP doesn't provide to clients a digital option in their list of available products. Therefore, in order to build a digital payoff you have to combine the existing options they provide and try to construct synthetically the digital payoff.

The digital payoff can be constructed with a long knock-in call option with strike at K_1 that knocks in at K_2 and a short call option at K_2. Here we assume that $K_1 < K_2$ and that all options have the same maturity date.

A range payoff would be an even better vehicle to bet in future monetary policies, which could be constructed with a long call digital at K_2 and a short put digital at K_3. The long call digital at K_2 can be constructed as mentioned above. The short put digital at K_3 could be constructed with a short put IDI option at strike K_4 that knocks-in at K_3 only, and a long put IDI option vanilla at strike K_3. Again, it's assumed here $K_1 < K_2 < K_3 < K_4$ and all options with same maturity date. Usually, K_2 and K_3 are chosen so that the IDI index falls inside the range K_2 to K_3 if the future monetary policy bet is realized and stays outside the range if not.

Regarding which IDI index to select, clients have the IDI2009 or ITC2012 as the available options. It would be better to construct the range payoff with all IDI options based on ITC2012 index, as it's underlying is the Selic O/N rate. This choice can be corroborated based on figure 24, that displays the spread of SETA rates to Selic O/N rates.

It's also common to leave some room inside the range when selecting K_2 and K_3 in case the spread of Selic target O/N rate to Selic O/N rate diverges a bit from its current level.

Another possibility in the IDI digital options market is to select option premium payment one business day after trading in a BMF calendar like it occurs for IDI vanilla options or to pay the option premium at the same date that occurs option payoff payment. In the second case, only the net payment of payoff and premium occurs at digital option payoff payment date.

Being the digital IDI option a good vehicle to bet in future monetary policy, then the next question is how they could be priced. To price an option you need a model, so which model would be suitable to price IDI digital options? Most market participants would be interested in trading short term maturities of IDI digital options, in order to bet in the next or the following Central Bank meeting decision. Therefore, the best model to price it should be similar to what was proposed in the IDI discrete tree model subsection previously presented. In the authors' opinion, a diffusive model could be difficult to be calibrated and would be problematic, since the nature of the Selic O/N forward rates is much more discrete than diffusive for short term maturities.

7.1.15 OTC IDI Options at Cetip

Not that relevant to the market, as most banks will only trade with funds through cleared contracts.

7.2 DI Future Options

The underlying of a DI Future Option is BVMF's DI1 Future contract. The option is European and deliverable. This means that exercise occurs only at maturity date and upon exercise you will enter into a DI1 Future contract. The notation used in this book will refer the maturity date as T_1 and the DI1 Future underlying maturity date T_2. So typically at maturity date T_1 you compare the prevailing DI1 Future price $FUT_{DI}(T_1, T_2)$ with a unitary price strike K to decide to exercise it or not.

The outline to cover DI Future Options will begin with a subsection explaining the basic information for trading them. The next topic will cover how BVMF defines the codes to represent DI Future Options.

The following topic will manipulate algebraically the DI Future Option payoff in order to represent it like a swaption. Then, we will discuss what are the popular strategies usually traded in the BVMF exchange involving DI Future options. Next subsections will derive a simple Black pricer for DI Future options and the SABR model will be proposed to fit the volatility surface that's observed in the market. Other models will be also used to derive DI Future option prices like HJM and BGM, but it will be pointed out that those models are more efficiently used for payoffs that involve term structure moves in the yield curve and not just a simple forward rate like it's the case of DI Future options. Because of this fact, it's common practice among local practitioners to use the SABR model for DI Future options pricing and risk management.

7.2.1 Basic trading information and definition of the contract codes

DI Future Options are exchange traded, with maturity dates T_1 usually being on January, April, July or October first business day. Maturity dates could be defined in other months – February, say – although this happens less frequently. In terms of DI1 underlyings usually available when trading DI Future options, BVMF created 4 types. Type I has an "approximate" 3M underlying. This means that a January maturity month DI Future Option of Type I will have its DI1 underlying maturity date at April for instance. It's said that the underlying has approximate 3M because the first business day of the maturity month and DI1 underlying maturity dates may fall into different dates. One example would be a Type I DI Future Option with maturity date at 02-Jan-2015. A perfect 3M tenor rule would say that the DI1 underlying maturity date would be 02-Apr-2015. However, the April DI1 maturity date is 01-Apr-2015, which is the first business day of the April 2015 month. A Type II and III DI Future option would have an approximate 6M and 1Y DI1 underlying maturity tenor respectively. A Type IV DI Future Option has a flexible DI1 underlying maturity. It can be 1M, 2M or 1Y6M for instance. It just have to be different than Type I, II and III underlying tenors of 3M, 6M and 1Y.

The contract codes defined at BVMF are based on the following rule. The first 2 characters will always be DI to represent that the underlying of the option is a DI1 contract. The next character will be used to identify if it's a type I, II, II or IV DI Future Option. It will be represented by 1,2,3 or 4 respectively. The next 3 characters will be used to represent the maturity of the option. So F15 means that the option maturity month is F which is January and the maturity year is 2015. As all other future or option contracts in the exchange, the maturity date is always the first business day of the month in a BMF calendar. The next character represents if it's a call or put option, being c short for call and p short for put option. The next 6 digits are used to represent the strike rate. Since DI Future options only use 4 digits to represent the strike rate, because it's traded as a rate with 2 decimal digits, then for DI Future options the first 2 digits of the last 6 on the code will always be 00 and the next 4 will be used to represent the strike rate. One example is DI2F15C001100, which is used to represent a DI1 Future option (DI), of Type II (2), with maturity date on 02-Jan-2015 (F15), a call option (C) and finally with a strike rate of 11,00% (001100).

7.2.2 DI Future Options payoff – smells like swaption?

The delivery mechanism of the DI Future Option can be translated into a payoff in BRL at maturity date T_1 given by:

$$Payoff[T_1] = Q \cdot M \cdot max\left(cp \cdot \left[FUT_{DI}(T_1, T_2) - \frac{100{,}000}{(1+K_R)^{\tau^{252}_{T_1,T_2}}}\right], 0\right) \tag{272}$$

where,

Q: is the quantity of contracts.

M: M is a multiplier of points for a DI Future Option, currently set to 1.

$max(A,B)$: is the operator that computes the maximum value of A and B.

cp: variable to define if it's a call or put option. It's equal to 1 if it's a call and equal to −1 if it's a put.

$FUT_{DI}(T_1,T_2)$: has been previously defined as the DI1 Future unitary price seen at date T_1 for a DI1 contract with maturity date at T_2. It's assumed its face value is 100,000 BRL.

K_R: DI Future option strike traded in interest rate format. The unitary price strike $K = \frac{100{,}000}{(1+K_R)^{\tau^{252}_{T_1,T_2}}}$.

$\tau^{252}_{T_1,T_2}$: day count fraction in Bus252 day count basis from DI Future option maturity date T_1 and its underlying DI1 maturity date T_2.

The idea of this subsection is to try to transform (272) into a BRL Fixed X Float swaption payoff with a little bit of algebra. This will be derived in the following equations:

$$Payoff[T_1] = Q \cdot M \cdot 100{,}000 \cdot max\left(cp \cdot \left[\frac{1}{\left(1+R^{CDI}_{T_1,T_2}\right)^{\tau^{252}_{T_1,T_2}}} - \frac{1}{(1+K_R)^{\tau^{252}_{T_1,T_2}}}\right], 0\right)$$

$$Payoff[T_1] = Q \cdot M \cdot 100{,}000 \cdot max\left(cp \cdot \left[\frac{(1+K_R)^{\tau^{252}_{T_1,T_2}} - \left(1+R^{CDI}_{T_1,T_2}\right)^{\tau^{252}_{T_1,T_2}}}{\left(1+R^{CDI}_{T_1,T_2}\right)^{\tau^{252}_{T_1,T_2}} . (1+K_R)^{\tau^{252}_{T_1,T_2}}}\right], 0\right)$$

Recalling that $(1+K_R)^{\tau^{252}_{T_1,T_2}}$ is a constant and may be taken out of the *max* operator yields:

$$Payoff[T_1] = Q \cdot M \cdot \frac{100{,}000}{(1+K_R)^{\tau^{252}_{T_1,T_2}}} \cdot max\left(cp \cdot \left[\frac{(1+K_R)^{\tau^{252}_{T_1,T_2}} - \left(1+R^{CDI}_{T_1,T_2}\right)^{\tau^{252}_{T_1,T_2}}}{\left(1+R^{CDI}_{T_1,T_2}\right)^{\tau^{252}_{T_1,T_2}}}\right], 0\right)$$

We could also use the fact that the unitary price strike $K = \frac{100{,}000}{(1+K_R)^{\tau^{252}_{T_1,T_2}}}$ to simplify the above equation to:

$$Payoff[T_1] = Q \cdot M \cdot K \cdot max\left(cp \cdot \left[\frac{(1+K_R)^{\tau^{252}_{T_1,T_2}} - \left(1+R^{CDI}_{T_1,T_2}\right)^{\tau^{252}_{T_1,T_2}}}{\left(1+R^{CDI}_{T_1,T_2}\right)^{\tau^{252}_{T_1,T_2}}}\right], 0\right) \quad (273)$$

Some further cancellation may be obtained if the exponential strike rate K_R and forward rate $R^{CDI}_{T_1,T_2}$ are converted to linear rates by:

$$(1+K_R)^{\tau^{252}_{T_1,T_2}} = 1+K_{R_L}\cdot\tau^{252}_{T_1,T_2} \tag{274}$$

$$\left(1+R^{CDI}_{T_1,T_2}\right)^{\tau^{252}_{T_1,T_2}} = 1+R^{L}_{T_1,T_2}\cdot\tau^{252}_{T_1,T_2} \tag{275}$$

By plugging (274) and (275) into (273) yields:

$$Payoff[T_1] = Q\cdot M\cdot K\cdot\tau^{252}_{T_1,T_2}\cdot max\left(cp\cdot\left[\frac{K_{R_L}-R^{L}_{T_1,T_2}}{\left(1+R^{CDI}_{T_1,T_2}\right)^{\tau^{252}_{T_1,T_2}}}\right],0\right) \tag{276}$$

The next step towards obtaining a swaption payoff can be obtained from acknowledging that a payoff that occurs at time T_1 can be converted to a payoff that occurs at T_2 by dividing the T_1 payoff by $P^{CDI}_{T_1,T_2} = \frac{1}{\left(1+R^{CDI}_{T_1,T_2}\right)^{\tau^{252}_{T_1,T_2}}}$, canceling thus the denominator $\left(1+R^{CDI}_{T_1,T_2}\right)^{\tau^{252}_{T_1,T_2}}$ inside the *max* operator of (276). This yields:

$$Payoff[T_2] = Q\cdot M\cdot K\cdot\tau^{252}_{T_1,T_2}\cdot max\left(cp\cdot\left[K_{R_L}-R^{L}_{T_1,T_2}\right],0\right) \tag{277}$$

It can be verified from (272) and (277) inspection that a DI Future call option specified in unitary price can be converted to a DI Future put option in interest rate units that can be understood as a receiver swaption with Notional in BRL equal to $Q\cdot M\cdot K$. If that last substitution is performed our swaption payoff can be specified as:

$$Payoff[T_2] = Not_{BRL}\cdot\tau^{252}_{T_1,T_2}\cdot max\left(cp\cdot\left[K_{R_L}-R^{L}_{T_1,T_2}\right],0\right) \tag{278}$$

7.2.3 DI Future Options most common trading strategies

Similarly to what happens in IDI options, it's common for market participants to build payoff graphs based on their bets on the forward rate through DI call and put option combinations.

7.2.4 A simple Black pricing formula for DI Future Options

Assuming the linear BRL equivalent forward rate from T_1 to T_2, namely $R^{L}_{T_1,T_2}$, to be log-normally distributed with σ_R volatility, and based on the T_2 zero coupon swaption payoff given by (278), it's possible to derive a Black type pricer for DI Future options by:

$$c = Q\cdot M\cdot K\cdot\tau^{252}_{T_1,T_2}\cdot\left(R^{L}_{t,T_1,T_2}\cdot N(d1_{DIOPT}) - K_{R_L}\cdot N(d2_{DIOPT})\right)\cdot P^{CDI}_{t,t+1^*,T_2} \tag{279}$$

where,

$$d1_{DIOPT} = \frac{ln\left(\frac{R^L_{t,T_1,T_2}}{K_{R_L}}\right)+0.5\cdot\sigma_R^2\cdot T_{vol}}{\sigma_R\cdot\sqrt{T_{vol}}}$$

$$d2_{DIOPT} = \frac{ln\left(\frac{R^L_{t,T_1,T_2}}{K_{R_L}}\right)-0.5\cdot\sigma_R^2\cdot T_{vol}}{\sigma_R\cdot\sqrt{T_{vol}}}$$

$P^{CDI}_{t,t+1^*,T_2}$: is the forward discount factor seen at date t, that discounts from $t+1^*$, which is the premium payment date to T_2.

The put would be priced as:

$$p = Q\cdot M\cdot K\cdot \tau^{252}_{T_1,T_2}\cdot\left(K_{R_L}\cdot N(-d2_{DIOPT}) - R^L_{t,T_1,T_2}\cdot N(-d1_{DIOPT})\right)\cdot P^{CDI}_{t,t+1^*,T_2} \tag{280}$$

We considered again negligible the convexity correction due to the fact that the option premium is paid the next business day in a BMF calendar.

In case one is interested in quoting an equivalent swaption in *BRL*, then the formula would be simply changed by noting that $Q*M*K\cdot\tau^{Bus252}_{T_1,T_2}$ is equal to the Notional in BRL Not_{BRL} for the swaption.

7.2.5 Can DI Future Options smile with the SABR model?

Yes, they can exactly like the IDI options case previously mentioned. The model is still the same and it will be based on stochastic differential equations for the linear forward rate R^L_{t,T_1,T_2} and its instantaneous stochastic volatility α. The equations are again presented below:

$$dF = \alpha\cdot F^{\beta}\cdot dW_1$$

$$d\alpha = \nu\cdot\alpha\cdot dW_2$$

$$dW_1\cdot dW_2 = \rho\cdot dt$$

To represent the model, F will be substituted by R^L_{t,T_1,T_2} in the first of the 3 above stochastic differential equations. Again, the implied volatility will be computed through:

$$\sigma_b(K,F) = \frac{\alpha}{(F\cdot K)^{\frac{(1-\beta)}{2}}\left\{1+\frac{(1-\beta)^2}{24}\cdot log^2\frac{F}{K}+\frac{(1-\beta)^4}{1920}log^4\frac{F}{K}+\ldots\right\}}\cdot\left(\frac{z}{x(z)}\right)\cdot$$
$$\cdot\left\{1+\left[\frac{(1-\beta)^2}{24}\cdot\frac{\alpha^2}{(FK)^{1-\beta}}+\frac{1}{4}\cdot\frac{\rho\beta\nu\alpha}{(FK)^{\frac{(1-\beta)}{2}}}+\frac{2-3\rho^2}{24}\nu^2\right]t_{ex+\ldots}\right\}$$

where,

$$z = \frac{\nu}{\alpha}(FK)^{\frac{(1-\beta)}{2}} \cdot log\frac{F}{K}$$

$$x(z) = log\left\{\frac{\sqrt{1-2\rho z+z^2}+z-\rho}{1-\rho}\right\}$$

Also, the calibration procedure is similar and usually $\beta = 1$ or chosen by historical investigation of a log-log plot of F and σ_{ATM} pairs. For ρ, ν and α usually a numerical procedure is conducted given market prices or implied volatilities for a range of strikes for the same maturity date.

7.2.6 DI Future Options pricing under HJM model – where's the smile?

To price DI Future options using the HJM model, the most suitable payoff is:

$$Payoff[T_1] = Q \cdot M \cdot 100{,}000 \cdot max\left(cp \cdot \left[\frac{1}{\left(1+R^{CDI}_{T_1,T_2}\right)^{\tau^{252}_{T_1,T_2}}} - \frac{1}{(1+K_R)^{\tau^{252}_{T_1,T_2}}}\right], 0\right)$$

The payoff occurs at T_1 time, so we need to figure out the dynamics under HJM model of the underlying $\frac{1}{\left(1+R^{CDI}_{T_1,T_2}\right)^{\tau^{252}_{T_1,T_2}}}$ in the $\mathbb{Q}^{T_1}_{\mathbb{CDI}}$ probability measure, where its numéraire is P^{CDI}_{t,T_1}.

Our starting point will be the CDI discount factor stochastic differential equation, derived previously in the IDI HJM pricing subsection and just displayed below:

$$dP^{CDI}_{t,T} = r_t \cdot P^{CDI}_{t,T} \cdot dt - \int_t^T \sigma_{t,u} \cdot du \cdot P^{CDI}_{t,T} \cdot dW^{CDI}_t \tag{281}$$

We can express the DI Future option underlying $\frac{1}{\left(1+R^{CDI}_{t,T_1,T_2}\right)^{\tau^{252}_{T_1,T_2}}}$ as a ratio of 2 CDI discount factors, one until T_1 and another until T_2 as:

$$\frac{1}{\left(1+R^{CDI}_{t,T_1,T_2}\right)^{\tau^{252}_{T_1,T_2}}} = \frac{P^{CDI}_{t,T_2}}{P^{CDI}_{t,T_1}} \tag{282}$$

We can derive the dynamics of $\frac{P^{CDI}_{t,T_2}}{P^{CDI}_{t,T_1}}$ which is our underlying by using Ito's Lemma of the initial SDE in (281) and a quotient function $\frac{X}{Y}$ representing $\frac{P^{CDI}_{t,T_2}}{P^{CDI}_{t,T_1}}$. This yields:

$$d\frac{P^{CDI}_{t,T_2}}{P^{CDI}_{t,T_1}} = -\frac{P^{CDI}_{t,T_2}}{P^{CDI}_{t,T_1}} \cdot \left(\int_{T_1}^{T_2} \sigma_{t,u} \cdot du\right) \cdot \left[dW^{CDI}_t + \left(\int_t^T \sigma_{t,u} \cdot du\right) \cdot dt\right] \tag{283}$$

Applying Girsanov theorem:

$$dW_t^{CDI} + \left(\int_t^{T_1} \sigma_{t,u} \cdot du\right) \cdot dt = dW_t^{T_1 CDI} \tag{284}$$

Finally:

$$d\frac{P^{CDI}_{t,T_2}}{P^{CDI}_{t,T_1}} = -\frac{P^{CDI}_{t,T_2}}{P^{CDI}_{t,T_1}} \cdot \left(\int_{T_1}^{T_2} \sigma_{t,u} \cdot du\right) \cdot dW_t^{T_1 CDI} \tag{285}$$

Solving the SDE yields:

$$P^{CDI}_{T_1,T_2} = P^{CDI}_{t,T_1,T_2} \cdot exp\left\{-\frac{1}{2} \cdot \int_t^{T_1} \left(\int_{T_1}^{T_2} \sigma_{s,u} \cdot du\right)^2 \cdot ds - \int_t^{T_1} \left(\int_{T_1}^{T_2} \sigma_{s,u} \cdot du\right) \cdot dW_s^{T_1 CDI}\right\} \tag{286}$$

It can be seen that $P^{CDI}_{T_1,T_2}$ is a martingale under the $\mathbb{Q}^{T_1}_{\mathbb{CDI}}$ probability measure, where its numéraire is P^{CDI}_{t,T_1}. Its expected value is given by:

$$\mathbb{E}^{\mathbb{Q}^{T_1}CDI}\left[P^{CDI}_{T_1,T_2} | \mathcal{F}_t\right] = P^{CDI}_{t,T_1,T_2} \tag{287}$$

with quadratic variation given by $\int_t^{T_1}\left(\int_{T_1}^{T_2} \sigma_{s,u} \cdot du\right)^2 \cdot ds$. Also, $P^{CDI}_{T_1,T_2}$ follows a lognormal distribution under $\mathbb{Q}^{T_1}_{\mathbb{CDI}}$. Therefore, a Black pricer can be used to come up with the DI Future option price under HJM. This formula is given by:

$$c^{HJM}_{DIOPT} = Q \cdot M \cdot 100{,}000 \cdot \left(P^{CDI}_{t,T_1,T_2} \cdot N(d1_{DIOPT_{HJM}}) - \frac{1}{(1+K_R)^{\tau^{Bus252}_{T_1,T_2}}} \cdot N(d2_{DIOPT_{HJM}})\right) \cdot P^{CDI}_{t,t+1^*,T_1} \tag{288}$$

where,

$$d1_{DIOPT} = \frac{ln\left(P^{CDI}_{t,T_1,T_2} \cdot (1+K_R)^{\tau^{252}_{T_1,T_2}}\right) + 0.5 \cdot \int_t^{T_1}\left(\int_{T_1}^{T_2} \sigma_{s,u} \cdot du\right)^2 \cdot ds}{\sqrt{\int_t^{T_1}\left(\int_{T_1}^{T_2} \sigma_{s,u} \cdot du\right)^2 \cdot ds}}$$

$$d2_{DIOPT} = \frac{ln\left(P^{CDI}_{t,T_1,T_2} \cdot (1+K_R)^{\tau^{252}_{T_1,T_2}}\right) - 0.5 \cdot \int_t^{T_1}\left(\int_{T_1}^{T_2} \sigma_{s,u} \cdot du\right)^2 \cdot ds}{\sqrt{\int_t^{T_1}\left(\int_{T_1}^{T_2} \sigma_{s,u} \cdot du\right)^2 \cdot ds}}$$

$P^{CDI}_{t,t+1^*,T_1}$: is the forward discount factor in CDI onshore curve seen at date t, that discounts from date $t+1^*$, which is the premium payment date to T_1. Note that the discounting only occurs from T_1 in the HJM price derivation because the underlying $P^{CDI}_{T_1,T_2}$ is a martingale under $\mathbb{Q}^{T_1}_{CDI}$, differently than the swaption derivation based on a linear rate which was a martingale under the probability measure $\mathbb{Q}^{T_2}_{CDI}$, which resulted in discounting the option payoff from T_2.

Also, please bear in mind that c^{HJM}_{DIOPT} is the price of a call option with the unitary price $P^{CDI}_{T_1,T_2}$ as the underlying, which should be converted to a put option when changing to swaption format as derived previously. The put option price with the unitary price $P^{CDI}_{T_1,T_2}$ as the underlying is given by:

$$p^{HJM}_{DIOPT} = Q \cdot M \cdot 100{,}000 \cdot \left(\frac{1}{(1+K_R)^{\tau^{252}_{T_1,T_2}}} N(-d2_{DIOPT_{HJM}}) - P^{CDI}_{t,T_1,T_2} N(-d1_{DIOPT_{HJM}}) \right) \cdot P^{CDI}_{t,t+1^*,T_1} \tag{289}$$

One interesting fact is that the HJM Black pricing formulas for DI Future options don't display any dependency of its volatility terms to the strike. So a volatility smile would hardly be reproduced, even with a multi-factor HJM model.

7.2.7 What about DI Future Options under the BGM a.k.a Libor Market Model?

Some of you may have asked how reasonable is the assumption that the linear rate $R^L_{T_1,T_2}$ is lognormally distributed used in the subsection that derives the simple Black pricer for DI Future options. It's a good question and the BGM model will be able to confirm that the assumption is consistent with an arbitrage free interest rate model.

We start things again with the HJM model. More precisely back to the following equation:

$$d\frac{P^{CDI}_{t,T_2}}{P^{CDI}_{t,T_1}} = -\frac{P^{CDI}_{t,T_2}}{P^{CDI}_{t,T_1}} \cdot \left(\int_{T_1}^{T_2} \sigma_{t,u} \cdot du \right) \cdot dW^{T_1 CDI}_t$$

Following the same approach used to derive the above SDE we could derive the one for its reciprocal underlying $\frac{P^{CDI}_{t,T_1}}{P^{CDI}_{t,T_2}}$ which is given by:

$$d\frac{P^{CDI}_{t,T_1}}{P^{CDI}_{t,T_2}} = \frac{P^{CDI}_{t,T_1}}{P^{CDI}_{t,T_2}} \cdot \left(\int_{T_1}^{T_2} \sigma_{t,u} \cdot du \right) \cdot \left[dW^{CDI}_t + \left(\int_t^{T_2} \sigma_{t,u} \cdot du \right) \cdot dt \right] \tag{290}$$

Applying Girsanov theorem we can say that:

$$dW^{CDI}_t + \left(\int_t^{T_2} \sigma_{t,u} \cdot du \right) \cdot dt = dW^{T_2 CDI}_t \tag{291}$$

By plugging (291) into (290) yields:

$$d\frac{P^{CDI}_{t,T_1}}{P^{CDI}_{t,T_2}} = \frac{P^{CDI}_{t,T_1}}{P^{CDI}_{t,T_2}} \cdot \left(\int_{T_1}^{T_2} \sigma_{t,u} \cdot du \right) \cdot dW_t^{T_{2CDI}} \tag{292}$$

We also know that:

$$\frac{P^{CDI}_{t,T_1}}{P^{CDI}_{t,T_2}} = \left(1 + R^{CDI}_{t,T_1,T_2}\right)^{\tau^{252}_{T_1,T_2}} = 1 + R^{L}_{t,T_1,T_2} \cdot \tau^{252}_{T_1,T_2} \tag{293}$$

Plugging (293) into (292) yields:

$$d\left(R^{L}_{t,T_1,T_2} \cdot \tau^{252}_{T_1,T_2}\right) = \left(1 + R^{L}_{t,T_1,T_2} \cdot \tau^{252}_{T_1,T_2}\right) \cdot \left(\int_{T_1}^{T_2} \sigma_{t,u} \cdot du \right) \cdot dW_t^{T_{2CDI}} \tag{294}$$

If the HJM volatility function satisfies

$$\int_{T_1}^{T_2} \sigma_{t,u} \cdot du = \frac{R^{L}_{t,T_1,T_2} \cdot \tau^{252}_{T_1,T_2}}{1 + R^{L}_{t,T_1,T_2} \cdot \tau^{252}_{T_1,T_2}} \cdot \gamma_{t,T_1} \tag{295}$$

where γ_{t,T_1} is a deterministic volatility function, It proves that the linear rate $R^{L}_{T_1,T_2}$ could become lognormally distributed under the probability measure $\mathbb{Q}^{T_2}_{\mathbb{CDI}}$, which has as its numéraire P^{CDI}_{t,T_2}. (295) is the key step to move from HJM to BGM model and call and put option formulas presented previously in (279) and (280) respectively are validated under the BGM model.

By plugging (295) into (294) yields the following SDE for R^{L}_{t,T_1,T_2} under the BGM model:

$$dR^{L}_{t,T_1,T_2} = R^{L}_{t,T_1,T_2} \cdot \gamma_{t,T_1} \cdot dW_t^{T_{2CDI}} \tag{296}$$

The BGM model is also not capable of creating a volatility smile if used in its original format. A bit of skew can be created using a displaced diffusion version of BGM, sometimes called shifted BGM like in (Brace, 2007), but it would still not be sufficient to fit a volatility smile for DI Future options. Only an extended stochastic volatility version of BGM would be able to fit the volatility smile in DI Future options. In essence, BGM (like HJM) is is a term structure model that should be used to price exotics that depend on the whole term structure of the yield curve. Their basic purpose is not to price vanilla options. However, deriving the basic equations and option formulas for DI and IDI options under HJM and BGM still helps in the understanding of those 2 products.

7.2.8 DI Future Options historical volatility computation – how to price a DI Future option if only the DI Futures market was liquid

Another interesting question is how to compute the historical volatility σ_R to be used as input in (279). But a more appropriate question could be what's the value of the quadratic variation term $\sigma_R^2 \cdot T_{Vol}$ that enters (279), as in this formula always it's the value of this quantity or its square root that matters? We will go back to the BGM derivation above to try to answer that question.

As seen in the previous subsection, the linear forward rate R^L_{t,T_1,T_2} follows the dynamics under (296) in the BGM model. Solving this SDE yields:

$$R^L_{T_1,T_2} = R^L_{t,T_1,T_2} \cdot exp\left\{-\frac{1}{2}\int_t^{T_1} \gamma^2_{s,T_1} \cdot ds + \int_t^{T_1} \gamma_{s,T_1} \cdot dW_s^{T_{2CDI}}\right\} \tag{297}$$

This means that

$$\mathbb{E}^{\mathbb{Q}^{T_2}_{\mathrm{CDI}}}\left[R^L_{T_1,T_2}\right] = R^L_{t,T_1,T_2} \tag{298}$$

With quadratic variation given by $\int_t^{T_1} \gamma^2_{s,T_1} \cdot ds$. This is the quantity that has to be estimated using historical data supposing that only DI Futures information is available. So first we will estimate γ_{t,T_1} and in a second stage try to integrate it from t to T_1 using an approximation of the integral over business days, in a very similar way that was done in the IDI historical volatility subsection.

We know from (293) that we just need the DI with maturity date on T_1 and T_2 to calculate R^L_{t,T_1,T_2}. So the steps to obtain an estimate for $\sigma_R = \sqrt{\frac{\int_t^{T_1} \gamma^2_{s,T_1} \cdot ds}{T_{Vol}}}$ can be achieved by:

1. Compute the number of business days $BD_{t,T_1} = K_1$ between your DI Future option pricing date t (usually today's date) and your DI Future option expire date T_1. Compute the number of business days $BD_{T_1,T_2} = K_2$ between DI Future option maturity date T_1 and DI Future underlying maturity date T_2. Initialize a loop variable $j = 0$ that will increment until $j = K_1$.
2. Define the start date ($T^{(1)}$) and end date ($T^{(n)}$) to construct your DI Futures historical time series and a business days window called *window*. Start at $T^{(1)}$ and for each T_i ranging from $T^{(1)}$ to $T^{(n)}$ construct a time series of linear forward rates $R^L_{T_i,T_i+K_1-j,T_i+K_1+K_2-j}$ based on (293).
3. From 2 construct a log return time series of $R^L_{T_i,T_i+K_1-j,T_i+K_1+K_2-j}$. After this operation your first result will be at $T^{(1)}+1$ because the log return needs 2 dates to calculate one value.
4. Estimate the instantaneous volatility of the forward rate $R^L_{T_i,T_i+K_1-j,T_i+K_1+K_2-j}$ by taking the standard deviation of the time series obtained in 3 in a rolling window of size *window*. Now our time series of instantaneous volatilities estimates starts at $T^{(1)}+1+window$. Save these estimates in a vector V_1.
5. Increase j by 1 and repeat steps 2 to 4 until $j = K_1 - 1$. Each Vector V_j obtained at the end of 4 will be used to construct a matrix M with K_1 columns and $n - window - 1$ rows. Each column of matrix M can be understood as rolling instantaneous volatilities estimates of linear forward rates

$R^L_{T_i,T_i+K_1-j,T_i+K_1+K_2-j}$. When $j = K_1 - 1$, the last column of M is a vector containing rolling instantaneous volatility estimates of linear forward rates seen one business day in the future, with a tenor of $T_2 - T_1 = K_2$. The first column contains estimates of linear forward rates seen at K_1 business days in the future, also with tenor $T_2 - T_1 = K_2$. The elements of the matrix M will be denoted $m_{i,j}$.

6. For each i-th row of the matrix M, compute the rolling DI Future implied volatility estimate $\sigma_R(i) = \sqrt{\frac{\sum_{j=1}^{K_1} m_{i,j}^2 \cdot \frac{1}{252}}{T_{Vol}}}$
7. Plot $\sigma_R(i)$

The reader may be thinking why we are not simply calculating an estimate of σ_R directly as a standard deviation from a log-return time series of $R^L_{T_i,T_i+K_1-j,T_i+K_1+K_2-j}$. We don't follow this approach as we think that for the same row of matrix M, the instantaneous volatilities estimates could be a bit different for columns 1 to K_1. Moreover, we expect that the instantaneous volatilities estimates are smaller in the right side of the matrix than on the left side of it. This results from the fact that there's a tendency that spot rates with a tenor τ have less volatility than forward rates seen in a future time for same tenor τ. Therefore, there could be a tendency that instantaneous volatilities suffer a decay when the linear forward rate is changing towards a linear spot rate and unfortunately only this more complex approach could capture this effect.

A simple way of testing it is by modeling a term structure in which most of the volatility comes from changes in the slope on a daily basis. Simplifying our rates model as:

$$r_t = \alpha + \beta \cdot t \tag{299}$$

And looking at the variance of the rate as:

$$Var[r_t] = Var[\alpha] + 2 \cdot t \cdot Cov[\alpha, \beta] + t^2 \cdot Var[\beta] \tag{300}$$

For the traditional forward rate we have:

$$(1 + r_1)^{t_1} (1 + r_{12})^{t_{12}} = (1 + r_2)^{t_2} \tag{301}$$

$$t_1 \cdot \ln(1 + r_1) + t_{12} \cdot \ln(1 + r_{12}) = t_2 \cdot \ln(1 + r_2) \tag{302}$$

Approximating $\ln(1 + x) \approx x$:

$$t_1 \cdot r_1 + t_{12} \cdot r_{12} = t_2 \cdot r_2 \tag{303}$$

$$r_{12} = \frac{t_2 \cdot r_2 - t_1 \cdot r_1}{t_{12}} \tag{304}$$

$$r_{12} = \frac{t_2 \cdot (\alpha + \beta \cdot t_2) - t_1 \cdot (\alpha + \beta \cdot t_1)}{t_{12}} \tag{305}$$

$$r_{12} = \frac{\alpha \cdot t_{12} + \beta \cdot (t_2^2 - t_1^2)}{t_{12}} \tag{306}$$

$$r_{12} = \frac{\alpha \cdot t_{12} + \beta \cdot t_{12} \cdot (t_2 + t_1)}{t_{12}} \tag{307}$$

$$r_{12} = \alpha + \beta \cdot (t_2 + t_1) \tag{308}$$

The variance of this rate would be:

$$Var\left[r_{t_{12}}\right] = Var[\alpha] + 2 \cdot (t_2 + t_1) \cdot Cov[\alpha, \beta] + (t_2 + t_1)^2 \cdot Var[\beta] \tag{309}$$

For the case in which $Cov[\alpha, \beta] \approx 0$, it is easy to see how forward rates have higher volatility than spot rates.

7.3 IR Option Strategies - VTF and VID

VTF is a strategy defined by BVMF to trade a DI Future option already delta hedged. VID is another strategy defined that enables market participants to trade delta hedged IDI options. Delta hedge amounts are calculated by BVMF through formulas specified in each strategy documentation.

7.3.1 VTF

In the same case as for DI Future options, the VTF strategy has a BVMF code that defines all relevant information about the option. The code specifies the underlying of the option (type I, II, III, or IV), if it's a call or put, what's the option maturity date and its strike. The VTF strategy goal is to enable market participants to trade delta hedged DI Future options.

The way this strategy is traded is that the exchange fixes the T_1 and T_2 maturity date DI1 rates, R_{t,T_1}^{CDI*} and R_{t,T_2}^{CDI*} respectively, and the delta computed by the exchange Δ_{BMF}^{VTF} before trading. If market participants agree with the provided values by the exchange, than trading starts. Let's suppose one goes long Q_{VTF} contracts for DI Future call options. Here it means it's a call option assuming the underlying is the forward rate, not the unitary price as we have seen previously. Going from one trading view to the other flips the call to put characterization of the contract as discussed in previous sections of this book.

The delta hedge provided by the exchange will be based on a quantity of DI1 contracts for maturity date T_2 and another quantity for maturity date T_1. Let's define 2 variables to define those quantities by $Q_{DI}^{T_2}$ and $Q_{DI}^{T_1}$ respectively.

Based on the VTF contract, the quantities $Q_{DI}^{T_2}$ and $Q_{DI}^{T_1}$ are given by:

$$Q_{DI}^{T_2*} = -Q_{VTF} \cdot \Delta_{BMF}^{VTF} \tag{310}$$

$$Q_{DI}^{T_2} = round2(Q_{DI}^{T_2*}, 5) \tag{311}$$

where,

*round*2$(Q_{DI}^{T_2*}, 5)$: is a function that rounds the quantity $Q_{DI}^{T_2*}$ to the nearest multiple of 5 contracts.

$$Q_{DI}^{T_1*} = -Q_{DI}^{T_2*} \cdot P_{t,T_1,T_2}^{CDI*} \tag{312}$$

$$Q_{DI}^{T_1} = round2(Q_{DI}^{T_1*}, 5) \tag{313}$$

where,

$P_{t,T_1,T_2}^{CDI*} = \frac{\left(1+R_{t,T_1}^{CDI*}\right)^{\frac{\tau_{t,T_1}}{252}}}{\left(1+R_{t,T_2}^{CDI*}\right)^{\frac{\tau_{t,T_2}}{252}}}$, based on the previously fixed DI1 rates R_{t,T_1}^{CDI*} and R_{t,T_2}^{CDI*} announced by the exchange and agreed by market participants prior to trading.

The rates which you enter the DI1 futures with quantities $Q_{DI}^{T_2}$ and $Q_{DI}^{T_1}$ are respectively R_{t,T_2}^{CDI*} and $R_{t,T_1}^{CDI*}$to be consistent with the whole process.

For a VTF strategy based on a DI Future put option, the quantities are given by:

$$Q_{DI}^{T_2*} = Q_{VTF} \cdot |\, \Delta_{BMF}^{VTF} \,| \tag{314}$$

$$Q_{DI}^{T_2} = round2(Q_{DI}^{T_2*}, 5) \tag{315}$$

The T_1 quantity of contracts $Q_{DI}^{T_1}$ for the VTF strategy on a put follows the same procedure as for a call once $Q_{DI}^{T_2*}$ is obtained.

7.3.2 DI Future delta hedge computation by BVMF

The delta hedged provided by the exchange on VTF strategies for call options is given by the following formula:

$$\Delta_{BMF}^{VTF} = N(d1_{BMF}) \cdot \frac{K}{P_{t,T_1,T_2}^{CDI*}} \tag{316}$$

For VTF strategies based on DI Future put options, the delta hedge provided by the exchange is given by:

$$\Delta_{BMF}^{VTF} = [N(d1_{BMF}) - 1] \cdot \frac{K}{P_{t,T_1,T_2}^{CDI*}} \tag{317}$$

where,

$$d1_{BMF} = \frac{ln\left(\frac{R_{t,T_1,T_2}^{CDI*}}{K_R}\right) + 0.5 \cdot \sigma_{BMF}^2 \cdot T_{vol}}{\sigma_{BMF} \cdot \sqrt{T_{vol}}}$$

$$d2_{BMF} = \frac{ln\left(\frac{R_{t,T_1,T_2}^{CDI*}}{K_R}\right) - 0.5 \cdot \sigma_{BMF}^2 \cdot T_{vol}}{\sigma_{BMF} \cdot \sqrt{T_{vol}}}$$

$$R_{t,T_1,T_2}^{CDI*} = \left[\frac{\left(1+R_{t,T_2}^{CDI*}\right)^{\frac{\tau_{t,T_1}}{252}}}{\left(1+R_{t,T_1}^{CDI*}\right)^{\frac{\tau_{t,T_2}}{252}}}\right]^{\frac{1}{\frac{\tau_{T_1,T_2}}{252}}} - 1$$

σ_{BMF}: is the forward rate implied volatility calculated by the exchange based on yesterday's market quotes.

One interesting thing to note is that BMF uses an assumption that the exponential rate R^{CDI}_{t,T_1,T_2} is lognormally distributed to derive its formula with same mean R^{CDI}_{t,T_1,T_2} and volatility σ_{BMF} . On the other hand, we verified that under BGM model it's the linear rate R^{L}_{t,T_1,T_2} which is lognormally distributed under probability measure $\mathbb{Q}^{T_2}_{\mathbb{CDI}}$. Moreover, it's a martingale under $\mathbb{Q}^{T_2}_{\mathbb{CDI}}$, thus its mean is equal to R^{L}_{t,T_1,T_2}. But the conversion from the linear rate to exponential rate is computed by a non linear function shown below:

$$R^{CDI}_{t,T_1,T_2} = \left(1 + R^{L}_{t,T_1,T_2} \cdot \tau^{252}_{T_1,T_2}\right)^{\frac{1}{\tau^{252}_{T_1,T_2}}} - 1 \tag{318}$$

Therefore, based on Ito's Lemma, under probability measure $\mathbb{Q}^{T_2}_{\mathbb{CDI}}$, R^{CDI}_{t,T_1,T_2} cannot be a martingale and would present a drift term based on the convex function (318).

7.3.3 VID

The way this strategy trades is very similar to what was described in the VTF strategy section. The exchange fixes prior to trading a DI1 rate $R^{CDI*}_{t,T}$ for IDI option maturity date T and proposes the DI1 hedge quantity Δ^{VID}_{BMF} for the same maturity date T as the IDI option. If market participants agree with values, then trading starts. One key difference is that for the VID strategy the delta hedge that the exchange provides is just in one DI1 contract instead of 2 for the VTF case. For the case that the VID strategy is based on a call IDI option, the quantity of contracts for the DI1 Futures, namely Q^{T}_{DI}, will be calculated by:

$$Q^{T*}_{DI} = -Q_{VID} \cdot \Delta^{VID}_{BMF} \cdot \frac{IDI_t}{P^{CDI*}_{t,T}} \tag{319}$$

$$Q^{T}_{DI} = round2(Q^{T*}_{DI}, 5) \tag{320}$$

where,

Q_{VID}: is the quantity of VID contracts traded.

Δ^{VID}_{BMF}: is the delta hedge calculated by the exchange for the VID strategy.

IDI_t: is the IDI spot value.

$P^{CDI*}_{t,T} = \frac{1}{\left(1+R^{CDI*}_{t,T}\right)^{\tau^{252}_{t,T}}}$: the discount factor computed based on the fixed DI1 rate $R^{CDI*}_{t,T}$ agreed prior to trading.

For the case that the VID strategy is based on a put IDI option, the quantity of contracts for the DI1 Futures, namely Q_{DI}^{T}, will be calculated by:

$$Q_{DI}^{T*} = Q_{VID} \cdot \mid \Delta_{BMF}^{VID} \mid \cdot \frac{IDI_t}{P_{t,T}^{CDI*}} \tag{321}$$

$$Q_{DI}^{T} = round2(Q_{DI}^{T*}, 5) \tag{322}$$

7.3.4 DI Future delta hedge computation by BVMF

The delta hedged provided by the exchange on VID strategies for call options is given by the following formula:

$$\Delta_{BMF}^{VID} = N(d1_{BMF}) \tag{323}$$

For VID strategies based on IDI put options the delta will be given by:

$$\Delta_{BMF}^{VID} = N(d1_{BMF}) - 1 \tag{324}$$

where,

$$d1_{BMF} = \frac{ln\left(\frac{IDI_{t,T*}}{K}\right) + 0.5 \cdot \sigma_{BMF_{IDI}}^2 \cdot T_{vol}}{\sigma_{BMF_{IDI}} \cdot \sqrt{T_{vol}}}$$

$$d2_{BMF} = \frac{ln\left(\frac{IDI_{t,T}}{K}\right) - 0.5 \cdot \sigma_{BMF_{IDI}}^2 \cdot T_{vol}}{\sigma_{BMF_{IDI}} \cdot \sqrt{T_{vol}}}$$

$IDI_{t,T*} = \frac{IDI_t}{P_{t,T}^{CDI*}}$: is the IDI forward value divided by the discount factor obtained using the agreed DI1 rate $R_{t,T}^{CDI*}$.

$\sigma_{BMF_{IDI}}$: is the implied volatility calculated by the exchange for IDI options considering it's underlying the IDI index based on yesterday's market quotes.

7.4 Jabuticabas: Risk Management of Options on Interest Rates

A discussion on some aspects of modeling and managing risk

7.4.1 IDI options

What are they? A price-based approach will tell you that they are pricing a payoff based on the future value of an accrued index. As Brazil is quite far from negative rates, this index will always go up (not good to be used on barriers; a problem in general for interest rate options in Brazil). Another problem with a price-based approach is that there is no connection among different maturities, and although a parabolic pattern might be observed, there's no underlying structure behind it.

No, really? A rate-based approach works better; given all the algebra to go from prices to rates, we reap some benefits; now we can use existing work on the modeling of rates to build a better and more robust model for the term structure of IDI options.

I can see clearly Volatility of rates presents a trend of volatility decay (think back to the "slope is what changes" discussions), and most of the time the volatility bursts have a very short duration (especially when coming from COPOM jumps). Unexpected decisions will bring new information almost instantaneously, and there should not be any further volatility comparable to a 40bp move in the curve. Typically more persistent volatility is associated with stops of receiver positions when rates go up. The art here is in decomposing volatility into trends, being aware about where in the monetary cycle we are, and guessing right on changes of regime.

Continuity and discreteness Unless the CDI moves in mysterious and unexpected ways, there is a good idea about the possible values that the IDI can have at a certain date, as the result of 2 or 3 different products. So you should really spend 5 minutes double-checking that the payoff of the structure you're pricing is good or bad when it comes to the placement of these possible values within the payoff.

This is left as an exercise for the reader A transition-matrix approach to pricing should be the standard, but as seen above it is not easy to implement. But if there is anywhere where resources should be devoted to research (both from a theoretical perspective and from a computational perspective), this is the place to look for improvements in algorithm efficiency.

DI future options (smell like swaptions)

Do I have a choice ? Exercise rules leave one with the right to exercise the option during a certain time window; be prepared for a quick exercise or to be unexpectedly exercised. Make sure that Back-Office and Operations can handle exercises that look like they're losing money.

Not exactly Trading and hedging forward rates is not an exact exercise; you will need some adjustments over time, and do not underestimate execution costs (both implementation shortfall and exchange fees).

Imperfect thoughts Hedging the correlation risk is kind of impossible. Think about the calculation of the sensitivities; for each of the 2 spot rates, you calculate the partial derivative. Hedging the option in this way is assuming zero covariance. But the realized covariance will be different. Perhaps the time to be more creative on hedging and managing this risk has arrived.

7.5 $\frac{BRL}{USD}$ Listed FX options

In this subsection we will discuss the $\frac{BRL}{USD}$ FX listed options contract details, payoff and we will revisit what's called the 3 T's for option pricing (Time of volatility,

Time of FX forward value computation and Time for discounting the option payoff). Later in this subsection we will derive a Black pricer for $\frac{BRL}{USD}$ Listed FX options and 2 methods will be proposed in order to generate a volatility smile.

7.5.1 Contract details

A $\frac{BRL}{USD}$ Listed FX option contract has a Notional of 50,000 USD. The option is European and cash settled, meaning that it can be exercised only at maturity date T and that upon exercise the option payoff is not delivered but cash settled. Proceeds from option payoff occur at $T+1^* = T_{Pay}$, which is one business day later than maturity date T in a BMF calendar, whereas the option premium payment occurs at $t+1^* = t_{pay}$, which is one business day after trading date t in a BMF calendar. Maturity dates are always in the first business day in a BMF calendar of a particular month. Strikes and option premium quotes are specified in the contract in *BRL* per 1,000 *USD*. The option payoff is settled based on the PTAX FX rate published one business day in a CDI calendar before maturity date T, in the same way that occurs for $\frac{BRL}{USD}$ FX Futures contracts in the exchange.

Regarding the exchange contract code, it follows the same mechanism for all options. The first 3 letters represent the option underlying, that for $\frac{BRL}{USD}$ FX options would be DOL. The next 3 characters would represent the usual maturity month and year. As an example, F15 would represent a contract which has a maturity date as the first business day in a BMF calendar of January 2015. The next character represents if it's a call or put option, represented by a C or P and the following 6 digits are used for the strike specification (strike is quoted in *BRL* per 1,000 *USD* units with 2 decimals). One example is code DOLF15C250000 which represents a $\frac{BRL}{USD}$ FX listed option with maturity date on first business day of January 2015 and with 2500,00 quoted strike.

7.5.2 $\frac{BRL}{USD}$ Listed FX options payoff

The payoff for a $\frac{BRL}{USD}$ Listed FX option is given by:

$$Payoff_{BRL}[T_{pay}] = Q \cdot M \cdot max\left(cp \cdot \left[PTAX_{T-1} \cdot 1{,}000 - K^*\right], 0\right) \quad (325)$$

where,

$Payoff_{BRL}[T_{pay}]$: is the payoff of the $\frac{BRL}{USD}$ Listed FX option computed in *BRL* currency and paid at T_{pay}, which is one business day after maturity date Tin a BMF calendar.

Q: is the quantity of contracts.

M: M is a multiplier of points for a FX listed option, currently set to 50.

$max(A,B)$: is the operator that computes the maximum value of A and B.

cp: variable to define if it's a call or put option. It's equal to 1 if it's a call and equal to -1 if it's a put.

$PTAX_{T-1}$: PTAX FX rate published one business day in a CDI calendar before maturity date T.

K^*: FX option strike quoted in *BRL* per 1,000 *USD* units. If used the strike simply in $\frac{BRL}{USD}$ units it will be referred to as $K = \frac{K^*}{1000}$.

The multiplier value of 50 combined with the fx fixing and strike quoting convention of the listed FX option that pays at maturity based on *BRL* per 1,000 *USD* units basically states that the *USD* Notional of one contract is 50,000 *USD*. A more user friendly way to rewrite (325) might be:

$$Payoff_{BRL}[T_{pay}] = Q \cdot 50,000 \cdot max\left(cp \cdot [PTAX_{T-1} - K], 0\right) \tag{326}$$

7.5.3 A simple Black pricing formula for $\frac{BRL}{USD}$ Listed FX options

In Section 3 we described the 3 T's used for option pricing and their effect on option premium calculation under a Black type formula. The 3 T's are summarized again briefly by:

1. Time of volatility -> This is computed from today's date t until fx option expiry date T_{ex}. In the specific case of $\frac{BRL}{USD}$ listed FX options, the expiry date is one business day prior to maturity date T in a CDI calendar because this is the date that $PTAX_{T-1}$, which is the option's underlying, is published.
2. Time of expected cashflow discounting -> This is computed from fx option price payment date t_{pay} to option payoff date T_{pay}. t_{pay} occurs one business day after trading date t in a BMF calendar and T_{pay} occurs also one business day after maturity date T in a BMF calendar.
3. Time of fx forward calculation ->This is computed from fx spot date t_{FX} to fx spot date obtained from fx fixing date, sometimes also called settlement date) T_{Settle}. In the specific case of $\frac{BRL}{USD}$ listed FX options, T_{Settle} is computing applying the fx spot settlement rule on $T-1$ which is the date that its underlying is fixed. Following the notation used throughout this book, $T_{Settle} = T - 1_{FX}$.

Based on the arguments outlined in Section 3, it yields that the Black type pricer for a $\frac{BRL}{USD}$ onshore listed option would be given by:

$$c = Q \cdot 50,000 \cdot \left(FXFWD^{ON}_{t,T-1_{FX}} \left[\frac{BRL}{USD}\right] \cdot N(d1) - K \cdot N(d2) \right) \cdot P^{CDI}_{t,t_{pay},T_{pay}}$$

All variables used in the above formula were defined and explained previously at Section 3 of this book. The put option price would be given by:

$$p = Q \cdot 50,000 \cdot \left(K \cdot N(-d2) - FXFWD^{ON}_{t,T-1_{FX}} \left[\frac{BRL}{USD}\right] \cdot N(-d1) \right) \cdot P^{CDI}_{t,t_{pay},T_{pay}}$$

7.5.4 Volatility surface based on SABR model

Again, one possibility to generate a volatility smile is to use the SABR model with same SDE equations as below:

$$dF = \alpha \cdot F^{\beta} \cdot dW_1$$

$$d\alpha = \nu \cdot \alpha \cdot dW_2$$
$$dW_1 \cdot dW_2 = \rho \cdot dt$$

To represent the model, F will be substituted by the FX forward value of $\frac{BRL}{USD}$ onshore, namely $FXFWD^{ON}_{t,T-1_{FX}}[\frac{BRL}{USD}]$, in the first of the 3 above stochastic differential equations. The implied volatility will be computed by:

$$\sigma_b(K,F) = \frac{\alpha}{(F\cdot K)^{\frac{(1-\beta)}{2}}\left\{1+\frac{(1-\beta)^2}{24}\cdot log^2\frac{F}{K}+\frac{(1-\beta)^4}{1920}log^4\frac{F}{K}+\ldots\right\}}\cdot\left(\frac{z}{x(z)}\right)\cdot \left\{1+\left[\frac{(1-\beta)^2}{24}\cdot\frac{\alpha^2}{(FK)^{1-\beta}}+\frac{1}{4}\cdot\frac{\rho\beta\nu\alpha}{(FK)^{\frac{(1-\beta)}{2}}}+\frac{2-3\rho^2}{24}\nu^2\right]t_{ex+\ldots}\right\}$$

where,

$$z = \frac{\nu}{\alpha}(FK)^{\frac{(1-\beta)}{2}}\cdot log\frac{F}{K}$$

$$x(z) = log\left\{\frac{\sqrt{1-2\rho z+z^2}+z-\rho}{1-\rho}\right\}$$

Also, the calibration procedure is similar and usually $\beta = 1$ or chosen by historical investigation of a log-log plot of F and σ_{ATM} pairs. For ρ, ν and α usually a numerical procedure is conducted given market prices or implied volatilities for a range of strikes for the same maturity date.

7.5.5 Volatility surface based on polynomial on FX delta

This topic uses a similar notation as in (Iain, 2011), which is a very good reference book for any kind of question related to FX options pricing. It assumes a quadratic polynomial can be constructed by:

$$\sigma_X(K) = exp\{f(x)\} \tag{327}$$

with,

$$f(x) = c_0 + c_1\cdot\delta(x) + c_2\cdot\delta(x)^2 \tag{328}$$

and

$$\delta(x) = N\left(\frac{x}{\sigma_0\cdot\sqrt{T_{Vol}}}\right) \tag{329}$$

with,

$$\sigma_0 = exp(c_0) \tag{330}$$

and

$$x = ln\left(\frac{FXFWD_{t,T_{Settle}}}{K}\right) \tag{331}$$

x plays the role of a moneyness quantity. $\delta(x)$ is a simpler Black-Scholes delta parametrization obtained by arithmetic average of $N(d1)$ and $N(d2)$ using a constant value for volatility number σ_0 which is not a function of strike. $f(x)$ is the quadratic function that when exponentiated yields the implied volatility for a given strike K and moneyness x. The idea of this parametrization is to solve the system of equations described above given 3 pairs of $\{K, \sigma_x(K)\}$ for unknowns c_0, c_1 and c_2.

If one is interested to better fit the wings of the vol surface, then another possibility would be to use a quartic polynomial instead of a quadratic one. The idea would be based on the same procedure and equations (except for a quartic polynomial instead of quadratic to define $f(x)$), however, it would require 5 pairs of $\{K, \sigma_x(K)\}$as input to solve constants c_0, c_1, c_2, c_3 and c_4. The 2 extra equations would be adding the missing information in order to fit better the wings of the volatility surface.

7.6 $\frac{BRL}{USD}$ Listed FX options with daily margining

The previously mentioned $\frac{BRL}{USD}$ listed FX options had one particular problem for market participants. BVMF's margin calculations didn't net exposure on $\frac{BRL}{USD}$ FX Future contracts with positions on $\frac{BRL}{USD}$ listed FX options. To overcome this issue, BVMF created a new listed FX option contract where there's daily margining and where netting occurs on exposures of $\frac{BRL}{USD}$ FX Future contracts against positions on $\frac{BRL}{USD}$ listed FX options. However, this contract never really traded like the exchange was hoping and they decided simply to create a new methodology for margin calculation that enabled netting of exposures on $\frac{BRL}{USD}$ FX Future contracts with positions on $\frac{BRL}{USD}$ listed FX options.

7.7 $\frac{BRL}{USD}$ FX options: strategies

In the same way that there are strategies of IR options delta hedged, namely the VTF and VID strategies, there's one strategy called VTC for $\frac{BRL}{USD}$ FX options that enables market participants to trade delta hedged $\frac{BRL}{USD}$ listed FX options.

7.7.1 VTC

The VTC strategy trades the following way. First, the exchange will agree with market participants on a value for the $\frac{BRL}{USD}$ FX Future value for FX option maturity date T, namely $FXFUT^{ON}_{t,T_1-1_{FX}}\left[\frac{BRL}{USD}\right]$, and its delta Δ^{VTC}_{BMF}. If market participants agree with the proposed values by the exchange, than trading starts. Let's suppose one goes long Q_{VTC} contracts of VTC strategy for a *USD* call FX listed option at maturity date T. This means that he will be long the same Q_{VTC} quantity of listed FX options for maturity date T and given a delta hedge amount Q^{T*}_{FXFUT}

calculated by the exchange by:

$$Q^{T*}_{FXFUT} = Q_{VTC} \cdot \Delta^{VTC}_{BMF} \quad (332)$$

$$Q^{T}_{FXFUT} = round2(Q^{T*}_{FXFUT}, 5) \quad (333)$$

If one goes long Q_{VTC} contracts of VTC strategy for a *USD* put FX listed option at maturity date T, then the delta hedge amount Q^{T*}_{FXFUT} calculated by the exchange will be given by:

$$Q^{T*}_{FXFUT} = Q_{VTC} \cdot | \Delta^{VTC}_{BMF} | \quad (334)$$

$$Q^{T}_{FXFUT} = round2(Q^{T*}_{FXFUT}, 5) \quad (335)$$

7.7.2 FX Future delta hedge computation by BVMF

The delta hedge Δ^{VTC}_{BMF} calculated by the exchange is given by the following formula for a *USD* call listed fx option:

$$\Delta^{VTC}_{BMF} = N(d1_{BMF(FX)}) \cdot \frac{1}{(1 + R_{t-1^*,T})^{\tau^{252}_{t,T}}} \quad (336)$$

For VTC strategies based on *USD* put options the delta will be given by:

$$\Delta^{VTC}_{BMF} = (N(d1_{BMF(FX)}) - 1) \cdot \frac{1}{(1 + R_{t-1^*,T})^{\tau^{252}_{t,T}}} \quad (337)$$

where,

$$d1_{BMF(FX)} = \frac{ln\left(\frac{FXFUT^{ON}_{t,T_1-1_{FX}}[\frac{BRL}{USD}]}{K}\right) + 0.5 \cdot \sigma^2_{BMF_{FX}} \cdot T_{vol}}{\sigma_{BMF_{FX}} \cdot \sqrt{T_{vol}}}$$

$$d2_{BMF(FX)} = \frac{ln\left(\frac{FXFUT^{ON}_{t,T_1-1_{FX}}[\frac{BRL}{USD}]}{K}\right) - 0.5 \cdot \sigma^2_{BMF_{FX}} \cdot T_{vol}}{\sigma_{BMF_{FX}} \cdot \sqrt{T_{vol}}}$$

$\sigma_{BMF_{FX}}$: is the implied volatility calculated by the exchange for FX listed options based on yesterday's market quotes.

$\frac{1}{(1+R_{t-1^*,T})^{\tau^{252}_{t,T}}}$: discounting term that uses previous date closing rate $R_{t-1^*,T}$ from trading date t in a BMF calendar for maturity date T, but uses the day count fraction term based on start date t and end date T in Bus252 DCB. This avoids having to agree with market participants on a DI1 rate as well prior to trading.

7.7.3 Do you believe you are delta hedged?

It is a lively debate: What will happen with the volatility surface when the price moves? Dupire's local volatility will say one thing, SABR will say another, a linear regression will say a different thing, a regression using only large moves will have a different result.

One can always look at *Regimes of Volatility* (Derman, 1998) for a good explanation of the "Sticky Strike", "Sticky Delta" and other rules for calculating the delta in different regimes.

For FX, which is typically parametrized as a function of Delta, one can also write the Total Delta as the sum of the Black Delta and an adjustment:

$$TotalDelta = \frac{\partial c}{\partial F} + \frac{\partial c}{\partial \sigma} \cdot \frac{\partial \sigma}{\partial F} \tag{338}$$

$$TotalDelta = BlackDelta + Vega \cdot \frac{\partial \sigma}{\partial F} \tag{339}$$

If the implied volatility is a function of the (Black) Delta:

$$TotalDelta = BlackDelta + Vega \cdot \frac{\partial \sigma}{\partial \delta} \cdot \frac{\partial \delta}{\partial F} \tag{340}$$

$$TotalDelta = BlackDelta + Vega \cdot Gamma \cdot \frac{\partial \sigma}{\partial \delta} \tag{341}$$

For a simple parametrization of the smile such as in "Option-Implied Probability Distributions and Currency Excess Returns" (Malz, 1997), we have:

$$\sigma(\delta) = ATM - 2 \cdot RR \cdot \left(\delta - \frac{1}{2}\right) + 16 \cdot ST \cdot \left(\delta - \frac{1}{2}\right)^2 \tag{342}$$

$$\frac{\partial \sigma}{\partial \delta} = -2 \cdot RR - 32 \cdot ST \cdot \left(\frac{1}{2} - \delta\right) \tag{343}$$

This is a simple example of an adjustment to the Black Delta based not on a change of the market's quotes (ATM, ST and RR) stay the same, but on the fact that the moneyness (and therefore the delta) of that particular strike has changed, while volatility as a function of delta has not (Sticky Delta).

Depending on the chosen dynamics (plug your stochastic volatility model here), the term $\frac{\partial \sigma}{\partial F}$ will be different (you can use a regression here as well). This has been covered in "Foreign Exchange Option Pricing: A Practitioner's Guide" (Clark, 2011), but the hard part is applying a framework typically developed for OTC markets (Sticky Delta, ATM vols, fixed terms) and applying it to listed options.

7.8 OTC IR and FX options

As mentioned before, the market in Brazil has some peculiar characteristics. Due to high volatility, regime changes and bank failures, most of the interbank market moved from OTC trading to listed contracts. So the FX market is driven by the DOL and the IR market is driven by the DI1 contracts.

As for funds, they don't have a lot of good choices. Banks won't extend credit to funds as a rule, and therefore OTC trades between a bank and a fund are typically traded OTC but registered and cleared at BVMF, and therefore restricted to what the clearing will price, process and accept. Unfortunately, at the time of writing intraday monitoring of the USDBRL spot price (even defined as DOL–Casado) and market rates such as the different DIs is not performed. This makes OTC options with a barrier restricted to using the PTAX as the variable monitored for FX and the IDI as the variable used in IR. For Index options, monitoring of barriers uses the maximum and minimum of the Spot Ibovespa calculated periodically by BVMF itself. This can lead to unexpected situations at the opening of the market, as an opening price will be calculated with stale prices depending on the time taken by the opening auctions, and it might not be correlated with the futures price for this small time window. Now, the IDI, with its positive drift, is not suitable for this kind of use, although some have come with uses of different combinations to arrive at a desired payoff.

As for the consequences of using the PTAX as a barrier, we will look at it in a later chapter.

And the true OTC options? Those are traded between a bank and a customer, and registered at Cetip. Back in 2008, this is where TARFs were found ... or weren't? At that time, TARFs and other structures were bundled under "Others", and there was no easy way to get a dump of all the trades in the system in a way that was useful (calculate PV or Delta). So the BCB (and everyone else) was left trying to guess the size of the iceberg. This has also had an influence in the creation of the CED, and now different payoff formulas must be approved and implemented by Cetip. In here one can use USDBRL Spot as a barrier, and Cetip can also act as a calculating agent.

But ... be aware that the tax treatment of OTC contracts might be different from listed instruments. Always check what the current tax treatment is with a lawyer, the lawyer's lawyer, and sacrifice a bird to the gods, burning its entrails and looking at which direction the smoke blows in order to predict what Brazil's authorities will do next.

8

The Mountain Goes to ... Foreign Exchange Contracts Offshore

CME holds a great variety of listed FX Futures contracts. In the first subsection we focus on its FX Futures contracts for the $\frac{BRL}{USD}$ currency pair.

The next subsection will discuss $\frac{BRL}{USD}$ outright NDF's in OTC market. We will start with this contract's payoff, highlighting the differences for the equivalent $\frac{BRL}{USD}$ outright NDF's payoff in the onshore market. One key difference is the possibility of a fallback FX Fixing rate to EMTA in the offshore contract. Because of this fact, we will show how offshore markets require another market risk factor, commonly called by market participants NDF OnOff spread. We will plot the time series for this market factor since 2010 and discuss why values went from positive to negative and what drives them.

Another interesting fact is that payoff is settled in USD and paid offshore and there's often collateralization based on CSA (Credit Support Annex) between the 2 involved parties in the transaction. So a little detour will happen to explain briefly why collateralized contracts need to discount their expected payoff based on the collateral index rate. After the brief detour, pricing of $\frac{BRL}{USD}$ outright NDF's offshore can be finally derived.

The following subsection describes that typically NDF's offshore outright X BMF 1st available FX Future spreads are traded with reasonable liquidity for a range of tenors. However, even though it's often encouraged throughout this book to use liquid market instruments to calibrate a curve, in the BRL offshore curve calibration it's better to use NDF's offshore outright X NDF onshore outright spreads for same tenor. This choice is based on the different trading hours for this NDF spread market traded OTC to BMF closing prices.

The last subsection explains the BRL offshore curve calibration. It assumes NDF OnOff spreads are quoted as the pips difference of the NDF offshore to NDF onshore. However, this choice means that once FX spot is changed, the calibrated BRL offshore discount factors will change also a bit. So a pure BRL offshore cashflow will display some fx risk due to BRL offshore curve calibration.

8.1 CME $\frac{BRL}{USD}$ FX Futures

8.1.1 Contract details

The contract code for trading the Brazilian Real Futures Contracts at CME is 6L for CME Globex Eletronic Markets, BR for Open Outcry. The Bloomberg code is BRA. To fully describe each one of the available contracts for all month listings it's also required the usual 3 characters to describe the month and year of the contract. One example would be F15 that represents the January 2015 contract. The Notional of one contract is 100,000 *BRL* and trade block minimum is 50 contracts. Contract daily fixings are traded and published in $\frac{USD}{BRL}$ units. It's worth noting that this is an inverted quotation of the usual $\frac{BRL}{USD}$ currency pair.

The last cashflow is paid based on the reciprocal PTAX value published one previous day in a CDI calendar than the contracts maturity date. If there is a price source disruption and the Central Bank of Brazil BRL PTAX rate is not published by the Central Bank of Brazil on the last cashflow day, then the CME Group may determine a final settlement price based upon the reciprocal of either the EMTA BRL Industry Survey Rate or the EMTA BRL Indicative Survey Rate, rounded to 5 decimal places. Even though the EMTA FX rate have never been fixed different than PTAX, this fallback FX rate means that this contract could have as its FX fixing a rate completely different than an onshore contract, like a FX Future at BVMF.

Each contract's maturity date will be the first business day of the contract's month in a CDI calendar and cashflow payments occur one business day after cashflow computation date in a *USD* and *CME* combined calendar, as payments must occur on dates that CME is opened but it must also be a non US bank holiday.

8.1.2 Payoff

The payoff for one $\frac{BRL}{USD}$ FX Future contract at CME on trading date t is given by:

$$MCF_t^T = CS \cdot \left(CP_t^T - TP_t^T\right) \tag{344}$$

where

MCF_t^T: is the margin cashflow computed in *USD* currency for date t for a $\frac{BRL}{USD}$ FX Future contract with maturity date T. Please bear in mind that the margin cashflow is computed at date t, but only paid the next business day in a *USD* and *CME* combined calendar.

CP_t^T: is the closing price for $\frac{BRL}{USD}$ FX Future contract with maturity date T, published by CME at t.

TP_t^T: is the traded price at date t for a $\frac{BRL}{USD}$ FX Future contract with maturity date T.

CS: is the contract size, currently set to 100,000 *BRL* Notional.

The next equation demonstrates how daily cashflows are computed on any other given non trading date t_N:

$$MCF_t^T = CS \cdot \left(CP_{t_N}^T - CP_{t_{N-1}}^T\right) \tag{345}$$

where,

$CP_{t_{N-1}}^T$: is the closing price for a $\frac{BRL}{USD}$ FX Future contract with maturity date T, published at date t_{N-1}, which is one business day previous to date t_N in a *USD* and *CME* combined calendar.

8.1.3 Pricing

Assuming the CME $\frac{BRL}{USD}$ fx futures to fx forward convexity to be negligible, which often happens for the most liquid CME fx future contracts that are short dated, the pricing of a CME $\frac{BRL}{USD}$ fx future collapses to the pricing of a fx forward contract. In the next subsection we will derive the pricing of OTC $\frac{BRL}{USD}$ offshore NDF contracts and the only difference between the strike of a CME $\frac{BRL}{USD}$ fx future contract and its equivalent $\frac{BRL}{USD}$ NDF strike is the quotation units that are inverted.

8.2 OTC – NDFs

8.2.1 $\frac{BRL}{USD}$ offshore NDFs – payoff and differences for the equivalent onshore NDF contract

There's a very liquid market for $\frac{BRL}{USD}$ offshore NDFs. Daily volume is around 8 billion *USD*. But what's different in the payoff of $\frac{BRL}{USD}$ NDF's offshore to onshore? Mainly the possibility to have a FX Fixing fallback rate on the offshore contract and the currency in which the payoff is paid. Let's begin with the payoff for an onshore $\frac{BRL}{USD}$ contract:

$$Payoff_T^{NDFOn}[BRL] = Not_{USD} \cdot (PTAX_{T-1} - K) \tag{346}$$

where,

$Payoff_T^{NDFOn}[BRL]$: is the payoff of a NDF onshore contract with FX Fixing date occurring at date $T-1$, which is one business day in a *CDI* calendar prior to payoff cash settlement date T. The payoff is settled in *BRL* currency.

K: is the NDF onshore agreed forward price (strike) at trade date t.

$PTAX_{T-1}$: FX Fixing of the NDF onshore contract published at date $T-1$.

The offshore $\frac{BRL}{USD}$ NDF contract also has as its fixing the *PTAX* FX rate. However, like the CME $\frac{BRL}{USD}$ FX Futures contracts described in the previous subsection, it has as its fallback FX rate *EMTA*. This means essentially that we can consider for pricing purposes that the FX Fixing rate is in fact *EMTA*, instead of *PTAX*, because of its fallback feature. The offshore $\frac{BRL}{USD}$ NDF contract payoff is given by:

$$Payoff_T^{NDFOff}[USD] = Not_{USD} \cdot \frac{(EMTA_{T-2_{FX}} - K)}{EMTA_{T-2_{FX}}} \tag{347}$$

where,

$Payoff_T^{NDFOff}[USD]$: is the payoff of a NDF offshore contract with FX Fixing date occurring at date $T - 2_{FX}$, which is 2 business day in a combined *CDI* and *US* holidays calendar prior to payoff cash settlement date T. The payoff is settled in *USD* currency.

K: is the NDF offshore agreed forward price (strike) at trade date t.

$EMTA_{T-2_{FX}}$: FX Fixing of the NDF offshore contract published at date $T - 2_{FX}$.

Comparing (346) and (347) one could note 2 major differences. One is the FX Fixing source which is different. As pointed out, the offshore NDF fixes with *EMTA* FX rate instead of *PTAX*. The other major difference is the location where payoff settlement occurs. The NDF onshore contract settles in *BRL* inside Brazil. The NDF offshore settles in *USD* outside Brazil.

Those 2 major differences explain partially why we have different fx forward prices agreed on onshore and offshore NDF contracts with same FX Fixing date. If there was a major crisis in Brazil, there's a large possibility that the NDF onshore *BRL* cash settled by the contracts payoff may not be able to be sent outside Brazil because of restrictions that could be imposed by the government. On the other hand, offshore contracts are already settled in *USD* outside Brazil, so no need to worry regarding the same government imposition that might happen regarding money outflows. On top of that, the offshore contract could be settled with its fallback FX rate which is *EMTA*. In the case of an inconvertibility event, the offshore NDF contract will certainly have lots of long *USD* positions when compared to onshore equivalent contract. Therefore, one could say that under that particular situation the *EMTA* published FX rate most likely will diverge considerably from *PTAX*. This means that under that specific scenario, not only the payment of the offshore contract is settled safely outside Brazil in United States, but also the payoff amount will be larger (for a long USD position) given that *EMTA* would be fixed higher than *PTAX*.

This difference in NDF prices for offshore to onshore contracts is commonly called NDFOnOff spread by market participants. It's quoted in pips and defined by:

$$NDFOnOff_t^T = \left(FXFWD_{t,T}^{OFF}\left[\frac{BRL}{USD}\right] - FXFWD_{t,T}^{ON}\left[\frac{BRL}{USD}\right]\right) \cdot 10000 \qquad (348)$$

where,

$NDFOnOff_t^T$: is the NDF OnOff Spread seen at date t for both NDF's with settlement date T.

Figures 68, 69, 70 and 71 show the NDFOnOff spreads historically for 3M, 6M, 1Y and 2Y NDFs since 2010.

One natural question by looking at the plots above is why the NDF offshore prices trade with a lower price than its equivalent NDF onshore. Isn't it providing more protection than its onshore equivalent based on the possible fallback to

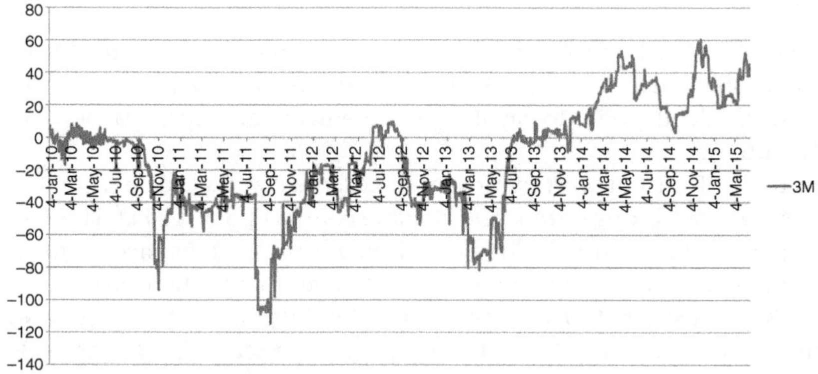

Figure 68 NDFOnOff Spread for 3m since 2010

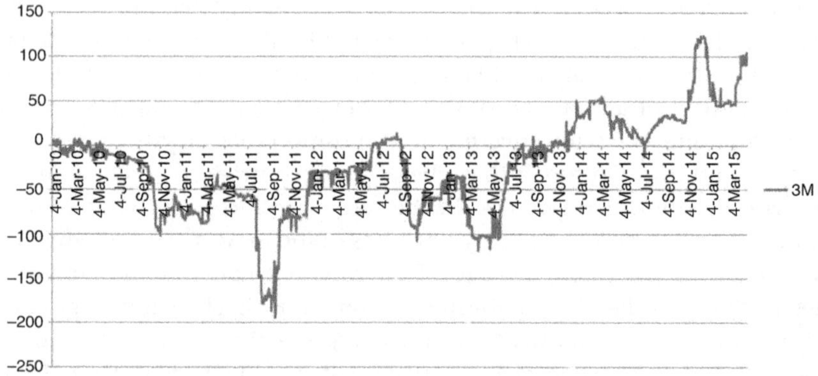

Figure 69 NDFOnOff Spread for 6M since 2010

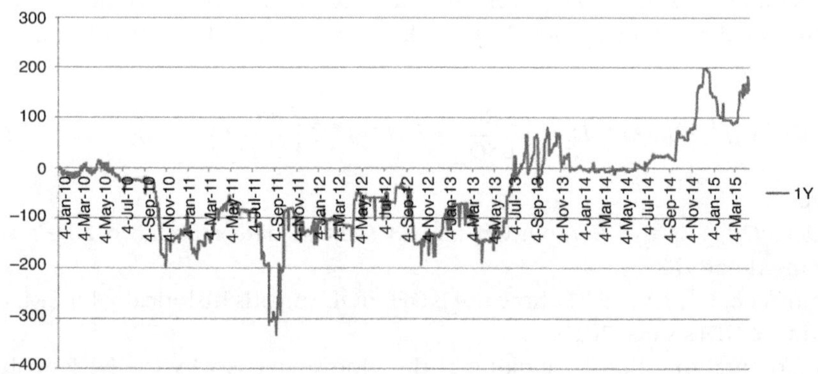

Figure 70 NDFOnOff Spread for 1Y since 2010

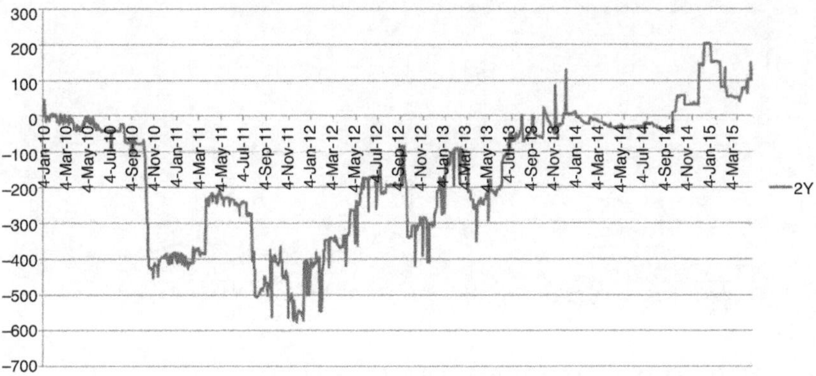

Figure 71 NDFOnOff Spread for 2Y since 2010

EMTA FX fixing? And also because it settles outside Brazil and it's not subject to currency outflow restrictions that could be imposed by the government? It sounds natural by looking solely to those 2 ingredients that the NDF offshore price should be higher.

On the other hand, there are many offshore market participants willing to be long BRL (and short USD) and receive the high BRL interest rate associated with a BRL trade. But for them to trade locally in Brazil is difficult. To accomplish that, they have to open a 2689 account that enables them to trade locally in Brazil; but, it's unfortunately not that easy to setup the infrastructure to open this account. This means that trading a NDF onshore is really hard for offshore players and often not the adopted way when trying to be long BRL. This limitation is also acknowledged by Brazilian banks that have no limitation on their side to open an offshore account to trade against offshore clients. However, they ask for a "premium" for entering into an NDF offshore transaction and the offshore counterparties have to sell USD with a NDF offshore price lower than its onshore equivalent. And this offshore short USD flow is what drives the NDFOnOff spread to be negative for most of the time.

There are periods however when the NDFOnOff spread can become positive. Figure (72) shows that during a crisis period such as the one we had at the end of 2008, the flow of offshore market participants willing to be long BRL diminishes, mostly because it's an emerging market that has lower liquidity and appetite during any crisis. Under that circumstance, the NDFOnOff becomes positive since it's not negatively skewed anymore by the offshore flow.

Another interesting effect on NDFOnOff spread happened around January 2011. During that month, it was announced by BCB that financial institutions with a net short USD position would have a compulsory deposit applied. With this measure, any market participant willing to be short USD would have 2

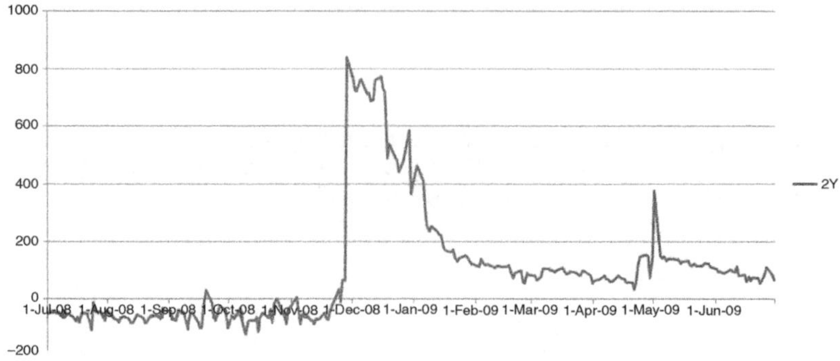

Figure 72 NDFOnOff Spread for 2Y from Jul-2008 to Jul-2009

options. Go short USD on the NDF offshore market or be short USD onshore and be subject to the compulsory deposit. And most of them chose to be short USD offshore for obvious reasons. Because of this fact, there was a great change in the NDFOnOff spread values, as almost only the NDF offshore market was receiving orders to sell USD. This caused the negative shift in the NDFOnOff spreads around January 2011 as seen in Figure (70). At 01-Jul-2013, BCB revoked the measure and a little bit prior to it the NDFOnOff spread started to climb back to around the levels when the measure was first announced in 2011.

8.2.2 A quick detour for pricing collateralized derivatives

In this subsection, we are interested in the effect that bilateral collateral agreements have on the pricing of OTC derivative trades. A collateral agreement between 2 counterparties A and B means that when a positive present value for counterparty A is computed, it's deposited by counterparty B in cash into counterparty A's account. There are other possible forms of posting collateral but here for simplicity we assume it can be only posted in cash without any loss of generality. A better guide for studying collateralization, pricing under collateral assumptions and counterparty credit risk is *Counterparty Credit Risk, Collateral and Funding: With Pricing Cases For All Asset Classes* (Brigo, Morini and Pallavicini, 2013).

In this book, it's assumed that such contracts are bilateral, so collateral is posted both ways, depending on which counterparty has the negative present value on the derivative contract which has to post collateral to the counterparty with positive present value.

The major pricing impact of bilateral collateral agreements into OTC derivatives is:

- Collateral payments introduce additional cashflows based on the collateral account accrued given the rate specified by the collateral agreement, being it typically Fed Funds, EONIA, MUTAN, etc. Thus, collateralized trades have exposure to the collateral rate.

The simplest question that we may ask is "What's the present value of 1 unit of fixed cashflow to be paid in a future date T under a collateral agreement?" The answer is that the present value must be equal to the discount factor

$$P_{t,T}^{Coll} = \frac{1}{\prod_{T_i=t}^{T-1}\left(1 + C_{t,T_i,T_{i+1}} \cdot \tau_{T_i,T_{i+1}}\right)}$$

based on the collateral index, where

$P_{t,T}^{Coll}$: is the discount factor based on collateral index *Coll* from date t to date T.

$\tau_{T_i,T_{i+1}}$: one accrual period between time T_i and time T_{i+1}. For most collateral indices it's expressed in Act360 DCB.

$C_{t,T_i,T_{i+1}}$: collateral forward rate seen at date t for accrual period between T_i and T_{i+1} given a collateral calibrated curve.

Below follows the proof for the above statement.

Assume that we are at date $T-1$ and we will receive 1 unit of cashflow in the next O/N accrual period T, which is typically 1 day over 360 but when weekends or holidays enter it may be some number n over 360. Let's say we have to figure out the present value amount X that have to be posted in collateral today so that, after the O/N accrual period, we pay back $X \cdot (1 + C_{T-1} \cdot \tau_{T-1,T})$, where C_{T-1} is the collateral index published at time $T-1$ under the contract CSA (Credit Support Annex). But also after this accrual O/N period, we will receive for sure 1 unit. Thus,

$$1 = X \cdot (1 + C_{T-1} \cdot \tau_{T-1,T})$$

which enables to write that

$$X = \frac{1}{(1 + C_{T-1} \cdot \tau_{T-1,T})}$$

Now assume that we are at date t and the cashflow will be received at the same future date T, which is now more than one accrual O/N period in the future. One day before T we will ask for a payment $X = \frac{1}{(1+C_{T-1}\cdot\tau_{T-1,T})}$. Recursively we ask for at time t for the amount $X = \frac{1}{\prod_{T_i=t}^{T-1}\left(1+C_{T_i}\cdot\tau_{T_i,T_{i+1}}\right)}$. Thus, the amount X which is the present value of unit of cashflow to be paid at future time T is given by the realized compounding of discount factors of O/N published collateral rates, from t to date $T-1$. But the OIS (Overnight index swap) market allows us to hedge the realized compounding discount factors into the forwards seen today. Thus,

$$X = \mathbb{E}^{\mathbb{Q}}\left[\frac{1}{\prod_{T_i=t}^{T-1}\left(1 + C_{T_i} \cdot \tau_{T_i,T_{i+1}}\right)}\middle|\mathcal{F}_t\right] = \frac{1}{\prod_{T_i=t}^{T-1}\left(1 + C_{t,T_i,T_{i+1}} \cdot \tau_{T_i,T_{i+1}}\right)} \tag{349}$$

where as stated above,

$C_{t,T_i,T_{i+1}}$: are the collateral forward rates seen at date t for accrual between period T_i and T_{i+1}.

$\mathbb{E}^{\mathbb{Q}}$: is an expectation under the probability measure that has $\prod_{T_i=t}^{T-1}\left(1+C_{T_i}\cdot \tau_{T_i,T_{i+1}}\right)$ as its numéraire.

In case the collateral index is based on a different currency than the cashflow currency the proof is a bit more elaborated and we refer the reader to *Counterparty Credit Risk, Collateral and Funding: With Pricing Cases For All Asset Classes* (Brigo, Morini and Pallavicini, 2013) again for a detailed explanation. But let's try to see what our intuition tell us about a simple example where collateral index is Fedfunds which is in USD and we will receive in a future date T one unit of BRL. Let's say the present value of the 1 unit BRL amount with collateral index FedFunds is called X again.

We can convert X, which is in BRL, to USD by doing a 0-day fx forward offshore $\frac{USD}{BRL}$ collateralized trade. This trade will result in an amount of $X\cdot FXFWD_{t,t}^{OFF}[\frac{USD}{BRL}]$ in USD. From date t to date $T-1$ this amount will be capitalized by the FedFunds O/N published rate and hedged in OIS market. This will result in a future date T amount of $X\cdot FXFWD_{t,t}^{OFF}[\frac{USD}{BRL}]\cdot\prod_{T_i=t}^{T-1}\left(1+C_{t,T_i,T_{i+1}}\cdot\tau_{T_i,T_{i+1}}\right)$ in USD. This amount can be hedged back to BRL by doing a fx forward offshore $\frac{BRL}{USD}$ trade for settlement date T. This generates the amount:

$$X\cdot\frac{FXFWD_{t,T}^{OFF}[\frac{BRL}{USD}]}{FXFWD_{t,t}^{OFF}[\frac{BRL}{USD}]}\cdot\prod_{T_i=t}^{T-1}\left(1+C_{T_i}\cdot\tau_{T_i,T_{i+1}}\right)$$

which must equal to 1 BRL unit at future date T. This yields:

$$1=X\cdot\frac{FXFWD_{t,T}^{OFF}[\frac{BRL}{USD}]}{FXFWD_{t,t}^{OFF}[\frac{BRL}{USD}]}\cdot\prod_{T_i=t}^{T-1}\left(1+C_{T_i}\cdot\tau_{T_i,T_{i+1}}\right) \tag{350}$$

Rearranging a bit (350) yields:

$$\frac{FXFWD_{t,t}^{OFF}[\frac{BRL}{USD}]}{FXFWD_{t,T}^{OFF}[\frac{BRL}{USD}]\cdot\prod_{T_i=t}^{T-1}\left(1+C_{T_i}\cdot\tau_{T_i,T_{i+1}}\right)}=X \tag{351}$$

This means that one cashflow in BRL for one offshore trade collateralized in Fedfunds must have the BRL cashflow converted to USD by a NDF with settlement date for the date that BRL will be paid, discount this cashflow until t with FedFunds OIS curve and convert back to BRL with a T+0 day FX forward offshore.

8.2.3 Pricing a collateralized NDF contract offshore

Recall that the payoff for the NDF offshore contract was given by:

$$Payoff_T^{NDFOff}[USD]=Not_{USD}\cdot\frac{(EMTA_{T-2_{FX}}-K)}{EMTA_{T-2_{FX}}} \tag{352}$$

We can rearrange a bit (352) to

$$Payoff_T^{NDFOff}[USD] = Not_{USD} \cdot \left(1 - \frac{K}{EMTA_{T-2_{FX}}}\right) = Not_{USD} - \frac{Not_{BRL}}{EMTA_{T-2_{FX}}} \quad (353)$$

where we used the fact that the Notional in BRL is given by:

$$Not_{BRL} = Not_{USD} \cdot K$$

Pricing can be done based on the following equation, assuming that collateral index currency is USD which is the same currency that payoff is defined:

$$PV_t[USD] = P_{t,T-2_{FX}}^{Coll} \cdot \left(Not_{USD} - \mathrm{Not_{BRL}} \cdot \mathbb{E}^{\mathbb{Q}_{\mathrm{Coll}}^{\mathrm{T-2_{FX}}}}\left[\frac{1}{EMTA_{T-2_{FX}}} | \mathcal{F}_t\right]\right) \quad (354)$$

where,

$P_{t,T-2_{FX}}^{Coll}$: is the discount factor based on a collateral index curve from date t to payoff payment date $T - 2_{FX}$.

$\mathbb{E}^{\mathbb{Q}_{Coll}^{T-2_{FX}}}$: is the expectation under the probability measure that has as its numéraire $P_{t,T-2_{FX}}^{Coll}$. It's worth mentioning again that we are assuming collateral index to be in *USD*.

Following the same route taken on previous sections of this book, we will substitute $EMTA_{T-2_{FX}} = FXFWD_{T-2,T-2_{FX}}^{OFF}\left[\frac{BRL}{USD}\right]$, which states that the *NDF* value seen at its fixing date $T - 2_{FX}$ collapses to its fixing $EMTA_{T-2_{FX}}$ value published on that date. This yields:

$$PV_t[USD] = P_{t,T-2_{FX}}^{Coll} \cdot \left(Not_{USD} - \mathrm{Not_{BRL}} \cdot \mathbb{E}^{\mathbb{Q}_{\mathrm{Coll}}^{\mathrm{T-2_{FX}}}}\left[\frac{1}{FXFWD_{T-2,T-2_{FX}}^{OFF}\left[\frac{BRL}{USD}\right]} \middle| \mathcal{F}_t\right]\right) \quad (355)$$

A very good paper to understand pricing of fx products under collateral assumptions is *Cooking with Collateral* (Piterbarg, 2012). In this paper he develops HJM type pricing in a dual currency economy and concludes that:

$$\frac{1}{FXFWD_{t,T-2_{FX}}^{OFF}\left[\frac{BRL}{USD}\right]} = \mathbb{E}^{\mathbb{Q}_{\mathrm{Coll}}^{\mathrm{T-2_{FX}}}}\left[\frac{1}{FXFWD_{T-2,T-2_{FX}}^{OFF}\left[\frac{BRL}{USD}\right]} \middle| \mathcal{F}_t\right] \quad (356)$$

Essentially, (356) is telling us that the reciprocal of $FXFWD_{t,T-2_{FX}}^{OFF}\left[\frac{BRL}{USD}\right]$ is a martingale under $\mathbb{Q}_{\mathrm{Coll}}^{\mathrm{T-2_{FX}}}$.

By plugging (356) into (355) yields:

$$PV_t[USD] = P_{t,T-2_{FX}}^{Coll} \cdot \left(Not_{USD} - \frac{Not_{BRL}}{FXFWD_{t,T-2_{FX}}^{OFF}\left[\frac{BRL}{USD}\right]}\right) \quad (357)$$

The final result in (357) is intuitive. The present value of an NDF discounts the Notional in USD with the collateral discount factor $P^{Coll}_{t,T-2_{FX}}$. This goes along what was presented in the previous subsection: a fixed cashflow in the same currency as the collateral index currency should be discounted with a curve based on the collateral forward rates. The second component is also intuitive. The Notional in BRL is converted to USD by the NDF value and also discounted by the collateral curve.

What if the same trade had EONIA as collateral instead?

In that case, the Notional in USD would be a future cashflow in USD, that would need to be converted to EUR based on $\frac{EUR}{USD}$ FX forward for settlement date $T-2_{FX}$. This amount would be then discounted by EONIA OIS curve and the result would be converted back to *USD* by the T+0 FX Forward of $\frac{USD}{EUR}$. For the Notional in BRL equivalent amount, it could be converted to EUR based on the offshore $\frac{EUR}{BRL}$ FX forward with settlement date at $T-2_{FX}$. It would be then discounting the same way based on EONIA OIS curve and converted back to USD based on the T+0 FX Forward of $\frac{USD}{EUR}$.

8.2.4 How offshore NDFs are usually traded in the interbank market?

$\frac{BRL}{USD}$ offshore NDF's are usually not traded as an outright NDF trade. They are traded based on spread strategies which are a combination of trades where usually one is long(short) one onshore trade against a short(long) offshore NDF outright. The onshore trade could be traded on the exchange based on a BMF date or as a NDF onshore based on a maturity tenor. The most common choice when traded as a BMF contract is to select the nearest maturity FX Future contract, except for dates where the nearest contract liquidity is rolled to the second nearest one. When other BMF dates are traded, usually the trade is executed as a combination of a DDI and a DI trade. This happens because usually the liquidity is smaller for FX Futures contracts longer than 3 months and to avoid complications due to convexity adjustments that FX future contracts may display and DDI and DI contracts don't.

However, when onshore trade is executed based on a maturity tenor, it needs to be registered at CETIP which is the clearing house for OTC trades in Brazil. But, regardless of being exchange traded or OTC, the trade will always be registered with a traded price such that the first cashflow of the exchange traded trade or present value of the OTC is zero.

The NDF offshore trade is usually traded with a settlement date derived from a BMF date or a tenor, similarly to the onshore case. In case it's based on BMF dates, usually it's based on BMF FX Fixing dates for its FX related contracts like DDI or DOL. When it's a tenor like 1Y, the settlement date for the NDF is obtained from a relatively complex algorithm (at least when thinking about simply adding a tenor) that is described in Subsection 1.5 of [11]. It's similar to adding 1Y to the current fx spot date to yield the corresponding NDF fx settlement date, but not exactly like that.

Tenors typically traded for the NDFs based on maturity tenors are 3M, 6M, 9M, 1Y, 2Y.

8.2.5 Revisiting the cupom curve construction based on NDF spread strategies

If liquidity is large for NDF spread strategies, a cupom curve could be calibrated based on 2 different strategies prices. Given a BRL CDI onshore calibrated curve and the closing nearest maturity FX Future price, namely $FXFUT^{ON}_{t,T_1}\left[\frac{BRL}{USD}\right]$, the calibration procedure could be implemented with the following equations:

$$NDFOnOff^{T}_{t} = \left(FXFWD^{OFF}_{t,T}\left[\frac{BRL}{USD}\right] - FXFWD^{ON}_{t,T}\left[\frac{BRL}{USD}\right]\right)\cdot 10000 \tag{358}$$

$$NDFOnOffBMF^{T}_{t} = \left(FXFWD^{OFF}_{t,T}\left[\frac{BRL}{USD}\right] - FXFUT^{ON}_{t,T_1}\left[\frac{BRL}{USD}\right]\right)\cdot 10000 \tag{359}$$

Based on (359) and the knowledge of $FXFUT^{ON}_{t,T_1}\left[\frac{BRL}{USD}\right]$, one could imply the value of $FXFWD^{OFF}_{t,T}\left[\frac{BRL}{USD}\right]$. But we are interested in calibrating the cupom curve and we need to use (358) to be able to imply our desired unknown which is $FXFWD^{ON}_{t,T}\left[\frac{BRL}{USD}\right]$. After this step we would use the fact that:

$$FXFWD^{ON}_{t,T}\left[\frac{BRL}{USD}\right] = FXFUT^{ON}_{t,T_1}\left[\frac{BRL}{USD}\right]\cdot\frac{P^{USB}_{t,T-1_{FX},T}}{P^{CDI}_{t,T-1_{FX},T}} \tag{360}$$

And calibrate cupom forward discount factor $P^{USB}_{t,T-1_{FX},T}$, by:

$$P^{USB}_{t,T-1_{FX},T} = \frac{FXFUT^{ON}_{t,T_1}\left[\frac{BRL}{USD}\right] + \frac{NDFOnOffBMF^{T}_{t}}{10000} - \frac{NDFOnOff^{T}_{t}}{10000}}{FXFUT^{ON}_{t,T_1}\left[\frac{BRL}{USD}\right]}\cdot P^{CDI}_{t,T-1_{FX},T} \tag{361}$$

8.2.6 The mythical offshore BRL discounting curve

The NDF offshore price is based on the following equation:

$$FXFWD^{OFF}_{t,T}\left[\frac{BRL}{USD}\right] = FXFWD^{ON}_{t,T}\left[\frac{BRL}{USD}\right] + NDFOnOff_{t,T} \tag{362}$$

But the NDF offshore $FXFWD^{OFF}_{t,T}\left[\frac{BRL}{USD}\right]$ can also be expressed based on the CSA collateral index curve discount factor and an implied BRL offshore discount factor calibrated by:

$$FXFWD^{OFF}_{t,T}\left[\frac{BRL}{USD}\right] = \frac{BRL}{USD}[t]\cdot\frac{P^{BRU}_{t,t_{fx},T}}{P^{Coll}_{t,t_{fx},T}} \tag{363}$$

where,

$P^{BRU}_{t,t_{fx},T}$: is the BRL (BRU first 2 letters are short for BRL and the U that follows indicate that it's used for USD settlement) offshore forward discount factor seen at date t, with start date at t_{fx} and end date at T.

Plugging (363) into (362) yields:

$$\frac{BRL}{USD}[t] \cdot \frac{P^{Coll}_{t,t_{fx},T}}{P^{BRU}_{t,t_{fx},T}} = \frac{BRL}{USD}[t] \cdot \frac{P^{USB}_{t,t_{fx},T}}{P^{CDI}_{t,t_{fx},T}} + NDFOnOff_{t,T} \tag{364}$$

Rearranging (364) a bit yields:

$$P^{BRU}_{t,t_{fx},T} = \frac{\frac{BRL}{USD}[t] \cdot P^{Coll}_{t,t_{fx},T}}{\frac{BRL}{USD}[t] \cdot \frac{P^{USB}_{t,t_{fx},T}}{P^{CDI}_{t,t_{fx},T}} + NDFOnOff_{t,T}} \tag{365}$$

Equation (365) is one possible modeling choice to imply a discount factor of BRL offshore, but please bear in mind that it's calibrated based on the collateral curve, so trades with same payoff but different collateral indexes on their CSA would imply in different BRL offshore discounting curves. Therefore, equivalent *BRU* rates calculated based on $P^{BRU}_{t,t_{fx},T}$ would be different when collateral is FedFunds, EONIA or US Libor 3M for instance.

Good luck trying to trade this curve on its own though. This is an implied curve, not observable directly in the market, and therefore difficult to hedge on its own. This is why sometimes it is better to model the two NDFs (onshore and offshore) in the same risks (onshore BRL – Pré – and USD – Cupom Cambial – curves), adding the spread as a basis risk. Yes, this risk is a function of the spread between the onshore USD rate and the funding rate in USD (offshore), but is also a function of supply and demand, of convertibility risk (oh the old days of 1998 and 2002, when selling the spread at 6% per year looked like a really good idea! Of course the spread shot to 40% later before going down, creating reports of "stored" P&L that would surely – yes, no doubt about it – come back still in the same year).

8.3 OTC – BRL/USD Options

There was a time in which this market was a function of:

1. Offshore demand for carry-related trades:
   a. A spread where the customer (hedge fund or pension fund) buys an ATMF USD Put BRL Call – struck at the NDF price – and sells an ATMS USD Put BRL Call – struck at the Spot price
   b. Customer (hedge fund) buys a RKO USD Put BRL Call, where the barrier of the reverse knock out is below a level seen by the market as "defended" by

the BCB. RKOs have a terrible way of bleeding a dealer to death, and they can lead to selling more gamma than it would be healthy.

2. Hedging for onshore-related hedging activity, because corporates would sell FX options embedded in swap that would make for a lower borrowing cost on a paired loan, and the local market was not big enough to hedge it.
   a. If in 2004/2005 forward settling strike options were popular, strings of OTM USD Calls and then TARFs became the preferred structures later.

When the onshore activity dried up after the consequences of the 2008 devaluation, the liquidity offshore was reduced, but with time it started gaining on the market share of the onshore market, due to the bigger costs of trading in the exchange. These included not only transaction costs (the consequences of a monopoly) but also the increasing costs of margin for both options and futures (there was no netting of margins between options and futures, as discussed on the subsection abut options with daily margining). For foreign banks in Brazil, where liquidity had to come from outside the country, this was not good.

And the nail in the coffin came with the IOF on Derivatives in Jul-2011; rules that clarified that Delta Hedging a portfolio would not pay taxes came until Sep-2011, but by then the rationale for keeping an onshore desk for options market-making was hard to defend.

How are these instruments different from the onshore options?

First, their payoff is in USD:

$$Payoff_T^{OptOff}\,[USD] = Not_{USD} \cdot Max\left[\phi \cdot \left(\frac{EMTA_{T-2_{FX}} - K}{EMTA_{T-2_{FX}}}\right), 0\right] \tag{366}$$

Although on the NDF we used a distinction between the EMTA and the PTAX to explain the spread between onshore and offshore NDFs, let's return to the PTAX for now, as the PTAX is the fixing that is going to be used on a daily basis, with some consequences for pricing of options.

In order to understand how these are quoted, let's look at the standard OTC maturities:

O/N, 1w, 2w, 1m, 2m, 3m, 6m, 9m, 1y, (18m?), 2y, ... First: There is an algorithm to find out the dates (fixing and settlement) corresponding to these maturities (one for days and weeks, another for months and years), and we refer the reader to [11] 1.5 for the algorithm; we would just correct the source by adding BRL to list of special Latam countries that treat the interim dates in the same way as the end date, as explained in 2.1.3; the holidays calendar for USDBRL is the combined calendar. Always confirm the dates with brokers or a knowledgeable source each morning before finding deals that seem too good to be true.

Ok, now the next part: What is being quoted?

First, all USD Calls are BRL Puts, all USD Puts are BRL Calls.

Second, the discounting here will be some USD rate as described above for the NDFs. Which rate? Well, before 2008 there was not much difference in the "depo" rate and Libor, and there was not much dispute among traders about which rate to use.

But during the crisis banks started discussing a lot which rates to use; and because of the BRL devaluation a lot of options were deep in the money, and customers tried to sell their ITM options trying to get cheap funding.

The market's answer was to change the settlement of the premia, so when trading an option you confirmed with the broker and the counterparty (another bank) the premium for the same settlement date as the payoff settlement date (no discounting necessary).

Third: Choice of strikes. Strikes are quoted in BRL per USD (same as outright NDFs and the Spot). The next step is defining what an ATM option is. For USD-BRL (and again we refer the reader to [11] for more details on other currencies) the ATM is an ATMF (At-the-money forward), with a strike equal to the forward (in this case, the NDF offshore).

Let's follow the rest of the calculations for the ATMF. Typically what is traded for ATM options is the straddle (+1 Call, +1 Put). The USD Call is a BRL Put, and the forward premium is first calculated using the Black formula and inverting parameters (to find a value expressed in USD/BRL):

$$fwdpr_{BRLPut} = BlackPremium\left(-1, \frac{1}{NDF}, \frac{1}{K}, \sigma, t\right) \tag{367}$$

Then the final forward premium (in percentage points) is equal to:

$$fwdpr_{USDCall} = fwdpr_{BRLPut} \cdot K \tag{368}$$

And the forward value in USD is equal to:

$$fwdpr\,[USD] = Not_{USD} \cdot fwdpr_{USDCall} \tag{369}$$

The delta (in percentage points) considering the forward (not the spot) is calculated in a similar way:

$$deltafwd_{BRLPut} = BlackDelta\left(-1, \frac{1}{NDF}, \frac{1}{K}, \sigma, t\right) \tag{370}$$

$$deltafwd_{USDCall} = -delta_{BRLPut} \cdot \frac{K}{NDF} \tag{371}$$

This delta is the one used in the market conventions and the one that dictates the notional of the NDF that would be traded together with the option in order to make it delta hedged.

As discussed before, this doesn't mean that when you trade the option and the delta hedge calculated in this manner that your book will show zero delta; the real delta of the option in your book will depend on how you model the joint dynamics of spot and implied volatility.

Now let's come back to the ATMF straddle. The delta forward of the USD Call is equal to (after some algebra using K=NDF and N(x) as the cumulative standardized normal distribution):

$$deltafwd_{USDCallATMF} = N\left(-\frac{\sigma\sqrt{t}}{2}\right) \tag{372}$$

And the delta forward for the USD Put is equal to:

$$deltafwd_{USDPutATMF} = -N\left(\frac{\sigma\sqrt{t}}{2}\right) \tag{373}$$

Now, the sum is not equal to zero. Even using the market convention for the deltas, trading the ATMF straddle will leave you with delta risk.

Is there any intuition for this result?

Yes, there is. Consider first that we can express the premium of an ATMF option as:

$$fwdpr_{USDCallATMF} = fwdpr_{USDPutATMF} = K\cdot\phi\cdot\left(N\left(\phi\cdot\frac{\sigma\sqrt{t}}{2}\right) - N\left(-\phi\cdot\frac{\sigma\sqrt{t}}{2}\right)\right) \tag{374}$$

And that for small values (like $\phi\frac{\sigma\sqrt{t}}{2}$) we can approximate:

$$N(x) \approx \frac{1}{2} + 0.4\cdot x \tag{375}$$

We now have:

$$\begin{aligned} fwdpr_{USDCallATMF} &= fwdpr_{USDPutATMF} \\ &= K\cdot\phi\cdot\left(\left(\frac{1}{2} + 0.4\cdot\phi\cdot\frac{\sigma\sqrt{t}}{2}\right) - \left(\frac{1}{2} - 0.4\cdot\phi\cdot\frac{\sigma\sqrt{t}}{2}\right)\right) \end{aligned} \tag{376}$$

$$fwdpr_{USDCallATMF} = fwdpr_{USDPutATMF} = K\cdot\phi\cdot\left(2\cdot 0.4\cdot\phi\cdot\frac{\sigma\sqrt{t}}{2}\right) \tag{377}$$

Because $\phi^2 = 1$ we can write:

$$\frac{fwdpr_{USDCallATMF}}{K} = \frac{fwdpr_{USDPutATMF}}{K} = 0.4\cdot\sigma\sqrt{t} \tag{378}$$

Looking at the deltas again:

$$deltafwd_{USDCallATMF} = N\left(-\frac{\sigma\sqrt{t}}{2}\right) = \frac{1}{2} - 0.4 \cdot \frac{\sigma\sqrt{t}}{2} = \frac{1}{2} - \frac{1}{2} \cdot \frac{fwdpr_{USDCallATMF}}{K} \tag{379}$$

$$deltafwd_{USDPutATMF} = -N\left(\frac{\sigma\sqrt{t}}{2}\right) = -\frac{1}{2} - 0.4 \cdot \frac{\sigma\sqrt{t}}{2} = -\frac{1}{2} - \frac{1}{2} \cdot \frac{fwdpr_{USDCallATMF}}{K} \tag{380}$$

And therefore the delta of the straddle is:

$$Not_{USD} \cdot deltafwd_{StraddleATMF} = \frac{1}{2} \cdot Not_{USD} \cdot deltafwd_{USDCallATMF} + \frac{1}{2} \cdot Not_{USD} \cdot deltafwd_{USDPutATMF} \tag{381}$$

$$deltafwd_{StraddleATMF} = \frac{1}{2} \cdot \left(-\frac{fwdpr_{USDCallATMF}}{K}\right) = -0.2 \cdot \sigma\sqrt{t} \tag{382}$$

Considering the notional of the straddle as the sum of the notional of each option.

This is what is meant by "premium adjustment" – the premium itself will have a risk when compared with the onshore options. Do not consider the delta onshore as a proxy of the delta offshore.

We could go on for pages and pages, but there is a whole chapter dedicated to FX options, the onshore/offshore mismatch, volatility surfaces, and other stuff.

9

Start from Where? Constructing Markets for FX Forwards, Futures, Onshore USD Interest Rates and Offshore Instruments

Here the goal is to create a framework for a consistent market scenario choosing among different market prices and conventions.

9.1 Observability of contracts

9.1.1 Spot x DOL

What is the best choice as the main input for FX Forward calculations?

The answer should be: Where is liquidity? Where can you execute?

For most the audience of this book (all of you smart people), chances are that the first future is the answer.

So you'll monitor the first future, the casado and the roll (you will need to roll the position, and try to do it before the last business day of the month). If you wait until the last day, you are trading the PTAX, not the roll.

If you are approaching a fixing, look at the casado more carefully.

If you really want to run the fixing / PTAX risk, wait for a further section on modeling the risk of the fixing.

9.1.2 FRC x Forward x DOL

In a perfect world, there would be a market for forwards and another for the DOL, due to the convexity described in other chapters.

That the world is not perfect only makes it more interesting. BVMF does not marks the longer-dated DOLs where they should trade, and therefore trading longer-dated DOLs against either a forward or the package 1st DOL + DIs + FRC at something other than a zero spread is likely to give you an undesired 1st day P&L due to Product Control teams marking everything at the prices published by BVMF. Brazil is not an easy country.

Do not trust closing prices blindly - ask which criteria was used to produce them.

Also, the FRC+DDI markets are not really liquid; chances are that the NDF market is the most liquid and more informative of all.

9.1.3 NDFs and forward points

NDFs have adapted to Brazil's conventions. Now there is an active market in NDFs for the date of first future, and a roll market as well. Also now other NDFs are quoted against the first future. Either way, you can look at the outright NDFs and interpolate them (geometrically as shown before), or you can look at the forward points (outright minus spot or outright minus NDF for first future date) and interpolate them (arithmetically perhaps?). Again, both models could be valid, as long as one is aware of the potential issues and failures of each (and remember, remember, the 31st of December!).

9.2 Structures

9.2.1 Dates

Always, always design structures where contracts have separate dates for fixing and settlement, even if you write a default rule for linking both. Remember the date rules for tenors in NDFs and FX options (go forward to spot settlement, jump forward the relevant interval, come back from settlement to fixing, then count how many business days you have).

Two other date-related rules must be ready:

1. How to deal with BVMF holidays (and other holidays as well, as offshore trading is even more important these days). If your choice of architecture has market data streaming directly to your scenario builder, think again: maybe an option for a parametrized input? We will talk about "The Triangle" below.
2. How to roll scenarios for the following day (it helps if you have decided what to do on holidays first). Here the main decision is what is kept constant from one day to another: Spot or First Future? We know what is not constant: the Casado (remember the sawtooth pattern). Most participants will keep the Spot constant, with DOL (and the forward curve) drifting down. This will have implications (a lot of implications when it comes to options).

9.2.2 Events (Breaks, Fixings, Market points)

Your calendar structure must have flexibility to seamlessly go from unknown market variable (Spot) to fixing (PTAX) intraday; you must have a good solution for cases like 31-Dec, the presence of holidays within the interval from Fixing Date to Settlement Date should be clear. You should be able to choose which points are there only as calculated values and which points should be considered as market inputs, because not all contracts have the same informational level (some drive, some follow).

Also, the averaging characteristic of the PTAX forces you to look at your fixing risk in a different way:

When you start the day at 9h the spot is the best estimate of the PTAX; but as the first of the four fixings is determined, the spot is not the best estimate of the PTAX anymore; that estimate should now be a weighted average of past fixings (1/4 now) and the spot (3/4) now. As time goes by, the weights change:

- Before 10h: {4/4 for spot}
- After 10h: {1/4 for the 10h fixing, 3/4 for spot}
- After 11h: {1/4 for the 10h fixing, 1/4 for the 11h fixing, 2/4 for spot}
- After 12h: {1/4 for the 10h fixing, 1/4 for the 11h fixing, 1/4 for the 12h fixing, 1/4 for spot}
- After 13h: {1/4 for the 10h fixing, 1/4 for the 11h fixing, 1/4 for the 12h fixing, 1/4 for the 13h fixing} - congratulations: all your fixings are done (by now the final average will have been published as well)

Pay attention to Ash Wednesday (a shorter trading day that starts later in the day).

9.2.3 "The Triangle"

Spot, Casado, DOL. Pick 2, the 3rd is determined. But the frequency in which data is updated for each of them is different, their volatility is different, and the value of the information that each update brings is different. So one has to establish a priority by which one updates the others. A suggestion for normal trading days:

1. Updates on DOL: Keep Casado constant, calculate Spot (most "robots" work this way to calculate Spot)
2. Updates on Casado: Keep DOL constant, calculate Spot (Casado does not change that much intraday, but it does change)
3. Updates on Spot: Keep DOL constant, change Casado (these typically will be manual updates, as using Spot coming from 1. just produces a feedback loop)

For days with no trading in DOL, please see below (NDFs).

A similar rule applies to the onshore/offshore spread:

1. Updates on DOL: Keep OnOff Spread constant, calculate NDF
2. Updates on OnOff Spread: Keep DOL constant, calculate NDF (OnOff Spread does not change that much intraday, but it does change)
3. Updates on NDF: Keep DOL constant, change OnOff Spread (these typically will be manual updates)

For days in which there's no trading on the DOL but NY is open for business, the rule changes to:

1. Updates on NDF: Keep OnOff Spread constant, calculate DOL
2. Updates on OnOff Spread: Keep NDF constant, calculate DOL
3. Updates on DOL: Keep NDF constant, change OnOff Spread (these typically will be manual updates)

One needs some flexibility to change these rules without having to ask IT for a change in the code.

9.3 Curve construction

9.3.1 Cupom Cambial

You went through door 1 and chose to interpolate the onshore USD curve. Now, please choose the curve that you want to interpolate:

1. The linear, "dirty" curve of the DDIs
2. The linear, "clean" curve of the FRCs composed in some way with the DOL and the casado (FRC+)
3. An exponential, actual days equivalent of the FRC+

Whatever your choice (not restricted to the above), good luck - you will need it.

9.3.2 Forwards

As explained before, it's not that there are elements enough that would lead us to reject other interpolation methods in favor of interpolating the forwards. But in practice one might want to control directly the forwards and imply the onshore USD curve.

It is important to note that because the BRL curve works in business days and typically the onshore USD curve works in actual days, either the forward curve is bumpy or the onshore USD curve is bumpy, depending on which curve is the interpolated curve and which curve is the implied curve.

9.4 The offshore x onshore spread

9.4.1 Changing standards

As mentioned before, the traded term structure of the NDF market has adapted to the onshore market (when it comes to the dates structure). This also helps in solving a similar mismatch problem: should we interpolate the outright NDFs and imply the spread? Should the interpolation follow the same dates and formula as in the onshore NDFs? Or should we interpolate the spread? Again, hard to just say which choice is the best in all situations. One could backtest the hedged portfolio, but the answers might not be clearly different, and some choices might be driven by qualitative opinions.

9.4.2 Convertibility, demand and taxes

The spread was really high in previous years (with 1998 and 2002 showing nasty spikes); during the past decade the growth of USD reserves and the demand for NDFs pushed the spread down into negative territory. So if before we used to speak about the "NDF premium", now we speak about the "NDF spread". A rate that was supposed to be positive is now negative. It's not as big of a modeling problem as negative nominal interest rates are, but still ... Also worth noticing is that this rate is highly sensitive to taxes, and new legislation might lead to jumps and discontinuities in the time series, and backtesting might need a good context to justify the differences in P&L compared with risk. The necessity to distinguish between structural breaks and volatility is a common theme in Brazil.

9.5 The mythical offshore BRL discounting curve

Which curves to represent YC risk? BRL offshore curve and LIBOR/FF or DI, cupom cambial and NDF OnOff spread? That was the choice we faced years ago, when the world was young. As discussed before, there are benefits in mapping the risks as spreads, and if one is a market maker with huge positions on each side of the convertibility frontier, it draws attention to the buildup of convertibility/basis instead of focusing into a non-observable rate. But we will focus carefully on the products traded offshore based on the BRL interest rates and CDI fixings.

10
Offshore IR Products Based on CDI Fixings

The offshore market for FX products has been explained in previous sections of this book. But what about IR related products offshore? Are there Fixed-Float swaps and swaptions offshore being traded? Is there any basis to quote onshore swaps and swaptions to their offshore equivalent contracts? After reading the previous sections of this book we believe that the reader might be inclined to say yes, and that's indeed the correct answer.

10.1 Offshore BRL Fixed-Float swaps

Similarly to what happened in the FX offshore market, there's currently a great number of market participants that want to be long BRL interest rates. One possibility for them would be to open a 2689 account locally in Brazil and trade DI Futures against the exchange. However, as discussed previously in the NDF offshore subsection, to open the 2689 account is not straightforward. And margin posting in the exchange is an additional problem. This fact created a great demand for offshore BRL Fixed X Float swaps.

First we will discuss the payoff of BRL Fixed X Float swaps. We will explain that the main difference is that trade is settled offshore in USD, and doesn't incur any possible outflow restriction that may happen to an equivalent onshore swap payoff that is settled in BRL. But for both the onshore and offshore swap payoffs, the floating index is the same, which is CDI.

The next subsection will debate what's the direction side of the flow for market participants willing to trade BRL interest rates and how it reflects in the swap rate basis of onshore to offshore swaps.

The last subsection will derive the mathematical pricing of an offshore BRL Fixed X Float swap. We will highlight that for an appropriate pricing, future convexity expectations have to be modeled based on covariances between BRL X cupom rates, BRL X US libor 3M and BRL X $NDFOnOff_{t,T}$. Transaction costs based on cupom and $NDFOnOff_{t,T}$ dynamic PV01 rebalancing could be added as well. The last possible component to be included in pricing is how much extra margin posting for the DI1 hedge could distort the offshore swap rate.

10.1.1 Offshore BRL Fixed-Float swaps payoff

The payoff for BRL Fixed-Float swaps is given by:

$$Payoff_{USD}[T_{Pay}] = Not_{BRL} \cdot \frac{(CapFac_{Fixed}(t,T) - CapFac_{Float}(t,T))}{EMTA_{T_{FIX}}} \tag{383}$$

where,

T_{Pay}: is the payoff payment date which is one business day later than maturity date T in a combined CDI and New York calendar.

T_{FIX}: is the FX Fixing date to convert the BRL cashflow to USD, which occurs 2 business days backwards from T_{Pay} in a combined CDI and New York calendar.

The other variables have been defined in previous sections of this book.

One interesting case was 01-Sep-2014 maturity date offshore BRL Fixed-Float swap. The payment date T_{Pay} was at 2-Sep-2014. But 1-Sep-2014 was a holiday in New York. Therefore, the FX Fixing date was at 28-Aug-2014. But the last interest accrual date was on 29-Aug-2014. In that particular case, the FX Fixing was published without the final BRL payment being fixed as one CDI fixing was still required.

As can be noticed by looking at (383), the payoff is very similar to the onshore swap payoff. The only 2 differences are that in the offshore swap the payoff occurs one business day after maturity date T in a combined CDI and New York holidays calendar, whereas in the onshore case, the payment occurs typically at maturity date. The second difference is that the offshore payoff is converted to *USD* by *EMTA* published at FX Fixing date T_{FIX} and paid outside Brazil. Thus a foreign investor does not have any outflow restriction concern regarding the offshore contract, but he should have for the onshore swap.

10.1.2 Foreign market participants appetite for offshore BRL Fixed-Float swaps

Like said previously, many market participants outside Brazil like to receive the high BRL fixed swap rates offshore to avoid having to setup the infrastructure to open a 2689 account locally in Brazil to trade the very same swap (to be more accurate it would be a DI1) onshore. This one-sided flow direction allows banks with an onshore infrastructure to only enter the offshore swap paying a lower swap rate than what's required for the onshore equivalent swap rate. At 05-May-2015, the offshore swap rate has a spread to onshore swap rate of -1.5 bps for maturity 04-Jan-2016, -5.5 bps for 02-Jan-2017 and -28 bps for 04-Jan-2021 and because of this one sided flow it's expected the basis of offshore to onshore swap rate to be negative in most common market situations.

10.1.3 Which discounting curve to use for offshore BRL Fixed-Float swaps pricing?

In the same way as for NDF's offshore, the offshore swaps are usually collateralized. Therefore, the procedure adopted in Section (8.2.2) has to be adopted here again where you convert your expected BRL cashflow into the collateral index currency, and later discount this quantity by the collateral index agreed upon the CSA of the swap with the counterparty. But maybe the most difficult question is how to compute the expectation of the BRL cashflow of the floating leg under an offshore probability measure associated with the collateral index discount factor as its numéraire.

10.1.4 Is this a quanto swap? Let's analyze it from a hedging perspective

A quanto swap is defined as a swap which has typically a floating leg based on an index associated with $CCY1$, but payment is done in $CCY2$, with $CCY1$ and $CCY2$ being different currencies. One example would be a Fixed Float USD-Libor-3M swap which makes payments of the USD based cashflows directly in EUR instead of USD. To hedge this quanto swap, one is subject to the covariance of the USD-Libor-3M discount factor with the $\frac{USD}{EUR}$ FX forward value. This particular feature can be seen alternatively (it's perhaps easier) when one think in terms of the required hedge for the quanto swap, which involves a vanilla USD Fixed Float swap paying in USD and a $\frac{USD}{EUR}$ FX Forward trade. But the FX Forward trade needs to have its Notional rebalanced dynamically, driven by the vanilla swap payoff equivalent value. When the vanilla swap expected payoff increases, it requires also a larger FX Forward Notional to be hedged, and depending of the sign of the covariance of the FX Forward value with the vanilla swap underlying it could incur in a cost or gain.

In our particular BRL Fixed Float swap offshore, the BRL cashflows are based on a BRL onshore index, namely CDI, but converted by a offshore FX rate and paid in *USD*. Another way to see it would be to not convert the BRL cashflows to *USD*, but to view it paying directly in *BRL* offshore units (BRU). By looking at things based on this perspective, and based on the familiar quanto swap example above, to hedge this offshore swap one would be subject to the covariance of the CDI discount factor with the $\frac{BRL}{BRU}$ FX forward value. One could argue that the $\frac{BRL}{BRU}$ FX rate has no vol and we will consider this to be true, as the conversion FX rate is always 1. However, what matters is the covariance of the CDI discount factor with the $\frac{BRL}{BRU}$ FX forward value, not with the FX spot value. Considering the $\frac{BRL}{BRU}$ FX forward to be based on:

$$FXFWD_{t,T}\left[\frac{BRU}{BRL}\right] = \frac{BRU}{BRL}[t] \cdot \frac{P^{CDI}_{t,t_{fx},T}}{P^{BRU}_{t,t_{fx},T}} \tag{384}$$

Considering $\frac{BRU}{BRL}[t]$ to be a constant with value 1 yields:

$$FXFWD_{t,T}\left[\frac{BRU}{BRL}\right] = \frac{P^{CDI}_{t,t_{fx},T}}{P^{BRU}_{t,t_{fx},T}} \tag{385}$$

We could express $NDFOnOff_{t,T}$ as a multiplicative spread rate instead of an additive spread and change (365) to:

$$P^{BRU}_{t,t_{fx},T} = \frac{\frac{BRL}{USD}[t] \cdot P^{Coll}_{t,t_{fx},T}}{\frac{BRL}{USD}[t] \cdot \frac{P^{USB}_{t,t_{fx},T}}{P^{CDI}_{t,t_{fx},T}} \cdot (1 + NDFOnOff_{t,T})} \tag{386}$$

Assuming the trade to be collateralized in USD-Libor-3M yields:

$$P^{BRU}_{t,t_{fx},T} = \frac{P^{CDI}_{t,t_{fx},T}}{(1 + NDFOnOff_{t,T})} \cdot \frac{P^{USD}_{t,t_{fx},T}}{P^{USB}_{t,t_{fx},T}} \tag{387}$$

Thus the ratio of $\frac{P^{CDI}_{t,t_{fx},T}}{P^{BRU}_{t,t_{fx},T}}$ is given by:

$$\frac{P^{CDI}_{t,t_{fx},T}}{P^{BRU}_{t,t_{fx},T}} = (1 + NDFOnOff_{t,T}) \cdot \frac{P^{USB}_{t,t_{fx},T}}{P^{USD}_{t,t_{fx},T}} \tag{388}$$

Therefore, the hedge for the offshore BRL Fixed-Float swap is a function of the covariance of the CDI discount factor with the NDF spread and the cupom over libor discount factor spread $\frac{P^{USB}_{t,t_{fx},T}}{P^{USD}_{t,t_{fx},T}}$.

10.1.5 Now let's analyze it from a mathematical perspective

We can start based on the payoff of the receiver swap given by:

$$Payoff_{USD}[T_{Pay}] = Not_{BRL} \cdot \frac{(CapFac_{Fixed}(t,T) - CapFac_{Float}(t,T))}{EMTA_{T_{FIX}}} \tag{389}$$

Assuming that the collateral index currency to be in *USD*, without loss of generality it yields that the fixed leg term can be priced based on the collateral pricing equation in (8.2.2):

$$PV^{USD}_t[Fixed] = \frac{Not_{BRL} \cdot CapFac_{Fixed}(t,T)}{FXFWD^{OFF}_{t,T_{Pay}}\left[\frac{BRL}{USD}\right]} \cdot P^{Coll}_{t,T_{Pay}} \tag{390}$$

where,

$PV^{USD}_t[Fixed]$: is the PV seen at date t in *USD* of the Fixed leg of the swap.

$FXFWD^{OFF}_{t,T}\left[\frac{BRL}{USD}\right]$: is the NDF value to convert BRL offshore (BRU) into *USD*.

The floating leg pricing is where the convexity arises though. We can start by taking the following expectation:

$$PV^{USD}_t[Float] = Not_{BRL} \cdot P^{Coll}_{t,T_{Pay}} \cdot \mathbb{E}^{\mathbb{Q}^{T_{Pay}}_{Coll}}\left[\frac{CapFac_{Float}(t,T)}{EMTA_{T_{FIX}}}|\mathcal{F}_t\right] \tag{391}$$

We can assume that the NDF offshore value $FXFWD^{OFF}_{T_{Fix},T_{Pay}}[\frac{BRL}{USD}]$ for settlement date T_{Pay} seen at date T_{Fix} is equal to the EMTA FX Fixing value $EMTA_{T_{FIX}}$ and replace it inside (391). This yields:

$$PV^{USD}_t[Float] = Not_{BRL} \cdot P^{Coll}_{t,T_{Pay}} \cdot \mathbb{E}^{\mathbb{Q}^{T_{Pay}}_{Coll}}\left[\frac{CapFac_{Float}(t,T)}{FXFWD^{OFF}_{T_{Fix},T_{Pay}}\left[\frac{BRL}{USD}\right]}|\mathcal{F}_t\right] \tag{392}$$

We can use the Radon-Nikodym derivative to change to the BRL offshore T_{Pay} forward measure, associated to discount factor $P^{BRU}_{t,T_{Pay}}$ as its numéraire by:

$$\frac{d\mathbb{Q}^{T_{Pay}}_{Coll}}{d\mathbb{Q}^{T_{Pay}}_{BRU}}|\mathcal{F}_{T_{Fix}} = \frac{FXFWD^{OFF}_{T_{Fix},T_{Pay}}\left[\frac{BRL}{USD}\right]}{FXFWD^{OFF}_{t,T_{Pay}}[\frac{BRL}{USD}]} \tag{393}$$

Plugging (393) into (392) yields:

$$PV^{USD}_t[Float] = Not_{BRL} \cdot P^{Coll}_{t,T_{Pay}} \cdot \mathbb{E}^{\mathbb{Q}^{T_{Pay}}_{BRU}}\left[\frac{CapFac_{Float}(t,T)}{FXFWD^{OFF}_{T_{Fix},T_{Pay}}[\frac{BRL}{USD}]} \cdot \frac{d\mathbb{Q}^{T_{Pay}}_{Coll}}{d\mathbb{Q}^{T_{Pay}}_{BRU}}|\mathcal{F}_{T_{Fix}}|\mathcal{F}_t\right] \tag{394}$$

$$PV^{USD}_t[Float] = Not_{BRL} \cdot P^{Coll}_{t,T_{Pay}} \cdot \mathbb{E}^{\mathbb{Q}^{T_{Pay}}_{BRU}}\left[\frac{CapFac_{Float}(t,T)}{FXFWD^{OFF}_{T_{Fix},T_{Pay}}[\frac{BRL}{USD}]} \cdot \frac{FXFWD^{OFF}_{T_{Fix},T_{Pay}}[\frac{BRL}{USD}]}{FXFWD^{OFF}_{t,T_{Pay}}[\frac{BRL}{USD}]}|\mathcal{F}_t\right] \tag{395}$$

$$PV^{USD}_t[Float] = \frac{Not_{BRL}}{FXFWD^{OFF}_{t,T_{Pay}}[\frac{BRL}{USD}]} \cdot P^{Coll}_{t,T_{Pay}} \cdot \mathbb{E}^{\mathbb{Q}^{T_{Pay}}_{BRU}}\left[CapFac_{Float}(t,T)|\mathcal{F}_t\right] \tag{396}$$

By looking at (396) we see an intuitive result. The PV in USD of the floating leg of the swap is given by taking the expectation of the CDI capitalization factor $CapFac_{Float}(t,T)$, dividing it by the NDF offshore value for settlement date T_{Pay}, namely $FXFWD^{OFF}_{t,T_{Pay}}[\frac{BRL}{USD}]$, and discount this USD based quantity given the USD collateral index discount factor $P^{Coll}_{t,T_{Pay}}$ from pricing date t to payment date T_{Pay}. But be careful of which probability measure leads to the expectation.

The next step on the derivation is to recall that under the HJM model,. the CDI capitalization factor SDE is given by:

$$CapFac_{Float}(t,T) = \frac{1}{P^{CDI}_{t,T_{Pay}}} \cdot exp\left\{ -\frac{1}{2} \cdot \int_t^{T_{Pay}} \left(\int_s^{T_{Pay}} \sigma_{s,u} \cdot du \right)^2 \cdot ds + \int_t^{T_{Pay}} \left(\int_s^{T_{Pay}} \sigma_{s,u} \cdot du \right) \cdot dW_{1_t}^{T^{CDI}_{Pay}} \right\} \quad (397)$$

We need, however, to explicit the $CapFac_{Float}(t,T)$ dynamics under the probability measure associated with $P^{BRU}_{t,T_{Pay}}$ as numéraire.

The Radon-Nikodym derivative to change from the measure where $P^{CDI}_{t,T_{Pay}}$ is its numéraire to $P^{BRU}_{t,T_{Pay}}$ is given by:

$$\frac{d\mathbb{Q}^{T_{Pay}}_{CDI}}{d\mathbb{Q}^{T_{Pay}}_{BRU}} |\mathcal{F}_{T_{Fix}} = \frac{FXFWD_{T_{Fix},T_{Pay}}\left[\frac{BRU}{BRL}\right]}{FXFWD_{t,T_{Pay}}\left[\frac{BRU}{BRL}\right]} = exp\left\{ -\frac{1}{2} \int_t^{T_{Fix}} \sigma^2_{FWD\left[\frac{BRU}{BRL}\right]} \cdot ds + \int_t^{T_{Fix}} \sigma_{FWD\left[\frac{BRU}{BRL}\right]} \cdot dZ_t^{T^{BRU}_{Pay}} \right\} \quad (398)$$

where,

$\sigma_{FWD\left[\frac{BRU}{BRL}\right]}$: is the FX Forward volatility for currency pair $\frac{BRU}{BRL}$.

$dZ_t^{T^{BRU}_{Pay}}$: is the Brownian Motion that shocks the FX Forward for currency pair $\frac{BRU}{BRL}$.

Let's assume that the 2 Brownian Motions $dW_{1_t}^{T^{BRU}_{Pay}}$ (that shocks $CapFac_{Float}(t,T)$) and $dZ_t^{T^{BRU}_{Pay}}$ (that shocks $FXFWD_{t,T_{Pay}}[\frac{BRU}{BRL}]$) are correlated by:

$$dW_{1_t}^{T^{BRU}_{Pay}} \cdot dZ_t^{T^{BRU}_{Pay}} = \rho_1 \cdot dt \quad (399)$$

We can rewrite

$$dZ_t^{T^{BRU}_{Pay}} = \rho_1 \cdot dW_{1_t}^{T^{BRU}_{Pay}} + \sqrt{1-\rho_1^2} \cdot dW_{2_t}^{T^{BRU}_{Pay}}$$

where $W_{1_t}^{T^{BRU}_{Pay}}$ and $W_{2_t}^{T^{BRU}_{Pay}}$ are independent Brownian Motions. So we can rewrite (398) as:

$$\frac{d\mathbb{Q}^{T_{Pay}}_{CDI}}{d\mathbb{Q}^{T_{Pay}}_{BRU}} |\mathcal{F}_{T_{Fix}} = exp\left\{ -\frac{1}{2} \int_t^{T_{Fix}} \sigma^2_{FWD\left[\frac{BRU}{BRL}\right]} \cdot ds + \int_t^{T_{Fix}} \sigma_{FWD\left[\frac{BRU}{BRL}\right]} \cdot \left(\rho_1 \cdot dW_{1_t}^{T^{BRU}_{Pay}} + \sqrt{1-\rho_1^2} \cdot dW_{2_t}^{T^{BRU}_{Pay}} \right) \right\} \quad (400)$$

Applying Girsanov Theorem

$$dW_{1_t}^{T_{Pay}^{CDI}} = -\sigma_{FWD\left[\frac{BRU}{BRL}\right]} \cdot \rho_1 \cdot dt + dW_{1_t}^{T_{Pay}^{BRU}} \tag{401}$$

Plugging (401) into (397) yields:

$$CapFac_{Float}(t,T) = \frac{1}{P_{t,T_{Pay}}^{CDI}} \cdot exp\left\{-\frac{1}{2} \cdot \int_t^{T_{Pay}} \left(\int_s^{T_{Pay}} \sigma_{s,u} \cdot du\right)^2 \cdot ds\right\} \cdot \tag{402}$$

$$\cdot exp\left\{\int_t^{T_{Pay}} \left(\int_s^{T_{Pay}} \sigma_{s,u} \cdot du\right) \cdot \left(-\sigma_{FWD\left[\frac{BRU}{BRL}\right]} \cdot \rho_1 \cdot dt + dW_{1_t}^{T_{Pay}^{BRU}}\right)\right\} \tag{403}$$

And the expectation of $CapFac_{Float}(t,T)$ under the probability measure where $P_{t,T_{Pay}}^{BRU}$ is its numéraire is given by:

$$\mathbb{E}^{\mathbb{Q}_{BRU}^{T_{Pay}}} \left[CapFac_{Float}(t,T)|\mathcal{F}_t\right]$$
$$= \frac{1}{P_{t,T_{Pay}}^{CDI}} \cdot exp\left\{-\int_t^{T_{Pay}} \left[\left(\int_s^{T_{Pay}} \sigma_{s,u} \cdot du\right) \cdot \sigma_{FWD\left[\frac{BRU}{BRL}\right]} \cdot \rho_1\right] dt\right\} \tag{404}$$

So now we have a drift term given by $exp\{-\int_t^{T_{Pay}} [(\int_s^{T_{Pay}} \sigma_{s,u} \cdot du) \cdot \sigma_{FWD[\frac{BRU}{BRL}]} \cdot \rho_1]dt\}$. One could try to calculate this convexity term based on historical data, by calculating historically the volatility of a synthetic $\frac{BRU}{BRL}$ FX forward, and its correlation with BRL onshore rates. The HJM volatility term $\left(\int_s^{T_{Pay}} \sigma_{s,u} \cdot du\right)$ for BRL rates could be calibrated to IDI options or also computed based on historical data as described in Section (7.1.13). But we could still try to investigate a bit further by breaking down the $\frac{BRU}{BRL}$ FX forward into its underlying components based on a multiplicative NDF spread rate like below:

$$FXFWD_{t,T_{Pay}}\left[\frac{BRU}{BRL}\right] = (1 + NDFOnOff_{t,T}) \cdot \frac{P_{t,t_{fx},T}^{USB}}{P_{t,t_{fx},T}^{USD}} \tag{405}$$

The equation above states that the $FXFWD_{t,T_{Pay}}[\frac{BRU}{BRL}]$ value will go up if $NDFOnOff_{t,T}$ multiplicative spread rate goes up, or if USD rates go up or if cupom rates go down. On the other hand we also know by looking at (405) that the drift term is short correlation of BRL rates (from the variable $CapFac_{Float}(t,T)$) and $FXFWD_{t,T_{Pay}}[\frac{BRU}{BRL}]$. So essentially one could say that the drift term derived in (404) could be viewed as:

- Short covariance of USD and BRL rates
- Short covariance of $NDFOnOff_{t,T}$ multiplicative spread rate and BRL rates
- Long covariance of cupom and BRL rates

The statement above says that a payer BRL Fixed-Float offshore swap position (that is long the floating leg and therefore the term $CapFac_{Float}(t,T)$) would generate a convexity where you are:

- Short covariance of USD and BRL rates
- Short covariance of $NDFOnOff_{t,T}$ multiplicative spread rate and BRL rates
- Long covariance of cupom and BRL rates

And obviously the receiver swap position would generate:

- Long covariance of USD and BRL rates
- Long covariance of $NDFOnOff_{t,T}$ multiplicative spread rate and BRL rates
- Short covariance of cupom and BRL rates

10.1.6 BRL Fixed-Float offshore breakeven historical swap rate

One could argue that his view of covariances indicate a non negative basis between the offshore to onshore equivalent BRL swap rates. Is he wrong? Or is the market wrong? What other ingredients may be missing in this calculation?

As seen previously, the cupom curve is not very liquid and concentrate its liquidity around the afternoon call that happens once a day. The same could be said about trying to hedge the $NDFOnOff_t$ spread. As we have seen in the previous subsections, an offshore swap needs to be dynamic rebalanced, and what we are focusing now is that the illiquid cupom and $NDFOnOff_t$ spread need to be dynamic rebalanced. Therefore, even if we assume that all correlations that matter for pricing are zero, still the correct price needs to be corrected by the expected transaction costs to hedge dynamically through time those 2 market factors. To calculate the expected transaction costs, one possibility would be to run a Monte Carlo simulation. For each simulation path, and at each time step, the PV01 of cupom and the NDF Spread are dynamically hedged, with the assumption of a bid-mid charge in bps.

Another more intangible and hard to quantify ingredient is the fact that usually banks with local presence inside Brazil will hedge the BRL and cupom rates risk with FRC and DI1 instruments, that are exchange traded and require margin posting. Margin posting is usually done by buying Brazil government bonds, which involves cash disbursement. But if the market moves in such a way that margin posting exceeds the cash that the particular bank has available as capital inside Brazil, it may need to fund extra cash or, in the case of foreign banks with local presence, the bank would need to ask treasury to send more cash. But the treasury will typically have USD outside Brazil, and a fx spot transaction would need to be done in order to internalize the BRL. Currently, there's no tax applied for this type of fx spot transaction, but in the recent past, a tax rate of 6% was applied.

Is there a way to try to identify what is the breakeven swap rate that should be charged? One approach would be to try to build a breakeven historical swap rate tool, in the same spirit of the breakeven historical vol tool (BEVL) in Bloomberg. The BEVL assumes that everyday in the past, hedging was done based on Black-Scholes model and a historical breakeven smile could be constructed for underlyings that don't have a developed vol market. In our offshore swap case, we could try to follow the same idea. We would construct a portfolio with the offshore swap, the DI, DOL,FRC and NDF spread hedges and dynamic rebalance it every day. We could also apply the fact that after a particular cupom PV01 threshold is breached, there would be transaction costs applied based on the multiplication of a bid-mid charge times the PV01. Something similar could be done for the NDF spread market factor which is illiquid also. After carrying the offshore swap plus hedges portfolio until the maturity of the swap, it will have a P&L value from the dynamic rebalancing strategy that occurred every day. And finally a swap rate could be implied from this P&L value to make the final P&L from hedging plus underlying swap offshore equal to 0.

Obviously if one believes based on the breakeven historical swap rate method that the swap rate traded in the market could be somehow different, and even if the future behaves like the past and his view is correct, one would be subject to eventual large P&L fluctuations based on the foreign market participants flow that is currently the predominant driver of the basis between offshore to onshore equivalent swap rates.

10.1.7 Calibrating an offshore BRL Fixed-Float swap basis curve

The procedure for calibrating this basis curve is straightforward. In the OTC offshore swap market it's observed the liquid swap rates for DI1 equivalent maturity dates. Let's say we have N dates and call those the associated offshore swap rates $R_{t,T_i}^{CDI(OFF)}$ for $i = 1$ to N. The curve is then calibrated with N instruments where its quote are $R_{t,T_i}^{CDI(OFF)} - R_{t,T_i}^{CDI}$, which is the difference of the offshore swap rate to the onshore DI1 rate used to calibrate the CDI onshore curve.

Regarding risk management, it's preferred to construct the basis curve this way as a long position of an offshore swap combined with a short position on a DI1 hedge would yield only a basis risk at trade inception.

10.2 Offshore BRL Fixed-Float swaptions

The DI Option section discussed how it could be viewed as a swaption after some algebra. And it was mentioned that currently the most widely used model for pricing DI Options is the SABR model. In the previous subsection, on the other hand, we discussed how offshore swaps are priced and which convexity terms arise because of the fact that the swap is paid offshore and typically collateralized. So how we combine those 2 things together to derive offshore swaption prices?

10.2.1 BRL Fixed-Float offshore swaption payoff and specification

Differently to the swaptions commonly traded in G10 currencies, the BRL Fixed Float swaption is zero coupon. The swaption is deliverable and by exercising the option you enter into a zero coupon swap offshore. The authors haven't seen cash settled payoff versions of BRL swaptions and the exercise is European, which means that it can be exercised only at one exercise date.

To exercise the swaption, one will compare the offshore forward swap rate $R^{CDI(OFF)}_{T_1,T_2}$ seen at exercise date T_1 for swap maturity date T_2 with the strike rate K. Those rates are exponential and what matters is the capitalization factor computed using them from T_1 to T_2. Therefore, the T_2 payer swaption equivalent payoff would be:

$$Payoff_{USD}[T_{Pay}] = Not_{BRL} \cdot max\left(\frac{\left(1+R^{CDI(OFF)}_{T_1,T_2}\right)^{\tau^{252}_{T_1,T_2}} - (1+K)^{\tau^{252}_{T_1,T_2}}}{EMTA_{T_{Fix}}}, 0\right) \tag{406}$$

where,

$Payoff_{USD}[T_{Pay}]$: is the offshore swaption payoff, paid in USD at date T_{Pay}.

T_{Pay}: payoff payment date of the swaption underlying swap, which is typically one business day forward than underlying swap maturity date T_2 in a combined CDI and NY holidays calendar.

T_{FIX}: is the FX Fixing date of the underlying swap, obtained moving backwards 2 business days from T_{Pay} in a combined CDI and NY holidays calendar.

But for pricing purposes we want to change (406) to represent linear forward rates instead of exponential rates. This yields:

$$Payoff_{USD}[T_{Pay}] = Not_{BRL} \cdot \tau^{252}_{T_1,T_2} \cdot max\left(\frac{R^{L(OFF)}_{T_1,T_2} - K_L}{EMTA_{T_{Fix}}}, 0\right) \tag{407}$$

where,

$$R^{L(OFF)}_{T_1,T_2} = \frac{\left(1+R^{CDI(OFF)}_{T_1,T_2}\right)^{\tau^{252}_{T_1,T_2}} - 1}{\tau^{252}_{T_1,T_2}}$$

and

$$K_L = \frac{(1+K)^{\tau^{252}_{T_1,T_2}} - 1}{\tau^{252}_{T_1,T_2}}$$

Now we can proceed with pricing:

$$c_{t+2}^{USD} = Not_{BRL} \cdot \tau_{T_1,T_2}^{252} \cdot P_{t,t+2,T_{Pay}}^{Coll} \cdot \mathbb{E}^{T_{Pay}^{Coll}} \left[max\left(\frac{R_{T_1,T_2}^{L(OFF)} - K_L}{EMTA_{T_{Fix}}}, 0 \right) | \mathcal{F}_t \right] \tag{408}$$

where,

c_{t+2}^{USD}: is the payer swaption premium to be paid in *USD* at $t+2$ in a combined CDI and NY holidays calendar. Discounting of payoff occurs only until $t+2$ which is the option premium payment date.

Again we could use the Radon-Nikodym derivative to change to the BRL offshore T_{Pay} forward measure, associated to discount factor $P_{t,T_{Pay}}^{BRU}$ as its numéraire by:

$$\frac{d\mathbb{Q}_{Coll}^{T_{Pay}}}{d\mathbb{Q}_{BRU}^{T_{Pay}}} | \mathcal{F}_{T_{Fix}} = \frac{FXFWD_{T_{Fix},T_{Pay}}^{OFF}\left[\frac{BRL}{USD}\right]}{FXFWD_{t,T_{Pay}}^{OFF}\left[\frac{BRL}{USD}\right]} \tag{409}$$

Plugging (409) into (392) yields:

$$c_{t+2}^{USD} = Not_{BRL} \cdot \tau_{T_1,T_2}^{252} \cdot P_{t,t+2,T_{Pay}}^{Coll} \cdot \mathbb{E}^{\mathbb{Q}_{BRU}^{T_{Pay}}} \left[max\left(\frac{R_{T_1,T_2}^{L(OFF)} - K_L}{EMTA_{T_{Fix}}}, 0 \right) \right.$$

$$\left. \cdot \frac{d\mathbb{Q}_{Coll}^{T_{Pay}}}{d\mathbb{Q}_{BRU}^{T_{Pay}}} | \mathcal{F}_{T_{Fix}} | \mathcal{F}_t \right] \tag{410}$$

$$c_{t+2}^{USD} = \frac{Not_{BRL}}{FXFWD_{t,T_{Pay}}^{OFF}\left[\frac{BRL}{USD}\right]} \cdot \tau_{T_1,T_2}^{252} \cdot P_{t,t+2,T_{Pay}}^{Coll} \cdot \mathbb{E}^{\mathbb{Q}_{BRU}^{T_{Pay}}} \left[max\left(R_{T_1,T_2}^{L(OFF)} - K_L, 0\right) | \mathcal{F}_t \right] \tag{411}$$

Now, we can arrive at Black type formulas again under the SABR model and price the swaption by:

$$c_{t+2}^{USD} = \frac{Not_{BRL}}{FXFWD_{t,T_{Pay}}^{OFF}\left[\frac{BRL}{USD}\right]} \cdot \tau_{T_1,T_2}^{252}$$

$$\cdot \left(R_{t,T_1,T_2}^{L(OFF)} \cdot N(d1_{SWPT}) - K_L \cdot N(d2_{SWPT}) \right) \cdot P_{t,t+2,T_{Pay}}^{Coll} \tag{412}$$

where,

$$d1_{SWPT} = \frac{ln\left(\frac{R_{t,T_1,T_2}^{L(OFF)}}{K_L}\right) + 0.5 \cdot \sigma_b(K,F)^2 \cdot T_{vol}}{\sigma_b(K,F) \cdot \sqrt{T_{vol}}}$$

$$d2_{SWPT} = \frac{ln\left(\frac{R_{t,T_1,T_2}^{L(OFF)}}{K_L}\right) - 0.5 \cdot \sigma_b(K,F)^2 \cdot T_{vol}}{\sigma_b(K,F) \cdot \sqrt{T_{vol}}}$$

with implied volatility parameter $\sigma_b(K,F)$ given by:

$$\sigma_b(K,F) = \frac{\alpha}{(F\cdot K)^{\frac{(1-\beta)}{2}}\left\{1+\frac{(1-\beta)^2}{24}\cdot log^2\frac{F}{K}+\frac{(1-\beta)^4}{1920}log^4\frac{F}{K}+\ldots\right\}}\cdot\left(\frac{z}{x(z)}\right)\cdot$$
$$\cdot\left\{1+\left[\frac{(1-\beta)^2}{24}\cdot\frac{\alpha^2}{(FK)^{1-\beta}}+\frac{1}{4}\cdot\frac{\rho\beta\nu\alpha}{(FK)^{\frac{(1-\beta)}{2}}}+\frac{2-3\rho^2}{24}\nu^2\right]t_{ex+\ldots}\right\}$$

where,

$$z=\frac{\nu}{\alpha}(FK)^{\frac{(1-\beta)}{2}}\cdot log\frac{F}{K}$$
$$x(z)=log\left\{\frac{\sqrt{1-2\rho z+z^2}+z-\rho}{1-\rho}\right\}$$

with $F=K_L$ and $K=K_L$ inside the SABR implied volatility formulas.

The receiver swaption would be priced as:

$$p_{t+2}^{USD}=\frac{Not_{BRL}}{FXFWD_{t,T_{Pay}}^{OFF}\left[\frac{BRL}{USD}\right]}\cdot\tau_{T_1,T_2}^{252}$$
$$\cdot\left(K_L\cdot N(-d2_{SWPT})-R_{t,T_1,T_2}^{L(OFF)}\cdot N(-d1_{SWPT})\right)\cdot P_{t,t+2,T_{Pay}}^{Coll} \quad (413)$$

11
The Dual Case – US Libor Onshore Swaps

We've seen that an offshore BRL Fixed Float swaption is paid offshore in USD, but the fixings are CDI which are associated to BRL currency. The dual trade is the so-called US Libor onshore swaps, which are paid onshore in BRL, but fixings are US Libor which are associated with USD currency. In the previous section we derived that the offshore BRL Fixed Float swap can be viewed as a quanto swap. And based on the same arguments, we will derive in this section that US Libor onshore swaps also are quantos.

11.1 Payoff of US Libor onshore swaps

Here we will consider a swap which has only one US Libor payment left, to simplify things without any loss of generality:

$$Payoff_{BRL}[T_2] = Not_{USD} \cdot L^{USD}_{T_1,T_2} \cdot \tau^{Act360}_{T_1,T_2} \cdot PTAX_{T_{Fix}} \tag{414}$$

Let's assume that US Libor fixings occur at T_1 without the usual $T-2$ lag to ease the notation.

11.2 Pricing of US Libor onshore swaps

The present value of the payoff specified in (414) is given by:

$$PV^{BRL}_t = Not_{USD} \cdot P^{CDI}_{t,T_2} \cdot \tau^{\mathrm{Act360}}_{\mathrm{T_1,T_2}} \cdot \mathbb{E}^{\mathbb{Q}^{\mathrm{T_2}}_{\mathrm{CDI}}}\left[L^{USD}_{T_1,T_2} \cdot PTAX_{T_{Fix}} | \mathcal{F}_{\mathrm{t}}\right] \tag{415}$$

We can change to the probability measure associated with P^{USB}_{t,T_2} as numéraire, in order to cancel the $PTAX_{T_{Fix}}$ inside the expectation. This yields:

$$PV^{BRL}_t = \frac{Not_{USD}}{FXFWD^{ON}_{t,T_2}\left[\frac{BRL}{USD}\right]} \cdot P^{CDI}_{t,T_2} \cdot \tau^{\mathrm{Act360}}_{\mathrm{T_1,T_2}} \cdot \mathbb{E}^{\mathbb{Q}^{\mathrm{T_2}}_{\mathrm{USB}}}\left[L^{USD}_{T_1,T_2} | \mathcal{F}_{\mathrm{t}}\right] \tag{416}$$

The forward US Libor rate $L^{USD}_{T_1,T_2}$ is a martingale under the probability measure associated with numéraire P^{USD}_{t,T_2}, but not P^{USB}_{t,T_2}. Therefore, there will be also a quanto adjustment in the US Libor forward rate when priced onshore.

The Radon-Nikodym derivative together with Girsanov theorem will again be applied to help us to obtain the drift adjustment for the US Libor forward rate under the required probability measure.

$$\frac{d\mathbb{Q}^{T_2}_{USD}}{d\mathbb{Q}^{T_2}_{USB}}|\mathcal{F}_{T_{Fix}} = \frac{FXFWD_{T_{Fix},T_2}[\frac{USB}{USD}]}{FXFWD_{t,T_2}[\frac{USB}{USD}]}$$

$$= exp\left\{-\frac{1}{2}\int_t^{T_{Fix}} \sigma^2_{FWD\left[\frac{USB}{USD}\right]}\cdot ds + \int_t^{T_{Fix}} \sigma_{FWD\left[\frac{USB}{USD}\right]}\cdot dZ_t^{T_2^{USB}}\right\} \quad (417)$$

where,

$\sigma_{FWD\left[\frac{USB}{USD}\right]}$: is the FX Forward volatility for currency pair $\frac{USB}{USD}$.

$dZ_t^{T^{USB}_{Pay}}$: is the Brownian Motion that shocks the FX Forward for currency pair $\frac{USB}{USD}$.

Let's assume that the 2 Brownian Motions $dW_{1_t}^{T_2^{USB}}$ (that shocks $L^{USD}_{T_1,T_2}$) and $dZ_t^{T_2^{USB}}$ (that shocks $FXFWD_{t,T_{Pay}}[\frac{USB}{USD}]$) are correlated by:

$$dW_{1_t}^{T_2^{USB}}\cdot dZ_t^{T_2^{USB}} = \rho_1\cdot dt \quad (418)$$

We can rewrite

$$dZ_t^{T_2^{USB}} = \rho_1\cdot dW_{1_t}^{T_2^{USB}} + \sqrt{1-\rho_1^2}\cdot dW_{2_t}^{T_2^{USB}}$$

where $W_{1_t}^{T_2^{USB}}$ and $W_{2_t}^{T_2^{USB}}$ are independent Brownian Motions. So we can rewrite (417) as:

$$\frac{d\mathbb{Q}^{T_2}_{USD}}{d\mathbb{Q}^{T_2}_{USB}}|\mathcal{F}_{T_{Fix}} = exp\left\{-\frac{1}{2}\int_t^{T_{Fix}} \sigma^2_{FWD\left[\frac{USB}{USD}\right]}\cdot ds + \int_t^{T_{Fix}} \sigma_{FWD\left[\frac{USB}{USD}\right]} \cdot\left(\rho_1\cdot dW_{1_t}^{T_2^{USB}} + \sqrt{1-\rho_1^2}\cdot dW_{2_t}^{T_2^{USB}}\right)\right\} \quad (419)$$

Applying Girsanov Theorem

$$dW_{1_t}^{T_2^{USD}} = -\sigma_{FWD\left[\frac{USB}{USD}\right]}\cdot\rho_1\cdot dt + dW_{1_t}^{T_2^{USB}} \quad (420)$$

Plugging (420) into (397) yields:

$$L^{USD}_{T_1,T_2} = L^{USD}_{t,T_1,T_2}\cdot exp\left\{-\frac{1}{2}\cdot\int_t^{T_1}\sigma_L^2\cdot ds + \int_t^{T_1}\sigma_L\cdot\left(-\sigma_{FWD\left[\frac{USB}{USD}\right]}\cdot\rho_1\cdot dt + dW_{1_t}^{T_2^{USB}}\right)\right\} \quad (421)$$

where,

σ_L: is a lognormal volatility of $L^{USD}_{T_1,T_2}$, assuming that L^{USD}_{t,T_1,T_2} follows a geometric Brownian motion.

And the expectation of $L^{USD}_{T_1,T_2}$ under the probability measure where P^{USB}_{t,T_2} is its numéraire is given by:

$$\mathbb{E}^{\mathbb{Q}^{T_2}_{USB}}\left[L^{USD}_{T_1,T_2}|\mathcal{F}_t\right] = L^{USD}_{t,T_1,T_2} \cdot exp\left\{-\int_t^{T_1}\left[\sigma_L \cdot \sigma_{FWD\left[\frac{USB}{USD}\right]} \cdot \rho_1\right]dt\right\} \tag{422}$$

Similarly to the FX forward of $\frac{BRU}{BRL}$ currency pair, the FX forward of $\frac{USB}{USD}$ currency pair can be viewed as:

$$FXFWD_{t,T_2}\left[\frac{USB}{USD}\right] = \frac{P^{USD}_{t,t_{fx},T}}{P^{USB}_{t,t_{fx},T}} \tag{423}$$

The equation above states that the $FXFWD_{t,T_2}[\frac{USB}{USD}]$ value will go up if cupom rates go up or if USD rates go down. On the other hand we also know by looking at (423) that the drift term is short correlation of US Libor rates (from the variable $L^{USD}_{T_1,T_2}$) and $FXFWD_{t,T_2}[\frac{USB}{USD}]$. So essentially one could say that the drift term derived in (422) could be viewed as:

- Long variance of USD rates
- Short covariance of cupom and USD rates

The statement above says that a receiver USD Fixed-Float onshore swap position (that is short the floating leg and therefore the term $L^{USD}_{T_1,T_2}$) would generate a convexity where you are:

- Short variance of USD rates
- Long covariance of cupom and USD rates

And obviously the payer swap position would generate:

- Long variance of USD rates
- Short covariance of cupom and USD rates

Most banks that have a local presence usually quote US Libor onshore swaps for clients on receiver side, and since usually the short variance of USD rates component is larger than the long covariance of cupom and USD rates, by not adjusting the swap rate at start would typically incur into dynamic rebalancing costs during the life of the trade and most likely a negative P&L accumulated until the maturity date of the swap when hedges are included.

12
FX Trading (Interest Rate and Fixing) Market and Credit Risk

12.1 Fixing

Here are some of the shortcuts to find the FX Delta of the derivatives contracts covered above, depending on your funding currency.

Swaps and NDFs: FX Delta is equal to the PV in BRL of the foreign currency leg divided by the FX Spot; for Brazilians, the USD-indexed leg; for offshore investors, the BRL-indexed leg will represent FX risk.

DDI futures: At the close, the number of contracts multiplied (including the 0.5 factor) by the unitary price (this product is equivalent to the PV of a leg of a FX Swap); the receivables or payables from the daily margining process will represent an additional FX risk for offshore investors. This is obviously less than the notional in USD.

DOL futures: Because the daily variation of the fx future price is paid/received "today" (the following day, to be precise), the FX Delta can be approximated by the number of contracts multiplied by the ratio between the price of the future (divided by 1000) and the FX Spot price. That alone means the trading a Casado (same notionals on both the FX Spot and the DOL) leads to a residual FX risk. And here we say approximately, as the correct valuation would include the covariance of the fx forward and the discount factor. Alas, the wait for a transparent market for both fx futures and fx forwards, with the fx futures EOD price reflecting the implied covariance in the market, has been long and it has not given any hope for a resolution. Most of the time the FX Delta will be greater than the notional, but for both DOL and DDI the FX Delta will approach the notional as we approach the maturity of the contract.

For the exposure to FX Spot on the day of fixing, please see 9.2.2.

12.2 The term structure of the Cupom Cambial

12.2.1 Slope

The slope will be very different depending on the rate chosen (the traded FRC, the implicit DDI, or a calculated exponential rate, adjusted or not). As it seems that most market participants model some kind of exponential rate, and that there should be some relationship with USD funding rates, expect an upward sloping rate most of the time.

12.2.2 Casado

Usually the time series follows a sawtooth pattern. The last time the Casado was negative (2002), reserves were not as big as they were now, and there was a significant lack of USD; the present level of reserves in 2015 (greater than USD 300 billion) makes unlikely that for next 2 years we will see a similar situation. And even then, the forwards time series was like an almost horizontal hockey stick: a short leg downward from spot to first future, then upwards for the rest of time.

12.3 Potential exposures

We were lucky last time we looked at Potential Exposures, because in IR Swaps we're dealing with only one question: What will be the path taken by the CDI? The MTM paths are a function of the path and how much that path differs from its expectation at the inception.

For a NDF (USD Fixed x BRL Fixed) or a FX Swap (USD Fixed x BRL Float), we have now another question: What will be the path taken by the Spot (up until its fixing at the PTAX)?

Earlier we wrote for an IR Swap:

$$Payoff_{BRL}[T] = \phi \cdot Not_{BRL} \cdot \left(CapFac_{Fixed}(t,T) - CapFac_{Float}(t,T)\right) \tag{424}$$

And defined:

$$f(t,\tau,T) = \prod_{T_i=t}^{\tau} (1+CDI_{T_i})^{\frac{1}{252}} \cdot \prod_{T_i=\tau}^{T} (1+CDI_{T_i})^{\frac{1}{252}} \tag{425}$$

Writing the payoff as:

$$Payoff = \phi \cdot Not_{BRL} \cdot \left(f(t,t,T) - f(t,T,T)\right) \tag{426}$$

Now we must write the payoff of a NDF as:

$$Payoff = \phi \cdot Not_{BRL} \cdot \left(g(t,T,T)h(t,t,T) - f(t,t,T)\right) \tag{427}$$

And the payoff of a FX Swap as:

$$Payoff = \phi \cdot Not_{BRL} \cdot \left(g(t,T,T)h(t,t,T) - f(t,T,T)\right) \tag{428}$$

Defining:

$$g(t,\tau,T)=\prod_{T_i=t}^{\tau}\left(\frac{FX_{T_i}}{FX_{T_{i-1}}}\right)\cdot\prod_{T_i=\tau}^{T}\left(\frac{FX_{T_i}}{FX_{T_{i-1}}}\right) \tag{429}$$

And representing the yield associated with the FX index, the Cupom Cambial:

$$h(t,t,T)=\frac{f(t,t,T)}{g(t,t,T)} \tag{430}$$

The PV of a NDF is:

$$PV_\tau=\phi\cdot Not_{BRL}\cdot\left(\frac{g(t,\tau,T)h(t,t,T)-f(t,t,T)}{f(\tau,\tau,T)}\right) \tag{431}$$

And the PV of a FX Swap is:

$$PV_\tau=\phi\cdot Not_{BRL}\cdot\left(\frac{g(t,\tau,T)h(t,t,T)-f(t,\tau,T)}{f(\tau,\tau,T)}\right) \tag{432}$$

Developing the formula for the NDF, we find:

$$PV_\tau=\phi\cdot Not_{BRL}\cdot\left(\frac{g(t,\tau,T)\frac{f(t,t,T)}{g(t,t,T)}-f(t,t,T)}{f(\tau,\tau,T)}\right) \tag{433}$$

$$PV_\tau=\phi\cdot Not_{BRL}\cdot\frac{f(t,t,T)}{f(\tau,\tau,T)}\cdot\left(\frac{g(t,\tau,T)}{g(t,t,T)}-1\right) \tag{434}$$

Which makes a lot of sense; if the NDF price has not changed from its initial price, there is no effect from the changes in the BRL curve.

But on a FX Swap, the "strike" price can be seen as a floating price, and changes in the BRL curve change the strike, and then we find the formulas:

$$PV_\tau=\phi\cdot Not_{BRL}\cdot\left(\frac{g(t,\tau,T)\frac{f(t,t,T)}{g(t,t,T)}-f(t,\tau,T)}{f(\tau,\tau,T)}\right) \tag{435}$$

$$PV_\tau=\phi\cdot Not_{BRL}\cdot\frac{f(t,t,T)}{f(\tau,\tau,T)}\cdot\left(\frac{g(t,\tau,T)}{g(t,t,T)}-\frac{f(t,\tau,T)}{f(t,t,T)}\right) \tag{436}$$

From both formulas we can conclude that most probably the Potential Exposure calculations will be dominated by the FX component rather then the interest rates (unless you have a really long transaction).

There are various approaches to estimate the adequate Potential Exposure, including historical and Monte Carlo simulations, scaling the volatility of FX and Rates or using stressed scenarios for an "envelope" for the FX paths. We don't want to be forcing upon you our opinion about which method works best, but we recommend you keep a long history of moves and please also remember that we've had several 10% devaluations in one month (8% for 1 week and 15%

for 1 month looks like a good rule of thumb). Or you can mix a shock with a diffusive ($\sigma\sqrt{t}$) behavior.

One would also expect a slightly higher Potential Exposure for the NDF than for the FX Swap if the expected correlation between the FX Forward and the BRL Curve is positive.

12.4 Interpolation and sensitivities

Unfortunately the Cupom Cambial does not have the same structure as the BRL curve, and it is harder to argue that one interpolation is markedly better than the other. Be always aware of the shortcomings of each choice (we advise against interpolating directly linear rates, even though they are directly traded). If you need to create a layer in which you model the dynamics of a exponential curve and therefore use (even indirectly or numerically) the chain rule to calculate DV01s, so be it.

Most textbooks will assume you will calculate a FX Delta against the Spot and DV01s for the zero curves; but here you can find alternatives:

1. FX Delta against DOL, PV01s for the forward curves (BRL and Cupom Cambial) that start at the DOL, and a combined IR Risk for the Casado
2. FX Delta against Spot, PV01s for the zero curves (BRL and Cupom Cambial) - the conventional view

One still needs to determine in this second case how to interpolate the Cupom Cambial between Spot and DOL, and this veers into the USD funding costs territory. For a good period of time, excess USD for Brazilian banks had to be deposited at the BCB at zero interest (when interest rates in the G10 were higher). We will not go into the detail of how each international bank funds its Brazilian operations, or how each Brazilian bank finds the cheapest way to borrow in USD, as this is subject to changes due to taxes, risk tolerance and other details. However, this might influence how the short part of the curve is interpolated for each institution.

Here the choice of interpolating using the Cupom Cambial or the Forwards will also be important; would it be coherent to interpolate forwards and use rates as risk factors? This is another layer of modeling between market inputs and risk factors, and knowledge about the response functions of the model is important for everyone (Traders, Product Control and Risk Management), and it could lead to interesting discussions at the end of each month when it's time for Price Testing – which points are liquid in the FRC? 2 or 3 perhaps ?

Not that expressing your exposure as sensitivities to different points of the FX Forwards curve is much better or easier; maybe it could be modeled directly the discount factors implied in the forward curves and get the Cupom Cambial from that and the discount factors from the BRL curve; or interpolate (linearly?) the forward points in the NDFs, interpolate (linearly?) the OnOff spread and then find the onshore forwards?

In one way or another you would like to be able to have a structure in which the DV01 for the short rates has more or less the same impact as the DV01 for long rates (not easy). The same applies for the OnOff spread. Because this spread can be negative or positive, there's not much to gain by looking at relative (%) moves and volatilities; absolute moves (bp) are better suited to the task.

12.5 A framework for risk

Now one has a triangle of risk factors: FX Spot (or DOL), BRL rates and USD-indexed rates (or forward points – BRL rates). The hard part is not estimating volatilities; it is estimating covariances. These would be crucial in pricing longer dated DOLs, and not always the behavior from the past will be a good guide. If typically for risk one assumes a positive correlation between Spot and the BRL Curve (as in 2008), the movements in the second half of 2011 (BRL devaluation and the BCB forcing rates down) showed how hard it is to manage covariance.

Step 1 is always calculating the sensitivities to each risk factor; but this is only the beginning.

Step 2 is a bit more risky: performing some kind of dimensionality reduction without losing too much detail; you should already have something like this for the BRL curve; just add FX and maybe level + slope for the Cupom Cambial.

Step 3 is to generate risk estimates for different scenarios, with and without correlation among the different risk factors, using Step 2 (and Cholesky) to generate correlated scenarios.

Step 4 is to look at the scenarios and despair ... sorry, not yet; you're likely to have quite different results on your calendar spreads here; you'll have to look at the implied covariance for each scenario and decide whether you should act based on the comparison with the historic covariance, the likelihood the scenario in question and the result of a 20-sided dice ... The despair will come after you pick one scenario and the world delivers you the opposite of that scenario. All choices will be hard, regret will happen, but it is a bit naive to manage risk as if all risk factors are uncorrelated; this is also a decision on correlation, and depending on the market behavior more likely to be risk mismanagement than risk management.

12.6 Trading forwards

Well, it is likely that this is what you're doing in this world (more than trading pure Cupom Cambial risk or just Spot risk); the logic of trying to find a hedge such that the variance of the combined portfolio is as low as possible is still valid. As described before, the dynamics of the risk factors (Spot, BRL curve and Cupom

Cambial) was not always the same; the 2nd half of 2008 was very different than the 2nd half of 2011.

The main difference with our approach to IR Swaps is that fixing risk on these was diluted and, in practice, ended at the last COPOM meeting before the maturity of the swap. But for NDFs or FX Swaps the fixing risk at maturity is still significant. So if at inception you hedged a 16 month NDF with 1y and 2y NDFs, as time went on you rolled the original 1y NDF (maybe from 3m to 9m), getting out of the original 2y NDF; and again 1m before the maturity you already picked this trade up in your upcoming expiries report, trading FRPs or similar trades to manage the fixing risks. Maybe the customer will roll the trade, and will ask you one week before to roll it at PTAX plus forward points. This means that one week from now the NDF will have its price fixed as this day's PTAX plus the agreed forward points. An accurate risk model for this kind of trade is also necessary if you plan on being active on this market.

12.7 Risk and P&L attribution

Now things are more interesting, given:

1. The choices of modeling:
   a. Spot or DOL?
   b. Interpolate the Cupom Cambial for the short term against a funding rate in USD? Or interpolate the Casado?
   c. Interpolate the Cupom or the Forwards?
   d. Dirty or clean rates (at least this one is easy: clean)
2. The contact with cash instruments (USD in the bank, not just as an index, and maybe your own foreign currency debt) which certainly brings different funding rates into play (e.g. reserve requirements and Central Bank-mandated rates for foreign currency deposits)
3. The cross variations of FX and rates introducing second order effects
4. Taxes (like the IOF on derivatives)
5. Choices on the roll of the scenarios

One of the most interesting decisions is whether to map the risk from a linear rate that is traded but carries too much noise into an exponential rate that is adjusted to settlement dates but is not observed directly in the market; the latter is better suited for a covariance analysis.

For now we will leave the questions above open, but some of answers will come when we examine the FX options.

We want to tackle two issues; we alluded to them before, but we should formalize them better.

The first point relates to illiquid prices, and we discussed this for the DIs and the BRL curve. Not all points are equal, and there is another situation where

Table 20 Limits hit by DOL in October 2008

Day	Upper	Lower
6	2,192.00	
7	2,323.50	
8	2,462.00	
10	2,328.00	
13		2,188.00
13		2,142.00
14		2,057.00
15	2,241.00	
22	2,390.00	
23	2,530.50	2,244.50
24	2,405.00	

exchange prices should not be used blindly: when they hit the daily oscillation limits. This has been more common in FX than in interest rates. We discussed the 1999 devaluation, which was a classic case of the need to use a price that reflected what the market was trading. But October 2008 was rich in such episodes (Table 20).

There were two additional near misses for the Upper limits (02-Oct and 21-Oct). What happens when the DOL hits such a limit? More often than not other markets (these days the offshore NDF market would be ready) would be trading (with less liquidity, of course). We would need to be ready with the Triangle structure; there would be a (stronger) disconnection between the expected P&L on the DOL and related instruments, leading to a bigger number on the payables/receivables expected for D+2 (the expected cashflow for D+1 is the one using the settlement price for the day, which is likely to be the limit in question).

It is very important to ensure that everything is valued with the same scenario (we would write it in all caps if our editor let us do it). Do not value OTC with a higher USDBRL and leave the P&L and expected cashflows from the BVMF frozen at the limit. Most likely you'll forget to hedge that bigger cashflow and become very angry 2 weeks later.

The second point deserves its own number.

12.8 DOL convexity correction to a FX forward price

The DOL contract first margin call is given by:

$$MCF_t^T = M \cdot \left(CP_t^T - TP_t^T\right) \tag{437}$$

When we enter a futures contract, we are expecting this cashflow to be 0 in a risk neutral world. The last cashflow occurs at T and it's based on $PTAX_{T-1}$ FX

Fixing, which gives us the following boundary condition:

$$MCF_T^T = M \cdot \left(PTAX_{T-1} - CP_{T-2}^T\right) \tag{438}$$

The fact that the futures contract have a 0 expectation under the discrete time risk neutral probability measure $\mathbb{Q}^*$, with the boundary condition gives us that:

$$\mathbb{E}^{\mathbb{Q}^*}\left[M \cdot \left(PTAX_{T-1} - CP_{T-2}^T\right) | \mathcal{F}_{T-2}\right] = 0 \tag{439}$$

Thus,

$$\mathbb{E}^{\mathbb{Q}^*}\left[PTAX_{T-1} | \mathcal{F}_{T-2}\right] = CP_{T-2}^T \tag{440}$$

Similarly to what was done in DI and DDI pricing, we could do a recursive iteration process that would yield:

$$\mathbb{E}^{\mathbb{Q}^*}\left[PTAX_{T-1} | \mathcal{F}_t\right] = FXFUT_{t,T_1-1_{FX}}^{ON}\left[\frac{BRL}{USD}\right] \tag{441}$$

So the Futures price seen at date t, namely $FXFUT_{t,T_1-1_{FX}}^{ON}[\frac{BRL}{USD}]$ is the conditional expectation of $PTAX_{T-1}$ under $\mathbb{Q}^*$.

We can again use the fact that $PTAX_{T-1} = FXFWD_{T-1,T-1_{FX}}^{ON}[\frac{BRL}{USD}]$, which states that the FX forward value collapses to the fixing value at contract maturity date. Thus,

$$\mathbb{E}^{\mathbb{Q}^*}\left[FXFWD_{T-1,T-1_{FX}}^{ON}\left[\frac{BRL}{USD}\right] | \mathcal{F}_t\right] = FXFUT_{t,T_1-1_{FX}}^{ON}\left[\frac{BRL}{USD}\right] \tag{442}$$

We know that the FXFWD value $FXFWD_{t,T-1_{FX}}^{ON}[\frac{BRL}{USD}]$ is a martingale under the $\mathbb{Q}^{T_{CDI}}$ probability measure, associated with numéraire $P_{t,t_{FX},T-1_{FX}}^{CDI}$. But we need to perform a change of measure to probability measure $\mathbb{Q}^*$. The Radon-Nikodym derivative is given by:

$$\frac{d\mathbb{Q}^*}{d\mathbb{Q}_{CDI}{}^T} | \mathcal{F}_T = \frac{\beta_T}{\beta_t} \cdot \frac{P_{t,T}^{CDI}}{P_{T,T}^{CDI}} = \prod_{T_i=t}^{T} \left[1 + CDI_{T_i}\right]^{\frac{1}{252}} \cdot P_{t,T}^{CDI} \tag{443}$$

Which with use of (262) yields:

$$\frac{d\mathbb{Q}^*}{d\mathbb{Q}_{CDI}{}^T} | \mathcal{F}_T = exp\left\{-\frac{1}{2} \cdot \int_t^T \left(\int_s^T \sigma_{s,u} \cdot du\right)^2 \cdot ds + \int_t^T \left(\int_s^T \sigma_{s,u} \cdot du\right) \cdot dW_{1_t}^{T_{CDI}}\right\} \tag{444}$$

Now we can change (442) to be based on $\mathbb{Q}^{\mathrm{T_{CDI}}}$ probability measure by:

$$\mathbb{E}^{\mathbb{Q}^{\mathrm{T_{CDI}}}}\left[FXFWD^{ON}_{T-1,T-1_{FX}}\left[\frac{BRL}{USD}\right]\cdot exp\left\{-\frac{1}{2}\cdot\int_t^T\left(\int_s^T\sigma_{s,u}\cdot du\right)^2\cdot ds\right.\right.$$
$$\left.\left.+\int_t^T\left(\int_s^T\sigma_{s,u}\cdot du\right)\cdot dW^{T_{CDI}}_{1_t}\right\}|\mathcal{F}_{\mathrm{t}}\right]=FXFUT^{ON}_{t,T_1-1_{FX}}\left[\frac{BRL}{USD}\right] \quad (445)$$

Assuming a lognormal model for the FX Forward based on:

$$dFXFWD^{ON}_{t,T-1_{FX}}\left[\frac{BRL}{USD}\right]=FXFWD^{ON}_{t,T-1_{FX}}\left[\frac{BRL}{USD}\right]\cdot\sigma_{FXFWD}\cdot dZ^{T_{CDI}}_{1_t} \quad (446)$$

And assuming

$$dZ^{T_{CDI}}_t=\rho_1\cdot dW^{T_{CDI}}_{1_t}+\sqrt{1-\rho_1^2}\cdot dW^{T_{CDI}}_{2_t}$$

with $dW^{T_{CDI}}_{1_t}$ and $dW^{T_{CDI}}_{2_t}$ as independent Brownian Motion yields:

$$FXFUT^{ON}_{t,T_1-1_{FX}}\left[\frac{BRL}{USD}\right]=FXFWD^{ON}_{t,T-1_{FX}}\left[\frac{BRL}{USD}\right]$$
$$\cdot exp\left(\int_t^{T-1}\rho_1\cdot\sigma_{FXFWD}\cdot\left(\int_s^T\sigma_{s,u}\cdot du\right)\cdot dt\right) \quad (447)$$

This proves that if one assumes BRL onshore interest rates to be positive correlated to the FX FWD value, then there's a positive convexity correction on the FXFutures price $FXFUT^{ON}_{t,T_1-1_{FX}}[\frac{BRL}{USD}]$ given by $exp\left(\int_t^{T-1}\rho_1\cdot\sigma_{FXFWD}\cdot\left(\int_s^T\sigma_{s,u}\cdot du\right)\cdot dt\right)$.

And if you're trading longer dated DOLs against a replicating portfolio, please remember that there should be a market price for it, even though BVMF is not marking it correctly. Please schedule an appointment with whoever is marking your books and/or controlling your risk. Ask them to buy this book. Discuss with them the alternatives to value adequately the portfolio and control the risk that you are running (yes, you have a market risk).

13
A Skewed Perspective of the World: FX Options

13.1 Starting from the end (Market standards for Offshore FX options)

13.1.1 Weightlifting

There are two markets for USDBRL options: One that is liquid and follows (for the most part) the modeling described in (Clark, 2011) (the offshore market), and the curious mix of FX options and listed markets (the onshore listed FX options). Let's start with the offshore market first (notation is this chapter follows mostly the source articles, not previous chapters).

We described some standards earlier, but let's review then:

1. Dates:
   a. Shorter maturities counted in days or weeks follow a rule that counts days from today to the Expiry Date
   b. Longer maturities counted in months or years follow a rule that counts months from the settlement corresponding to a trade today to the settlement corresponding to an Expiry Date
2. Daycounts:
   a. Actual/365 between today and the Expiry Date is used for the volatility to calculate the forward Black Price (given the Forward Price); remember the discussion on the 3 Ts of Option Pricing
   b. As for the other two Ts: one is implicit in the Forward Price, and another is used for discounting; as discounting is not the standard for interbank trades, we will leave this process (discounting) to the reader, as this will change based on each institution's methodology

Brazilians have a habit of thinking about business days most of the time (and no, it's not about trying to avoid them); and volatility should happen on business days; how to deal with the Actual/365 standard?

The answer is to use weights in your calendar.

Weekends: weight 0

Normal business days: weight 1

As Clark (2011) describes, this weight is applied to each 1-day forward volatility in a formula for the effective variance:

$$\sum_{i=1}^{N}\left(\left(w_{t_i}\sigma_{t_i}^{fwd}\right)^2 \cdot (t_i - t_{i-1})\right) = \left(\sigma_{t_N}^{impl}\right)^2 \cdot t_N \tag{448}$$

Now one could get really confident and start playing around with weights, but this is unlikely to end well without looking at the mirror (or the market).

But do not despair: Here are some suggestions that you can backtest to see whether a weight different than 1 is justified:

1. Last business day of the month (typically a day in which there is a lot of interest in the fixing): could be more volatile
2. Last business day of the year (BVMF trading holiday): a perfect candidate for a zero weight
3. Other BVMF holidays: The DOL is not trading, but you can observe (but not all participants can trade) markets like offshore NDFs and Spot. There will be volatility, but it might be difficult to extract value from your gamma; perhaps a lower weight can be justified by backtesting against intraday volatility (How much of the volatility comes from the gap between close and open? How much comes from intraday movements? More on this later)
4. Ash Wednesday has less minutes of trading, but there are not many Ash Wednesdays to do a robust backtesting. Maybe give it a try.

On G10 currencies is not uncommon to see FOMC meetings on other macroeconomic relevant scheduled announcements to carry weights higher than 1. Perhaps in Brazil every day there is a surprise and this distinction is not as relevant.

Ok, so now we kind of know how to go back and forth between the traded maturities and some kind of model that we might have for the 1-day forward volatilities. Is it over? No, the fun has just started. We will need:

1. A way to model how much of the volatility is due to the gap between the closing price and the opening price and how much of it comes from intraday movements (and how to model this intraday volatility into the PTAX)
2. A way to deal with these distinctions (moving from 3 Ts to 5 Ts?) when pricing options
3. A way to store this information so that I will know what the market was on that day
4. A way to process that information so I can roll my volatility surface from a quite low overnight volatility at 18:00 to a higher overnight volatility at 9:00

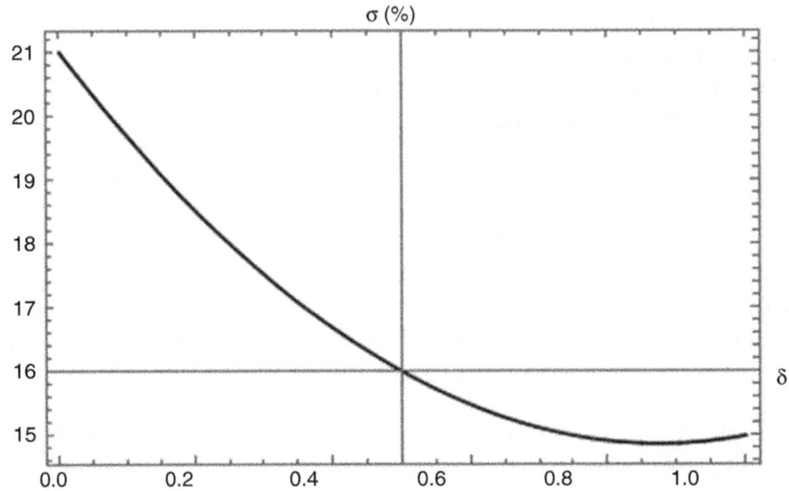

Figure 73 A simple smile using Malz

And of course we will need a model to describe the co-movement of the forward volatilities, but there are a lot of papers and models for that.

13.1.2 Reversal of fortune

Coming back to "Option-Implied Probability Distributions and Currency Excess Returns" (Malz, 1997):

$$\sigma(\delta) = ATM - 2 \cdot RR \cdot \left(\delta - \frac{1}{2}\right) + 16 \cdot ST \cdot \left(\delta - \frac{1}{2}\right)^2 \tag{449}$$

For parameters like: ATM=16%, RR=3%, ST=0.5%, we might have a chart like Figure 73.

For those used to see higher volatilities on the right of the chart, remember that higher strikes correspond to lower deltas (seen from a call's perspective).

For the 25 delta call, we have:

$$\sigma_{\delta=0.25} = ATM - 2 \cdot RR \cdot \left(-\frac{1}{4}\right) + 16 \cdot ST \cdot \left(-\frac{1}{4}\right)^2 \tag{450}$$

$$\sigma_{\delta=0.25} = ATM + \frac{1}{2} \cdot RR + ST \tag{451}$$

For the 25 delta put (here equivalent to a 75 delta call), we have:

$$\sigma_{\delta=0.75} = ATM - 2 \cdot RR \cdot \left(\frac{1}{4}\right) + 16 \cdot ST \cdot \left(\frac{1}{4}\right)^2 \tag{452}$$

$$\sigma_{\delta=0.75} = ATM - \frac{1}{2} \cdot RR + ST \tag{453}$$

A 25 delta Risk Reversal would be equal to buying a 25 delta call and selling a 25 delta put.

In volatility, this is equal to:

$$\sigma_{rr25\delta} = \sigma_{\delta=0.25} - \sigma_{\delta=0.75} = RR \tag{454}$$

A 25 delta Strangle would be equal to buying a 25 delta call, buying a 25 delta put and selling the ATM straddle, all divided by 2.

In volatility, this is equal to:

$$\sigma_{st25\delta} = \frac{\sigma_{\delta=0.25} + \sigma_{\delta=0.75} - 2 \cdot \sigma_{ATM}}{2} = ST \tag{455}$$

So far so good. The OTC FX market trades not only the 25 deltas but also the 10 deltas.

Within this model the 10 delta calls would be priced as:

$$\sigma_{\delta=0.10} = ATM - 2 \cdot RR \cdot (0.10 - 0.50) + 16 \cdot ST \cdot (0.10 - 0.50)^2 \tag{456}$$

$$\sigma_{\delta=0.10} = ATM + 0.80 \cdot RR + 2.56 \cdot ST \tag{457}$$

Comparing this with:

$$\sigma_{\delta=0.25} = ATM + 0.50 \cdot RR + 1.00 \cdot ST \tag{458}$$

Leads us to write:

$$\sigma_{\delta=0.25} = ATM + 0.50 \cdot RR_{25} + 1.00 \cdot ST_{25} \tag{459}$$

And:

$$\sigma_{\delta=0.10} = ATM + 0.50 \cdot RR_{10} + 1.00 \cdot ST_{10} \tag{460}$$

With the parameters for the 10 deltas defined as:

$$RR_{10} = 1.60 \cdot RR_{25} \tag{461}$$

And:

$$ST_{10} = 2.56 \cdot ST_{25} \tag{462}$$

This gives us a first idea of the ratios between the 10 delta and the 25 delta quotes.

Now, how does Brazil fit into this? Like a square peg in a round hole - not much.

First problem: ATMs are not 50 delta; remember that in Brazil ATMs are ATMFs, and that:

$$deltafwd_{StraddleATMF} = \frac{1}{2} \cdot \left(-\frac{fwdpr_{USDCallATMF}}{K} \right) = -0.2 \cdot \sigma \sqrt{t} \tag{463}$$

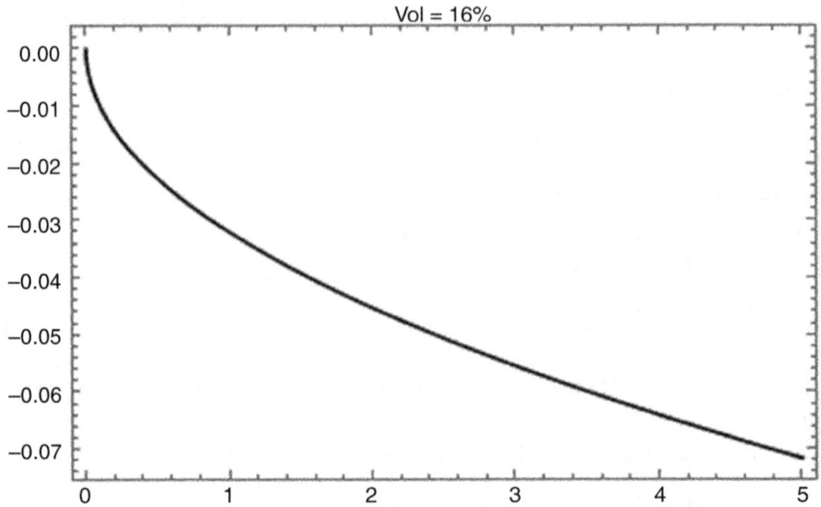

Figure 74 Delta Forward of an ATMF Straddle with Implied Volatility=16%

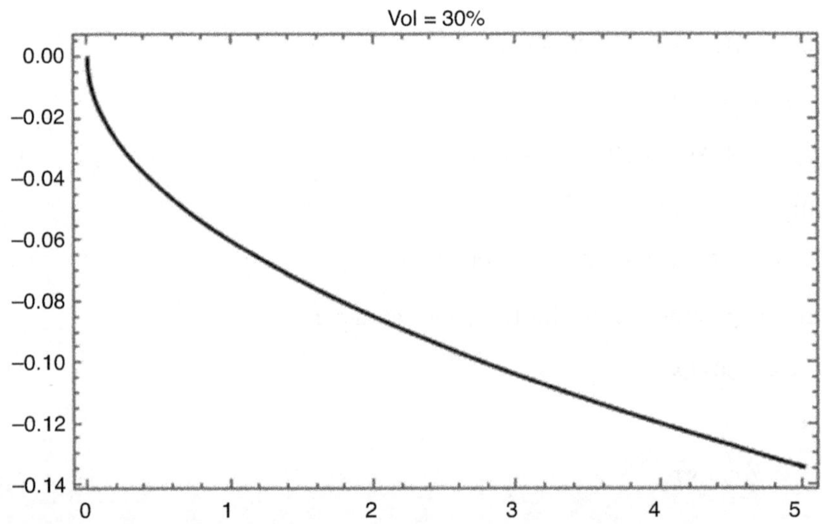

Figure 75 Delta Forward of an ATMF Straddle with Implied Volatility=30%

For a 16% ATMF implied volatility, we have Figure 74.

But for a 30% ATMF implied volatility (think 2008), we have Figure 75.

So your 2y ATM straddle is giving you a delta 40 call and a delta 60 put ... and the symmetry around the ATM implicit in the simple Malz formula is gone.

Also the deltas for onshore and offshore options with the same strike are not the same.

And the 10 deltas trade higher than the expected values given the 25 deltas and a quadratic model.

We're going to need a better model and more inputs.

If you want the same number of inputs and a different model, one could try the Vanna-Volga model (see *FX Options and Smile Risk* (Castagna, 2010)). Similar heuristics are used in United States Patent 7315838, filled by SuperDerivatives. One can see also the works of Uwe Wystup, like the paper available on this link: http://mathfinance2.com/mf_website/useranonymous/company/papers/wystup_vannavolga_eqf.pdf. These models focus also on the adjustments needed to price exotics.

Another choice is what Murex calls the Tremor Model, in which the 15 deltas are the inputs.

What do you need?

If all you want is a simplified model for some risk management and exact pricing is not needed, by all means use something simple like the Tremor Model, or maybe even try to fit Gatheral's SVI.

If you want to really delve into the mysteries of USDBRL options, pick up some sheets of paper, breathe deeply, and keep on reading.

Let's look again at market conventions, but now it is important to understand how the figures (Straddle, Strangles, Butterflies and Risk Reversals) are traded.

1. Straddle:
   a. Used for the ATMF and priced with the ATMF implied volatility σ_{ATMF}
   b. Traded with no Delta Hedge (no NDF packaged together)
   c. But have a residual delta as described above and also depending on

$$TotalDelta = BlackDelta + Vega \cdot Gamma \cdot \frac{\partial \sigma}{\partial \delta} \tag{464}$$

   d. A Notional of USD 10MM (the standard size on a broker's screen) is equal to USD 5MM of an ATMF USD Call BRL Put and USD 5MM of an ATMF USD Put BRL Call
2. Strangle:
   a. Used within the Market Strangle (in fact a Butterfly) and priced with a volatility $\sigma_{STR} = \sigma_{ATMF} + \sigma_{FLY}$
   b. The chosen deltas (the pair {25, -25} or {10, -10}) is calculated using $\sigma_{STR} = \sigma_{ATMF} + \sigma_{FLY}$ and the unknown strikes; with that we find the strikes and the total value (in USD) of the strangle
   c. Traded with no Delta Hedge (no NDF packaged together)
   d. But might have a residual delta depending on the risk reversal and the parametrization of the dynamics of the implied volatility as Equation 464 shows

3. Butterfly:
   a. A Strangle priced with a volatility $\sigma_{STR} = \sigma_{ATMF} + \sigma_{FLY}$ against (opposite signs) a straddle priced with the ATMF implied volatility σ_{ATMF}
   b. Traded with no Delta Hedge (no NDF packaged together)
   c. The existence of a σ_{RR} will lead to different strikes for the 25 delta calls and puts in practice; what matters is that the total value (in USD) of the fly is the same both with the traded volatilities and the model volatilities
4. Risk Reversal:
   a. Long (Short) an OTM USD Call BRL Put and Short (Long) an OTM USD Put BRL Call, priced with volatilities:

      - $\sigma_C = \sigma_{ATMF} + \frac{1}{2} \cdot \sigma_{RR} + \sigma_{FLY}$
      - $\sigma_P = \sigma_{ATMF} - \frac{1}{2} \cdot \sigma_{RR} + \sigma_{FLY}$

   b. The chosen deltas (the pair {25, -25} or {10, -10}) is calculated using σ_C and σ_P and the unknown strikes; with that we find the strikes and the total value (in USD) of the risk reversal
   c. Traded with a Delta Hedge (a NDF packaged together with a Notional in USD equal to the opposite delta, but with the opposite sign, trying its best to hedge the options)
   d. But might have a residual delta depending on the risk reversal and the parametrization of the dynamics of the implied volatility as Equation 464 shows
   e. Again, the cost equation will say that what matters is that the total value (in USD) of the risk reversal is the same both with the traded volatilities and the model volatilities

Now, you might have a really nice superinterpolation method, but it has to obey a simple rule: It needs to price correctly the traded structures above.

So just the 25 delta structures will generate 2 cost equations (one for the volatilities and strikes for the Risk Reversal and another for the volatilities and strikes for the Butterfly). In each cost equation the options are priced using the parameters of your pricer and the total value. Whatever you have programed (or bought) within your model, it must price correctly the traded structures.

With just 25 deltas, you need two parameters beyond the ATMF. With 25 and 10 deltas, you need 4 parameters beyond the ATMF.

Your choice of parametrization for the curve (implied volatility as a function of delta) must have some properties:

- Quick to calculate (to calculate a delta you need a volatility, but to know the volatility you need the delta, ...)
- In delta space it should look like Figure 73; it should have only one value of the delta for which the derivative of the implied volatility as a function of delta is equal to zero.

- It should not allow arbitrages:
  - USD Calls with lower strikes (expressed as BRL per USD) should we worth more
  - No butterfly should be worth less than zero
- This asks for some smoothness and therefore one should avoid cubic splines; the warning about looking for the real meaning of the numbers (a representation of something that follows a process) is very useful here. Some kind of polynomial interpolation and some dampening to avoid kinks might be the best solution.
- But then again a curve like Figure 73 will not necessarily give you good results for lower delta values. This kind of curve generates an inverted omega in volatility as a function of strike, with a flattening happening too early. One might need an alternative such as SABR, on increasing the 10 delta Flies. Not a single best answer here (besides "Thou shall not sell 2 or 3 deltas" as a matter of principle).

13.1.3 The locals are friendly

Now that we know how to approach the interpolation problem for a particular maturity, we will worry about interpolating those slices.

The first step is to interpolate ATMs looking at the implied 1-day forward volatilities. Try to avoid imaginary forward volatilities. The easiest way to do it is to calculate the effective variance and interpolate and extrapolate in that space. The monotonicity of this curve will help in avoiding kinks.

One can also look at the local volatility, less as an interpolation method and more as a monitor of possible arbitrages.

These include:

$$\frac{\partial c}{\partial K} > 0 \tag{465}$$

$$\frac{\partial^2 c}{\partial K^2} > 0 \tag{466}$$

$$\frac{\partial c}{\partial (T-t)} > 0 \tag{467}$$

One trick involves calculating local volatilities which are noisy; smooth the local volatility surface with a filter, then come back to the implied volatility space and recalculate the implied volatility based on the new and smoothed local volatility. Sometimes just 5bp here and there can help.

But to interpolate between known slices (standard NDF and options expiries) outside the ATMF strikes involves choices. The first choice is: interpolate parameters and create a new slice with interpolated parameters (like RR and FLY), interpolate outright implied volatilities and then try to extract parameters or interpolate effective variances? The best choice seems to be to interpolate effective variances, and here the particular method to find an intermediate point in the surface could use either the delta or the strike as the space for the interpolation. Using delta and monitoring the result in both strike and delta might be reasonable.

For the ATMF, we already saw that longer-dated straddles have deltas that deviate significantly from 0.50; this presents a challenge, because market flies/strangles can become negative. Why? Because the ATMF will be much closer to the 25 delta (USD) call than to the 25 delta (USD) put; if the Risk Reversal is high, this effect will increase. So, because we are taking (due to the slope or RR) more vol from the ATM to arrive at the 25 delta put than we're adding to arrive at the 25 delta call, the market strangle will be negative.

Large skews (values of RR) do "skew up" the smile calculations in this and other ways.

How high can the skew go? We remember the 10 delta 1y Risk Reversal trading at 41% in the 2008/2009 crisis, corresponding to the 10 delta USD put trading at 20% (a strike closer to 2.00 than to 2.50) and the 10 delta USD Call trading at 61% volatility (strike 5.92 or something close to it) and a 3% premium.

13.1.4 Thin tails wagging the dogs

The best source for managing barrier risks is still *Dynamic Hedging* (Taleb, 1997), and what we have to add is simple. Sometimes the BRL has appreciated more than the government desired, and the BCB acted in a way that led the market to believe that a particular level was seen by the BCB as an informal floor (something like 3.10, 2.00, 1.55 – this led to the IOF, etc.). This has an effect in the market dynamics, and a particular trade became very popular: customers (hedge funds) buying Reverse Knock-Out USD Puts with short maturities (1 to 3 months).

An example of the evolution of a RKO is in Figure 76; when it hits the barrier the option is in the money. The trick is to ask for an option where the barrier is a bit below the informal floor and wait for the theta, the friend of hedge funds and foe of banks' exotic desks.

The (usually high) Risk Reversal conspires to make this option cheaper; dealers buying Risk Reversal from customers through RKOs, OTM USD calls is a common theme, and leads to a crowded market of sellers of Risk Reversal when times are good. A common trade is also one when the dealer is selling a USD Put Spread ATMF x ATMS, and the theta here is mainly due to the carry (interest rate differential); we hope the reader remembers the discussion about how to roll the FX scenario: Spot same, Forward down.

In the same way that the NDF spread moved from positive to negative more than 10 years ago due mainly to demand for long BRL short USD positions, the

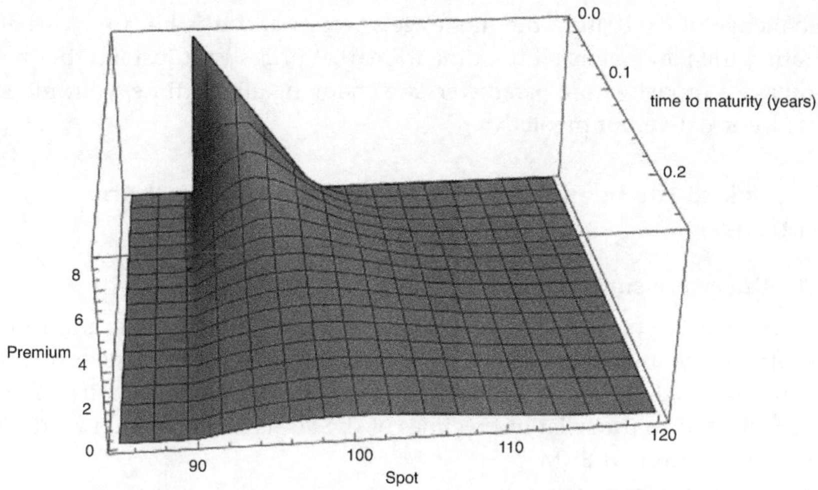

Figure 76 RKO, Strike 100, Barrier 90

volatility surface is not simply an unbiased estimator of future volatility or simply a reflex of historical volatility: it responds to supply and demand.

In 2008, all corporates were selling TARFs or OTM USD Calls, and the RR was under heavy selling pressure. In a certain way, one could think of a contrarian strategy that identifies such a flow, and bets against it after 6 months of such flow, benefiting from lower prices for this bet.

13.1.5 The couple, decoupled

How to model the volatility of the spot and the forward? There are different ways to do it, but the most common is the Stochastic Local Volatility Model or SLVM. For USDBRL, this seems a bit of a hack. The original idea of SVMs (Stochastic Volatility Models) is that there are two random processes (the FX Spot and its instantaneous volatility) and that these two might be correlated. This typically explains the smile (the strangle premium), but not always the skew (the RR). That part is then fit through a local volatility mapping, as explaining the usually big skews is hard using a simple SVM.

Obviously introducing such a model has consequences:

1. A new dynamic for the the volatility given co-movements of Spot and instantaneous volatility will change the Total Delta for vanilla options
2. Exotic options will have (very) different prices (and hedges as well)

Is it better to "complicate" things in this way? The answer is yes, given the improvement in the hedge that is implicit in adopting a more realistic process. But any time we include more parameters and a more complicated dynamic, the challenge of calibrating the model gets worse; and it is fair to ask whether calibrating the parameters all the time to market prices isn't just another hack - if you have a model whose parameters are changing all the time, your model is neither informative nor predictive.

13.2 Back to the beginning (What is different in onshore FX options?)

13.2.1 Uncertain smile

Sticky deltas are typically used in FX due to the OTC parametrization of the traded structures, and sticky strikes are typically used in listed markets like equities. But as argued at *Regimes of Volatility* (Derman, 1998), this choice of deltas should be linked to the volatility regimes of the assets. What should we do with the listed FX options at BVMF?

There are several answers:

1. Build a grid for the listed maturities and strikes (like equities), find the implied vol for each strike individually without necessarily parameterizing the time slice or the surface ... not good (no dynamics, you'll probably be forced to use sticky strike)
2. Build a grid for the listed maturities and strikes (like equities), find the implied vol for each strike individually but try your best to fit a functional form for the time slice given some parameters (now you can use sticky delta)
3. Build a grid for the offshore maturities and strikes, change parameters to match the implied vol for each strike (try your best, exact fit is probably impossible) for each time slice (now you can use sticky delta)

The fact that you're using offshore dates and strikes doesn't mean the parameters will be the same (more on this later), but at least you can compare both.

13.2.2 Fixing the averaging

Now it's time to gather data ... a lot of data.

Start with all trades for the 1st and 2nd maturities of DOL (tick by tick data, but no need for orders - most of the time the DOL will move 1 tick at a time) with time stamps. Then the Casado (if you have intraday, nice. If not, try to get 3 or 4 intraday samples and the range (min and max).

Now it is time to measure the volatility of the currency using that data, and try to assign a value for the volatility of the gap between the closing price and the opening price of the following day.

Then measure the intraday volatility (use "A New Approach for the Dynamics of Ultra High Frequency Data: the Model with Uncertainty Zones" (Robert and Rosenbaum, 2011)), and use this method to estimate the volatility that is relevant for the PTAX (think about a process that run for 9 hours sampled every hour for the first 4 hours, then averaged).

By the time you finish, you will have:

1. An estimate of the appropriate overnight (gap) vol given the current volatility regime
2. An estimate of an hourly volatility
3. Some idea of the correlation between both (given the current volatility regime)

With those inputs, you can automate the pricing of an overnight option:

1. In the morning, you have:
   a. A full trading day
   b. An overnight gap
   c. 4 hours of trading and averaging
2. At the end of the day, you have:
   a. An overnight gap
   b. 4 hours of trading and averaging
3. At the start of the fixing date, you still have some value:
   a. 4 hours of trading and the averaging

The correct way to model this decay is by having the gap and hourly volatilities and correlation as an input, and let the system deal with the decay; changing a single input during the day and storing it just once (and the closing value, which is worse for interpolating to the next point) is not a good way to deal with this risk.

Also pay attention to the roll on the next to last business day of the month. For the last business day of the month, the second future is the one that moves in tandem with the spot; the first future will track the PTAX.

13.2.3 I'd risk everything

OTC options and structured products linked to FX left a trail of tears from 2005 to 2009, as corporates tried to benefit from a strong BRL. From a string of monthly forward settling strike options to a string of OTM USD Calls to the infamous TARF, corporates took on leverage to "lower" funding costs, hedge exports or just play. With improved registration at CETIP, now the governance around suitability and transparency for regulators is much improved these days.

Some OTC trades (with funds mainly) are cleared through BVMF, and barriers must be linked to the PTAX, which presents a bit of a challenge for modeling. Although there is a widely accepted discretization correction for discretely monitored barriers ("A Continuity Correction for Discrete Barrier Options" by Broadie and Glasserman, 1997), it is not a foregone conclusion that the same formula would apply for a barrier on the PTAX.

The solution?

Monte Carlo with the intraday volatility. Match Broadie and Glasserman's formula $\left(B_D = B_C \cdot \exp\left(\beta \cdot \sigma \cdot \sqrt{t}\right)\right)$ with the results of the intraday simulation. Once the simulation is calibrated, use it to calculate the PTAX (with the bigger sample and the averaging) and try to find the adequate multiplier to apply on the volatility (in fact, changing beta: $B_D = B_C \cdot \exp\left(\beta_{new} \cdot \sigma \cdot \sqrt{t}\right)$).

Chances are that you will find a discontinuity in the Present Value profile of such a product, as the Spot might be at a different value than the PTAX when it is established that the barrier was hit.

13.2.4 Look in the mirror

Ok, now we have:

1. Onshore
   a. "The Triangle": Spot, DOL (1st future), Casado
   b. DI1, OC1 and the realized spread between Selic and CDI
   c. The Cupom Cambial complex (DDI, FRC, SCS)
   d. Knowledge about the difference between DOL and a NDF
   e. A listed options market and a volatility surface (assume that it follows the offshore OTC structure for dates and parameters)
2. Offshore
   a. NDF prices and the relationship with the onshore forwards
   b. Different discounting practices depending on CSAs, venues
   c. A volatility surface (OTC structure for dates and parameters)

Now, we've seen triangle-like relationships among two trios: Spot, DOL and Casado, and Onshore NDFs, Offshore NDFs and the OnOff Spread. Is there anything similar for the onshore and offshore volatilities?

Let's start with the ATMFs. Why should they be different? Or, conversely, why should they be equal? Remember that the ATMF strike for the onshore surface is not the same as the ATMF strike for the offshore surface. In a simple world where volatility is flat and the OnOff Spread is constant (by constant we mean the rate per year is constant; the ratio between the Offshore and the Onshore NDFs would be equal to $(1+Spread)^{T-\tau}$ and therefore the average ratio is close to $(1+Spread)^{\frac{T-\tau}{2}}$. One could expect the ratio of the ATMF volatilities to be at least this value; adding stochasticity to the spread and guessing a covariance matrix should perhaps add an additional spread between the ATMF vols.

Now the fun begins. Remember all the ink spilled about parametrization of volatility by delta? Well, a 25 delta offshore is not the same thing as a 25 delta onshore.

Onshore the 25 delta strike is determined using:

$$\delta_{25c} = \phi \cdot N\left(\phi \cdot \left(\frac{\ln\left(\frac{F}{K}\right) + \frac{\sigma_{25c}^2 t}{2}}{\sigma_{25c}\sqrt{t}}\right)\right) = 0.25 \tag{468}$$

And substituting:

$$\sigma_{25c} = ATM + \frac{1}{2} \cdot RR + ST \tag{469}$$

We have:

$$\left(\frac{\ln\left(\frac{F}{K}\right) + \frac{\sigma_{25c}^2 t}{2}}{\sigma_{25c}\sqrt{t}} \right) = NInv(0.25) \tag{470}$$

Then:

$$\ln\left(\frac{F}{K}\right) = NInv(0.25) \cdot \sigma_{25c}\sqrt{t} - \frac{\sigma_{25c}^2 t}{2} \tag{471}$$

$$\left(\frac{F}{K}\right) = \exp\left(NInv(0.25) \cdot \sigma_{25c}\sqrt{t} - \frac{\sigma_{25c}^2 t}{2}\right) \tag{472}$$

$$K_{25c} = F \cdot \exp\left(-NInv(0.25) \cdot \sigma_{25c}\sqrt{t} + \frac{\sigma_{25c}^2 t}{2}\right) \tag{473}$$

$$K_{25c} = F \cdot \exp\left(-NInv(0.25) \cdot \sigma_{25c}\sqrt{t}\right) \cdot \exp\left(+\frac{\sigma_{25c}^2 t}{2}\right) \tag{474}$$

Which is a nice formula.
Offshore we have:

$$\delta_{25c} = -\left(\frac{K}{F}\right) \cdot N\left(-1 \cdot \left(\frac{\ln\left(\frac{K}{F}\right) + \frac{\sigma_{25c}^2 t}{2}}{\sigma_{25c}\sqrt{t}}\right)\right) = 0.25 \tag{475}$$

$$\left(-\frac{\ln\left(\frac{K}{F}\right) + \frac{\sigma_{25c}^2 t}{2}}{\sigma_{25c}\sqrt{t}}\right) = NInv\left(0.25 \cdot \frac{F}{K}\right) \tag{476}$$

$$\ln\left(\frac{K}{F}\right) = -NInv\left(0.25 \cdot \frac{F}{K}\right) \cdot \sigma_{25c}\sqrt{t} - \frac{\sigma_{25c}^2 t}{2} \tag{477}$$

$$\left(\frac{K}{F}\right) = \exp\left(-NInv\left(0.25 \cdot \frac{F}{K}\right) \cdot \sigma_{25c}\sqrt{t} - \frac{\sigma_{25c}^2 t}{2}\right) \tag{478}$$

$$K_{25c} = F \cdot \exp\left(-NInv\left(0.25 \cdot \frac{F}{K_{25c}}\right) \cdot \sigma_{25c}\sqrt{t} - \frac{\sigma_{25c}^2 t}{2}\right) \tag{479}$$

$$K_{25c} = F \cdot \exp\left(-NInv\left(0.25 \cdot \frac{F}{K_{25c}}\right) \cdot \sigma_{25c}\sqrt{t}\right) \cdot \exp\left(-\frac{\sigma_{25c}^2 t}{2}\right) \tag{480}$$

Which is not a nice formula (the strike is in both sides, and buried in the Inverse Cumulative Normal.

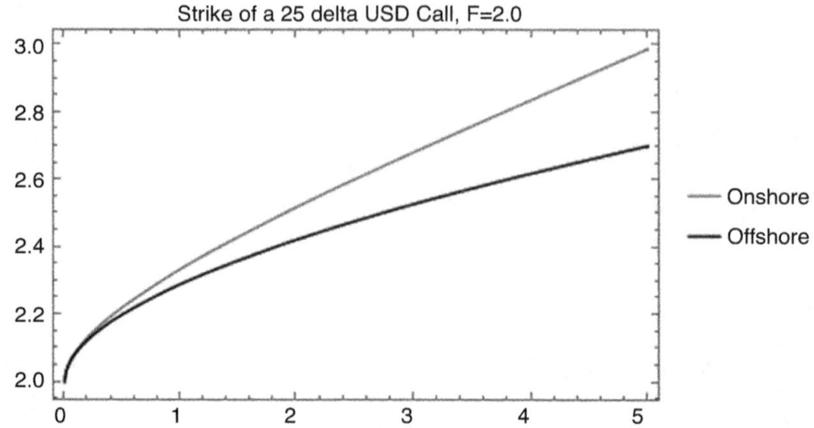

Figure 77 Strikes for a 25 delta USD Call

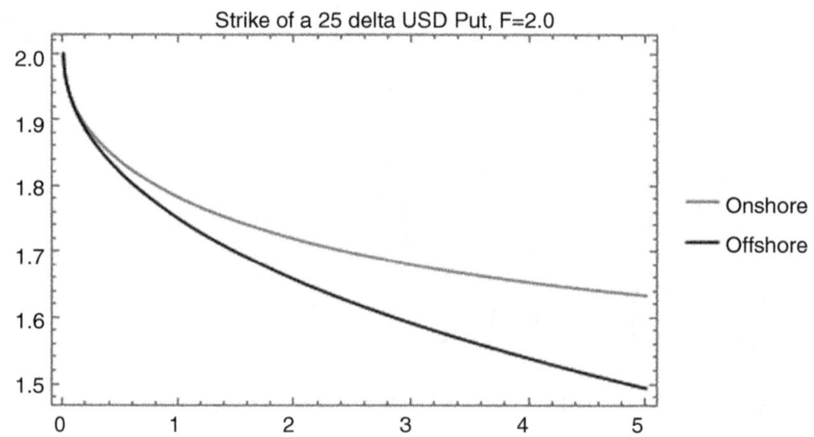

Figure 78 Strikes for a 25 delta USD Put

But Ok, this is why computers were invented, so they can run Newton-Raphson for us. A simple example from 2009 with: $F = 1.8592$; $\sigma = 20.70\%$; $t = \frac{94}{365}$; $\delta = +0.25$ returns K=2.00675 for the onshore 25 delta strike and K=1.99624 for the offshore 25 delta strike (with the same forward). And this gets worse with time (Figures 77 and 78).

And it is not only in the 25 or 10 deltas that we have a problem; coming back to the ATMFs, the deltas for the onshore options are determined by:

$$\delta_{ATMF} = \phi \cdot N\left(\phi \cdot \left(\frac{\ln\left(\frac{F}{K}\right) + \frac{\sigma_{ATMF}^2 t}{2}}{\sigma_{ATMF}\sqrt{t}}\right)\right); K = F \tag{481}$$

$$\delta_{ATMF} = \phi \cdot N\left(\phi \cdot \left(\frac{\sigma_{ATMF}\sqrt{t}}{2}\right)\right) \tag{482}$$

For the offshore options we have:

$$\delta_{ATMF} = -\frac{K}{F} \cdot \phi \cdot N\left(-\phi \cdot \left(\frac{\ln\left(\frac{K}{F}\right) + \frac{\sigma_{ATMF}^2 t}{2}}{\sigma_{ATMF}\sqrt{t}}\right)\right); K = F \tag{483}$$

$$\delta_{ATMF} = -\phi \cdot N\left(-\phi \cdot \left(\frac{\sigma_{ATMF}\sqrt{t}}{2}\right)\right) \tag{484}$$

From Equation 375, we can write for the onshore ATMF options:

$$\delta_{ATMF} = \phi \cdot \left(\frac{1}{2} + 0.4 \cdot \phi \cdot \left(\frac{\sigma_{ATMF}\sqrt{t}}{2}\right)\right) \tag{485}$$

And for the offshore ATMF options:

$$\delta_{ATMF} = -\phi \cdot \left(\frac{1}{2} - 0.4 \cdot \phi \cdot \left(\frac{\sigma_{ATMF}\sqrt{t}}{2}\right)\right) \tag{486}$$

Expanding, we have for the onshore options:

$$\delta_{ATMF} = \phi \cdot \frac{1}{2} + \left(0.4 \cdot \left(\frac{\sigma_{ATMF}\sqrt{t}}{2}\right)\right) \tag{487}$$

So onshore USD Calls have a delta greater than 0.5, and onshore USD puts have a negative delta with an absolute value lower than 0.5.

And for the offshore options:

$$\delta_{ATMF} = -\phi \cdot \frac{1}{2} + \left(0.4 \cdot \left(\frac{\sigma_{ATMF}\sqrt{t}}{2}\right)\right) \tag{488}$$

So offshore USD Calls have a delta lower than 0.5, and offshore USD puts have a negative delta with an absolute value greater than 0.5.

In delta space, the ATMFs are in different parts of the curve in relation with the 25 deltas. The whole set of reference points is shifted

Well, we played with algebra long enough, and just spoke about problems. What about solutions?

It should be clear that:

1. In the offshore markets the parameters (ATMF, RR, ST) are directly observable and liquid (screens)
2. Once the NDF OnOff Spread is accounted for, the two surfaces should present a small offset, more like a small parallel shift and a small sideways move
3. The curves should have approximately the same shape (easier said than done); after all, the dynamics of the spot should be the same for both
4. Therefore, the parameters used in the interpolation of the onshore should not be the same as the parameters used on the offshore interpolation; they should be a function of the whole offshore curve

Imagine the offshore world according to Malz. You have:

$$\sigma(\delta) = ATM - 2 \cdot RR \cdot \left(\delta - \frac{1}{2}\right) + 16 \cdot ST \cdot \left(\delta - \frac{1}{2}\right)^2 \tag{489}$$

And also:

$$\delta = -\frac{K}{F} \cdot \phi \cdot N\left(-\phi \cdot \left(\frac{\ln\left(\frac{K}{F}\right) + \frac{\sigma^2 t}{2}}{\sigma\sqrt{t}}\right)\right) \tag{490}$$

For $\phi = -1$ we have:

$$\delta = \frac{K}{F} \cdot N\left(\frac{\ln\left(\frac{K}{F}\right) + \frac{\sigma^2 t}{2}}{\sigma\sqrt{t}}\right) \tag{491}$$

So we can think that first we determine the curve of the volatility as a function of the delta by calculating a series of points corresponding to intervals (from delta 1 to 0). Like Figure 79.

Replacing the delta of the In-The-Money call by the delta of the OTM put, we find Figure 80.

Then we determine the strike corresponding to each pair {delta, volatility} (Figure 81) and find the chart (or grid) of the implied volatility as a function of the strike in Figure 82 and by changing the time to maturity to build the grid or surface.

The most important thing to notice in Figure 82 is how the implied volatility flattens after (or before) a high enough (or low enough) strike. That is a shortcoming of this model, and one could use alternative interpolation methods like SABR or SVI for extrapolation; it is better to use formulas that have been proved to avoid arbitrage than to extrapolate blindly.

Now we found the implied volatility per strike for the offshore market. How should we reconcile this curve with the onshore market? We have already discussed how the strikes are not the same for the same delta even if both forwards are the same (Figures 83, 84 and 85).

Ok, this is pure Malz (ATM = 50 delta), but we already saw how different the deltas of the ATMF are from an onshore and an offshore perspective. The

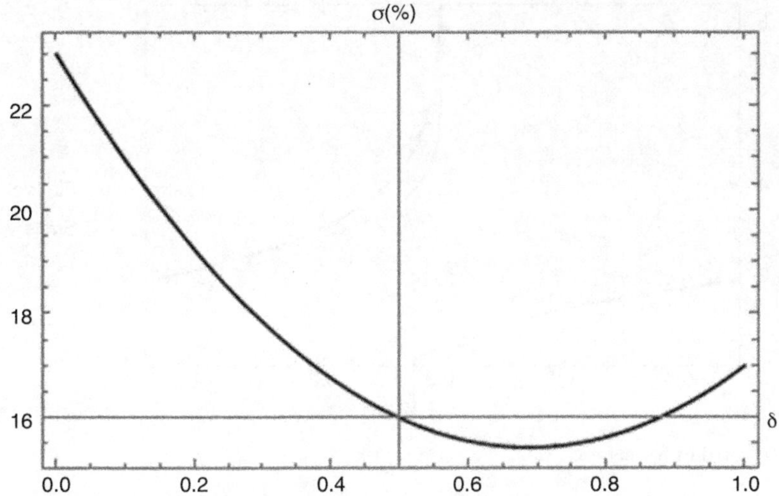

Figure 79 Interpolation according to Malz; (ATM, RR, ST)=(16, 3, 1)%

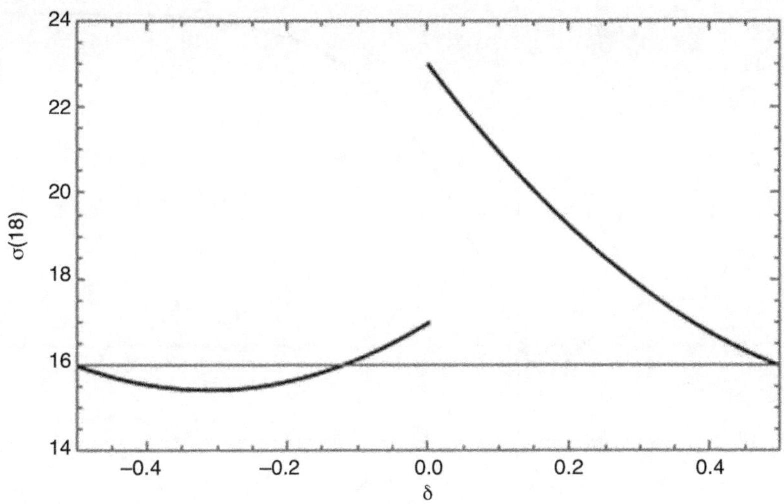

Figure 80 Modified Malz Interpolation

difference increases with time to maturity and with volatility (they're always together, of course), and it is easy to see how managing a book with both onshore and offshore options becomes interesting.

So using the same parameters for a delta-based interpolation will not produce the same smile. For the values used in the last charts (ATM=16%, RR=3%, ST=1%)

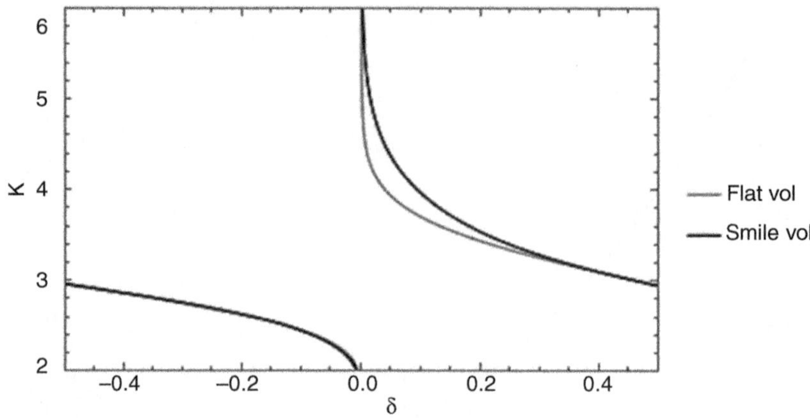

Figure 81 Strikes for each delta

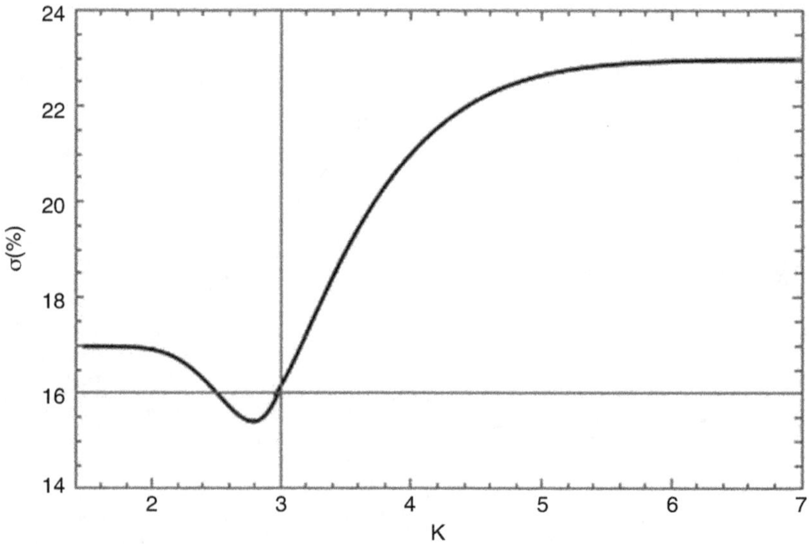

Figure 82 Implied volatility as a function of strike

the effect was not that dramatic, but what happens when ATM is 35% and RR is 20%? One might have to adjust the onshore parameters so the curves are rising and falling at more or less the same strikes, and the distance between the curves is not bigger than it should be.

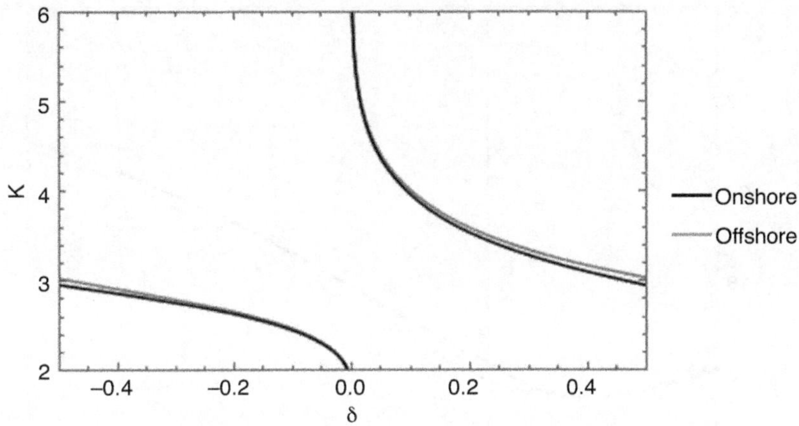

Figure 83 Strikes for Deltas (Onshore and Offshore)

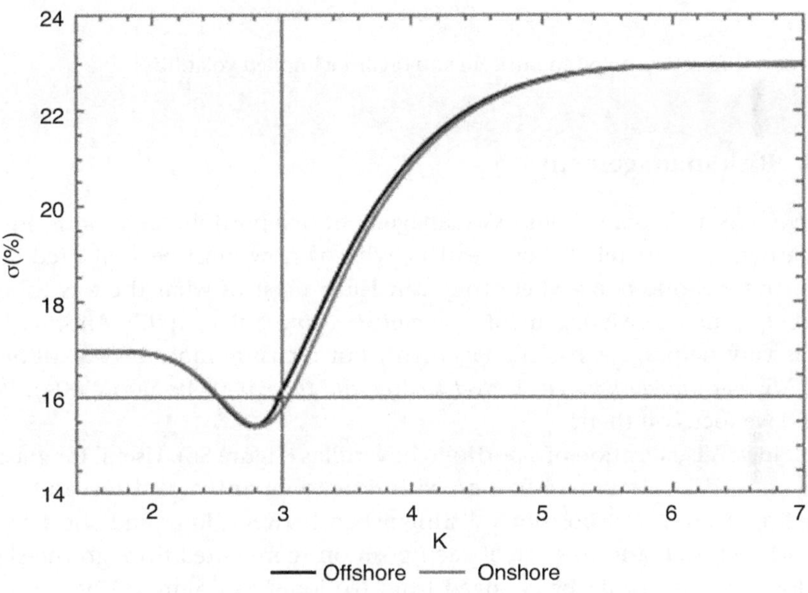

Figure 84 Implied volatility (Onshore and Offshore)

This is critical when RR is high; you need ST high enough that there is some smile, not only a smirk - or at least a flat curve on the left for lower strikes. This is where some other parametrization like SVI, SVI-JW and variants might help: drawing a curve that seems reasonable might be easier with this model. File fitting both curves in a reasonable way under "art, not a science".

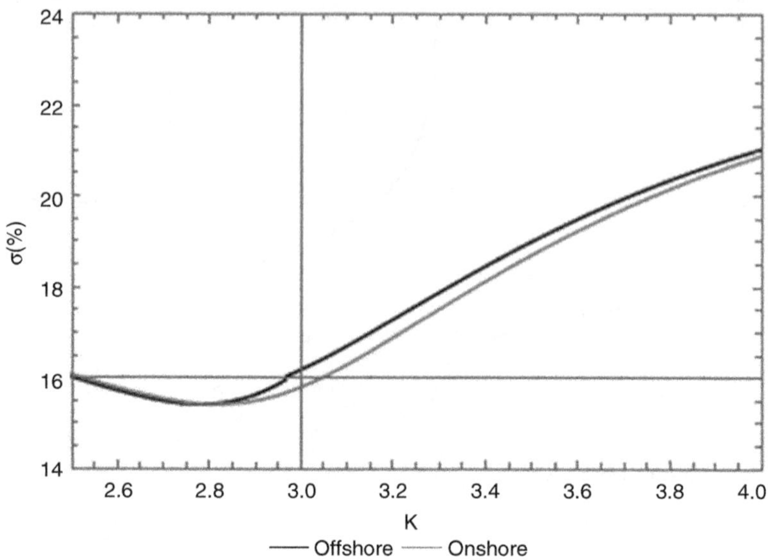

Figure 85 Differences between onshore and offshore implied volatilities

13.3 Risk management

There is a lot to be said about risk management of a portfolio of options, including barriers. Fortunately for our readers, who by now must be a bit tired of our jokes, there is one book where they can learn most of what there is to know about Options Risk Management: *Dynamic Hedging* (Taleb, 1997). Another book that is very helpful for risk management, but focusing more on volatilities, is *Volatility and Correlation: The Perfect Hedger and the Fox* (Rebonato, 2004). What should we focus on then?

First idea: Visualization of a portfolio of vanillas (Figure 86). Useful for grasping at a glance concentration of fixings, with time to maturity (or dates) and strikes providing a grid, and positions distinguished between long and short by the color of each dot, and the size of each position represented through the size of the dot. This size could be changed from Notional to Gamma, Vega, or other variable of interest.

We can also add more information to this chart with lines showing the strikes for the ATMF, 25 delta and 10 delta (Figure 87).

In fact, the placement of the ATMF, 25 delta and 10 delta strikes is perhaps the main risk from a modeling perspective for a book of vanillas. When the RR increases, the distance between these points increases much more on the USD Call side than in the USD Put side. This can be seen clearly in Figure 83, where in the USD Call side the range of strikes is quite wide compared with the

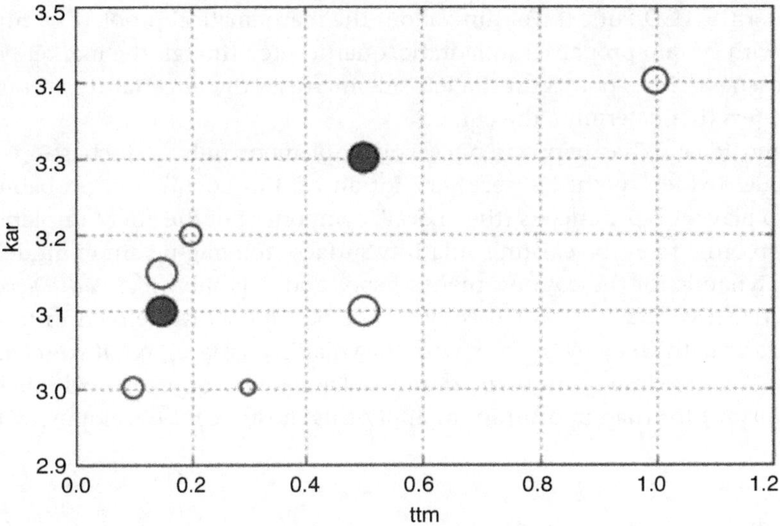

Figure 86 Visualization of vanillas

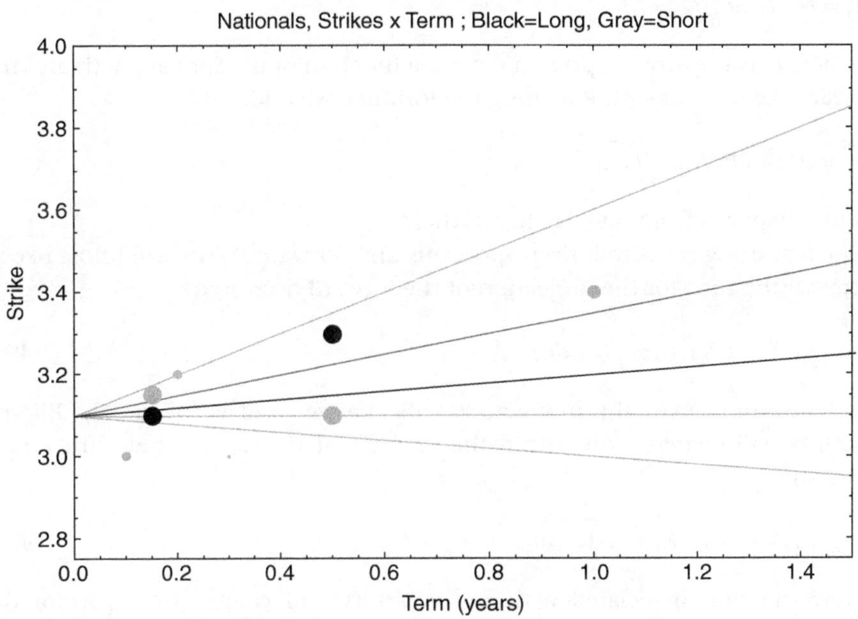

Figure 87 Vanillas and strikes

range for the USD Puts. If we think about the mathematical problem of fitting a curve with certain properties (quadratic, quartic, etc.) though the market points, the closeness of the points on the left side increases the uncertainty around the parameters that determine the curve.

Second idea: What happens once you implement fully a stochastic volatility model (which might be necessary for an exotics book)? You probably still need to play with parameters (the "Local" component of the SLVM implementations) in order to fit the existing volatility surface. You might gain in modeling a better dynamic for the co-movement of spot and volatility (like *Path-Dependent Volatility* (Guyon, 2014), which is by far the best model we've seen in terms of linking the path taken by the spot with the volatility surface), but if your "adjustments" are more important than your model you have not progressed much. We look forward for the opportunity to apply this most recent development to FX options.

13.4 Risk and P&L attribution

Let's go back to the 3 Ts and look at how the PV of a FX Option changes from one day (i) to the next day (j).

$$c_i = c(F_i, K, \sigma_i \sqrt{t_{\sigma,i}}, df_i) \tag{492}$$

Where F_i is the forward price at day (i), a function of the Spot at day(i) and the Forward Points at day (i). Rewriting the formula, we find:

$$c_i = c(S_i + FP_i, K, \sigma_i \sqrt{t_{\sigma,i}}, df_i) \tag{493}$$

What happens from one day to another?

The first thing is the roll. Keep Spot constant, Forward Points will (most likely) decrease (the time for the projection of the forward decreased):

$$c_{j,1} = c(S_i + FP_{j,1}, K, \sigma_i \sqrt{t_{\sigma,i}}, df_i) \tag{494}$$

As a consequence, the moneyness will change, and with our big RR the volatility will change (still within the scenario at the day (i), but with a new forward):

$$c_{j,2} = c(S_i + FP_{j,1}, K, \sigma_{j,2} \sqrt{t_{\sigma,i}}, df_i) \tag{495}$$

Now the time associated with the volatility will change (one part of the traditional theta):

$$c_{j,3} = c(S_i + FP_{j,1}, K, \sigma_{j,2} \sqrt{t_{\sigma,j,3}}, df_i) \tag{496}$$

And with the new time associated there will be a new volatility (mainly through the backbone of the ATMFs):

$$c_{j,4} = c(S_i + FP_{j,1}, K, \sigma_{j,4}\sqrt{t_{\sigma,j,3}}, df_i) \tag{497}$$

And finally there's a new time associated with the discounting (the second part of the traditional theta):

$$c_{j,5} = c(S_i + FP_{j,1}, K, \sigma_{j,4}\sqrt{t_{\sigma,j,3}}, df_{j,5}) \tag{498}$$

Phew! And the market has not opened yet! The main message is that due to the roll and the slope of the volatility surface we will have an unexpected theta (that can be estimated by calculating the slope of the volatility surface). All calculations against the closing price should start from this last formula. And there you have the most interesting of risks: The interplay of the high forward points and the high risk reversal. The secret for that relationship would make for a really good paper. Because good and synchronized data is typically not shared outside each institution, we'll avoid this kind of analysis in the book for now, but please note that it applies to forwards as well.

14
Some Cash is Better Than Nothing – What you Need to Know about Cash Products

Describing bonds and their relationship with the derivatives markets.

14.1 Local government bonds

14.1.1 Floating to the top – LFTs

There's nothing like Brazil's LFT (Letra do Tesouro Financeiro) to describe one of Brazil's economic problems (high interest rates on government debt making other investments look risky and unattractive).

This bond is a dream come true:

1. A floater, it accrues the Selic rate, so virtually no market risk (it might trade at a discount, though, as in 2001)
2. No other credit risk beyond the government, who can print money
3. Not much of a liquidity risk; it can be used as collateral on repurchase agreements with the BCB an the haircut is quite low
4. Bullet, no intermediate coupon payments subject to taxes

With these characteristics, it is easy to understand why it epitomizes Brazil's relative privileges for the rentiers: A government bond without market, credit or liquidity risk paying a high interest rate should not exist.

Although the government is trying to decrease the participation of these floaters within the total government debt, there is still a good chunk of money on overnight reverse repos (banks lending overnight to the BCB).

14.1.2 The name of the game – LTNs and NTN-Fs

Nominal rates, short and bullet (LTNs) or longer with semiannual 10% coupons (NTN-Fs), also know as Fixed-rate securities. Coupon fixed rates are in exponential accrual method with 30360 DCB (in order to guarantee a perfect 0.5 year day count fraction between 01-Jan and 01-Jul which are the coupon start and end dates). One interesting project would be to look at weekly intraday patterns in DI1 rates, as these mysteriously go up before weekly auctions, most of the time returning to previous levels after the results. Liquidity on the DI1 curve is typically related to the amount of bonds issued for that particular maturity date (2017, 2021).

14.1.3 Making it real – NTN-Bs

Real rates and a certain leap of faith (with maturities beyond 30 years). NTN-Bs pays coupons and principal linked to IPCA index, and because the IPCA

- (1) it is the index used in the inflation targeting regime
- (2) is less volatile than the IGP-M (3)

was chosen by the Treasury as the bond to be promoted while its brother, the NTN-C, is no longer issued (it paid linked to IGP-M instead of IPCA).

14.1.4 Living fossils – NTN-As

USD-linked and with funky cashflows, began life as the result of an exchange of old sovereign debt (EI Bonds and such). Not really liquid, and USD-indexed bonds (NTN-Ds) are no longer issued.

14.1.5 Reading the fine print

More details can be found at the BCB's website (http://www.bcb.gov.br/htms/demab/Domestic%20Federal%20Securities%20Characteristics.pdf). Most of these bonds will be priced by banks in Bloomberg; in Brazil, Anbima will publish reference prices as well (http://portal.anbima.com.br/informacoes-tecnicas/precos/taxas-tit-publicos/Pages/sobre.aspx). Be always aware of the tax treatment of the FX trades to buy them, and about what happens with coupon payments.

If you are trading at BVMF, most likely you are buying one of these bonds to deposit as margin (cash will not receive interest), and we think that by now you know that interest rates are high in Brazil; so be familiar with all the processes related to buying, holding and selling them, and receiving interest.

Some indices were developed using theoretical portfolios of bonds, like the IMA; because the IMA became popular, there is some demand to create an official (listed) market for it.

But alas! Values involved are high, but there is almost no secondary market in local government bonds, and weekly auctions don't really help in creating an environment that appeals enough for market-makers to invest time and money. The market (and associated CCP) for government bonds organized by BVMF never really took off.

14.2 Local corporate bonds

Well, if the secondary market for government bonds is not liquid, this "market" is more like a quagmire. Quotes will be published daily by Anbima, but a part of these securities could fail a more rigorous criteria of diversification among holders in order to classify as a traded security.

Most of these securities end up paying CDI + spread; good luck trying to attribute a stand-alone credit spread based in the information coming from these bonds. They will respond to major news and events, it is hard to observe changes on a day-to-day basis.

14.3 Local funding practices

Most banks issue CDs (known as CDBs) or LFs (longer term securities), paying a percentage of CDI. Some securities (like LCIs) pay less than 100% of the CDI because of their tax-exempt status. The use of cash as collateral is rare; securities like government bonds are the preferred collateral (composing more than 80% of the collateral deposited at BVMF).

14.4 Offshore government and corporate bonds

Brazil has a long history of sovereign debt (and problems paying it), but with international reserves at a relatively high level this ceased to be a sword hanging over the country. Of interest to us is what happens when the country issues a offshore sovereign bond denominated in BRL (like the BR 16 BRL bond, issued in 2005). The fact that it doesn't have any tax payments and that it has probably a larger number of potential investors than NTN-Fs might make it trade at a premium compared with the alternatives and curves discussed up to now.

As for offshore corporate bonds, they are always an interesting alternative of funding for local companies because of lower interest payments when compared to the local interest rates. They are important because of the associated flow of resources into the country when they are issued, and also because there is sometimes a demand for hedge associated with the maturity of these bonds that can distort the Cupom Cambial curve.

14.5 Liquidity (or lack thereof)

Most of the time, trading in bonds will react to market information from derivatives, not the opposite. If you plan on trading bonds and completed your training in the most recent developments of Brazil's arcane tax system, be aware that for big dislocations of rates the government will conduct auctions in which it will buy back bonds from investors, giving them a chance to avoid the illiquidity premium when exiting positions. That is why sometimes it is easier to hedge the exposure with derivatives and then try to unwind the package than just try and unwind the bonds position at once.

14.6 The Brazilian Repo market (Compromissadas)

In the onshore Brazilian market, a repo transaction, also called "compromissada," can be executed against Brazil Central Bank or against a bank. Here, we will describe the "compromissada" transaction against Brazil Central Bank, since the "compromissadas" done against banks may vary slightly between different banks.

All "compromissadas" are repo transactions collateralized with Brazil goverment bonds where the "compromissada" buyer gives cash to Brazil Central Bank and selects a minimum of 4 Brazil goverment bonds as collateral. The weights of each one of the selected goverment bonds are then defined and sent to Brazil Central Bank with a maximum weight of 25% of invested cash per selected goverment bond serving as collateral. The weights can vary from each selected goverment bond serving as collateral, always respecting the maximum weight per collateral bond of 25% mentioned above. The quantity of each one of the collateral bonds is defined based on a published unitary price released by BCB before the daily auction of "compromissadas".

The "compromissada" can be done with an O/N, 3M or 6M term currently. For the O/N type of "compromissada," the collateral can only be rehypothecathed to enter into another "compromissada" transaction. For the term "compromissada" of 3M and 6M, the collateral can be rehypothecated as the buyer wishes (could be sold in the bond market or posted as collateral at BVMF would be the most natural choices). The only condition is that at the end of the "compromissada" maturity, Brazil Central Bank gives back the original cash to the "compromissada" buyer adjusted by the repo rate, and the buyer of the "compromissada" delivers back to BCB the goverment bonds as collateral. Also, all "compromissada" trades are hold to maturity and cannot be early unwound.

The O/N type of "compromissada" is a spot transaction, meaning that the BCB auction occurs in the morning and the "compromissada" buyer has to deliver cash to BCB at transaction date t. Also, BCB has to post the goverment bonds as collateral also at transaction date t. The last step involves BCB having to deliver the adjusted cash back to the "compromissada" buyer at $t+1$, which is the next day in a CDI (and Selic) calendar. The term "compromissada" transactions of 3M and 6M are 1 day forward starting, meaning that the term "compromissada" buyer has to deliver cash one business day later than transaction date t in a CDI calendar. Also, goverment bonds serving as collateral will be posted on the "compromissada" buyer account at $t+1$ and maturity date (when BCB delivers cash adjusted back to the "compromissada" buyer) occurs 3M after the $t+1$ forward starting date.

There are 2 cases to adjust the cash to be paid back in the future by BCB. The easy case is when the collateral goverment bond doesn't pay any coupon during the period between the compromissada settlement date and its maturity date:

$$CashAdj_T = Cash_{t_s} \cdot (1 + Repo_{t_s,T})^{\tau^{252}_{ts,T}} \tag{499}$$

where,

t_S: is the "compromissada" settlement date, being the transaction date t for the O/N case and $t+1$ for the term "compromissada" case.

$CashAdj_T$: is the repo rate adjusted cash paid at "compromissada" maturity date T.

$Cash_{t_s}$: is the original cash paid by the "compromissada" buyer to BCB at settlement date t_s.

$Repo_{t_s,T}$: is the repo rate agreed in the transaction, that will be capitalized between settlement date t_s and maturity date T in Bus252 DCB.

The other case occurs when there's a coupon payment during the period between the compromissada settlement date and its maturity date:

$$CashAdj_T = Cash_{t_s} \cdot (1 + Repo_{t_s,T})^{\tau^{252}_{ts,T}} - C \cdot VNA_{t_c} \cdot (1 + Repo_{t_c,T})^{\tau^{252}_{tc,T}} \tag{500}$$

where,

t_C: is the collateral bond coupon payment date.

C: is the BRL cash payment of the collateral goverment bond, excluding any *VNA* adjustments. For NTN-Bs, it needs to be adjusted by VNA_{t_c}, which is the adjusted nominal value published by Anbima at coupon payment date t_C. The VNA adjustment represents the inflation correction to be paid over inflation coupon payments and is calculated as:

$$VNA_{t_c} = \frac{I_{t_c}}{I_{Issue}}$$

where,

I_{t_c}: is the IPCA index (not the monthly rate) published by IBGE

$I_{Issue} = 1614.62$ is the IPCA value effective for 15-Jul-2000.

NTN-Bs will be discussed in more detail in the next subsection for the interested reader.

For NTN-Fs, VNA is always equal to 1 and no adjustment needs to be done in the BRL coupon payments.

Typically, a rational investor would require the "compromissada" repo rate to have a premium over the regular goverment bond yield to allocate his cash for a term (could be up to 6M) in a hold to maturity fashion. But in Brazil there might be rare situations with large flow distortions that may not satisfy the rational investor condition stated above (unfortunately).

15
Index of Choice ... Inflation-Linked Products and Curves

In this section, we will first discuss government inflation linked bonds, more specifically NTNBs. We will describe how the coupons are paid and when they are paid, and explain the concept behind VNA, which is the updated nominal value, and the quoting convention for NTNBs.

The next subsection explains where inflation linked swaps are usually registered and their most usual payoffs. After that, it will be explained who's responsible for IGPM and IPCA indices publication and the lags that occur between their publication dates to effective dates.

15.1 Government Inflation-Linked Bonds

Government inflation linked bonds are NTNB's and NTNCs, but currently only NTNBs (Notas do Tesouro Nacional B) are liquid and we will only discuss them in this book. They are issued by Brazil National Treasury, pay semi-annual coupons linked to inflation based on a coupon rate $R = 6\%$, which is exponential based on 30360 DCB. Although many people in Brazil might think that it's based on Bus252 DCB, it must be on 30360 DCB in order to compute always exactly a 0.5 day count fraction between coupon accrual dates. For a 1 bond position, each i-th coupon payment is computed by:

$$Coupon[T_i] = 1,000 \cdot \left[(1+6\%)^{0.5} - 1\right] \cdot \frac{IPCA_{T_i}}{IPCA_{Issue}} \tag{501}$$

Principal payment for T_N date is calculated by:

$$Principal[T_N] = 1,000 \cdot \frac{IPCA_{T_N}}{IPCA_{Issue}} \tag{502}$$

where,

$IPCA_{Issue} = 1614.62$ is the IPCA value effective for 15-Jul-2000.

$IPCA_{T_i}$: is the IPCA value effective for date T_i related to the i-th coupon, which can be looked up in BBG BZCLVLUE historical prices (HP) page for every 15th day of the month.

Coupons and principal are paid based on the FOLLOWING rule in a CDI calendar for the end accrual date that falls on 15th day of coupon or principal payment months. NTNB's are traded for default settlement in $t+1$ in a CDI calendar, being t the trade date. But other settlement dates are possible like $t+2$, $t+3$ or any other case.

Their equivalent BRL face value for 1 bond is 1,000 BRL, but many market participants like to analyze the Updated Nominal Value (VNA), which is calculated by

$$1{,}000 \cdot \frac{IPCA_t}{IPCA_{Issue}} = VNA_t$$

VNA time series can be obtained at Anbima website and they have a procedure to obtain $IPCA_t$, which some market participants like to say it's the $IPCA$ spot value, based on last published IPCA value before trading date t based on:

$$IPCA_t = IPCA_{Last} \cdot (1 + IPCA_{Proj})^{\frac{\tau^{252}_{T_{Last},t}}{\tau^{252}_{T_{Last},T_{Next}}}} \tag{503}$$

where,

T_{Last}: 15th day of current month (if date of t is equal or greater than 15), or previous month (if date of t is smaller than 15).

T_{Next}: 15th day of current month (if date of t is smaller than 15), or next month (if date of t is equal or greater than 15).

$IPCA_{Last}$: is the last IPCA index published, effective for date T_{last}.

$IPCA_{Proj}$: is the IPCA monthly projection published on Anbima website.

$IPCA_t$: is the IPCA index projected for effective date t.

NTNBs quoting convention is based on yield and given by:

$$Price_t = 1{,}000 \cdot VNA_t \cdot \left(\sum_{T_i=1}^{N} \frac{\left[(1+6\%)^{0.5} - 1\right]}{(1+y)^{\tau^{252}_{t,T_i}}} + \frac{1}{(1+y)^{\tau^{252}_{t,T_N}}} \right) \tag{504}$$

where,

T_i: are the end accrual dates for the NTNB bond, that always fall in the 15th day of the respective coupon payment month.

y: NTNB exponential yield on a BUS252 DCB.

$Price_t$: price of NTNB for settlement at date t.

This quoting convention is used for any t, regardless of the settlement date of the NTNB. This is not strictly correct, as the price for other settlement dates, beside the default $t+1$ settlement, should be computed based on the default settlement price and then entering a repo transaction (Operação Compromissada).

The repo transaction would be described as selling the $t+1$ bond and buying the $t+2$ bond, and it's traded based on the repo rate, which is closely related to $Selic_t$ rate and is not related to y which is the bond yield. But given that quoting procedure is based on (504), one could still calculate it using the correct repo rate procedure adjusting $Price_t$, and goalseek later a yield to match the correct price.

15.2 Inflation-Linked Swaps

Inflation Swaps in Brazil can be linked to 2 different inflation indices, IPCA and IGPM. They are registered as OTC trades at CETIP or BVMF. When registered at BVMF, the exchange is responsible for any counterparty risk and will guarantee the payment of the swap payoff to the party which is expecting to receive the cashflow. Additionally, margin posting is required when the swap is traded on the exchange. On the other hand, the CETIP registered swap is not guaranteed and collateral posting can be achieved only when the 2 counterparties involved have a CSA agreement under the CGD (Contrato Global de Derivativos) between them.

Regarding inflation swaps, first we will discuss how the IGPM and IPCA publication occurs. Then we will discuss how their payoffs are computed. The next topic will highlight the fact that the IGPM and IPCA swap rates quoted in the market are usually dirty, except for a particular range of days of the month when swaps become trading forward starting.

Later it will be explained how the IGPM and IPCA swap market is organized, discussing the tenors usually traded and which ones have good liquidity.

The final topic explain different possible pricing models for inflation swaps with its pros and cons. Interpolation and seasonality will be also discussed. The last topic details how to calibrate jointly an IPCA curve with both NTN-B bond yields (subtracting the asset-swap spread) and IPCA swap quotes.

15.2.1 IGPM and IPCA publication

IGPM is published every month by FGV (Fundação Getúlio Vargas) 2 business days before the first business day of the month in a CDI calendar. So the May-2015 index will be published 2 business days in a CDI calendar before 1-Jun-2015, which is at 28-May-2015. The April-2015 IGPM index was published at 29-Apr-2015, which is 2 business days before 04-May-2015, since 01-May-2015 was a holiday and 02-May-2015 and 03-May-2015 were Saturday and Sunday .

The ratio of the May-2015 index to the April-2015 index gives the accrued monthly inflation effective from 04-May-2015 to 01-Jun-2015, which are the 2 first business days of each month in a CDI calendar. This feature of having an index published on a date and effective for some future date have similarities to FX Fixings, that when published in a date, usually represent exchange of cashflows happening in future dates because of the so-called fx settlement rules.

The foreign currency analogy approach uses this fact to build an inflation swap pricing model based on nominal and real rates.

The IPCA index is also published every month, but by IBGE (Instituto Brasileiro de Geografia e Estatística). But the publication dates don't follow a specific publication rule like in the IGPM case. The ratio of 2 IPCA indices published on adjacent months represent also the accrued monthly inflation, but effective from the 15th of one month to the 15th of the next month. Because it's not possible to obtain a publication rule that works for every month, the foreign currency analogy approach doesn't work as nicely for the IPCA curve calibration as for the IGPM case.

15.2.2 IGPM and IPCA swaps payoff

IGPM and IPCA swaps, when registered at BVMF, are usually zero coupon swaps. At Cetip it can be registered as a multi-cashflow swap. We will consider the payoff of zero coupon swaps because that's what have more liquidity, without any loss of generality. The payoff of an IGPM or IPCA receiver swap is given by:

$$Payoff_{BRL}[T] = \frac{Not_{BRL}}{I_{Last}} \cdot (1+R)^{\tau_{t,T}^{252}} \cdot I_T - Not_{BRL} \cdot CapFac_{Float}(t,T) \quad (505)$$

where,

$Payoff_{BRL}[T]$: is the payoff of the swap paid in BRL currency and settled at date T.

I_{Last}: is the last inflation index published before trade date t.

R: is the inflation exponential fixed leg swap rate in Bus252 DCB.

$\tau_{t,T}^{252}$: is the day count fraction from trade date t to swap maturity date T.

I_T: is the inflation index effective for maturity date$T$.

$CapFac_{Float}(t,T) = \prod_{T_i=t}^{T}\left[1+CDI_{T_i}\right]^{\frac{1}{252}}$ with the usual definition as in previous sections of this book.

It can be noticed by looking at (505) that the floating leg of both IPCA and IGPM swaps are floating and based on 100% CDI.

15.2.3 Dirty and Clean Rates ... again

We have seen previously that usually a cupom swap or a DDI Future trade a dirty rate because they are referenced to $PTAX_{t-1}$, which is set before trading/pricing date t. The same occurs for IGPM and IPCA swaps. They are referenced by I_{Last}, which is set before trading/pricing date t as well. One example would be an IGPM swap traded on 20-Apr-2015. The last published IGPM index seen on 20-Apr-2015 was published on 30-Mar-2015, which is already 20 days old.

15.2.4 Trading conventions for IGPM and IPCA swaps. Are they liquid?

Interbank trading for both IGPM and IPCA swaps is done via broker and registered usually at BVMF. Client trades are usually registered at CETIP and there's a larger flow of interbank trades than client trades.

The IGPM swap market usually quotes as the first tenor a 1M swap. Its start accrual date is at pricing date t and maturity date is one month later, adjusted by FOLLOWING convention based on the CDI calendar. As an example, let's assume t to be 6-May-2015. 06-June-2015 is a business day in CDI calendar and the maturity date of the swap, namely T would be that date. So interest accrual on both inflation and floating leg of swap are from 06-May-2015 to 06-Jun-2015. Regarding inflation variation, the variable I_{Last} would be the IGPM index published on 29-Apr-2015 and I_T would be published on 28-May-2015, but effective for 01-June-2015.

Other so-called tenors traded in the market are 2M up to 1Y every month, even though interest accrual is usually shorter than so-called tenor, as will be explained. For the so-called 2M swap tenor, maturity date is obtained as the first business day in a CDI calendar from the month of date t added by 2M tenor. In our same example, maturity would be obtained, first by adding 2M tenor to 06-May-2015, which yields 06-Jul-2015. And the first business day of the month of 06-Jul-2015 is 01-Jul-2015, which would be the swap maturity date T. By doing this now interest accrual goes from t to T still, but I_T will be fixed at 29-Jun-2015, but effective for 01-Jul-2015 which is T also. The only variable now not aligned is I_{Last} which is different than t, published on 29-May-2015 but effective for 04-May-2015 and is what makes the swap rate to be dirty when trade date t is at 06-May-2015.

Summarizing, that example has a trade with less than 2 months of interest accrual computation, but approximately 2M of inflation lag between I_T and I_{Last}, except for the first business day adjustment that occured in that particular example (01-May-2015 was a holiday). The same procedure happens for swaps of longer tenors than 2M.

After the 1Y tenor, it's usually quoted only tenors that fall on January maturity months every year. So on 06-May-2015, after the 1Y tenor it's quoted the 1Y8M tenor, which has as maturity date 02-Jan-2017. The next would be 2Y8M tenor and this procedure goes until around a 10Y tenor.

For IPCA swaps , maturity dates are obtained based on a similar process until the 1Y tenor, but with maturity dates ending on 15th of each month which is the effective date for all IPCA published indices, differently than the first business day of the month which is the effective date for all IGPM indices. For other tenors after 1Y, usually they trade swap maturity dates that match NTNBs maturity dates. So on 06-May-2015, after the 1Y tenor, the next tenor is 1Y4M that has as its maturity 15-Aug-2016, which a NTNB maturity date. The next maturity date traded would be 15-May-2017 which is also a NTNB maturity date and so forth.

From the IGPM and IPCA publication dates until the corresponding indices effective dates, the swaps start date changes and it start trading as forward starting swaps, where first accrual dates are usually the effective dates for each one of the indexes. So for 29-Apr-2015, IGPM swaps would have start date as 04-May-2015, and interest accrual periods would match perfectly with effective dates for I_{Last} and I_T. For that particular range of dates between index publication date and its effective date, the swap rate would be traded clean . The same procedure occurs for quoting IPCA forward starting swaps.

15.2.5 IPCA swaps pricing – the market approach

Many market participants like to price IPCA swaps similarly to the NTNBs quoting convention. The equation below describes how they usually price it:

$$PV_t^{BRL} = Not_{BRL} \cdot \frac{VNA_t^{NTNB}}{VNA_{t_{Last}}^{NTNB}} \cdot (1+R)^{\frac{\tau_{t,T}}{252}} \cdot P_{t,T}^{IPCA} - Not_{BRL} \tag{506}$$

where,

$P_{t,T}^{IPCA} = \frac{1}{\left(1+R_{t,T}^{IPCA}\right)^{\frac{\tau_{t,T}}{252}}}$: is the discount factor for IPCA curve calibrated to IPCA swap quote R.

$R_{t,T}^{IPCA}$: IPCA curve calibrated clean rate, from date t to date T.

Since a swap needs to have a 0 PV at inception it yields that:

$$P_{t,T}^{IPCA} = \left(\frac{VNA_t^{NTNB}}{VNA_{t_{Last}}^{NTNB}} \cdot (1+R)^{\frac{\tau_{t,T}}{252}}\right)^{-1} \tag{507}$$

Equation (506) is similar to NTNB quoting convention. Fixed inflation cash-flows are given by term $(1+R)^{\frac{\tau_{t,T}}{252}}$, discounted by an IPCA clean rate $R_{t,T}^{IPCA}$ (that could be compared with NTNB yield) inside $P_{t,T}^{IPCA}$, and then this inflation units quantity would be multiplied by the Notional in BRL times the ratio of 2 VNA values to update the Notional from T_{Last} to t.

There's a problem though with the proposed model. Imagine an IPCA swap with maturity date T on 15-May-2015, but let's assume that I_T was published at 07-May-2015. Based on the payoff given by (505), at 07-May-2015 you have all inflation related variables fixed and the payoff would be a known BRL quantity to be paid at date 15-May-2015. Therefore, at that particular date, the PV_t formula should be a function of the CDI onshore curve discount factor $P_{t,T}^{CDI}$ only, but that variable does not show up in (506). As a matter of fact, at date 07-May-2015 (506) would suggest that this trade still is a function of the IPCA curve discount factor $P_{t,T}^{IPCA}$, which suggests that something is odd with that pricing model.

15.2.6 IPCA swaps pricing – the foreign currency analogy approach and why it's complicated

As mentioned previously, the IPCA lag from publication date to its effective date doesn't follow a specific rule like in the IGPM case where the lag could be constructed based on a $T+2$ rule based on CDI calendar. The foreign currency analogy is based on the construction of a settlement rule, and because of this fact, it will be complicated to adopt this method for IPCA swaps calibration. The whole idea of the foreign currency analogy is to construct inflation index forwards as inflation index spot values time the ratio of discount factors in nominal and real rate curves. But usually in FX systems inside banks, the FX settlement rule is static (or hardcoded) and shouldn't be changing. Unfortunately, for the IPCA inflation case, it needs to be hardcoded every month.

To illustrate this fact let's give an example. Imagine that we are at 06-May-2015 and imagine that next IPCA fixing will be published tomorrow at 07-May-2015. The effective date for next IPCA index is at 15-May-2015. There are 6 business days between 07-May-2015 and 15-May-2015 in a CDI calendar. So one might be inclined to say that the rule is 6 business days in that calendar. IPCA spot would be computed by:

$$I_t = I_{Last} \cdot \left(1 + IPCA_{Proj}\right)^{\frac{\tau^{252}_{T_{Last_{Eff}}, t_{Eff}}}{\tau^{252}_{T_{Last_{Eff}}, T_{Next_{Eff}}}}} \tag{508}$$

where

I_t: is the IPCA spot value for date t (06-May-2015).

I_{Last}: value of the last IPCA index published.

$IPCA_{Proj}$: Anbima IPCA projection forecast.

Until now, nothing new, but the problem lies within the following variables used on FX forward calculations based on the lag between IPCA publication dates and effective dates:

$T_{Last_{Eff}}$: is the date effective date for last IPCA published which is always the 15th.
t_{Eff}: is the effective date obtained from t. This would add 6 business days in a CDI calendar to 06-May-2015, which would yield 14-May-2015.
$T_{Last_{Eff}}$: is the effective date for next period which always falls on the 15th day of the month.

Based on this analysis, it will be seen that given $IPCA_{proj}$, IPCA spot will be accrued for a full month from $IPCA_{Last}$ besides one business day which is correct.

Now assume that, in the following month, the IPCA publication occurs on the 8th day of the month which is 5 business days only from the 15th in a CDI calendar. Now you need to change the fx settlement rule for fake currency related to IPCA in order to capture correctly the fact that the lag between publication and effective dates have changed.

For anyone still interested in this method (we will present a better approach in the next subsection), the pricing can be done by:

$$PV^{BRL}_t = \frac{Not_{BRL}}{I_{Last}} \cdot (1+R)^{\tau^{252}_{t,T}} \cdot I_{t,T} \cdot P^{CDI}_{t,T} - Not_{BRL} \tag{509}$$

where,

$$I_{t,T} = I_t \cdot \frac{P^{IPCA}_{t,t_{Eff},T}}{P^{CDI}_{t,t_{Eff},T}} \tag{510}$$

$$I_t = I_{Last} \cdot (1 + IPCA_{Proj})^{\frac{\tau^{252}_{T_{Last_{Eff}},t_{Eff}}}{\tau^{252}_{T_{Last_{Eff}},T_{Next_{Eff}}}}} \tag{511}$$

Plugging (510) and (511) into (509) yields:

$$PV^{BRL}_t = Not_{BRL} \cdot (1+R)^{\tau^{252}_{t,T}} \cdot (1 + IPCA_{Proj})^{\frac{\tau^{252}_{T_{Last_{Eff}},t_{Eff}}}{\tau^{252}_{T_{Last_{Eff}},T_{Next_{Eff}}}}} \cdot \frac{P^{IPCA}_{t,t_{Eff},T}}{P^{CDI}_{t,t_{Eff},T}} \cdot P^{CDI}_{t,T} - Not_{BRL} \tag{512}$$

And calibration of the IPCA curve can be obtained by:

$$P^{IPCA}_{t_{Eff},T} = \frac{1}{P^{CDI}_{t,t_{Eff}} \cdot (1+R)^{\tau^{252}_{t,T}} \cdot (1 + IPCA_{Proj})^{\tau^{252}_{T_{Last_{Eff}},t_{Eff}} / \tau^{252}_{T_{Last_{Eff}},T_{Next_{Eff}}}}} \tag{513}$$

Now, one could calibrate a forward rate $R^{IPCA}_{t,t_{Eff},T}$, seen at date t, from date t_{Eff} to date T by:

$$R^{IPCA}_{t,t_{Eff},T} = \left(\frac{1}{P^{IPCA}_{t_{Eff},T}}\right)^{\frac{1}{\tau^{252}_{t_{Eff},T}}} - 1 \tag{514}$$

Under this approach, IPCA clean rates are obtained from t_{Eff} to T, so it's a forward curve, and not a spot curve as in the previous subsection. Any interpolation method could be applied to interpolate in rates space, however it carries the burden of updating the spot date settlement rule every month.

15.2.7 IPCA swaps pricing – the IPCA forwards calibration approach

This is the best approach, in the authors' opinion. It takes into account the lag between IPCA publication dates and its effective date, without the need to construct the settlement rules like in the foreign currency analogy approach. The key difference is that under this approach the present value equation calibrates the IPCA index forward values directly. So let's describe the method:

We start again from the IPCA receiver swap payoff below:

$$Payoff_{BRL}[T] = \frac{Not_{BRL}}{I_{Last}} \cdot (1+R)^{\tau^{252}_{t,T}} \cdot I_T - Not_{BRL} \cdot CapFac_{Float}(t,T) \tag{515}$$

We can price this payoff by taking the expectation under the probability measure associated to $P_{t,T}^{CDI}$ as numéraire. Under this measure, the variable $CapFac_{Float}(t,T)$ is a martingale , which yields:

$$PV_t^{BRL} = \frac{Not_{BRL}}{I_{Last}} \cdot (1+R)^{\tau_{t,T}^{252}} \cdot P_{t,T}^{CDI} \cdot \mathbb{E}^{\mathbb{Q}_{CDI}^{T}}[I_T|\mathcal{F}_t] - Not_{BRL} \tag{516}$$

We can substitute the term I_T by $I_{T_{Fix},T}$ which is the inflation forward value seen at its fixing date T_{Fix}, because the forward value converges to the fixing value at fixing date. By applying this change and defining $I_{t,T} = \mathbb{E}^{\mathbb{Q}_{CDI}^{T}}\left[I_{T_{Fix},T}|\mathcal{F}_t\right]$ yields the following present value equation:

$$PV_t^{BRL} = \frac{Not_{BRL}}{I_{Last}} \cdot (1+R)^{\tau_{t,T}^{252}} \cdot P_{t,T}^{CDI} \cdot I_{t,T} - Not_{BRL} \tag{517}$$

Until here there's no difference between the 2 methods. The PV_t^{BRL} of a swap is zero at inception and by no arbitrage it yields that:

$$I_{t,T} = \frac{I_{Last}}{P_{t,T}^{CDI} \cdot (1+R)^{\tau_{t,T}^{252}}} \tag{518}$$

Thus, given a calibrated CDI onshore curve, the historical value of I_{Last} and the swap rate R it's possible to calibrate directly the IPCA inflation forward value $I_{t,T}$ without having to construct it based on the IPCA spot value and the ratio of nominal and real rates discount factors, which is where the settlement rule we wanted to avoid enters.

15.2.8 IPCA index forwards interpolation without seasonality

As discussed previously, there are many liquid quotes for IPCA swap rates R for a range of tenors. Let's call the IPCA forward values computed by (518) the knot values associated to its dates which will be called the knot dates. Therefore, to determine a possible IPCA forward index value for any given date, one is essentially facing the problem of choosing an interpolation method for all dates between the knot dates.

One simple interpolation scheme is log-linear. Suppose we have the IPCA index forward values I_{t,T_i} calibrated by (518) for N knot dates T_i with i from 1 to N. Assuming $T_{i-1} < T < T_i$, the IPCA index forward value for effective date T will be given by:

$$I_{t,T} = I_{t,T_{i-1}} \cdot exp\left(\frac{\tau_{T_{i-1},T}^{252}}{\tau_{T_{i-1},T_i}^{252}} \cdot g_i\right) \tag{519}$$

where the growth rate g_i :

$$g_i = ln\left(\frac{I_{t,T_i}}{I_{t,T_{i-1}}}\right) \tag{520}$$

is constant for each period i.

15.2.9 Adding seasonality

Historical observations suggest that inflation indices exhibit a seasonal pattern, related to consumer habits. So why not add them?

Given an interpolated value $I_{t,T}$ by (519), one could multiply it by a seasonality factor

$$I^*_{t,T} = I_{t,T} \cdot exp\left\{a_{i-1} \cdot (T - T_{i-1})\right\} \tag{521}$$

with the requirement that

$$\sum_{m=1}^{12} a_m = 0 \tag{522}$$

Each a_m term is constant during months ranging from 1 to 12 and could be obtained by regression analysis of historical data to satisfy (522).

The requirement (522) also ensures that on knot dates the IPCA index forward value with seasonality collapses to the knot index forward value given by (518) .

15.2.10 Joint calibration of IPCA curve with NTN-B bond quotes (reduced by asset-swap spread) and IPCA swap rate quotes

One could argue that the large liquidity of IPCA linked products should be based on NTNB prices also, so let's try to add them to the calibration procedure and derive a joint calibration of IPCA index forward values based on IPCA swap rates, NTNB yields and asset swap basis quotes.

This approach is based on calibrating a vector of swap rate quotes R_i from i going from 1 to N and their maturity dates T_i, and a list of NTNB identifiers (could be based on CUSIP) together with its yield y_{CUSIP} and asset swap spread as_{CUSIP}.

Given that information, for each NTNB, an associated risk free price $NTNB_t^{CUSIP}$, seen at date t, could be constructed as:

$$NTNB_t^{CUSIP} = VNA_t \cdot \left(\sum_{T_i=1}^{N} \frac{\left[(1+6\%)^{0.5} - 1\right]}{\left(1 + y_{CUSIP} - as_{CUSIP}\right)^{\tau_{t,T_i}^{252}}} + \frac{1}{\left(1 + y_{CUSIP} - as_{CUSIP}\right)^{\tau_{t,T_N}^{252}}} \right) \tag{523}$$

Please bear in mind that we are using a similar equation to (504) adopted by the market but we are excluding the asset swap spread from the yield to arrive in sort of a risk-free NTNB bond price.

But $NTNB_t^{CUSIP}$ could also be computed based on inflation forwards, given that it could make use of (517) but on a multi cashflow format

$$NTNB_t^{CUSIP} = \frac{1,000}{I_{Issue}} \cdot \left(\sum_{T_i=1}^{N} \left\{ [1.06]^{0.5} - 1 \right\} \cdot I_{t,T_i} \cdot P_{t,T_i}^{CDI} + I_{t,T_N} \cdot P_{t,T_N}^{CDI} \right) \tag{524}$$

with,
$I_{Issue} = 1614.62$ which is the IPCA index used as reference for VNA calculations.

Thus, given a calibrated CDI onshore curve, y_{CUSIP}, as_{CUSIP}, I_{Issue} and VNA_t, one could calibrate all values of I_{t,T_i} given an interpolation constraint.

As an example, let's try to calibrate an IPCA curve on 8-May-2015 based on the following instruments:

1. Swap rates from 1M up to 1Y
2. NTNB maturity date 15-Aug-2016 yield and asset swap spread
3. NTNB maturity date 15-May-2017 yield and asset swap spread
4. NTNB maturity date 15-Aug-2018 yield and asset swap spread
5. NTNB maturity date 15-May-2019 yield and asset swap spread
6. NTNB maturity date 15-Aug-2022 yield and asset swap spread
7. NTNB maturity date 15-May-2023 yield and asset swap spread
8. NTNB maturity date 15-May-2035 yield and asset swap spread
9. NTNB maturity date 15-May-2045 yield and asset swap spread
10. NTNB maturity date 15-Aug-2050 yield and asset swap spread
11. NTNB maturity date 15-May-2055 yield and asset swap spread

As discussed previously in this book, in most practical cases, the best choice for computing risk is with respect to market tradable instruments, and the list of instruments selected above enable us to do exactly that.

For all 12 first swap rates (from 1M to 1Y), given (518) we can calibrate 12 IPCA inflation forward values up to 1 year. The next instrument in the bootstrapping procedure is the NTNB with maturity date 15-Aug-2016. The goal of the calibration of this instrument is to calibrate the IPCA inflation forward values for its coupon end accrual dates, which are on 15-Aug-2015, 15-Feb-2016 and 15-Aug-2016. The first 2 IPCA inflation forward values have been calibrated to the 4M and 10M swap rates and we are left only to calibrate the yield and forward for 15-Aug-2016. But this is achieved using a combination of (523) and (524), which will be 1 equation and 1 unknown and it's therefore straightforward. Alternatively, the 15-Aug-2016 IPCA inflation forward could be calibrated with the swap rate with equal maturity date as the NTN-B. Here we have to make a choice to either include only the swap rate or the NTN-B yield and its asset swap spread as both will be redundant on curve calibration as they are used to calibrate the same 15-Aug-2016 IPCA inflation forward value. Usually the bid–ask quotes for the NTN-Bs are tighter than the ones for the same maturity date swap, justifying therefore the selection of the NTN-B yield and asset swap spread as calibration inputs.

The next NTNB with maturity date on 15-May-2017 requires to solve the IPCA inflation forward values for its coupon dates at 15-Nov-2015, 15-May-2016, 15-Nov-2016 and 15-May-2017. The IPCA inflation forward value for 15-Nov-2015 can be calibrated to the 7M swap rate using (518) again. The last IPCA inflation forward value at 15-May-2017 can be calibrated to the swap rate with NTN-B maturity date, which is also 15-May-2017. However, the 15-May-2016 and 15-Nov-2016 IPCA inflation forward values have still to be calibrated. But (523) and (524) provide only one equation. To solve for the IPCA inflation forward values we will use an interpolation constraint that could say that inflation forward values are log-linearly interpolated; as in Subsection (15.2.8). The 15-May-2016 knot IPCA forward value can be interpolated based on the last calibrated knot date before it, which is calibrated from 1Y swap rate at 15-Apr-2016 and the next calibrated knot date at NTN-B maturity date on 15-Aug-2016. It's worth mentioning again that interpolation occurs based on IPCA inflation forward values as in (519). On the other hand, the 15-Nov-2016 inflation forward will be interpolated based on its preceding calibrated knot date at 15-Aug-2016 NTN-B maturity date and its next calibrated knot date that is at the next NTN-B maturity date at 15-May-2017. Here again we have to make a choice on using the swap rate at NTN-B maturity date or the NTN-B yield and its asset swap spread for calibration. If the latter is chosen, then 15-May-2016, 15-Nov-2016 and 15-May-2017 inflation forwards have to be calibrated based on (523) and (524). The way we circunvent the issue of 3 unknowns and only 1 equation is to rewrite 15-May-2016 and 15-Nov-2016 inflation forwards based on last calibrated knot date inflation forward at 15-Apr-2016 and the only unknown inflation forward at 15-May-2017 that (523) and (524) could solve given the interpolation constraint.

This process is repeated until all instruments are calibrated and permits a joint calibration between NTNB yield and swap rates that could be interesting for analyzing the 2 markets together, potentially to find good relative value trades based on the calibrated inflation forward values.

15.2.11 The IGPM market

The IGPM market is currently illiquid for bonds, so only the swap market has some liquidity. The approaches usually done for IGPM curve calibration are the same though. Many market participants tend to use the calibration method based on (507), but VNA values used are with respect to IGPM projections.

The foreign currency analogy approach works better for IGPM than IPCA, based on the fact that the lag between IGPM publication dates to effective dates can be defined by a settlement rule that never changes. Therefore, Equation (513) could be used for IGPM as well, only by changing the settlement rule applied from t to t_{Eff}. On the other hand, the calibration based on inflation forwards is still preferred to have a consistent calibration method for both inflation curves.

15.3 Exchange traded inflation-linked Futures

There are currently 2 exchange-traded contracts available the defined as Interest rate contracts in the BVMF website. They are the DDM contract for IGPM and DAP contract for IPCA. Their payoff is very similar to DDI futures, by changing *PTAX* in the contract equations to IPCA or IGPM spot values accrued from last published index based on (503). The margin cashflow equations are therefore based on unitary prices much alike the DDI case.

However, they trade a clean rate differently than the DDI contract because their opening price from closing price equation is based on the ratio of $\frac{I_t}{I_{t-1}}$ and not $\frac{PTAX_{t-1}}{PTAX_{t-2}}$ like it was the case for DDI. Currently, liquidity is very thin on those contracts.

The other 2 contracts listed as Index contracts at BVMF website are IGM and IAP. They behave similarly to a DOL or IND contract and the margin cashflows are based on index future values directly. There's also very thin liquidity currently on those contracts.

16 Microstructure of the Listed Derivatives

Durations and tick sizes, consequences and possible developments for the more liquid instruments.

16.1 Microstructure: concepts

Some definitions

- S : Spot price of asset/contract
- σ : Daily volatility (of intraday prices)
- H : Number of hours in the daily trading period (default: 7)
- σ_H : Volatility scaled in hours:

$$\sigma_H = \frac{\sigma}{\sqrt{H}} \tag{525}$$

- σ_S : Volatility scaled in seconds:

$$\sigma_S = \frac{\sigma}{\sqrt{H \cdot 3600}} \tag{526}$$

- α : Tick Size
- α_S : Relative Tick Size:

$$\alpha_S = \frac{\alpha}{S} \tag{527}$$

- Sz : Size of the contract (default: 1)
- MA : Minimum amount that can be traded (default: 1)
- TV: Tick Value, the minimum amount a trader can gain or lose, defined by the product:

$$TV = MA \cdot Sz \cdot \alpha \tag{528}$$

- C : Cost in currency units of trading one contract; it can be either defined as such, to change according to the volume traded, or to be defined as a percentage of the value (Sz * S) traded

- RTC : Round Trip Cost, equal to twice the cost C
  - Let's express RTC for trading the minimum amount of futures in Brazil as:

$$RTC = pct \cdot MA \cdot Sz \cdot \alpha \tag{529}$$

  - Let's express RTC for trading the minimum amount of equities in Brazil as:

$$RTC = pct \cdot MA \cdot Sz \cdot S \tag{530}$$

- D : Duration, the time between trades at different prices
- nPC : Number of price changes during the daily trading period
- M : number of trades during the trading hours H; is at least nPC by definition
- ET : Exit time for a GBM (see below)

16.2 Can durations be estimated?

- The exit time (in seconds) ET for a Geometric Brownian Motion from the band defined by $\{S_0, S_1\}$ with starting point S, volatility σ_S and zero drift (Wilmott) is:

$$ET = \frac{1}{\frac{1}{2} \cdot \sigma_S^2} \cdot \left(\log\left(\frac{S}{S_0}\right) - \frac{1 - \left(\frac{S}{S_0}\right)}{1 - \left(\frac{S_1}{S_0}\right)} \cdot \log\left(\frac{S_1}{S_0}\right) \right) \tag{531}$$

- Simplifying:

$$ET = \frac{2}{\sigma_S^2} \cdot \left(\log\left(\frac{S}{S_0}\right) - \frac{S - S_0}{S_1 - S_0} \cdot \log\left(\frac{S_1}{S_0}\right) \right) \tag{532}$$

- Defining the band by half of the tick size up and down:

$$S_0 = S - \frac{\alpha}{2} \tag{533}$$

$$S_1 = S + \frac{\alpha}{2} \tag{534}$$

$$ET = \frac{1}{\sigma_S^2} \cdot \left(2 \cdot \log\left(\frac{S}{S - \frac{\alpha}{2}}\right) - \log\left(\frac{S + \frac{\alpha}{2}}{S - \frac{\alpha}{2}}\right) \right) \tag{535}$$

- Expanding the logs:

$$\log\left(\frac{S}{S - \frac{\alpha}{2}}\right) \to \frac{1}{2} \cdot \left(\frac{\alpha}{S}\right) + \frac{1}{8} \cdot \left(\frac{\alpha}{S}\right)^2 + O[\alpha]^3 \tag{536}$$

$$\log\left(\frac{S + \frac{\alpha}{2}}{S - \frac{\alpha}{2}}\right) \to \frac{\alpha}{S} + O[\alpha]^3 \tag{537}$$

- And therefore:

$$D = ET = \left(\frac{\alpha}{2 \cdot S \cdot \sigma_S}\right)^2 \tag{538}$$

- In hours instead of seconds:

$$D_H = \left(\frac{\alpha}{2 \cdot S \cdot \sigma_H}\right)^2 \tag{539}$$

- How many trades (at least) in a day:

$$M \geq nPC = \frac{H}{D_H} \tag{540}$$

16.3 What happens in practice?

- It seems reasonable that a person should be able to watch a screen, read the last traded price and the current spread and process this information before a change in price happens.
- So something like 5 seconds seems adequate; 0.2 seconds or 500 seconds do not seem desirable.
- For an asset with a daily volatility of 1% (16% annualized, $\sigma_S = 0.0063\%$), the relative tick size α_S is 0.028%.
- For the S&P500 futures (in Oct 2012, S=1400, α=0.25), α_S is 0.018%.
- For a stock priced at 30 and with a tick of 0.01, α_S is 0.033%.
- Looking at most recent Tick Size tables of the FESE (Federation of European Securities Exchanges), discussed at Tick Size regimes , the new Table 2 (durations will probably fall in the 3 to 30 seconds range) seems better than Table 4 (durations lower than 5 seconds).
- Stocks priced at 600 with a tick size of 0.01 most probably won't have a spread of 0.01 and price changes will typically be higher than that as well.
- The main reason for this estimate to underestimate the realized durations is a spread higher than the tick size. There are two main reasons for that to happen:

  - The tick size is too small (as discussed above)
  - The tick size as defined is (theoretically) good, but the RTC is of the same order of magnitude than α

- Using the time-weighted average of the spread instead of the tick size in the formula above will lead to better results. In the next section a model that explains why this is a good approach will be described.
- Looking at the empirical studies in "Large Tick Assets: Implicit Spread and Optimal Tick Size" (Dayri and Rosenbaum, 2013), we can validate their

findings by estimating:

$$nPC = \frac{H}{D_H} = H\left(\frac{2 \cdot S \cdot \sigma_H}{\alpha}\right)^2 \tag{541}$$

$$\sqrt{nPC} \cdot \alpha = 2 \cdot \sqrt{H} \cdot S \cdot \sigma_H \tag{542}$$

$$\left(\eta \cdot \sqrt{nPC} \cdot \alpha\right) = \left(2 \cdot \sqrt{H} \cdot \eta\right) \cdot (S \cdot \sigma_H) \tag{543}$$

- Which fits the empirical results.

16.4 What is the importance of the tick size?

- Duel between market makers and investors
- Tick size = spread
  - Cost for investor for crossing the spread
  - Gain for market-maker (assuming it makes money also from OTC flows)
- Decimalization
  - HFT: Likes a lower tick size (faster price changes, benefits from speed)
- Exchange:
  - Sets up the contract and listing rules
  - Benefits from trading revenue
  - But wants a balanced market

From the point of view of (a very simple model of) a HFT:

- There are nPC price changes in a day
  - The trade size is small enough that you can enter a trade now, close it on the next move and enter another trade at the same time
  - So there are at most nPC trades per day, each with a P&L equal to:

$$P\&L = \pm TV - RTC \tag{544}$$

  - At the end of the day the expected P&L is:

$$\mathbb{E}[P\&L] = k[TV, RTC, p] \cdot nPC \cdot (p \cdot TV - (1-p) \cdot TV - RTC) \tag{545}$$

- Where p is the probability of winning TV on a trade (1−p) is the probability of losing TV on this trade, and k estimates the proportion of trade opportunities where the HFT will trade.

- For an estimate of the function k, for the HFT to trade we must have:

$$(2*p-1)\cdot TV - RTC \geq 0 \tag{546}$$

$$p^* = \frac{1+Min\left[1, \frac{RTC}{TV}\right]}{2} \tag{547}$$

$$k = Max\left[0, \frac{p-p^*}{1-p^*}\right] \tag{548}$$

- For futures in Brazil:

$$\mathbb{E}[P\&L] = k\cdot\frac{(2\cdot S\cdot\sigma)^2\cdot MA\cdot Sz\cdot((2\cdot p-1)-pct)}{\alpha} \tag{549}$$

The exchange receives the revenue of investors, market makers and HFTs:

$$\mathbb{E}[Revenue] = (Q_{inv} + Q_{mm} + Q_{HFT})\cdot RTC \tag{550}$$

- Let's assume that investors and market makers do not change their amounts based on the fees or the tick size (market makers mainly working through customer orders and hedging OTC flow).
- Because of that, as long as the fees are reasonable, there's no need to lower fees to increase demand for investors and market makers.
- But lowering the fees for HFTs (or whatever they might be called) can increase revenues, by maximizing:

$$Rev_{HFT} = Q_{HFT}\cdot RTC_{HFT} \tag{551}$$

- For futures in Brazil:

$$Rev_{HFT} = k\cdot\frac{(2\cdot S\cdot\sigma)^2\cdot MA\cdot Sz\cdot pct}{\alpha} \tag{552}$$

- The challenge is then to maximize both the expected value of the P&L of the HFT and the exchange's revenue simultaneously, by adjusting α and pct, without changing any of them so much that it affects investors and market makers.
- In fact, the revenue for the exchange only exists if the RTC is low enough for the expected P&L to be positive.
- In futures, for 2 different values of the probability p, we can see that there's a value for pct that maximizes the exchange revenue while keeping the trade profitable for the HFT, since multiplying k by pct leads to an inverted parabola.

16.5 The model with uncertainty zones (Robert and Rosenbaum)

16.5.1 Description of the model

- Start with: $\varepsilon_t = \log P_t - \log X_t$ where:
- X_t is the efficient price (the model price)
    - P_t is the transaction price (in the grid defined by the tick value)
    - ε_t is the microstructure noise process
- The model allows:
    - Price discreteness
    - Price movements of one or several ticks
    - A behavior depending of several factors such as features of the order book
    - Delays caused by the reaction times of the market participants are not null
- If a transaction occurs at some value and leads to a price change, it means that the efficient price process has been close enough to this value shortly before the transaction time.
- How, when and where trades happen ?
    - Suppose the tick size α is 0.10, so mid-ticks would be: 100.05, 100.15, 100.25, ... and allowable transaction prices would be: 100.00, 100.10, 100.20, 100.30, ...
    - Uncertainty band: bands $\pm\, \eta\, \alpha$ around the mid-ticks, with $0 < \eta < 1$ and α equal to the tick size
    - In the example above, make $\eta = 0.20$
    - The bands will be: {100.03,100.07}, {100.13,100.17}, ...
    - A necessary condition for a trade to happen at 100.10 would be for the efficient price to have left the zone {100.03,100.07} on the way up (through 100.07) or to have left the zone {100.13,100.17} on the down (through 100.13)
    - Market conditions still need to allow the trade to happen though, which might lead to price movements of several ticks (efficient price moves through several zones before a trade happens)
- What does η mean ?
    - η quantifies the aversion to price changes
    - The larger the η, the farther from the last traded price the efficient price has to be so that a price change may occur

- The main advantage of $\eta > 0$: The return of the traded price to a previous level is not instantaneous as in the pure rounding model.

16.5.2 What can we do with this model?

- By counting the alternations and continuations of the traded price, we can estimate η, and from that estimate the efficient price from the traded price. Then we estimate the realized volatility on the efficient price, rather than the traded price.
- We can also test the effects of different values for α and for η, and test different dynamics (delays between the time when the efficient price leaves the uncertainty zone and the time a trade happens).

$$N_{\alpha,t,k}^{(a)} = \sum_{t_i \le t} \mathbb{I}_{\left\{ \left(P_{t_i} - P_{t_{i-1}}\right) \cdot \left(P_{t_{i-1}} - P_{t_{i-2}}\right) < 0 \, AND \, \left|P_{t_i} - P_{t_{i-1}}\right| = k \cdot \alpha \right\}} \tag{553}$$

$$N_{\alpha,t,k}^{(c)} = \sum_{t_i \le t} \mathbb{I}_{\left\{ \left(P_{t_i} - P_{t_{i-1}}\right) \cdot \left(P_{t_{i-1}} - P_{t_{i-2}}\right) > 0 \, AND \, \left|P_{t_i} - P_{t_{i-1}}\right| = k \cdot \alpha \right\}} \tag{554}$$

$$\frac{N_{\alpha,t,k}^{(c)}}{N_{\alpha,t,k}^{(a)}} \; is \, an \, estimator \, of \; 2 \cdot \eta \tag{555}$$

- If $\eta < 1/2$, we have more alternations; if $\eta > 1/2$, we have more continuations.

$$\hat{\eta}_{\alpha,t} = Min \left[Max \left[\sum_{k=1}^{m} \left(\lambda_{\alpha,t,k} \cdot u_{\alpha,t,k} \right), 0 \right], 1 \right] \tag{556}$$

$$\lambda_{\alpha,t,k} = \frac{N_{\alpha,t,k}^{(c)} + N_{\alpha,t,k}^{(a)}}{\sum_{j=1}^{m} \left(N_{\alpha,t,j}^{(c)} + N_{\alpha,t,j}^{(a)} \right)} \tag{557}$$

$$u_{\alpha,t,k} = \frac{1}{2} \cdot \left(k \cdot \left(\frac{N_{\alpha,t,k}^{(c)}}{N_{\alpha,t,k}^{(a)}} - 1 \right) + 1 \right) \tag{558}$$

- The efficient price can be calculated as:

$$\hat{X}_{\tau_i} = P_{t_i} - \alpha \cdot \left(\frac{1}{2} - \hat{\eta} \right) sign\left(P_{t_i} - P_{t_{i-1}}\right) \tag{559}$$

- And the realized volatility estimated as:

$$\hat{RV}_{\alpha,t} = \sqrt{\sum_{t_i \le t} \left(\log\left(\hat{X}_{\tau_i}^{t}\right) - \log\left(\hat{X}_{\tau_{i-1}}^{t}\right) \right)^2} \tag{560}$$

16.6 DOL

- Large tick (η around 0.16)
- Average spread: 1.1 tick
- Average price change: 1 tick
- Duration: 25 seconds
- It is the contract that closer to the ideal duration and spread dynamics
- The diversity of participants is key to this relative success (banks as makers and takers)

16.7 DI

- Large tick (η around 0.10)
- Average spread: 1.1 tick
- Average price change: 1 tick
- Duration: 3 minutes
- The liquid maturities look like a sumo match ... a lot of potential energy accumulating, then a sudden release and the price changes
- As for the less liquid contracts, this analysis cannot be easily applied

17

Unlucky End: On the Obsolescence of Products and Books

As this book was being written, BVMF decided to allow more open contracts in its interest rate futures, not just every 3 months. It also changed almost all of the details of its inflation-linked futures.

The relationship between the CDI and the Selic rate has also changed. Since the end of 2013, the number of contributions to the formation of the CDI rate dropped dramatically (the incentives to contributing to the formation of benchmark rates are lower than the costs of implementing a whole governance policy around it); because of that CETIP has implemented a fallback that models the CDI using a linear regression with the Selic rate as the independent variable (not the best available choice, in our opinion). The consequences of choosing such a model are left to the reader.

Brazil being Brazil, the only thing we can be sure about is that we cannot be sure about anything else. If we had written this book 5 years ago, we would have missed a lot of developments like the IOF on Derivatives or the CDI fallback. 10 years ago we would be heralding a new era, oblivious to what would happen in 2008. We will continue to monitor relevant events on taxes, convertibility, market and regulatory changes, and will keep improving and updating models. Please visit the book's website to keep yourself informed of these developments, of upcoming new editions, of interesting snippets of code and analysis.

Books on financial markets will by its nature become obsolete. We hope to have written a book that, rather than just list facts, will have increased your interest in Brazil's financial markets and encouraged you to develop your own solutions and models. If we have helped you to avoid obsolescence, our goal will have been achieved.

References

Andersen, Leif and Vladimir Piterbarg, 2010. "Interest Rate Modeling (Volumes 1, 2, 3)". Atlantic Financial Press.

Brace, Alan, 2007. "Engineering BGM". CRC Press.

Bartlett, Bruce, 2006. "Hedging Under the SABR Model". *Wilmott Magazine*, July/August.

Brigo, Dmiano and Fabio Mercurio, 2006. "Interest Rate Models - Theory and Practice: With Smile, Inflation and Credit". Springer Finance.

Brigo, Damiano, Massimo Morini and Andrea Pallavicini, 2013. "Counterparty Credit Risk, Collateral and Funding: With Pricing Cases For All Asset Classes". Wiley.

Castagna, Antonio 2010. "FX Options and Smile Risk". Wiley.

Clark, Iain, 2011. "Foreign Exchange Option Pricing: A Practitioner's Guide". Wiley.

Dario, Alan De Genaro and Marco Avellaneda, 2012. "Pricing Interest Rate Derivatives Under Monetary Policy Changes", http://papers.ssrn.com/sol3/papers.cfm?abstract_id=2039730

Dayri, Khalil and Mathieu Rosenbaum, 2013. "Large Tick Assets: Implicit Spread and Optimal Tick Size". http://arxiv.org/pdf/1207.6325.pdf

Emanuel Derman, 1998. "Regimes of Volatility". Risk.

Filho, Emilio Garofalo, 2000. "Cambio no Brasil – As Peripécias da Moeda Nacional e da Política Cambial, 500 anos depois". Editora de Cultura.

Filho, Emilio Garofalo, 2002. "Cambio, Ouro e Divida Externa – De Figueiredo a FHC". Saraiva Editora.

Guyon, Julien, 2014. "Path-Dependent Volatility". Risk.

Gyorgy Varga, 2000. "Interpolaçnao por Cubic Spline paraa Estrutura a Termo Brasileira". Resenha BM&F – no 140.

Hagan, S. Patrick, Deep Kumar, Andrew Lesniewski and Diana E. Woodward, 2002. "Managing Smile Risk". *Wilmott Magazine*, September/October.

Hagan, Patrick S. and Graeme West, 2006. "Interpolation Methods for Curve Construction". *Applied Mathematical Finance,* 13, (2).

Heath, David, Robert Jarrow and Andrew Morton, 1992. "Bond Pricing and the Term Structure of Interest Rates: A New Methodology", *Econometrica,* 60 (1) (January): 77–105.

Hull, John C., 2005. "Options, Futures and Other Derivatives", 6th edition. Prentice Hall.

Lord, Roger and Antoon Pelsser, 2008. "Level-Slope-Curvature: Fact or Artifact". Tinbergen Institute Discussion Paper TI 2005-083/2.

Malz, Allan M., 1997. "Option-Implied Probability Distributions and Currency Excess Returns". Federal Reserve Bank of New York, Staff Reports, Number 32, November.

Mark Broadie and Paul Glasserman, 1997. "A Continuity Correction for Discrete Barrier Options". *Mathematical Finance,* 7 (4) (October): 325–348.

McKinney, Wes, 2012. "Python for Data Analysis: Data Wrangling with Pandas, NumPy, and IPython". O'Reilly Media.

Piterbarg, Vladimir, 2012. "Cooking with Collateral". Risk.

Rebonato, Riccardo, Kenneth McKay and Richard White, 2009. "The SABR/LIBOR Market Model: Pricing, Calibration and Hedging for Complex Interest-Rate Derivatives". Wiley.

Riccardo Rebonato, 2004. "Volatility and Correlation: The Perfect Hedger and the Fox", 2nd edition. Wiley.

Robert, Yann Christian and Mathieu Rosenbaum, 2011. "A New Approach for the Dynamics of Ultra High Frequency Data: the Model with Uncertainty Zones". *Journal of Financial Econometrics* 9 (2): 344–366.

Rossant, Cyrille, 2014. "IPython Interactive Computing and Visualization Cookbook". Packt Publishing.

Shreve, Steven, 2010. "Stochastic Calculus for Finance II: Continuous-Time Models". Springer Finance.

Taleb, Nassim Nicholas 1997. "Dynamic Hedging". Wiley.

Index

Printed and bound by CPI Group (UK) Ltd, Croydon, CR0 4YY